THE ABINGDON PREACHING ANNUAL 2002

THE ABINGDON PREACHING ANNUAL 2002

EDITED BY

Charles Bugg

ABINGDON PRESS
Nashville

THE ABINGDON PREACHING ANNUAL 2002

Copyright © 2001 by Abingdon Press

ISBN 0-687-08198-X
ISSN 1075-2250

01 02 03 04 05 06 07 08 09 10—10 9 8 7 6 5 4 3 2 1

MANUFACTURED IN THE UNITED STATES OF AMERICA

CONTENTS

MARCH

CONTENTS

OCTOBER

NOVEMBER

DECEMBER

CONTENTS

INTRODUCTION

The church where I'm presently interim preaching has a sign affixed to the pulpit. The sign simply says, "We would see Jesus." Those are good words. In fact, they are New Testament words. While not originally used in the context of proclamation, those words have made their way to more than one pulpit where I've preached.

"We would see Jesus." What does that mean for preaching? On the one hand, this phrase sounds oversimplistic. Go to an Academy of Homiletics meeting in the United States, and you will come away with the clear impression that preaching is complex. Homileticians ponder, debate, and discuss thorny issues such as how a text is exegeted, what are possible structures for sermons, do we need more narrative, what's the best way to deliver a message, and so forth. After a weekend at the academy meeting, we all leave knowing that effective preaching requires thoughtful, prayerful, hard work.

"We would see Jesus." If only our listeners knew the anguish we preachers often go through to bear some kind of witness. However, those rather simple and straightforward words do remind us of something important. Whatever else preaching is, it is the attempt to make all of us aware of God. We don't see God physically. At least, I don't. However, in the busyness or dullness of our lives, most of us need to be reminded that there is "another" dimension to life.

Seeing Jesus helps to calm our overwhelming anxieties. Seeing Jesus brings hope when life is draining. Seeing Jesus stirs the church and calls us to the oppressed, the impoverished, and the marginalized. Seeing Jesus helps us to remember others and the Divine "otherness," and helps us to understand that life isn't "just about me." So next Sunday, I will walk to the pulpit and preach. Greeting me will be the sign, "We would see Jesus." After all is said and done, that is my prayer.

Charles Bugg

SERMONS
ON THE PSALMS

PREACHING THE PSALMS: WHY?

We believe the Psalms should be preached, that they can be preached, that the life of the church is impoverished if we do not include the Psalms in our proclamation of the Word of God. But for many clergy, there is nothing obvious about preaching the Psalms. Not often does a psalm serve as a text for a sermon, and the reasons for this omission are varied. Christian preaching inevitably gravitates toward the New Testament, and even though publishers have for centuries printed handy editions of "The New Testament and Psalms," those Psalms are still in the Old Testament, and are riddled with bulls and altars, pleas for vengeance, kings and priests, a passion for the Temple—all the agenda we think the New Testament has left in the dust.

In the liturgy, the Psalms function as a means of responding to Scripture. But they may also be preached. Clearly by the end of the Old Testament era, psalms were being collected, suggesting that the leadership of Israel's religious life conceived of a broader application of the entire batch of psalms beyond their original deployment as liturgies or individual prayers. The resulting "Psalter" has the character of a hortatory or instructional book.

We have to reckon with the fact that, through the long history of the church, psalms most certainly *have* been preached. The Psalms are very much a part of our canon of Scripture, a fair enough warrant for the preacher who would weave a sermon around a psalm. To anyone who wonders whether to preach on the Psalms, or to anyone who wonders how to preach on the Psalms, we have sermons from Barth and Bonhoeffer, Luther and Calvin, Augustine and Jerome, virtually every giant in the history of the church, which are both our warrant and our tutor in this enterprise.

THE BEAUTY AND
URGENCY OF MY SONG
❧

PSALM 42

"As a deer longs for flowing streams, so my soul longs for you, O God." This psalmist had seen a deer, probably many of them, thirsty, nosing about, peering into dry riverbeds, searching for water—and he knew that he thirsted for God in the same way. You can create your own image for this quest. In Pat Conroy's novel, *The Lords of Discipline*, young Will McLean laments his lack of a romantic life in words that may reflect our anxiety about God:

> I once read in a book that traced the natural history of blue whales that the great creatures often had to travel thousands of miles through the dark waters of the Pacific to find a mate. They conducted their search with the fever and furious attention of beasts aware of the imminence of extinction. As whaling fleets depleted their numbers, scientists conjectured that there were whales who would exhaust themselves in fruitless wandering and never connect with any mate at all. When I read about those solitary leviathans, I feared I had stumbled on an allegory of my own life, that I would spend my life unable to make a connection, unable to find someone attracted by the beauty and urgency of my song.[1]

There's a psychology to this thirst. Our seeking, our song, is indeed urgent—but it has a beauty about it. You don't need me to tell you that we walk around with this gaping hole in our souls, and we will pour anything and everything into it to fill it: stuff, diversions, booze, you name it. We view this thirst as a problem, and one to be solved, and quickly. But maybe that hole isn't a curse so much as a gift. That hollowness is God crying out to you; your song is God's song first! God's Spirit has burrowed out a place, so you would seek after him. Otherwise, you might never sense any need for God. It gets mislabeled—but it is God's call. And the answer isn't something far away. St. Augustine said, "The divine mystery is closer to me than I am to myself." And he also said, "O Lord, you have made us for yourself, and our hearts are restless until they find rest in you."

It may be we miss out on this because of the economics of the psalm. We are utterly unacquainted with thirst. At the Howell house, we have water in multiple locations, in six rooms, and in several spigots outside. We also have bottles of Midas Spring Water, superior water, there for our choosing. We know nothing of what the ancients knew all too well: what it was like to fall on your knees, look upward to the heavens, and know that the gathering clouds and what God might shower on the earth were matters of life and death, not just bad news for an impending picnic. Water, even for us, is no luxury, but a necessity. It permeates all that we are. But as affluent as we are, we take all that for granted, and it is hard to glimpse our dependence upon God. To figure it out, we need to go to school, we need some discipline.

There is an aspect of time and effort to this psalm. The psalmist prays this prayer in the far north of Israel, at the foot of snowcapped Mt. Hermon, where even today there is a spectacular waterfall that forms the source of the Jordan River. He prays there, but he longs to go up to Jerusalem—and that will take some time, some labor, a lot of energy, a plan. There is a time lapse, and the need for some exerted effort, between when he prays and when the fulfillment might come.

Prayer, connecting with God, is never quick and easy. It's like learning a foreign language. Fifteen years ago I studied Italian, in some depth. Then I flew to Italy, thinking I'd be proficient. But prowling around Rome, I soon was lost, getting just bits and pieces, here and there. But I kept at it, immersed myself in my confusion, took even embarrassing stabs at it—and finally, in about the fourth week, something clicked. A real conversation, back and forth, in Italian. I even began to have some Italian thoughts!

Now it's no use trying Italian on me—because I have spoken and listened to virtually no Italian since then. I am having no Italian thoughts at all. Prayer is like that, like a muscle. It requires use, discipline. All the great masters of prayer teach us this. Dom John Chapman said, "The only way to pray is to pray; the only way to pray well is to pray much."[2] Catherine of Siena wrote, "You, O God, are a deep sea into which, the more I enter, the more I find, and the more I find, the more I seek." Joseph Cardinal Bernardin, while dying of cancer, gave us who suddenly fire off those 911 prayers when we are in trouble this shrewd advice: "Pray while you're well, because when you're sick you will not feel well enough to pray."[3] And Georges Bernanos said we must block out a time for prayer each day: even if not well used, don't give it to anybody else!

This leads us to the geography of Psalm 42. The psalmist knows that God is everywhere; he is praying, after all, near Mt. Hermon. But there is a place, somewhere he needs to go. Henry David Thoreau in *Walden* wrote that he went into the woods "because I wished to live deliberately, to front only the essential facts of life, and see if I could not learn what it had to teach, and not, when I came to die, discover that I had not lived." The Israelites came out of the woods, and went to the temple, on Mt. Zion, God's holy city. When they thought of that temple, they subscribed to what Amos Wilder once said about church: "Going to church is like approaching an open volcano, where the world is molten and hearts are sifted. The altar is like a rail that spatters sparks, the sanctuary like the chamber next to an atomic oven. There are invisible rays, and you leave your watch outside."[4]

They knew God certainly was everywhere, but they were aware of it because of what happened in the temple, in those special meetings in public worship. Nowadays, attendance at worship is regarded as utterly optional; in fact, some feel you can probably be a better Christian if you don't go and suffer the distractions and hypocrisy and parking stress. Church is treated as a matter of convenience, something you do on Sunday if there's not too much else going on. And you might even enjoy it, if the choir sings pretty, if the preacher is funny.

But we are wired by God in such a way that we need to be in worship. We owe it to God. And we need the pace, and the impact of the words uttered only there. As an English author wrote, "Why should men love the Church? Why should they love her laws? She tells them of life and death, and of all that they would forget. She is tender where they would be hard, and hard where they like to be soft. She tells them of evil and sin, and other unpleasant facts."

The psalmist poignantly remarks that tears have been my

bread day and night. Have tears, sorrow, been your bread? At the temple there was another bread, called the bread of presence, just a loaf of bread that somehow signified to the Jews the very face of God. I wonder if Jesus had that in mind at the Last Supper when he took a loaf of bread, blessed it, broke it, and gave it to them, saying, "This is my body, given for you." It was Jesus who said, "I am the living water, and I am the bread of life. The bread I give for the life of the world is my body." And on the cross, when Jesus flung open a window into the very heart of God, to show us his mercy, his side was pierced, and out flowed water—a sign, a symbol, that this Jesus, whom we worship in this place, around this table, is what we are thirsty for.

Flannery O'Connor was once asked what really mattered in her life. She said that it was this bread: "Holy Communion is the center of existence for me. All the rest is expendable." And so it is. "As a deer longs for flowing streams, so my soul longs for you, O God." "When shall I come and behold the face of God?" God is here. Now. Today. Your beautiful song has been heard.

Notes

1. Pat Conroy, *The Lords of Discipline* (New York: Bantam, 1982), p. 55.

2. Quoted by Henri Nouwen, *The Road to Daybreak: A Spiritual Journey* (New York: Doubleday, 1988), p. 117.

3. Joseph Cardinal Bernardin, *The Gift of Peace: Personal Reflections* (Chicago: Loyola, 1997), p. 67.

4. Amos Wilder, "Electric Chimes or Rams' Horns," in *Grace Confounding* (Philadelphia: Fortress, 1972), p. 13.

TESTED BY ITS OWN DEFEAT

Surely God is good to the pure in heart. I mean, if we developed a job description for God, that should hover near the top. It is God's job to bless, to protect, to do good, and especially for those who are good.

The psalmist knows this saying, *God is good to the pure in heart*, quite well—but has also learned from the school of his own life that there is this anomaly at the epicenter of life. *But as for me, all the day long I have been stricken.* He has kept his heart pure, he has done the right thing, he has been faithful and good—but has been rewarded with nothing but suffering, physical pain, actual poverty. The number one theological question that lands in my office is this: If there is a good God, then why do people, and especially good people, suffer? Isn't God supposed to bless, and protect us?

Why is there suffering? C. S. Lewis, early in his career, traveled around England lecturing on the problem of evil. He said, "Sufferings are God's hammerblows to awaken and to discipline us." But then he got married, and his wife, Joy, suffered the brutality of cancer, and died. Lewis never again said, "Sufferings are God's hammerblows." He recognized the painful illogic of his words. God does not give cancer, or strike people with AIDS, or cause car accidents.

This view that the good are rewarded and the wicked are punished is absurd to anyone with eyes and ears. At my latest check, the rich and healthy are not especially holy. If so, you could just find the largest houses in a city, peer in the windows, and there you would find moral exemplars, saints, champions of good. You could check the obituaries each day, and the people with the high numbers next to their names you could assume to be very righteous, while any who died young must have been guilty of great sin. On that model, if God is "blessing" anybody in America, it

23

must be Bill Gates. But it was Gates who said he didn't understand why people would go to church; it seemed to him like an inefficient use of time. Better to be out working, and making money.

The psalmist tells the truth about our view of at least some of the wealthy—even though we know better. *Pride is their necklace . . . their hearts overflow with follies . . . their tongues range over the earth. Therefore the people turn and praise them, and find no fault in them* (vv. 6-10). We all know and love somebody who is wealthy, and we want to leap to their defense. But when someone is good, like this psalmist, but suffers, there is almost a resentment toward those who have plenty, and great ease. And there is an implicit warning that attaches itself to wealth, beautifully put by G. K. Chesterton: *There is one thing Christ and all the Christian saints have said with a sort of savage monotony: they have said simply that to be rich is to be in peculiar danger of moral wreck.*

We can explain much suffering, without blaming God. When there is an airplane crash, people always ask, "How could God allow this tragedy?" But God doesn't swat planes out of the air. Rather, when Orville and Wilbur Wright lifted off at Kitty Hawk, and people watched and said, "Now that's a great way to get around," then we signed a contract with death, knowing fully well that some hopefully small percentage of planes would malfunction and crash. Lots of suffering is like that—and I want to say to those who suffer, "Don't take it personally!"

But nothing could be more personal. The "problem of evil" is no intellectual head game, something intellectuals bat about in some ivory tower. Suffering is intensely personal. It strikes, like a fist to your midsection. It just deflates you. Teddy Roosevelt suffered the death of his wife, Alice, as she was giving birth, and his mother, Mittie, on the same day. At the end of that day, he wrote in his diary: *She was beautiful . . . when her life seemed just to be begun . . . when my heart's dearest died, the light went out of my life forever.*

When we suffer, there is a temptation to give up on God—and many have, and I cannot blame them. One of my early hospital visits years ago was with a young woman, in her twenties, whose doctor had just informed her that she would not survive. Late that night, her mother just kept staring out the hospital window, into the darkness. When I had to leave, I said, "Can I say a prayer?" She did not turn around, and dismissed the thought by saying, "Pray if you want. No one is listening."

I do not blame her. The psalmist stood with her when he said, *All in vain have I kept my heart clean.* But he doesn't give up. His faith survives, somehow, and he gives two reasons for this surprise.

But then I went to the sanctuary of God. He went to the temple, the holy place, and somehow, by being in that place, he caught some glimpse of hope. I wonder anymore what people think about church buildings. Once upon a time in America, the skylines of great cities featured towering church spires. Now they are dwarfed by towers that celebrate commerce, money. In our anti-institutional milieu, many people feel they can virtually be more spiritual outside the church. Many are cynical about church—and I might add, we have labored long and hard to earn that cynicism! But despite whatever may or may not go on inside a church, the very fact that they still stand is awesome. In Lorraine Hansberry's play, *Raisin in the Sun*, a suddenly grown-up girl announces to her mother that she no longer believes in God. Her mother makes a swift path across the room, slaps her daughter on the cheek, and commands, "Repeat after me: In my mother's house, there still is a God." A sanctuary is a protest, a dissenting voice in our culture of skepticism, that there still is a God. They are, admittedly, mere stone. But Jesus once said that even the stones would cry out.

But the psalmist also doesn't give up because of what I think verse 15 implies. He speaks of being *true to the generation of thy children.* He is not alone as a believer, a seeker, a doubter, but that he is woven into the fabric of a community, of a broader congregation, who have believed. Many have endured much worse, and doggedly hung on. I love to read of the lives of saints, and the stories of martyrs, how they clung to God in the face of vicious attacks and long nights of suffering.

In 1985 I went to China with Prof. Creighton Lacy, who was born there, the child of missionaries. They were driven from the country in 1948—all except Dr. Lacy's father, and we went in part looking for news of what had happened to him. After poking

SPIRITUAL PREPARATION FOR MINISTRY

An Introduction

The year begins, at least in the national calendar, with January. I once heard Ernest Campbell, former pastor of the Riverside Church in New York City, speak of the tensions in our calendars: the church calendar, the civic calendar, and the sports calendar! Some of us indeed live from Advent to Christmas to Epiphany; others from Christmas to New Year's; others from the World Series to the Super Bowl. These reflections assume that the preacher and the congregation also live in this same tension. And so, in these monthly devotionals you will also find there is some interplay between the different calendars. At times the focus is on the liturgical season: Lent, Easter, Pentecost; at other times, the emphasis might be on summer, or fall, or the beginning of the new year. And there is also some attention to congregational issues: the stewardship campaign, and issues of time management and conflict resolution. These devotionals are written out of a pastoral context, within the rhythms of work and rest, shepherding and preaching, giving and receiving.

But why should you read them? In a book entitled *Good News in Exile,* Anthony Robinson, a pastor from Seattle, describes his journey through depression. He writes:

> At first I didn't have any idea why I felt so overwhelmed and debilitated. I couldn't imagine what was going on. Understanding treatment, and learning came slowly, but they came. Part of the learning called for a different and deeper kind of faith, one that put less responsibility on me, and one that taught me of God's grace, and learning to trust the Spirit's leading. I came to see that I, like many churches shaped by civic faith, had turned a religion of grace into a religion of good works and achievement. We preached grace, but it was hard to receive it ourselves. In crucial ways this loss of grace, and its replacement with a religion of good works and activism, was destroying the mainline churches, even as it had contributed to my own terrifying experience of depression.

In this brief statement, Tony Robinson offers a prophetic word of judgment and hope. Have we taken a religion of grace and converted it into a religion of good works? Do we find ourselves depressed about the church's present and future mission? Do we overfunction, sensing that we are totally responsible for the completion of God's work? Do we find it hard to receive the grace of God? Are busyness and activism destroying the mainline church?

I invite you to spend time each month with the meditations entitled "Spiritual Preparation." Perhaps they will help you to make your way through the inevitable difficulties that arise in the pastoral ministry. Perhaps they will give you a glimpse of God's grace. Perhaps they will help you to trust in the Spirit's leading. And perhaps they will lead you into a deeper sense of your purpose and calling as a pastor.

May God use these meditations, and our ministries, in the year that is to come. (Ken Carter)

Source: *Good News in Exile* by Martin Copenhaver, Anthony Robinson, and William Willimon (Eerdmans).

SPIRITUAL PREPARATION

❦

JANUARY

We try, but we cannot live in the past. The apostle Paul knew something about this. He could rehearse his own past, claim his own tradition, tout his own credentials—circumcised on the eighth day, of the tribe of Benjamin, the favorite son of Jacob, a Hebrew of Hebrews, a Pharisee, blameless under the law—Paul could recall the past, but he was really a person who lived in the present and toward the future. He could even say, about his own past, that he had "counted it all as loss," for the sake of knowing Christ.

It is true that we cannot escape the past, but neither can we live there. Some of us cannot get over traumatic events, strange twists, and unexplainable turns that have shaped us—recall Paul's "thorn in the flesh"—while others among us look back to the glory days, "that championship season," to "the good old days when times were bad," as the country song has it.

A new year gives us the opportunity to think about the past even as we enter into the future. Paul knew how to reflect on and come to grips with the past, but his preoccupation was with the present, with the future, with what is and what is to come. His chief goal, his primary aim, was "to know Christ and the power of his resurrection and the fellowship of his suffering." But then, he would confess that he was not there yet; he was not yet whole, not yet perfect, but his mind was focused on the destination:

> I press on . . . forgetting what lies behind and straining forward to what lies ahead, I press on toward the goal for the prize of the heavenly call of God in Christ Jesus. (Phil. 3:12b-14)

In the days of January we can think about pressing on, about an upward call, about what lies ahead.

31

- Do you have any personal or spiritual goals for the coming year? Can you state them simply? How can these goals shape your ministry? How are these goals related to Paul's discipline of "forgetting what lies behind"? What do you need to put in the past?

This is, admittedly, a hopeful orientation. But hope is one of God's greatest gifts to us, one of our most helpful and necessary resources. Consider the Sundays and how they might lead us in the journey toward hope.

Baptism of the Lord. On this day we are reminded that we have been baptized. For pastors, this carries profound meaning. At a time when it is easy to be made a scapegoat or placed on a pedestal, to become isolated from the community or separated from other clergy, this day reminds us that we are a part of the baptized, that we are children of God, cleansed in the waters of the Jordan, empowered by the spirit, sent forth with the words of affirmation, "You are my beloved child; in you I am pleased" (Luke 3; Matthew 3). The remembrance of our baptisms can connect us with the community of God's people, and this can be a powerful corrective to our individualism and to our works of righteousness. Yes, we are often more comfortable in giving than receiving; and yet baptism is a sign that ministry is grace.

Martin Luther King Jr. Day. On this day we are reminded of a modern prophet who called us to our core convictions about justice and dignity. His presence among us, in recent memory, through his writings and in this annual remembrance, is a sign that God is not finished with us, that matters of race and class which divide and demoralize are under God's judgment, but also within a vision of God's kingdom. The Old Testament lection for the fourth Sunday after the Epiphany is appropriate: "He has told you, O mortal, what is good; and what does the LORD require of you but to do justice, and to love kindness, and to walk humbly with your God?" (Mic. 6:8).

- In the new year, it will help us to know that God's work is about grace and justice. How is God's grace present in your life? How is God's justice present, or absent, in your life?

In these Sundays the pastor will find guidance for moving forward by staying close to the Gospel texts. Jesus is baptized. Jesus calls disciples. Jesus proclaims a message of repentance. Jesus heals. Jesus teaches.

With a new year there is a possibility to begin anew. As pastors we can become involved in an infinite variety of tasks: some are important, others are trivial; some are rewarding, others are draining; some are intentional, others are accidental. Sometimes we are proactive and focused. At other times we are reactive and unfocused.

Staying close to the Gospel texts helps us to see again that our ministry is the ministry of Jesus. We baptize—we extend the grace of God to others. We call disciples—we share the ministry, which is not ours alone. We call for repentance—we urge our hearers to consider God's kingdom as the priority in their lives. We heal—we move toward the sick and the grieving; we touch them, we pray for them. We teach—we draw from the wisdom of Jesus in a culture enamored with self-help literature.

Staying close to the Gospel texts also helps us to see that our ministry is possible only as we allow Jesus to minister to us. We are baptized, recipients of God's grace, and we need to remember this daily. We were called, we left our nets somewhere, and we made a decision to follow. This also is a truth that we need to claim each day. We need to repent, to rearrange our priorities, to seek first the kingdom of God and his righteousness (Matthew 6). We need to be healed. Henri Nouwen's image of the "wounded healer" is one that continues to describe us. And we need to be taught. There are new insights and fresh revelations for those who open themselves prayerfully to the Word.

A new year begins. May it mark a turning point in your own life, as you forget what lies behind and press forward toward the goal of the upward call of God in Christ Jesus. (Ken Carter)

JANUARY 6, 2002

Baptism of the Lord

Worship Theme: God, who did a new thing among the Hebrews, who did a new thing in sending the Spirit upon Jesus at his baptism, who did a new thing in the time of the early church, acts still—do you not perceive it?

Readings: Isaiah 42:1-9; Acts 10:34-43; Matthew 3:13-17

Call to Worship (Psalm 29):

Leader:	Ascribe to the LORD, O heavenly beings, ascribe to the LORD glory and strength.
People:	**Ascribe to the LORD the glory of his name; worship the LORD in holy splendor.**
Leader:	The voice of the LORD is over the waters; the God of glory thunders, the LORD, over mighty waters.
People:	**The voice of the LORD shakes the wilderness; the LORD shakes the wilderness of Kadesh.**
Leader:	Ascribe to the LORD, O heavenly beings, ascribe to the LORD glory and strength.
People:	**Ascribe to the LORD the glory of his name; worship the LORD in holy splendor.**

Pastoral Prayer:
God, ever faithful, renew us as you renewed your covenant with your people Israel so that we may be a light to the nations.

God, ever faithful, send again your Spirit, light upon us like the dove that descended upon Jesus in the Jordan so that we might be about your work among our neighbors. God, ever faithful, give us new eyes as you transformed Peter's vision so that we might spread your good news among all people—showing no partiality. Establish justice. Heal the sick. Welcome the stranger. Use us as your instruments. All this we pray in the name of the One you called Beloved, who reigns with you and the Holy Spirit, One God, forever. Amen. (Scott Haldeman)

SERMON BRIEFS

TO BE A BLESSING

ISAIAH 42:1-9

Isaiah 42 is found in the portion of the book of Isaiah that scholars call Second Isaiah, which includes chapters 40–55. This part of Isaiah was most likely written during the Babylonian exile (sixth century B.C.E.) and was addressed to the Israelites living in exile. Second Isaiah opens with the words "Comfort, O comfort my people. . . . Speak tenderly to Jerusalem" (40:1-2), and in the verses that follow, God promises that Jerusalem will be restored as the dwelling place of God. Chapter 42 describes the servant of the Lord, a character who will play a key role in the restoration of Israel as the people of the Lord. Who is "the servant of the Lord"? A review of commentaries on the book of Isaiah shows that there are many ideas about the servant's identity. But we should not let that trouble us. Prophetic speech is poetry, filled with metaphor, imagery, and hyperbole. The result is a message with a multiplicity of meanings, a message relevant to many people in many times, but with a particular message to a particular people at a particular time.

How, then, might we understand the metaphor, the imagery, the hyperbole of chapter 42 of Isaiah? One understanding of the servant emerges from a study of the history of ancient Israel's relationship with the Lord. In Genesis 12, God calls Abraham and Sarah to leave their homeland and journey to a new place.

The reason for the journey was blessing—"in you all the families of the earth shall be blessed." Beginning in Genesis 12, God narrows the focus of relationship, from universal relationships in Genesis 1–11, to a relationship with a single family. The purpose of the narrowing, however, was not to exclude "all the families of the earth"; in the family of Abraham and Sarah "all the families of the earth shall be blessed." Through the Israelites, all the earth was to find the knowledge and blessings of God. But, as we read in the pages of the Old Testament, the Israelites broke covenant and, rather than realizing and passing along blessing, they obtained judgment.

In Second Isaiah, the prophet tells the people of Israel that judgment has come—the Israelites are in exile in Babylon. Jerusalem and the Temple have been destroyed. But now the penalty has been paid; God and Israel will have a new beginning. Jerusalem will be restored as the dwelling place of the Lord; the Israelites will again be the people of God, and the Lord will be their God. God promises restoration, but the restoration requires action on the part of the Israelites. They must do their part to fulfill the promise given to Abraham and Sarah. God will act, and the Israelites must act as well. They must fulfill their role as the servant of the Lord.

Israel must "bring forth justice to the nations," "open the eyes that are blind," "bring out the prisoners," and be "a light to the nations" (42:1, 6, 7), for that was the intent of God's call to Abraham and Sarah. Who is to be the servant of the Lord? The people of Israel, the descendants and heirs of Abraham and Sarah, are to be the servants of the Lord. God, the God of all creation, who ". . . created the heavens and stretched them out, who spread out the earth and what comes from it, who gives breath to the people upon it and spirit to those who walk in it" (v. 5)—this God called a people to be in special relationship, not for their own benefit, but for the benefit of all of humankind, even all of creation. The people of this special relationship violated the sacred terms of the relationship, and the wrath of God burned against them. They found themselves punished more harshly than they ever dreamed possible. But the God who punishes is the God of incredible love and compassion. God will restore Israel and Israel will be a blessing to the nations, in spite of itself. Let us forever be mindful of our mission, our role, in this world—"to be a blessing." And, we achieve that blessing by being "servants of the Lord." (Nancy L. deClaissé-Walford)

DOES GOD PLAY FAVORITES?

ACTS 10:34-43

An exciting and marvelous mystery unfolds before our eyes. If we fail to be impressed, it is because we can take it for granted. Christians in the first century were impressed, though. Life would never be the same. This was the kind of event that marked an epoch in their lives, much the way the advent of running water in the home marked an epoch in the lives of many of our families. What a big deal that was to a previous generation! Now, we expect running water. The magic and mystery are gone. In the same way, we expect God will not play favorites. Let's try to relive some of the excitement.

I. A Shocking Turn of Events

Despite Peter's opening remarks, the Jewish Christians who traveled with him were thunderstruck when, while Peter was still preaching this sermon, the Holy Spirit fell on Gentiles. You have to read a few verses past our text to find these results. Why the surprise? After all, they believed in one God, Creator and Ruler of all. Most of the Old Testament, however, is based on the idea that God plays favorites: Abraham over others, Jacob over Esau, Israel over the nations. God may rule over all, but God has favorites. Of course, there were always voices like the author of Jonah and the prophet Ezekiel, who suggested other nations have a place in God's plan. Israel's special status could be understood as a calling to be a light to the world. Nevertheless, the conviction remained, God favored Israel.

When the Spirit of God drove the good news about Jesus to a Gentile audience, cherished assumptions exploded in a blast that can still be felt to this day. God shows no partiality. The door was opened to Gentiles, and most of us would not be Christians if that door did not stand open.

II. But Does God Favor Christians?

This story changes things. Henceforth anyone can come to Jesus Christ, and they can come, in the words of the hymn, "Just as I am." But have we merely exchanged one form of favoritism for another? If God does not discriminate on the basis of race, does God judge on the basis of religion? This question demands an answer in a culture as religiously diverse as ours.

Peter's opening remark seems to work against any kind of favoritism: "God shows no partiality, but in every nation anyone who fears him and does what is right is acceptable to him." Peter goes on, however, to tell the story of Jesus, mentioning that he is Lord of all and declaring him judge of the living and the dead. At the end we learn, "Everyone who believes in him receives forgiveness of sins through his name." Is he saying that anyone who wants to be acceptable to God has business to do with Jesus Christ?

Of all the ways to come at this problem, I'll focus on the one I find most helpful. In a world as diverse as ours, apostolic Christianity pointed to Jesus as the one way because of his close relationship to the God he called "Father." Our text today speaks of God anointing Jesus with the Spirit and power, raising him from the dead, and ordaining him judge of all. To say, then, that God shows no partiality is to say that Jesus does not. People of every nation who fear God and do right are acceptable to him, that is, to Jesus. To try to make the text say that religion does not matter is to force our categories onto the text.

Acts has excited and challenged us. Now we go forth as witnesses to all that God has done in Jesus Christ. (David C. Mauldin)

WHEN GOD BLESSED HIS OWN SON

MATTHEW 3:13-17

Jesus' unique relationship with his heavenly Father was confirmed, not bestowed upon him, at his baptism. Matthew reports that as soon as Jesus came up from the water, the heavens opened up, the Spirit of God descended like a dove upon Jesus, and a voice from heaven said, "This is my beloved Son, with whom I am well pleased" (3:16–17 RSV). This divine confirmation from God was an affirmation of God's being and behavior, and of acceptance and approval.

As Jesus began his public ministry, a three-year journey toward Jerusalem and a cross, it was absolutely critical that he receive the blessing from his heavenly Father. If God's beloved Son needed affirmation, how much more do you and I need to feel accepted and approved of by our earthly father or mother, as well as by God?

No other story in the Bible demonstrates the importance of a father's blessing as does the story of Jacob and Esau, twin sons of Isaac and Rebekah. Jacob and Esau were raised in a dysfunctional family. Before their birth, they wrestled with one another in the womb and God predicted that they would grow up hating each other. They were twins, but the two boys were as different as night and day. Esau loved the outdoors and Jacob preferred staying inside. Genesis 25:28 says Isaac loved Esau, and Rebekah loved Jacob. Rebekah and Jacob plot and succeed in stealing from Esau his father's blessing.

Although Isaac and Rebekah are not model parents, they do teach us that every child longs to receive the blessing of his or her parents and that parents and children have a deep stake in each other's destinies. How can we as parents or grandparents shape the destiny of our children and grandchildren?

I. The Bond of Generations

First, we must realize that generations are inalienably and terrifyingly bound together. Jacob and Esau duplicated the dysfunctional and deceitful personalities of their father and mother.

Generations are inseparably bound together. Responsible parents understand that their choices have lasting consequences upon their children. Perhaps that is why the prophet Ezekiel said, "The fathers have eaten sour grapes, and the children's teeth are set on edge" (Ezek. 18:2 RSV).

II. Symbolic Actions Have Lasting Power

Paul Tournier, the late Swiss psychiatrist and theologian, used the story of Esau to describe a psychological problem that he constantly dealt with in therapy. He called it "the unblessed child." It was the result of a child not being blessed, not feeling approved of by his or her parents, feeling that somehow they did not measure up, that somehow they never really pleased their parents.

There are no unblessed children in the church or the kingdom of God. When Jesus picked up the little children and blessed each of them, he communicated that God accepts and loves us just the way we are. Symbolic actions have genuine and abiding power.

III. Spoken Words Shape Human Life

Finally, the family of Isaac, Rebekah, Jacob, and Esau, as well as the relationship between Jesus and God, demonstrates that spoken words shape human life. Do you remember the line you were taught as a child? "Sticks and stones may break my bones, but words will never hurt me." If we are honest, we would rewrite that statement to say, "Sticks and stones may break my bones, but words will surely hurt me."

When it comes to parent-child communication, even the most loving and thoughtful parent sometimes puts his or her foot in the mouth. When was the last time you blessed your children by telling them that you love them?

The choices we make as parents and grandparents will affect many of the choices our children and grandchildren will make. Generations are inseparably bound together. Symbolic actions have genuine and lasting power. Our spoken words shape human life. (Bob Buchanan)

JANUARY 13, 2002

Second Sunday After the Epiphany

Worship Theme: God is the giver of all good gifts.

Readings: Isaiah 49:1-7; 1 Corinthians 1:1-9; John 1:29-42

Call to Worship (Psalm 40):

Leader:	Happy are those who trust God, who do not turn to the proud, to those who go astray after false gods.
People:	**I delight to do your will, O my God; your law is within my heart.**
Leader:	I have told the glad news of deliverance in the great congregation; see, I have not restrained my lips, as you know, O LORD.
People:	**I have not hidden your saving help within my heart, I have spoken of your faithfulness and your salvation.**
Leader:	I waited patiently for the LORD; God inclined to me and heard my cry.
People:	**God drew me up from the desolate pit, out of the miry bog, and set my feet upon a rock, making my steps secure.**
All:	**God put a new song in my mouth, a song of praise to our God.**

Pastoral Prayer:

O Fire of Redemption, send us as you sent your servant to be a light of the world. O Voice who calls prophets, who told Isaiah to proclaim the end of exile, call us and give us a sustaining word for those who are lost. O Lamb of God, visit us with mercy. Comfort those who grieve. Heal those who are ill. Fill those who hunger. Humble the arrogant. Bless the just. O Lamb of God, visit us with peace. O Dove who hovered above Jesus, announcing who he really was, speaking to us of our true name, children of the Most High. We praise your name with our voices and with our lives, as we are saints and co-heirs with you in the bounteous future of the heavenly reign. (Scott Haldeman)

SERMON BRIEFS

SERVANT OF THE LORD

ISAIAH 49:1-7

Isaiah 49:1-7 is described by scholars as "the second servant oracle" in the book of Isaiah. There are four: 42:1-9; 49:1-7; 50:4-11; and 52:13–53:12, and all are found in chapters 40–55, the portion of the book of Isaiah known as "Second Isaiah" (chapters 1–39 are called "First Isaiah," and chapters 56–66 are referred to as "Third Isaiah"). Second Isaiah most likely achieved the form we find in our canon of Scripture during the exilic period of ancient Israelite history, the mid-sixth century B.C.E.

What are the servant oracles? How might we describe the servant? In the four passages listed above, Isaiah describes a person who has been chosen by God (42:1; 49:1-3; 50:4-5), who has the Spirit of God (42:1), who upholds the covenant of God (42:4), who will be a light to the nations (42:6; 49:6; 53:11), who will be afflicted (53:4-10), and through whom the nations will be called to account (50:10-11; 52:14-15). Is the person a deliverer for Israel, either a supernatural being or a king from the line of King David? Is it the nation of Israel? Is it someone from outside the people of ancient Israel? All of these options, and a number of others, have been suggested as answers to the question.

The most satisfying answer to the question "Who is the servant?" is "The servant represents the people of ancient Israel." Beginning with Abraham and Sarah, the people of Israel were chosen by God to uphold the covenant and be a light to all the nations. The beginning of Isaiah 49 could certainly be understood as the words of ancient Israel to the nations surrounding it: "The LORD called me before I was born . . . and he said to me, 'You are my servant, Israel, in whom I will be glorified' " (49:1, 3). The words in verse 4, however, indicate frustration, defeat, and resignation on the part of the servant: "I have labored in vain, I have spent my strength for nothing and vanity."

In verses 5 and 6, we encounter a new voice, and the words of this voice suggest a different identity for "the servant of the Lord." This servant cannot be the people of ancient Israel, because this servant has been called to bring back, to raise up Jacob, and to gather and restore Israel to the Lord. Can the servant in the four servant songs in Second Isaiah have more than one identity? Probably. Remember that prophecy is poetry, and poetic language is metaphor and imagery, language that can always have more than one meaning. That is the wonder, that is the frustration, and that is also the danger in interpreting the prophetic texts of the Old Testament.

One way to arrive at an identification of the second servant voice in Isaiah 49 is to examine the historical circumstances in which the words were written. Jerusalem was captured by the Babylonians and the Israelites were relocated to Babylon in the early sixth century. Within fifty years, the Persians had destroyed the Babylonian Empire, leaving the Israelites under the control of yet another foreign power. But the Persian king Cyrus issued an edict that allowed the Israelites to return to Jerusalem and rebuild the city and the Temple. In Ezra 1:1-2, we read that "the LORD stirred up the spirit of King Cyrus . . . so that he sent a herald throughout all his kingdom, [saying,] "The LORD, the God of heaven, . . . has charged me to build him a house at Jerusalem." Many commentary writers understand the second voice in Isaiah 49 as that of a Persian leader who was used by the Lord—as a servant of the Lord—to accomplish the restoration of the Israelites to their land.

When the Israelites in exile were overwhelmed by what

seemed insurmountable obstacles to their calling to be the servant of the Lord (Isa. 49:4), God gave them renewed strength to accomplish the task in the form of permission and aid from the ruling peoples.

Our God is faithful and provides for us in more ways than we can ever know. And God continues to send servants of the Lord into the world to accomplish the fullness of the kingdom of God. Who is the servant of the Lord? The servant is the one who heeds the calling of the Lord at any time and in any place. (Nancy L. deClaissé-Walford)

GOD'S FAITHFULNESS

1 CORINTHIANS 1:1-9

Paul's greeting to the church in Corinth is a simple reminder of the grace that we have received and the gratitude that we need to return to our faithful God.

I. Salutation to the Corinthian Church and Beyond

The apostle Paul writes this letter to the church in Corinth. This letter is similar to the others he wrote. The fact that Paul emphasizes that he is an apostle of Christ Jesus is important. He is acknowledging his authority to the people of Corinth. Not only has Christ called him, but God also plays a part in his apostleship. The letter is specifically addressed to the church at Corinth, but Paul reminds them that they are only a part of the unified body of believers. The phrase *together with all those who in every place call on the name of our Lord Jesus Christ . . .* has the effect of making this letter timeless. This letter is for all Christians in the first century, but perhaps even more for all Christians to follow. God presents grace and peace to us anew each time we open our Bible to these passages.

II. Thanksgiving for the Grace Given and Received

Paul continues to praise the Corinthian church in this salutation. It is very easy to become deeply involved in our lives or the negativity we see on the six o'clock news and forget the abundant grace of our Lord Jesus Christ. Paul gives thanks to God for the grace that God bestows upon the church at Corinth. This grace empowered them in their service to God. What does God's grace do for Christians today? It enriches our relationships. As we grow in our understanding of the grace of God, we can begin to instruct others in the power of Christ. In many cases, the elders of the church that lead a congregation are those who best represent this knowledge and understanding of God's grace. Discipleship is a lifelong process and one not to take lightly. Those who trust in God and allow the power of grace to rule their lives are a strong witness to the power and glory of God to others.

III. The Results of a Relationship in Faith

The Corinthian church became a good witness for the new Christian movement. They spread the word of Jesus Christ and many new believers became a part of the fellowship. God gave them the spiritual gifts they needed to continue in ministry. God gives those same gifts to us as we develop our relationship of faith. God strengthens believers in all things. How do some people who are dying face death with little fear? These people know that God is with them. God comforts them. God gives them the strength they need. God's grace is the gift of our relationship to Christ Jesus. God's grace strengthens and nurtures that relationship with our Lord and Savior as we mature as Christians. The result of this relationship is when we share the grace of God with others in God's world. Paul concludes his salutation with a simple but profound statement, "*God is faithful.*" There is much power in those three words. It is God's faithfulness in the time of Paul's letter to the Corinthians and today that continues to call believers into fellowship with our Lord Christ Jesus. (John Mathis)

BECOMING A FOLLOWER OF JESUS CHRIST

JOHN 1:29-42

When did you and I decide we would follow Jesus? What was it that brought us to the decision to become disciples?

How can we convince others of who Jesus Christ is? These are all important questions, but the matter of being Christian is also an issue of *when, what, or how* we are Christians. An underlying question concerning our discipleship is, "Who helped bring us to Jesus Christ?" John's Gospel is very interested in this question.

I. Someone Points Us to Christ (v. 29)

The next day, the day after some of the religious orthodoxy cornered John the Baptizer, John runs into the One he had said would follow after his pronouncement and who was so powerful he couldn't even tie his sandals. When seeing Jesus, John is overcome and exclaims: "Here is the Lamb of God who takes away the sin of the world!" (v. 29).

The biblical witness is that we are found by God and this occurs with the help of others. John tells his disciples what he witnessed and points them in Jesus' direction. We need to think back from time to time and recall who it was that spoke to us about Christ and, in doing so, pointed us, not to themselves and their experience, but to Christ, so that we might meet and experience Christ for ourselves.

II. Christ Puts Our Lives in Perspective (vv. 30-34)

John's disciples must have been stretching their necks and standing on tiptoe, as all eyes turned to look at who was coming toward them. John is speaking to his disciples; he is not speaking to the religious orthodoxy. As Jesus passes by, John's huddled group of followers must have been stunned with the news that in the person who just passed by was the very fullness of God. And, this person John saw and pointed to was, as he put it, "the Lamb of God." Now, whether his disciples understand the ramifications of his pronouncement is not clear. What is clear is that John knew that Jesus would take the place of the temple sacrifices. Jesus, for John, would be the one and only sacrifice that would completely fulfill salvation for all generations—those that had come before and those that would follow.

III. Being Confronted by Christ (vv. 35-42)

Does the church make it too easy to follow Jesus Christ? This passage makes us think again about the ways and means by which we invite people to follow Christ. The first disciples, Andrew and Peter, are inspired by their rabbi, John, to leave and become disciples of Jesus. As they are following from a distance, Jesus turns around and confronts them with a question: "What do you want?" This is the question with which every would-be follower needs to be confronted.

The disciples' answer is interesting: "Where do you live?" Jesus makes them focus on why they are following. They must grapple with their reasons for becoming disciples. Are they following because John told them to follow? Are they just tagging along with no intention other than their inquisitiveness? Their interest in "where" Jesus lives is significant. Jesus invites them to discover for themselves where he takes up residence. What they will learn is that this Christ, this Messiah, will take up residence, not in a building of a town, a synagogue, or any other institution; but, this Christ has come to set up residence in the human heart and soul.

Becoming disciples of Jesus Christ is no simplistic matter, and we who are followers should not take lightly our calls to lead others to Christ. (Mike Childress)

JANUARY 20, 2002

Third Sunday After the Epiphany

Worship Theme: God breaks through our gloom to save. Jesus says, "Repent," calling us to join his work of teaching, telling good news, and curing.

Readings: Isaiah 9:1-4; 1 Corinthians 1:10-18; Matthew 4:12-23

Call to Worship (Psalm 27):

> *Leader:* The LORD is my light and my salvation; whom shall I fear?
>
> *People:* **The LORD is the stronghold of my life; of whom shall I be afraid?**
>
> *Leader:* One thing I asked of the LORD,
>
> *People:* **to live in the house of the LORD all the days of my life, to behold the beauty of the LORD, and to inquire in his temple.**
>
> *Leader:* The LORD is my light and my salvation; whom shall I fear?
>
> *People:* **The LORD is the stronghold of my life; of whom shall I be afraid?**

Pastoral Prayer:

Savior of all people, come again to save. Healer of all ills, come again to save. Joy of aching hearts, come again to save. You who breaks the yoke of drudgery, relieve our burdens, loose our bonds. Come again to save. To the alien. To the widow. To the orphan. Come again and save. To those in pain. To those who grieve. To those who weep. Come again and save. To the mighty. To the poor. To the homeless. Come again to save. Our light and our salvation, come again to save. (Scott Haldeman)

SERMON BRIEFS

WHAT A CALLING—TO BE A PROPHET!

ISAIAH 9:1-4

Isaiah lived and prophesied during one of the most troubling times in the life of ancient Israel. He received his call in the Jerusalem Temple in the year that King Uzziah died, probably about 740 B.C.E., and continued his prophetic career until about 680 B.C.E. (Isa. 6:1ff). At that time, every nation in the ancient Near East was under the threat of invasion by a new power in Mesopotamia, the Assyrians. One author writes, "From the time of the conquest of Canaan down to the Babylonian exile, Israel had many enemies varying from small tribal groups of raiders to the major world powers, but none can compare with Assyria for the destruction of property, the amount of tribute taken, or captives carried away to foreign lands." What a time to be in the prophetic business!

In addition, Ahaz became king of the southern kingdom of Judah early in the prophetic career of Isaiah. Ahaz was not the best person to lead Judah through a crisis such as the Assyrian threat. Fearful of retaliation by the Assyrian king Tiglath-Pileser, Ahaz refused to join a coalition of Syrian and Palestinian states that had banded together to fight against Assyrian incursions into their lands. In answer, the coalition, which included the northern kingdom of Israel, beseiged Jerusalem in 735 in order to overthrow Ahaz and place a king who was sympathetic to the coalition on the throne. Isaiah's words to Ahaz during this crisis are recorded in chapters 7–14 of the book of Isaiah. In 7:4 Isaiah says, "Take heed, be quiet, do not fear, and do not let your heart be faint because of these two smoldering stumps of firebrands [Israel and Damascus, the two major states of the coalition]." And then Isaiah tells Ahaz that a son will be born to him and that before his son "knows how to refuse the evil and choose the good, the land before whose two kings you are in dread will be deserted" (7:11-16). Isaiah counseled Ahaz to trust in God alone and to wait faithfully for God's deliverance.

Instead, Ahaz turned to Tiglath-Pileser for protection against the coalition. A short time later, as Isaiah had said, Assyria destroyed Damascus and the northern kingdom of Israel, and Ahaz and all of Judah were left at the mercy of the Assyrians, who had every intention of making Judah a province of the Assyrian state (Isa. 8:1-8).

Ahaz and his advisers had not heeded Isaiah's words. What a calling . . . to be a prophet! The prophets were intimately acquainted with God, knew the depth of God's love and compassion for the people, and knew the depth of God's anger at the people. Abraham Heschel writes, "To the prophet, God was overwhelmingly real and shatteringly present." In the days of Isaiah, this overwhelmingly real and shatteringly present God watched, as the people with whom God had covenanted to give land and blessing sought protection and blessing elsewhere.

God, through the words of the prophets, makes it clear to the Israelite people that they will be punished for their disobedience. But God also, through the prophets, speaks words of hope. The God with whom Isaiah was intimately acquainted loved Israel more than anyone could fully understand. Isaiah spoke words of condemnation: "The LORD will bring on you and on your people and on your ancestral house such days as have not come since the day that Ephraim departed from Judah" (7:17). And Isaiah spoke words of hope: "Do not be afraid of the Assyrians . . . for in a very little while my indignation will come to an end" (10:24-25). The two words are thoroughly interwoven in the texture of the book. God expects obedience; the result of disobedience is punishment; and God loves us more than we can understand.

In chapter 9, Isaiah takes comfort in the promise that Judah will survive the terrible assault of the Assyrians. To Ahaz and the Israelites, Isaiah says, "But there will be no gloom for those who were in anguish" (9:1). And in words of praise to God, Isaiah says, "The people who walked in darkness have seen a great light . . . you have multiplied the nation, you have increased its joy . . . for the yoke of their burden, and the bar across their shoulders . . . you have broken" (9:2-4).

On a rather bleak winter day, I walked around my garden inspecting the blackberry plants I trimmed back in November. They looked pretty dead, and I wondered if they would sprout in the spring. And then, next to one of the bare plants, I saw a daffodil shooting up out of the ground. (Nancy L. deClaissé-Walford)

A CHURCH UNITED

1 CORINTHIANS 1:10-18

As we read the opening of this chapter, we know that Paul commends the church at Corinth for all the good things they have accomplished, but we have the feeling that there is another side to the story.

I. Paul's Call for United Purpose

In verse 10 we learn that there are troubles in the church at Corinth. Paul appeals to the Corinthians *by the name of our Lord Jesus Christ.* Paul is again going to great length to ensure that the members of the church realize that he is relaying the message of Christ. Paul does not raise one teaching over another or call on others to follow only his teaching. Instead, Paul asks the Corinthians to reach an agreement and an accord between the different factions of the church. The church is to have a united understanding of Christ and share a united purpose. Paul has heard reports of arguments among the believers in Corinth. The arguments seem to stem from the question of who is the greatest teacher of the gospel message. This leads to two interesting questions. Do Paul, Apollos, and Peter each have a different message to present to the church? Are the people paying more attention to the person bringing the message than to the message itself? Moreover, Paul even compares the three to Christ. This only emphasizes his point that the brothers and sisters of the church at Corinth should unite in the message of the church and the purpose or mission of the church.

II. Has Christ Been Divided?

The key question in this passage is simple: *Has Christ been divided?* Who is responsible for the power and glory of the message that the Corinthian church is proclaiming? Paul speaks of the centrality of Christ in the gospel message. Christ has not been divided. The message of the gospel has not changed. There is much power in the message of Christ, even now. Also unchanged since the time of Paul's writing is the number of divisions within the church. How do we Christians continue to exist in our divisions, while also keeping the message of Christ the central focus of our teachings? It is not as important how we worship, as long as our message is united. We ought to keep Christ crucified at the center of our faith and practices. God sent Paul to the Corinthians to proclaim the good news of Christ Jesus. God sent Paul with a humble heart and a simple message. Christ Jesus perished on the cross for the redemption of humankind. This message is as powerful today as when Paul brought it to the people of Corinth.

III. The Message of the Cross

Paul goes to great length to give the glory and credit to God. God is responsible for salvation. Too often, we become enamored with our own abilities to witness or share the gospel message. We must always keep in mind that Christ brought salvation into the world and that salvation is by the power of God. In addition, the message of the cross is not a once-in-a-lifetime event. Paul speaks of salvation as a process, an ongoing action. In the cross, we continue to see the power of God. (John Mathis)

GOING FISHING WITH JESUS

MATTHEW 4:12-23

How are your fishing skills? Have you ever let "the big one" get away?

Soon after beginning his public ministry, Jesus was walking

beside the Sea of Galilee and invited two brothers to be his disciples. Jesus promised, "Follow me, and I will make you fish for people." These two brothers, Simon Peter and Andrew, were ordinary people.

Although we may not be attracted initially to this metaphor, it describes the expansive, all-embracing nature of the kingdom of God, which is proclaimed and enacted in Jesus Christ. Jesus does not call his people to some quiet, settled-down affair. Rather, he is always on the move, pushing out, calling forth, and reaching toward the whole world and the whole realm of humankind.

When was the last time you shared your faith with someone who is neither a believer nor a member of any church? Some of us have never been told or shown how. Others are reluctant, because they do not want to be perceived as "pushy," or they are afraid of being rejected. However, most people who don't go to church, when asked why, respond that nobody ever invites them. If you and I are honest, we have done a poor job of fishing with Jesus. We hesitantly cast our nets, and then quickly pull them in, satisfied with a meager catch.

Let's go fishing with Jesus and learn how to share our faith more effectively.

I. A New Location

When we go fishing with Jesus, location is extremely important. Unfortunately, most churches spend far too much time, energy, and money fishing in their own parking lots. To become fishers of people, we have to be willing to leave our comfortable pews, break out of our "holy huddles," and move back into the marketplace where people are hurting and searching for ultimate purpose.

After Jesus was crucified and buried, Simon Peter returned to his former profession—a fisherman on the Sea of Galilee. Peter was fishing offshore when Jesus walked up and called out, "Any luck?" Not knowing who was speaking, Peter and his fishing buddies mumbled, "We haven't caught a thing." Then Jesus said, "Throw your net on the other side of the boat." When they did, they were unable to haul in the net because the net was full (John 21).

II. A New Approach

Going fishing with Jesus also requires a new approach. Relationships are the key! We need to find ways to build better relationships with our neighbors and friends. After Matthew met Jesus, he threw a party and invited all his friends to come and meet his new friend.

Not only is a new approach required, but also a wide variety of baits. While walking through a fishing department, I was amazed at the fishing tackle area. There were literally hundreds of baits, and artificial worms of every imaginable color. Why in the world would a fisherman need all those different kinds of baits? Because every situation is different. A skilled fisherman selects a bait made for specific conditions: the season of the year, the time of day, the color of the water, the depth of the water, and the behavioral patterns of the fish.

III. A New Time

Going fishing with Jesus requires also that we are time sensitive. Luke's account of the disciples going fishing with Jesus has a few extra details. Early one morning, Peter and Andrew were washing their nets. After fishing all night, they had come back empty-handed. No matter how much you like to fish, that's not fun.

Jesus climbed into Simon Peter's boat and told him to push just off shore, so he could speak to the crowd. When Jesus finished speaking, he instructed Peter to move into deeper water and let down his nets again. Luke 5:6-7 reads, "They caught so many fish that their nets were beginning to break. So they signaled their partners in the other boat to come and help them. And they came and filled both boats, so that they began to sink."

Luke's account reminds us that to be successful in fishing, we must be sensitive to the time of day. Fish don't feed all day long. We must rely on the Holy Spirit to tell us when to cast our nets, when we need to listen, and when we need to speak. A common mistake in sharing our faith with a nonbeliever is moving ahead too fast.

IV. A New Direction

Finally, going fishing with Jesus will bring new direction and purpose in our lives. Jesus took the everyday, customary skills of Peter and Andrew and gave them a new direction. If Jesus said to two fishermen, "Come and I will make you fishers of people," what would he say to you? Benjamin Garrison says, "Every once in a while someone is called by God from the cash register to the pulpit . . . but more usually it is a call to stay at the cash register, to witness in business to kingdom business—a call to keep on fishing."

Will you go fishing with Jesus? Will you go and share your faith wherever he leads? (Bob Buchanan)

JANUARY 27, 2002

Fourth Sunday After the Epiphany

Worship Theme: God saves, turning creation right side up. The poor and the weak are God's instruments as the way of the cross leads not to defeat but to redemption.

Readings: Micah 6:1-8; 1 Corinthians 1:18-31; Matthew 5:1-12

Call to Worship (Psalm 15):

Leader: O LORD, who may abide in your tent?

People: **Who may dwell on your holy hill?**

Leader: Those who walk blamelessly, and do what is right,

People: **Those who speak the truth from their heart;**

Leader: We come into God's house with joy.

People: **Let us worship God.**

Pastoral Prayer:

All wise God, who acts in ways we call foolish, use our foolishness to serve your world. Bless all gathered here. Bless all those who gather in your name across the globe. Bless those who are poor with generous neighbors. Bless those who grieve with arms to hold them as they weep. Bless the hungry with full cupboards. Bless the lonely with friends. Bless those who do justice with endurance and firm hope. Bless those who make peace with courage to defy those who fuel hate. Bless the homeless with adequate shelter. Bless the sick with someone who heals. Bless the anxious with peace of mind. In the names of the One reviled and crucified who trusted you to the grave and who now lives and reigns

56

with you and the Holy Spirit, one God forever. Amen. (Scott Haldeman)

SERMON BRIEFS

A CALL BACK TO LOVE

MICAH 6:1-8

The presidential elections held in 2000 showed us how the legal process can take many twists and turns in a seemingly endless process that produces no easy solution. Although it was a contest between two sides, both sides took advantage of different positions and options that revealed how complex the legal system in the United States can be. It is a process that is open to appeals and even the court of public opinion, yet in the end one side is the winner, the other the loser. In this passage from Micah, God has a controversy with Israel. The case, God says, can be taken to the hills and mountains. Israel can plead its case to these immovable objects of nature, but they must answer the hard questions of faithfulness and justice that God is asking. The way in which Israel was living revealed unfaithfulness to God and to one another. Throughout their history, God has demonstrated to Israel the saving acts of a God who cares. These saving acts were meant not only to liberate, but also to instruct them on proper conduct in a relationship with God and with their brothers and sisters in the nation of Israel. Liberating the nation from slavery in Egypt was an act that included all the Israelites who would make the journey out of bondage into freedom. No one was excluded; indeed, all were invited and encouraged to attend. Even as the nation trekked across the wilderness, other people from different heritages joined them and became a part of the nation of Israel. The journey of becoming a community was one that would not end after crossing the final border into the promised land. It was a lifelong journey that would show to other nations the power and love of the one true God. Instead, the temptation was to become like other nations. The people rejected the idea of community in favor of individual greed and selfishness. Sharing was not as important as hoarding. Forgiveness and mercy were no longer as valued as revenge and vengeance. What troubled God was that their acts of worship to show forgiveness for wrongdoing were done more for show than to illustrate true inward change. For the people of Israel to be the people of God, their hearts had to be the heart of God. God is indeed not as interested in show as in true conversion of heart and spirit to a oneness with God and with each other. This text includes the powerful verse, "and what does the LORD require of you but to do justice, and to love kindness, and to walk humbly with your God?" The requirements of God have always been those that begin and stay in one's heart. In the passage about eating with unclean hands Jesus explained that it is not what goes into one's mouth that defies a person as much as it is what comes out, for the words that come out reflect what is inside the heart. God does not require rivers of oil, or exquisite livestock as sacrifices, but rather that one live a life that "does justice," and "loves kindness," and "walks humbly" with God. The application for us today is that we should not be simply content to follow acceptable form and structure in our worship and service, yet lack a true love for one another and a true love for God. We can do countless things as an expression of what we know is right and good, but unless we possess inside the true requirement, a love of God and our fellow humans, we have failed. God is calling us back to love. (Eradio Valverde Jr.)

KNOWLEDGE OF GOD

1 CORINTHIANS 1:18-31

Paul continues his message from the previous section of Scripture. He continues to talk of the *message about the cross* and our knowledge regarding the wisdom of God.

I. The Wisdom of God

In this continuation of his admonishment of the people of the Corinthian church, Paul struggles to make it known that their knowledge of God is a gift. Paul's questions are reminiscent of his

Jewish upbringing and the Old Testament Scripture. It is almost as if God is questioning Job once again. Where are those who claim to be wise, to be great debaters, or to be interpreters of the Law? Do they have full knowledge of God? Paul seems to confess that we cannot know God's wisdom.

II. Knowledge of God

At this point, Paul does a short reflection of the ministry of Jesus. Throughout his ministry, the Jewish people continue to believe in Jesus and follow him because of the miracles (or signs, as John proclaims in his Gospel) that he performs. We do not know God by the signs and miracles we see. Moreover, the people of the Greek world held wisdom and learning in high regard. Paul proclaims that we see the wisdom of God in *Christ crucified*. We know God through faith. The Jewish people who did not continue to follow Christ could not accept a Messiah who did not conquer the world. The Greek people saw the message of the cross as foolishness. However, to those who have faith, Christ is the power and the wisdom of God. Verse 25 serves as a reminder to Christians who believe that they have it all figured out and become perhaps a bit to smug in their knowledge of Christ. Paul reminds us of the infinite power of God. *God's foolishness is wiser than human wisdom, and God's weakness is stronger than human strength*. True knowledge of God is to respect and honor the infinite power of God.

III. Personal Knowledge of God

In order to explain further his message to the Corinthian believers, Paul personalizes the message. The people in the church at Corinth were ordinary people. They were not highly educated. They were not wealthy, or of royal birth. God uses the disenfranchised to show glory and power to the world. This is particularly important to believers now as they look to serve the Lord. God calls Christians to action and to use their spiritual gifts that God gives them through Christ Jesus. Some fear that they are not talented enough, rich enough, or strong enough. As we serve the Lord, let us not forget that our talents, our means, and our strengths are all gifts of the God who calls us. As Paul reclaims from the psalmist, *Let the one who boasts, boast in the Lord*. (John Mathis)

A HIGHER ROAD TO HAPPINESS

MATTHEW 5:1-12

Perhaps you have heard about the student going around campus wearing a big button with the letters BAIK. Someone stopped him and asked what it meant.

He replied, "That means, 'Boy Am I Confused.' "

"But don't you know that 'confused' is not spelled with a K?" he was reminded.

"Man," he replied, "you don't know how confused I am."[1]

You and I live in some rather confusing times. In the midst of this chaos, where do you look for happiness? Our text is the Beatitudes (Matt. 5:1-12), which introduce the Sermon on the Mount that Jesus delivered to his disciples or "students," as they embarked on their journey with him. Every beatitude begins with a blessing. *The Jerusalem Bible* translates the word *blessed* as "happy." Robert Schuller even refers to the Beatitudes as "The Be (Happy) Attitudes."[2]

Dennis Prager, author of *Happiness Is a Serious Problem*, has spent several years studying happiness, and concludes that there is little correlation between the circumstances of people's lives and how happy they are.[3] Let us consider how to take a higher road to lasting happiness by embracing nine life-changing attitudes. The first letter of each attitude spells the word *HAPPINESS*.

Jesus describes the first attitude in Matthew 5:3: "Blessed (Happy) are the poor in spirit, for theirs is the kingdom of heaven." Let's name the first attitude "**HONESTY AND HUMILITY**. To be "poor in spirit" means to be humble. To be humble is to be honest about our need for God. You and I are not self-sufficient, and there is nothing we can do to earn favor with God. God's favor is a gift called GRACE.

The second attitude appears in v. 4: "[Happy] are those who

mourn, for they will be comforted." Of all the roads leading to lasting happiness, this one sounds the strangest. Jesus says that true happiness begins with deep sadness. Max Lucado translates the second beatitude as, "Blessed are those who know they are in trouble and have enough sense to admit it."[4] This attitude encourages us to **ADMIT** our failures and **ACCEPT** God's grace. When we do this, God promises to comfort us in five ways: by giving us *courage* for the present, *calm* during the storm, *companionship* for the journey, *compassion* for our shortcomings, and *confidence* for the future.

The third attitude is the opposite of **POWER**. "[Happy] are the meek, for they will inherit the earth" (v. 5). Meekness is not synonymous with weakness. Moses is described as a very "meek" man (Num. 12:3 RSV), but it is clear from his life that he was no pushover! It was in his relationship with God that he was described as "meek," suggesting that he was humble, teachable, and submissive to God.[5] The third attitude is meekness—an openness to be taught and guided by the Master Teacher.

The fourth attitude is the **PURSUIT** of what is right. Mother Teresa was asked what she thought of America, and replied without hesitation, "I have never seen such poor people." On an earlier visit she said, "In India—people are dying of physical starvation. In America, people are dying of emotional starvation."[6]

The fourth Beatitude promises, "[Happy] are those who hunger and thirst for righteousness, for they will be filled."

The fifth attitude encourages us to **INITIATE FORGIVE-NESS.** "[Happy] are the merciful, for they will receive mercy." Resentment has been described as "the cocaine of emotions." The more you feed it, the more it demands. Resentment and anger can kill the embittered and angry. It can kill physically: chronic anger has been linked with elevated cholesterol, high blood pressure, and other deadly conditions. It can kill emotionally: it can raise anxiety levels and lead to depression. It can be spiritually fatal, too, because it can shrivel the soul.[7]

The sixth attitude is **INSIDE ("N" SIDE).** "[Happy] are the pure in heart, for they will see God" (Matt. 5:8). The sixth Beatitude says that God does the best work from the INSIDE ("N" SIDE) out, and advises us to look at what's on the INSIDE ("N" SIDE) of a person and not vice versa.

The seventh attitude is "[Happy] are the peacemakers, for they will be called children of God" (v. 9). Be **EMPATHETIC** to folks who are hurting. Our volatile and violent world needs more ambassadors of peace!

The eighth and ninth attitudes are so similar that many believe they belong together. They have the same first letter—"S," and both stand for **SACRIFICE**! "[Happy] are those who are persecuted for righteousness' sake, for theirs is the kingdom of heaven. [Happy] are you when people revile you and persecute you and utter all kinds of evil against you falsely . . . for your reward is great in heaven . . ." These two Beatitudes remind us that nothing comes easily. Everything worthwhile has a price and yes, some things are worth dying for!

Where will you search for lasting happiness? No matter what the world tells you, Jesus calls us to follow a higher road to happiness. (Bob Buchanan)

---

1. Robert Coleman, "Fools for Christ," *Preaching*, May/June 1999, p. 8.

2. Robert Schuller, *The Be (Happy) Attitudes* (Waco, Texas: Word Books, 1985), p. 15.

3. Dennis Prager, "A Simple Truth about Happiness," *Reader's Digest*, June 1998, p. 99.

4. Max Lucado, *The Applause of Heaven* (Dallas: Word Publishing, 1990), p. 53.

5. Allison Trites, "The Blessings and Warnings of the Kingdom," *Review and Expositor* (Spring 1992), p. 186.

6. Schuller, pp. 100 and 110.

7. Lucado, pp. 111-12.

SPIRITUAL PREPARATION

FEBRUARY

Jesus is in the wilderness for forty days. Moses had been on the mountain for forty days without food. Elijah had a forty-day flight to the mountain of God. Israel wandered in the wilderness for forty years. In Lent we focus on the temptations of Jesus and our own temptations. Lent is a forty-day journey through the wilderness. It is clear in the New Testament that Jesus identifies with us, as One who encounters testing. "We have [a high priest] who in every respect has been tested as we are, yet without sin," the writer of the letter to the Hebrews insists (4:15*b*).

In Lent we enter into a period of spiritual self-examination. The gospel lection on the first Sunday of Lent focuses on the temptation of Jesus in the wilderness (Matt. 4:1-11). In a wonderful book entitled *Living with Contradiction*, Esther de Waal poses a question:

> Those three temptations Jesus faced are equally my own temptations: to be relevant, to be spectacular, to be powerful. Am I able, like Christ, to put them down?

The first temptation: if you are the Son of God, command this stone to become a loaf of bread. *This is the temptation to be relevant*. It is the need, the drive, the desire, the compulsion, the obsession to do what is urgent, to be productive, to make a splash, to be known, to be helpful, to be useful.

Now, in one sense, there is nothing wrong with relevance. A loaf of bread is a wonderful thing to a person who is fasting, or to a starving world. But Jesus' mission was not to turn stones into bread. He had a clear sense of where he was headed in life, of his Father's purpose for him. And so he rejected the voice that urged him to transform stones into bread. He said "no" to what someone has called "the tyranny of the urgent."

Steven Covey, the best-selling author, has written about the urgent and the important. Some things are urgent and important: if my car doesn't start this morning, that's important and urgent. Some things are urgent, but not very important. This sale will last only three more days—but we know there will be another one. Some things are neither urgent nor important—they are simply a waste of time. But some aspects of life are important, and perhaps not urgent. What is important, but not urgent?

> Reading the Bible is not urgent, but it is important.
> Riding bikes with my children is not urgent, but it is important.
> Putting flowers on a grave is not urgent, but it is important.
> Taking a trip, just for fun, is not urgent, but it is important.
> Exercising is not urgent, but it is important.
> Having a date with your spouse is not urgent, but it is important.
> Prayer is not urgent, but it is important.

Jesus rejects the urgent, in favor of the important, as he resists the temptation to turn stones into bread. He says, quoting:

> One does not live by bread alone, but by every word that comes from the mouth of the LORD. (Deut. 8:3)

- Is your ministry focused on matters that are urgent but not important? Do you find yourself being asked to turn stones into bread?

There is a second temptation: if you are the Son of God, throw yourself down from the temple . . . the angels will catch you, you will not be harmed. *This is the temptation to be spectacular.* As pastors, if we are honest, we can identify with this temptation. We want to serve large, growing congregations. We want to impact the lives of persons in dramatic ways. We want to bring about visible change in our communities.

Sometimes this temptation can lead toward what a friend calls the "people-pleasing" syndrome. We begin to minister in ways that are pleasing to others. The actions may be right or wrong, good or bad. The bottom line becomes the adoration and the applause of others. This is a seductive temptation for pastors.

The tempter places the question before Jesus: Will you do this one thing for me, for us, for the cause? The danger in this request is that we can be distracted from our mission in life. Jesus did not come to throw himself from the temple. As Henri Nouwen notes: "Jesus refused to be a stunt man. He did not come to prove himself. He did not come to walk on hot coals, swallow fire, or put his hand in the lion's mouth to demonstrate that he had something to say."

Jesus came for another reason: to announce that the kingdom of God was here!

His temptation in life was to become distracted from this mission.

- In what ways are you distracted from your calling to follow Christ as a pastor? How are you tempted to do the spectacular?

There is a third temptation: *to be powerful*. The devil shows Jesus all the kingdoms of the world and says, "These can all be yours if you will fall down and worship me." The Bible speaks of the devil and temptation in a variety of ways: as tendencies within ourselves, as a personal being outside ourselves with whom we struggle, as a powerful angel gone astray, as an organized force at odds with the will and purpose of God. The word *devil* means "the slanderer"; the word *satan* means "the adversary."

If we are trying to live within God's will and purpose, we will encounter temptation. One of the strongest is the desire for power. We quickly adopt the world's definitions of power; we can trace this back to Israel's desire for a king, so that she could be like the other nations (read 1 Samuel 8).

Jesus rejects the world's forms of power. Again, Henri Nouwen has a wonderful reflection on this temptation: "What makes this temptation of power so irresible? Maybe it is that power offers an easy substitute for the hard task of love. It seems easier to be God than to love God, easier to control people than to love people, easier to own life than to love life. Jesus asks, 'Do you love me?' We ask, 'Can I sit at your right hand and your left hand?' Our painful history is that [we are] ever and ever again tempted to choose power over love, control over the cross, leading over being led."

- How are you tempted to seize power, to control others, to dominate?

These three temptations—to be relevant, to be spectacular, to be powerful—were the temptations of Jesus. As his representatives, as his followers, they are our temptations as well. In Lent we are challenged to confront them.

May the spirit of God sustain you in these forty days! (Ken Carter)

Sources: Esther de Waal, *Living with Contradiction* (Harrisburg, Penn.: Morehouse Publishing Co., 1998), p. 95; Henri J. Nouwen, *In The Name of Jesus: Reflections on Christian Leadership.* 2nd ed. (New York: Crossroad, 1993), pp. 38, 59-60; Steven Covey, *The Seven Habits of Highly Effective People* (S & S Trade, 1989, 1990).

FEBRUARY 3, 2002

Fifth Sunday After the Epiphany

Worship Theme: The fast that God requires is that we let the oppressed go free. In this way God uses us to be about God's just and peaceful reign.

Readings: Isaiah 58:1-9*a* (9*b*-12); 1 Corinthians 2:1-12 (13-16); Matthew 5:13-20

Call to Worship (Psalm 112):

Leader: Happy are those who fear the LORD,

People: **Happy are those who delight in his commandments.**

Leader: It is well with those who deal generously and lend, who conduct their affairs with justice.

People: **For the righteous will never be moved; they will be remembered forever.**

Leader: They are not afraid of evil tidings; their hearts are firm, secure in the LORD.

People: **Their hearts are steady, they will not be afraid; in the end they will look in triumph on their foes.**

Leader: Praise the LORD!

People: **Praise the LORD!**

Pastoral Prayer:

God of justice, you free slaves and feed the hungry. Free us. Feed us. God of justice, you spoke through the prophets, redefining a fast as an act of charity; speak now, transforming empty acts of devotion into gestures of liberation. Through us may the hungry eat. Through us may wounds be cleaned and bound. Through us may the imprisoned be visited. Through us may the grieving find their tears wiped away. God of justice who seeks the renewal of creation, visit us with power. Amen. (Scott Haldeman)

SERMON BRIEFS

THE DISCIPLINE OF FASTING

ISAIAH 58:1-9*a* (9*b*-12)

The discipline of fasting was practiced throughout biblical history. The one commanded day of fasting was appointed by the law on the Day of Atonement. The prophet Joel called for national repentance and exhorted the Israelites to be restored to favor in the eyes of God with fasting (Joel 2:12). There are numerous scripture references indicating that fasting was to be practiced by God's people. Their fasts included times of calamity and national danger (2 Chron. 20:3; Ezra 8:21), times of conflict (1 Sam. 7:6) and catastrophe (2 Sam. 1:12). Men of faith fasted at various times and for sundry reasons—David (2 Sam. 12:16), Moses (Deut. 9:18, 25). The length of fasting has no prescribed uniformity. Sunrise to sunset (Jud. 20:26; 1 Sam. 14:24). According to Daniel 6:18, it could be for a shorter period of time. A three-day fast was asked by Esther of Mordecai and "the Jews . . . in Susa" (Esther 4:16). Also, seven days was a fast period (1 Sam. 1:13) and on another occasion three weeks (Dan. 10:1-2). Moses fasted for forty days (Exod. 34:28).

Fasting was common, but in today's scripture the attitude of fasting was being challenged by Isaiah. Fasting should reflect the heart's motive through acts of righteousness. There is within this scripture text a rebuke, a warning, and a promise.

I. A Rebuke Concerning Fasting

The rebuke is over self-righteousness, the external religion of show instead of the inner act of humility. The Israelites did not possess a sincere heart. Fasting was done so that others could see and "admire" their commitment to God. This style would crystalize centuries later in the Pharisee party of Israel.

The people's hearts were not right with God. They still possessed sin in their lives and God knew it. God desired that their hearts would hunger and thirst for God's will, ways, purposes, and not just for food and drink. The psalmist wrote,

> As the deer pants for streams of water, so my soul pants for you, O God. My soul thirsts for God, for the living God (Ps. 42:1-2a NIV)

The stinging rebuke from God was well warranted for they did not "pant" for God! Do you crave to experience God?

II. A Promise Concerning Fasting

Isaiah lays down the promise principle of fasting for the people. Elmer Towns describes the purposes of fasting in his book *Fasting for Spiritual Breakthrough* (Falls Church, Va: Regal Books, 1996):

1. "To loose the chains of injustice" (v. 6a NIV). This fast frees both the individual and others from the addictions to sin.
2. "And untie the cords of yoke" (v. 6b NIV). This fast is to invite the Holy Spirit to lift the heavy load of problems we face and overcome barriers that keep us from walking joyfully with God.
3. "To set the oppressed free" (v. 6c NIV). This fast would be used to bring people out of the kingdom of darkness into God's holy light. It would bring revival and evangelism into our lives.
4. "And break every yoke" (v. 6d NIV). This fast is to make sure that God is in control of our lives in all areas.
5. "To share your food with the hungry" (v. 7a NIV). This fast focuses on the humanitarian and social needs of the world.

6. "Light will break forth" (v. 8*a* NIV). This fast will help in our decisions. "What does God want in life?" becomes the foundational question.
7. "Your healing will quickly appear" (v. 8*b* NIV). This fast will ask for physical healing and health for individuals.
8. "Then your righteousness will go before you" (v. 8*c* NIV). This fast is to give testimony to the influence Jesus has on our lives.
9. "The glory of the LORD will be your rear guard" (v. 8*d* NIV). This fast asks for God's protection from Satan's power.

III. A Warning Concerning Fasting

If we do not follow and approach God with a sincere heart, God gives a stern warning, "You cannot fast as you do today and expect your voice to be heard on high" (Isa. 58:4 NIV).

What God wants is the opposite—God desires our voices to be heard because God loves us! A warning is for our benefit, much like a yellow traffic light—it's a caution that this is a place to become alert because of danger. With the world in its mess, we need fasting to draw us close to God. We snuggle close to God as God comes close to us!

Let the restoration of the soul begin today! (Derl Keefer)

GIFTS OF THE SPIRIT

1 CORINTHIANS 2:1-12 (13-16)

Paul continues to call the Corinthians to a spirit of unity. He emphasizes that his message is simple, the power of the crucified Christ. Paul does not feel that his knowledge is sufficient to explain the mystery of God, but the experiences that he shares demonstrate the power of God. Our challenge is to share our experiences of Christ with others in simple, meaningful ways, rather than with big words or theological debate.

I. Where to Place Our Faith

As Christians, we need to be extremely careful to place our faith and trust in the power of God, as opposed to human wisdom. Are we to follow those who proclaim the message of Jesus Christ? As followers of Jesus, we need to be careful in the amount of praise we give to those who are Christ's messengers. We have had too many examples in the past of ministers who have gone astray, who have led others away from the flock. It is not a competition to see who can lead the most people to Christ. Does not God bring about salvation? This is the message that Paul is trying to impart to the believers in Corinth. Do not place your faith in Paul or in Paul's knowledge, but put your faith in God through Jesus Christ, crucified for humanity. Paul shares his belief in the power of Christ crucified and allows God to continue the work that he starts.

II. Proclaiming the Wisdom of God

We who proclaim the message of God should be trembling in our boots at all times. We confess to speak wisdom that our faith has allowed us to proclaim. Paul describes God's wisdom as secret and hidden. Revelation of God's wisdom is through the Holy Spirit. Paul ascribes most power to the Spirit by suggesting that *the Spirit searches everything, even the depths of God*. God is still at work today by the Spirit of Christ in the hearts of believers. The Spirit helps us to discern the gifts that God gives to us, and allows us to put these gifts to work for the Kingdom. As Christians mature in their relationship with God, they gain a better understanding of God's will and greater ability to share God's wisdom.

III. Gifts of the Spirit and the Example of Christ

Paul relays to us that our words and witness are not by our wisdom, but by the Holy Spirit. This passage of the Corinthian letter brings about several poignant questions. Why do some people refuse to see the power of Christ and even reject the teachings of God? Does the Spirit of God dwell in only a select few? I believe that the Spirit of God does exist in all human beings, so why does not everyone believe in the power of Christ crucified? Theologically, I struggle with this passage. What does Paul mean by 'unspiritual'? For me, God reveals the message of Christ through the Holy Spirit. Our witness is living out the Spirit in our words and actions. How do we discern how we are to live? We know the example that Jesus Christ gives us through his life in the world. Through the Holy Spirit, we have the mind of Christ. (John Mathis)

SALT AND LIGHT

MATTHEW 5:13-20

At the conclusion of the Sermon on the Mount, Jesus offers another teaching, and in a sense, an affirmation to the gathered crowds. He suggests the metaphors of salt and light for who and what those among him have come to be. Note that Jesus does not say, "You should be the salt," or "You should be the light." Rather, Jesus says, "You *are* the salt; you *are* the light." He does not give his listeners an option about what they are or are to be.

Salt and light alone are useless, but when combined with other resources they are fruitful and productive. Salt is that which gives taste to bland food. It is also a preserver of that which is fresh, healthy, and good nourishment for humanity. Alone, it is simply a grainy pile of elements, wasting space. Light, by itself, does little good if it has nothing to shine upon. It gives vision to eyes and illuminates all that surrounds it.

Jesus' charge is a critical one. He teaches those around him that they are the salt and light in a bland and dark world. The flavor and vision of the world are up to them. It is their responsibility to shine their light before others, for the glory of God.

Once Jesus tells his listeners who they are, he instructs them on how they should be. Those in the crowd would know that to be the salt and light of the world, one must follow the Law and the Prophets. Jesus' message is that the Law is no longer enough; he claims he has come to *fulfill* the Law, when in actuality what he does is *fill* the Law. The old laws should be followed and taught, but a new action is proposed. The commandments laid down in the Law and the Prophets are good, but things are different now that Jesus is there to fulfill them. Now, righteousness is built on the charge of being salt and light. Jesus is there to set a new standard—it is no longer good enough to be like the law-abiding scribes and Pharisees—those who traditionally knew the most about following the commandments in the Law and Prophets. A new era has dawned with the fulfillment of the Messiah.

Within a few quick sentences, Jesus names his listeners as the future of the faith—they are the salt and the light. He informs them that following the old laws is no longer enough to enter the kingdom of heaven, and he tells them that they now have to be more righteous than those they know to be the most righteous. Not only is this a surprising charge, but it seems like an impossible task, that is until you consider that the One who has obeyed all the laws is the One preaching to them. The perfect example of what it means to be righteous, even more righteous than the scribes and Pharisees, was standing in front of them. While Jesus does not directly say it, he beckons his listeners to follow his example in the Law and in righteousness to bring glory and honor to God. (Victoria Atkinson)

FEBRUARY 10, 2002

Transfiguration Sunday

Worship Theme: God performs signs of power and reveals that Jesus is the Messiah, showing us still that the divine promises are trustworthy.

Readings: Exodus 24:12-18; 2 Peter 1:16-21; Matthew 17:1-9

Call to Worship (Psalm 2):

Leader: Serve the LORD with fear and with trembling.

People: **We will serve the LORD with fear.**

Leader: I will tell of the decree of the LORD: He said to me, "You are my son; today I have begotten you.

People: **"Ask of me, and I will make the nations your heritage, and the ends of the earth your possession."**

Leader: Serve the LORD with fear and with trembling.

People: **Let us worship God.**

Pastoral Prayer:
Holy One of Israel, as you made Moses' face to glow on the mountain where you gave your people your Law, order our steps by your Word. As we praise you in this time and place, we offer you a sacrifice of thanksgiving and tell of your glory. Holy One, who transfigured Jesus upon the mountain, identifying him as your Beloved Child, transfigure us, the Body of Christ, in this time and place, so we might be a revelation of your grace this

day. Transfigure your church to be about your work. Transfigure our society according to your justice. Transfigure our budgets—denominational, federal, local, and personal—according to the needs of your poor ones. Transfigure our lives toward service. In the name of your Beloved, transfigured now beside you in glory and coming again in glory. Amen. (Scott Haldeman)

SERMON BRIEFS

GIVE ME CLOUDS AND FIRE (I THINK)

EXODUS 24:12-18

If you could go with Moses up onto the mountain, into the cloud of God's glory, would you do it? I cannot decide. On one hand, the opportunity is too wonderful to miss. On the other, I think I would be terrified.

A lot of things are happening in this part of the book of Exodus: the giving of the Law, and instructions for the tabernacle and Israel's worship. At the center of it all is a good, old-fashioned appearance of God. God initiates the action, which takes place on a mountain—a holy mountain. The people, even the elders, have to stay back. A cloud covers the mountain. After six days of waiting, God speaks on the seventh day. The glory of the Lord appears as a devouring fire in the sight of all the people.

Here Scripture struggles to describe the holiness of God. God is not like you and me, we are reminded. The presence of God calls forth awe, reverence, and even fear. I am intrigued by the possibility of experiencing the indescribable glory of God first-hand. If I were given the chance to do what Moses did, though, I might be more comfortable watching from a distance with everyone else.

This passage has a lot in common with Gospel narratives about the transfiguration of Jesus. There, too, Scripture struggles to describe God's holiness. There, too, we hear of a mountain, a cloud, a few chosen witnesses, and the glory of God. If these passages sound strange to you, you are not alone. Modern Christians have a tendency to look at them as fossils. The attempts to describe God in these texts are a bit crude; they are a touch less developed than our efforts. Like fossils, they show us how things used to be. This is how people imagined God before they learned better. Fossils, of course, are no longer living. This view becomes a problem precisely because these passages want to live. Most contemporary theology is abstract and ethical. You do not find a lot of clouds and fire. Our attempts to describe God are good and helpful, but we should not despise earlier efforts because they are different, especially when they are found in Scripture. What we lose when we give up clouds and fire and other pictures of God is the sense of awe and reverence and powerful presence that these stories want to express. We need to be reminded of God's transcendence. We need to feel again the power and the wonder.

Both the transfiguration of Jesus and the story of Moses on the mountain speak of more than just God's glory. They teach us that God reaches out to us. Yes, God is holy and majestic and far above us. Being finite creatures, we can neither understand nor even experience God. Nevertheless, God desires to reach us. So God accommodates our weakness. God comes to us in ways we can experience and comprehend. Moses was the mediator between God and Israel. Israel needed instructions for living and worship if they were to be God's people—if they were to know God and have a relationship with God. Moses' mission on the mountain was all about those things. The Gospels tell us that Jesus is greater than Moses, though he is about the same business. Jesus shows us God. We know God through him. We know God through him in a way that we could not without him. The better we comprehend the holiness of God, the more we will value what Jesus has done for us.

The Christian life balances the mystery of God with an intimate relationship with God. We may use words different from those of the writers of Exodus; but we share with them a common experience. The one true God, sovereign and holy, has reached out to us. We are overwhelmed and maybe a little frightened. But we go to the mountain because God has called us there. Amen. (David C. Mauldin)

TRUST THE TRADITION!

2 PETER 1:16-21

"Christianity did not begin with you!" It was a revealing revelation, really. To realize that there were other Christians before me was a sobering thought.

I think most of us most of the time realize that Christianity did not begin with us. But, it is so easy to forget! How easy it is to forget that others have opinions and theology that are just as valid as ours. It is so easy to fall into the trap of thinking that we have all the answers, that our theology is superior, and that God is going to ask our opinion about how to judge the rest of the world.

This attitude was prevalent to the church to which 2 Peter is written. In this predominantly Gentile church, many of the first-generation leaders, such as Peter, are passing away and false teaching is becoming more commonplace. Peter says, "Don't forsake your heritage. Trust the tradition!" In verses 16-18, he reminds followers of the faith that these formative events of the faith were witnessed firsthand. Peter and others saw the power of God descend on Jesus at his transfiguration, the same power that raised him from the dead and will bring him back a second time. These are not cleverly invented tales. They were there! They saw! Argue and debate our creeds and theological formation if you will, but we know what we saw. It is the power of personal testimony.

We owe those who gave us such a trusted tradition a great deal. Many fulfilled their calling by sitting in a dusty corner copying the Scriptures. Others preserved it at a great personal price. Because of them, this wonderful tradition has survived burnings and bannings.

How can we ever repay the community of faith who gave us its book? One way is to remember that this book can only be interpreted properly within the community out of which it was born (v. 20). Another way is to remember that the same Holy Spirit who guided its construction then (v. 21) is the same Holy Spirit who guides its interpretation now! The same Holy Spirit who revealed God's truth and gave men and women the power to perceive it then, is alive to steer its application today.

Here is the task of the church! Our vital mandate is to take our trusted tradition and show how it applies to our lives! Here is where a fresh wind blows across the face of contemporary biblical study. Why have we felt compelled to make biblical truth conform to every varied whim of culture and scientific theory? Why can't we simply show by word and deed that this stuff works! (v. 19).

A man who is drowning in a sea of alcohol and doesn't remember how his wife got that bruise on her face doesn't need a sermon on the different views of premillennialism—not when he comes to hear a word from God. When a sixteen-year-old finds that her boyfriend lied about "protection," she doesn't need to hear about current denominational controversies. How often, though, does this happen?

"I have some questions about the Old Testament," she said. "Can we talk?" "I have some questions, too," I replied. "Sure!" A frequent visitor to our church, this woman was prepared when she came to my study. She even started talking about the documentary hypothesis, a theory about the construction of the Torah. I was shocked but also wondering, *Why is she here?* Then she came to Jonah. "Did that really happen?" she asked. "I believe the story is true," I replied. "But even more so, I believe that it contains the truth. It is a story about a group of people, outside of God's love, who responded to God's Word when they heard it. It changed their lives. God's Word can change yours!" Then the dam broke and she told me the real reason she had come, and how she needed to let God change her life.

This stuff works! Let us show by our lives that this trusted tradition can turn people around! (Gary L. Carver)

ONE BRIEF SHINING MOMENT

MATTHEW 17:1-9

The disciples in our reading lived with an understanding of God peculiar to them. They understood Jesus in this way. Thanks to Peter's resourcefulness, they understood Jesus as the Christ, the anointed Son of the living God. And, it was because of this understanding and confession that Peter became the rock on which the church was to be built. But still, the meaning of our understanding of God is veiled in darkness; in other words, it withdraws into the mystery that surrounds it.

Today, we celebrate that mystery in one of its more profound moments: the Transfiguration. It is no fiction, cleverly articulated like a fairy tale from the Brothers Grimm or a saga like the Epic of Gilgamesh. It is more akin to the transformation of a caterpillar into a butterfly. The caterpillar crawls slowly about in its dull colors and shape, eating and molting as it goes. But at the right time, it encloses itself in a cocoon or chrysalis. Eventually, the chrysalis opens to reveal a magnificently colored Monarch or a Great Purple Hairstreak. The caterpillar undergoes a complete *metamorphosis,* which literally means "a change in form." That is the same word Matthew uses to describe Jesus in the Transfiguration. He completely changes form. Not only were his garments white as light, his face shone like the sun! For his disciples, he was changed forever.

They had witnessed what happened to him before when he went up to the mountain all those times alone to pray. Every time he did so, things were different. The last time Matthew recalls Jesus going to the mountain to pray, he missed the boat the disciples were on and walked across the water to meet them! When Jesus went to the mountain either alone or with his three closest companions, his experience of God helped him to let go of the things that constrained him: the fire he came to cast upon the earth, and his baptism as the Son of God. And his letting go changed everything for those around him. The first disciples were changed from fishermen to fishers of people. The lame walked. The blind saw. The deaf heard. The dead were raised. And the world's outlook on life was reversed; that is, God's salvation was at work in the world.

Martin Buber once observed that in each new eon, fate becomes more oppressive, reversal more shattering. We might add that the presence of God becomes ever nearer. It's disconcerting. Peter would go on to say in one of his letters that scoffers would come. And indeed, they are here in our time, fueling the passion of skepticism and our uncertainty about our future relationship with the Almighty. Indeed, the appearance of God is perverse; that is, it *turns away* from what we consider to be normal in our day-to-day lives. We live in a digital age where, "for the first time in human history, children are an authority on a central innovation in society. Their number, [coupled] with their digital mastery, is creating a power that will sweep over every firm and every economy."[1] Matter is beginning to matter less and less. Time is collapsing because the world is more interactive and is breeding unprecedented change at ever-increasing speed. Even our materialism has shifted dramatically, because the gap between desire and purchase has closed. Everything is available everywhere. What was it St. Paul said? "Do not be conformed to this age, but rather be transformed by the renewal of your minds that you may prove what is the good and acceptable and perfect will of God."

But when Jesus makes his presence felt, we discover that our lives are cleansed. The old pictures in our heads are gotten rid of and they're replaced by a new way of viewing ourselves and the world. It is little wonder then that Jesus reminds us that we, too, are the light of the world. That is because we, too, are transformed by his living presence. His fire takes us and changes us as the caterpillar changes into a butterfly. Who can explain it? It is as complex and astonishing as the stars that cover the universe, like dandelion seeds puffed by a child on a summer morning. And it is as simple as these words of Walt Whitman:

> A child said, "What is the grass?" fetching it to me with full hands;
> How could I answer the child? . . . I do not know what it is any-
> more than he.[2]

Because of that one brief, shining moment, we are, ourselves, transformed. We are freed to take our lives into more constructive ways of living. For the Day of Transfiguration is a new and fresh day. Today we are new people because of the change evoked by Jesus Christ. Today, we can meet life in a new way. (Eric Killinger)

---

1. Don Tapscott, "Minds over Matter," in *Business 2.0* (January, 1999), p. 90.

2. Walt Whitman, *Leaves of Grass.* Quoted in Stanley Romaine Hopper, *The Way of Transfiguration: Religious Imagination as Theopoesis* (Louisville: Westminster/John Knox, 1992), p. 155.

FEBRUARY 17, 2002

First Sunday in Lent

Worship Theme: Human sin is universal and breaks the harmony of creation; yet grace abounds and justifies sinners, bringing life instead of death.

Readings: Genesis 2:15-17; 3:1-7; Romans 5:12-19; Matthew 4:1-11

Call to Worship (Psalm 32):

Leader: Happy are we whose transgressions are forgiven, whose sins are covered.

People: **Happy are we to whom the Lord imputes no iniquity, and in whose spirit there is no deceit.**

Leader: I confessed my transgressions and you forgave.

People: **When we pray, you save us from trouble.**

Leader: Steadfast love surrounds those who trust in the Lord.

People: **Be glad in the Lord and rejoice, O righteous; shout for joy, all you upright in heart.**

Pastoral Prayer:

God of grace and God of glory, on your people pour your power. Our ancestors disobeyed your command, forgive us this day our transgressions. Our ancestors tasted death as they ate of the fruit of the knowledge of good and evil, bring us out of the valley of shadows and into the dawn of your age. God of grace

81

and God of glory, on your people pour your power. Even as you banished the first people from your garden, you provided them with clothes; provide us our bare necessities as we clothe the naked. Even as you decree punishment, you begin the work of salvation; visit us with your just mercy as we forgive those who sin against us. God of grace and God of glory, on your people pour your power. You who refuse to turn away from your people, turn again to us and renew within us your covenant of grace. You who came among us in flesh, living our life and suffering our death, be among us this day to justify us and to love us and to feed us that we might live your life and die your death, rising to live forever with you in the reign of justice and peace. Amen. (Scott Haldeman)

SERMON BRIEFS

WHO WE ARE

GENESIS 2:15-17; 3:1-7

What does it mean to be a human being? Are we fundamentally good beings? That can't be. We sometimes make unwise, even morally evil, choices. How can fundamentally good beings err so terribly? Human beings must be basically evil, then. But, if this is truly the case, how can we account for the many examples of devotion we have experienced in our lives—our parents' love and care for us, our spouses' companionship and partnership, our friends' constancy and support? How, then, do we explain the altruism of a Mother Teresa, or the thirst for justice of a Martin Luther King?

It is no wonder that all the world's religions have offered answers to the question of who we are as human beings, that entire branches of learning concentrate on some aspect of the question, that philosophers struggle with it, or that the answers vary so widely. If we are to live purposeful lives, we must begin with some idea of who we are!

The key biblical text on the question of human identity, of course, is found in the opening chapters of Genesis, perhaps one of the best-known passages in the Bible. Virtually every Sunday school almunus can summarize the story: God created Adam and Eve as sinless beings. But, tempted to disobedience by the serpent, they rebelled against God's explicit instruction not to eat the fruit of a certain tree found in the center of the Garden. For their rebellion—the origin of human sinfulness—God placed Adam, Eve, and their descendants under a number of penalties, including expulsion from the Garden and, ultimately, death.

Familiarity can breed oversimplification. This summary of the story of our first parents misses a number of features emphasized in the biblical text. What's more, it fails to account for why God prohibited the tree of the knowledge of good and evil, how sinless humans could have even contemplated rebelling against God's command, or how the knowledge of good and evil could have had such negative consequences (isn't it better to have a sense of morality than to remain naive?). Yes, the text shows us that we are disobedient sinners, but it also teaches us a great deal more about ourselves, as well.

It shows, for example, that from the very beginning of our race we have been limited creatures. It is not quite accurate to say that, according to the Bible, God created Adam and Eve in a state of "perfection." To be sure, humanity is the crowning act of God's creation, but human beings are creatures nonetheless—created, in fact, from a ball of clay (Adam from 'adamah, the Hebrew word for "earth, land, soil"). Indeed, according to the text, one of Adam's first insights was the awareness of his own state of incompleteness: he needed Eve. Our first parents did not even know right from wrong! Like infants, they could not make moral choices. They could do nothing malicious, to be sure; but neither could they do good. They were created, as the psalmist says, "a little lower than angels"—wondrous, but limited.

We sometimes tell our children that, with a dream driven by determination and fueled on hard work, they can be and do anything they choose. Of course, this is not true at all. Despite all the marvelous and magnificent potential inherent in any human life, each and every one of us is restricted and constrained by the traits of our species, by the accidents of our birth, by our particular amalgam of physical and mental capabilities, and, ultimately, by our mortality.

Like their descendants, however, our first parents were unwilling to accept these God-given limitations—they wanted to be more than human! Genesis details very clearly the thought process that culminated in the consumption of the forbidden fruit. It was not mere rebellion for rebellion's sake. The serpent pointed out to Eve—accurately, it should be noted—that were she and Adam to acquire the knowledge of good and evil, and thereby become morally competent agents, they would take a major step toward becoming more godlike. The idea of becoming like God fascinated Eve. She wanted to become God's peer. Mere humanity was no longer enough for her. And Adam, who was apparently privy to the entire discussion between Eve and the serpent, agrees.

What arrogance and presumption! "Desire conceived and brought forth sin" (see James 1:15). Ambition, properly oriented and motivated, is certainly good. Without it, we would never achieve, never accomplish. But ambition improperly oriented toward that which cannot, or ought not, be attained is dangerous. And ambition improperly motivated out of pure egocentrism—"I will be like God"—destroys. Why? In part because, no matter how strong our ambition, we remain limited creatures. We can attain more power than we can safely manage, more knowledge than we can wisely utilize. Like Icarus, we fly higher than our wings can safely take us.

Finally, our ancestors soon learned—as we all do early in life—that *overreaching our capacities inevitably brings unanticipated disaster.* Genesis narrates this truth very simply: Immediately upon consuming the fruit intended to give them godlike knowledge, Adam and Eve became aware of their own nakedness and vulnerability. One cannot gain knowledge of the good without also knowing evil. When we, who are but animated bits of clay, seek to usurp the place of God, if only briefly, how can we expect that our endeavor will have its intended result?

So, this is who we are: creatures made in the image of God, a vexing admixture of godlike potential and mortal limitation. Like our foreparents, we all struggle to maintain the balance, to realize our potential without arrogantly infringing on God's prerogatives. Only God can be God; we have our hands full being human. (Mark Biddle)

A STUDY IN CONTRASTS

ROMANS 5:12-19

Adam! Christ! Two significant individuals, but so different in their influence. This was the point Paul made in this section of Scripture. Simply put, through Adam, sin came into the world and brought terrible consequences to all. Through Christ, grace came into the world and cured all that had happened through Adam. Several contrasts were made.

I. Through Adam, sin that leads to death came into the world. Through Christ, grace that leads to life came into the world.

Adam chose to disobey God in the Garden of Eden, and ate the forbidden fruit. He did what he wanted, not what God asked, which seems to be the essence of all sin. As a result, death came into the world (v. 12). One of my seminary professors, seeking to explain this act, said that while we are not responsible for what Adam did, we are all affected by it. We reap the consequences of that deed. One consequence is that we all face death, both a physical one and a spiritual one. We die inside when we are cut off from God.

Jesus changed that. Jesus died our death. We now can have life (vv. 17-18). Grace brought forgiveness and love and eternal life. The death that came through Adam was overcome through Christ.

II. Through Adam, judgment came into the world. Through Christ, acquittal was offered.

The power of sin that came into the world through Adam's deed is so powerful, it catches everyone. All fall into its grip. As a result, we are judged guilty before God and condemned (vv. 16, 18). The record of our lives has been read, and it is not a pleasant one. There are no excuses to be given. We are without hope.

Christ brings acquittal. When the sentence is pronounced on us, Christ steps forward on our behalf and takes our judgment away. Christ died for our sins, Christ has forgiven our failure; Christ has taken our judgment. Instead of reaping the results of our judgment, we are escorted into eternal life with God. Through Adam, we find condemnation. Through Christ, we find acquittal.

III. Through Adam, disobedience came into the world. Through Christ, obedience to God was presented.

Adam disobeyed. He serves as an example of what it means to live on the wrong side of God, to go against God's will. To take matters into our own hands is costly. This is the lesson we can learn from Adam. Living disobediently brings consequences we do not want.

On the other hand, Christ gives us an example of what it means to obey God. When choices were presented, Jesus held on to God. It was not easy. In the Garden of Gethsemane, he sweated drops of blood that indicated how painful the struggle was. But he still held on to God and obeyed. The result? Salvation. Death was overcome and eternal life was offered to all. To obey God brings us the true life.

Adam or Christ? Which way is the way to life? Should there be any question about that? (Hugh Litchfield)

CONFLICTS LEADING TO THE CROSS: TEMPTATION

MATTHEW 4:1-11

Conflict is generally at the heart of most stories. Stories present several kinds of conflict. A character may be in conflict with herself or himself. A character may be in conflict with supernatural forces, such as Luke Skywalker in the *Star Wars* trilogy. A character may be in conflict with nature, such as the old man in Hemingway's *The Old Man and the Sea*. A character may even be in conflict with another individual or society.

The story of Jesus, whether told by Matthew, Mark, Luke, or John, is no exception. Conflict was at the very center of Jesus' life. In all four Gospels, Jesus engages in every imaginable conflict. He battles with unclean spirits. He overcomes threatening forces of nature. He confronts the Jewish and Roman authorities. He struggles with the disciples, and he agonizes within himself about his own death.

As we retrace the journey of Jesus, we can identify four specific conflicts that ultimately led to the cross. We begin with Jesus' temptation experience in the wilderness when he engaged in a face-to-face battle with Satan. Later, we will look at Jesus' conflict with the religious leaders (legalism), his conflict with Rome (the political power broker of his day), and his inner conflict in the Garden of Gethsemane.

Matthew, Mark, and Luke tell about Jesus' temptation. Mark's account is the shortest, only two verses. Matthew and Luke begin with the same first temptation, turning stones to bread, but they have a different order for the other two temptations.

One writer suggests that Luke's order has a more natural and geographical sequence. The same writer suggests that Matthew's order is more natural in logical sequence, moving from the lowest level of temptation to the highest level of temptation.

As we attempt to retrace the steps of Jesus and walk where he walked, what lessons can we learn from his temptation experience?

The first lesson: temptation often comes immediately after significant spiritual milestones. It should be no surprise that the temptation experience follows immediately Jesus' baptism when the heavens opened up, the Spirit of God descended upon Jesus, and his heavenly Father said, "This is my beloved Son, in whom I am well pleased." Perhaps that is why the apostle Paul warned about letting down our guard: "If you think you are standing, watch out that you do not fall" (1 Cor. 10:12).

The second lesson: temptation rears its head whenever we are at our lowest point and wherever we are most vulnerable. Jesus spent forty days and forty nights in the wilderness, and he ate absolutely nothing. Loneliness had taken its toll on him. Emotionally, he had fallen from high to low. Environmentally, he had been driven from the cheers of baptism to the dread of the desert. Physically, he had been weakened by hunger until he was dangerously open to any temptation.

Satan attacked Jesus from three different angles. The first temptation was a temptation for Jesus to use his powers selfishly. The second was a temptation for Jesus to become only a miracle-worker and thereby attract people to follow him for the wrong reason. The third temptation offered Jesus a shortcut to win the world other than the way of the cross.

The third lesson: temptation is common to everyone, but we do not have to face it alone. The Bible assures us that others have experienced temptation and that Jesus understood the full weight of temptation, yet he did not yield to the temptation of Satan (1 Cor. 10:13; Heb. 4:14-15). Someone once asked, "Why is it that opportunity knocks only once, yet temptation bangs on the door constantly?" I don't know the answer to that question, but I do know that even though we constantly struggle with temptation, God gives us one more promise: "for the one who is in you is greater than the one who is in the world" (1 John 4:4). (Bob Buchanan)

FEBRUARY 24, 2002

Second Sunday in Lent

Worship Theme: God's chosen are called to bring God's good news to all the people of the earth.

Readings: Genesis 12:1-4*a;* Romans 4:1-5, 13-17; John 3:1-17

Call to Worship (Psalm 121):

Leader: I lift up my eyes to the hills—from where will my help come?

People: **My help comes from the LORD, who made heaven and earth.**

Leader: He will not let your foot be moved; he who keeps you will not slumber.

People: **He who keeps Israel will neither slumber nor sleep.**

Leader: We delight in God's help.

People: **We delight in God's works.**

All: **Let us worship the God who saves.**

Pastoral Prayer:

   God who gives life to the dead, awaken us to the world of your promise. God who calls into existence things that are not, do a new thing among us. God who blesses us that we might be a blessing, send us among the nations to tell of your grace. God who pitches his tent among us, be present now with saving love. Love the unlovable. Heal the diseased. Comfort the anxious.

Welcome the stranger. Feed the hungry. Renew your church. In the name of the One you sent to show what love is, and who now lives and reigns with you and the Holy Spirit. Amen. (Scott Haldeman)

SERMON BRIEFS

A MODEL OF FAITH

GENESIS 12:1-4*a*

The book of Genesis begins at the beginning of and recounts the early history of the human race as a pitiful tale of firsts. The first pair of human beings commits the first sin. The story of the first pair of brothers is the story of the first murder. Within the first few generations of humanity, human evil and corruption reach such proportions that God finds it necessary to wipe the slate virtually clean and start anew with Noah, his descendants, and a few animals to repopulate the world. This same Noah, however, soon becomes the first drunkard, and, within very few generations, humanity, in its arrogance, undertakes the first folly of human technology—the Tower of Babel. In order to prevent further foolish attempts to gain heaven by human means, further attempts "to make a name for themselves," God must confuse their language. The human family fractures into nations and clans. From the outset, humankind seems bent on its own misery. But at precisely this low point, God intervenes once again—not now to wipe the slate clean in a purging destruction—but to begin a process of redemption by choosing to work through a single key figure, Abraham.

The biblical account is remarkable. God calls the otherwise insignificant Abraham to leave home and family for a new land to be God's bequest to him. God promises to make old and childless Abraham the founding ancestor of a great nation. God promises to protect and preserve Abraham and his offspring and, in the coup de grâce, God announces the intention to use Abraham and his offspring as the key for reversing human history's downward spiral. Pretty heady stuff!

But a careful reader of Genesis will soon note, not only what the text announces with such gravity, but also that this text is amazingly silent with respect to a number of details that the reader may think equally important. As it turns out, these silences speak volumes.

The text says nothing, for example, as to *why* God chose *Abraham,* of all people. Noah was the most righteous member of his generation. The Bible makes no such remark concerning Abraham. In fact, a number of factors would seem to contraindicate Abraham's selection: he was old—perhaps too old to survive the rigors of migration and nation-founding; he was old and childless, and his wife, Sarah, was herself well past the age of childbearing. Subsequent events in Abraham's life demonstrate that Abraham was neither particularly moral (Gen. 12:10-20) nor a model husband and father (Genesis 16; 21). Judging both from the names of members of Abraham's family and the testimony of other passages of Scripture (Josh. 24:2), Abraham was not even a monotheist at the time of his call!

Theologically, of course, the text's silence on this issue is tantamount to a statement of the fundamental biblical concepts of election and grace: God calls only those who are unworthy because no one truly merits God's call: not Abraham, not us. This truth is, or will be if we take it to heart, at the same humbling and encouraging. To be called of God is to receive a vocation for which none of us are truly qualified. Yet the call of God comes even to the Abrahams of the world.

The text is also strangely silent regarding the relationship between the privileges of election and the responsibilities attendant upon it. God slipped in a semi-disguised obligation among the four promises God made to Abraham. God promises land, offspring, protection, and that Abraham and his family will become key in God's efforts to bring the blessings that will reverse the downward trend of human history. God promises, in effect, to give Abraham a heavy responsibility. It is easy, given human arrogance and egocentrism, to focus on the privileges of election. But, even though the text does not spell it out explicitly, the sequence of the promises makes it clear that the privileges Abraham will enjoy are intended primarily to facilitate Abraham's ability to fulfill his responsibility. God will give Abraham a land so that Abraham can be a beacon of blessing to all the families of the earth. God will make Abraham a great nation so that the benefits to other nations may be perpetuated and expanded. God will protect Abraham so that his survival may ensure that he has the opportunity to fulfill his destiny.

Finally, the text is amazingly silent as to Abraham's reaction to God's call. Hebrew narrative typically eschews psychological characterization, preferring reports of behavior to accounts of a character's private thoughts. The Bible also typically refrains from offering the details of God's plans for fulfilling God's promises. The silence between verses 3 and 4 of our text is deafening. Just imagine the conversation that took place around the dinner table as Abraham recounted his call experience to his wife, Sarah.

Perhaps the most amazing feature of the story of Abraham is the fact that, despite the absurdity and vagueness of God's call, Abraham and Sarah left their homeland and set out on what many might have called a fool's errand. It is no accident that Abraham is known as a model of faith. (Mark Biddle)

WE ARE FAMILY

ROMANS 4:1-5, 13-17

There is a story about a woman who had several children through childbirth, and several others through adoption. One day, a visitor asked which children were "her own" and which had been adopted. The woman replied, "I don't remember."

The visitor's question may have been an innocent one, a simple matter of curiosity. However, perhaps more was involved. Did the visitor think that the natural-born children were the "real" children, that they were loved more or were entitled to more in this family? If this was the intent of the question, the mother quickly put any such notions to rest. She had chosen to grant all of the children equal standing in the family. The gift of her love meant that neither birth nor subsequent action could change the fact that they were now her descendants.

In the text, Paul shows that we are similar to the children in this story. Fortunately, we do not have to be genetic descendants of Abraham, or followers of "the Law" to become a part of God's family. We learn that if we have Abraham's faith and trust in God, then we become his true descendants and members of the family.

Imagine what it would be like to be without family and see a family picnicking in the park or worshiping together. Imagine wanting to be a part of that family so badly that it hurt, yet knowing that there is nothing you can do to earn a place there. Then, imagine, one day, you are summoned. The family you have longed to be a part of is there, and they have chosen you to become their newest family member. In order to be one of them, all you must do is accept their love, believe, and trust in their commitment to you. Imagine your joy, your sense of awe, perhaps even your feelings of humility and unworthiness that you have been chosen. Then you learn that not just you, but everyone without family has become a descendant and heir.

Now, imagine that you are a natural born child in this family. At first you are willing to welcome siblings into your home—it is a nice thing to do. But wait. All that you have now belongs to them, too? They get equal shares of the toys, the love, everything? Perhaps this is not what you bargained for after all. Perhaps you find yourself feeling like the early laborers in the vineyard—begrudging those who came late and received equal wages for far less work. But, your parents say, this is about family and about love, not about merit and fairness.

Fortunately, the offer of family membership is based on grace—God's grace and love for us. This means that, thankfully, there is nothing we can do in our sinful nature to corrupt the plan. As individuals, we can gratefully accept this outrageous offer. As church families, we can joyfully welcome our new siblings, no matter who they are or where they come from. Thanks be to God. (Tracy Hartman)

A SNEAK PREVIEW

JOHN 3:1-17

Nicodemus, "a leading Jew," sneaked away from his religious community to have one of the most profound, yet perplexing, conversations with Jesus that anyone had had with Jesus to date. Essentially, Nicodemus wants to know how one is able to discern the realm of God in the midst of the clamor of human activity. He is afraid of being embarrassed and chastised by his peers, so he seeks Jesus in the privacy of the evening hour when the religious community would have no way of knowing such an encounter was taking place. Nicodemus wants a sneak preview of this mysterious Galilean. What he needs is what we need, also—a relationship with Christ that is born from above.

I. We Still Seek Jesus, Privately (vv. 1, 2)

Why are we so afraid of others discovering that we are interested in Christ? Nicodemus's dilemma remains our dilemma. We still get sweaty palms at the thought that our friends, work associates, neighbors, even our fellow church members might find out we really do believe Jesus is God's Messiah, the One sent to save us from our sins and give us new life, even eternal life. The thought of someone finding out that we actually believe that he healed blind Bartimaeus, turned water into wine at a wedding reception, and raised Lazarus from the dead frightens us. We may nod our heads in the affirmative, or even say "amen" in worship to such claims in Scripture, but in private we are just not sure about all this stuff about the miracles Jesus performed. Like Nicodemus, we have our own reservations, and to confront them means to seek Jesus out in the privacy of our own darkness.

II. Born from Above (vv. 3-8)

Jesus is very serious about this matter of being born from above. In order to discern the activity of God in the midst of the clamor of human affairs, one must be given life from above, from God. In order to believe in just the work Jesus performed, we must have a relationship with God, first. For some folks, being born again is a once-in-a-lifetime experience, a mountaintop moment. And, it's usually an emotional, life-changing experience at some point in life. John's Gospel speaks of something quite different. What Nicodemus's sneak preview unveils is more about mystery than it is about chronology. Being born again is about looking back; being born from above is about looking inward.

III. The Need for Evidence (vv. 9-15)

It still seems impossible. We fill the baptismal font or pool and we baptize men, women, and children. At age twelve, the children are enlisted in confirmation class, and for a year or two they are instructed in the teachings of Jesus. Upon completion of their classes and going through the rigors of testing, the confirmands are paraded before the church and confirmed as members of the church of Jesus Christ. Baptized adults, while not going through the confirmation process, nevertheless, are signed up in orientation classes, and for a period of time are instructed about what it means to be a Christian and member of Christ's church. After all of this, where is the evidence that any of the above has any influence on people? Why are churches filled with people, but not filled with things from above? To take Jesus seriously, we are called to believe and not reject the evidence of Holy Scripture. To look around this world for evidence of things from above, things from God, we have to be disciples of God's Word and claim the evidence given in the Gospels as our own. And if we do not believe what we read and hear from Scripture, how are we going to believe when we hear things from above?

IV. A Return to the Basics (vv. 16, 17)

It is the most quoted, most familiar, and probably the most unbelievable of all that Jesus told Nicodemus in that sneak preview: "God loved the world so much that he gave his only Son, so that everyone who believes in him may not be lost but may have eternal life" (v. 16 JB). A ray of light begins breaking forth in Nicodemus's darkness. Something begins to be birthed from above. Nicodemus isn't being born again. Something begins to happen on the inside of him and it is coming from above, from God.

But there is another scripture that does not get quoted as much, and it follows in tandem with John 3:16: "For God sent his Son into the world not to condemn the world but so through him the world might be saved" (v. 17 JB). Born-again people can continue to condemn the world; people born from above cannot and will not condemn the world.

What a sneak preview! What has followed from that encounter at night between Jesus and Nicodemus has been breaking forth in the lives of people ever since that night. And, it is showing up over and over again, as disciples of Jesus Christ continue seeking a sneak preview every time we are confronted with believing in Jesus Christ. (Mike Childress)

SPIRITUAL PREPARATION

❧

MARCH

There is, in life, a persistent, ongoing spiritual struggle. The experience of struggle does not mean that we are not where God wants us to be, but that we are not doing what God wants us to do. Life is a test. "Lead me not into temptation," the bumper sticker reads, "I know the way already."

Christianity does not take us out of the world of struggle. Indeed, in life, a faithful life in following Jesus, we know that we live squarely in a world of struggle.

Pastors understand this. We move now more deeply into the season of Lent. In Lent we remember that Jesus was driven into the wilderness, by the Spirit, to be tempted by the devil, and he is there for forty days. A Lenten spirituality helps us to come to terms with wilderness. A Lenten spirituality helps us to make our way through struggle.

A couple of affirmations, as we define a Lenten spirituality for pastors:

First: when we have discovered our mission in life, a powerful force will come along to sidetrack or sabotage us. Jesus understands who he is: he is the Son of God. He is baptized. He is about to begin his public ministry. All is well, right? Actually, it is not quite that easy. Satan comes along, to test him, to sidetrack him, to sabotage him, to distract him. When we have found the right path, we can be sure that someone will come along to show us another route. For this reason testing and temptation are always signs that we are doing something right! If we do not care about God, if we do not want to serve Jesus, if we have no interest in the spiritual life, there will be no testings. Only when we are given a direction are we also given temptations to abandon that direction.

- Can you recall an experience that tested your call or direction in ministry?

97

A second affirmation: there is no spiritual growth without wilderness experience. Most of us would describe the wilderness of Israel as desert. Henri Nouwen has called the desert "the furnace of transformation." The rabbis of ancient Israel called the wilderness "the school of the soul." In the wilderness we grow spiritually. Edwin Friedman, the family systems theorist, posed this question in a group once: "What is your threshold for pain? Your answer to that question will teach me about your capacity for growth." The higher our capacity for pain, the greater our capacity for growth.

When all is well we are easily seduced into thinking we have no need for God.

In the wilderness we must place our trust in God. When we are in the midst of the wilderness we have a potential for growth. There is no spiritual growth without wilderness. There is no resurrection without death. There is no crown without a cross. There is no Easter without Lent.

- What does the season of Lent mean to you, spiritually? Can you think of victories and defeats that occur during these days? What does wilderness mean to you in light of your own struggles in life and ministry?

One of the most compelling descriptions of struggle in the Scriptures is Elijah. When Jesus posed the question "Who do people say that the Son of Man is?"(Matt. 16:13), one response was Elijah. In 1 Kings 19, Elijah finds himself in a struggle. He has won a great victory over the priests of Baal; now he flees for his life. He finds himself in the wilderness. The following meditation picks up the story there:

Are you afraid?
> Do you want to run to the wilderness,
> to die there, depleted, despondent, alone?
> You can escape from the enemy,
> but you can never flee from the Presence.
> Still, you make the attempt.
> But suddenly—surprise, grace, transition—
> suddenly you feel a Touch,
> and a Voice speaks,
> pointing you to Providence:

"eat it, it will nourish you;
drink it, you'll never thirst again."
This is all you need, at least for now.
You're tempted to push the food and drink aside.
Too hungry to eat, too thirsty to drink,
spiritually famished, emotionally dehydrated.
You are depleted, despondent, alone,
but the Voice cannot be silenced, even in the Silence.
"Without my Presence you'll never survive the journey
that is ahead."
You eat the bread and drink from the cup.
And you keep going.
What else can you do?
One step leads to the next,
one day to the next.
Forty days and forty nights later,
　　you're alive.
You reach the cave, and there you sleep
in the Presence, until the Voice speaks again.

- What is your greatest need, right now, in the ministry?

A Lenten spirituality helps the pastor to make his or her way through the inevitable struggles that come. Lent is the journey into the wilderness. It is the journey of Jesus, toward the cross. It is a journey of struggle. But it is, we are promised, the way that leads to life. May the days of March, these latter days of Lent that move through Holy Week and conclude with the celebration of the Resurrection, be the furnace of your own transformation, the school of your own soul, the experience of God's providence. The gospel hymn is both simple in content and profound in implication:

Trust and obey, for there's no other way
To be happy in Jesus, but to trust and obey.

(Ken Carter)

Source: "Trust and Obey," *United Methodist Hymnal* (Nashville: UMPH, 1989), p. 467.

MARCH 3, 2002

Third Sunday in Lent

Worship Theme: God answers our needs—water for the thirsty, living water for the perishing; if we drink we never need thirst again.

Readings: Exodus 17:1-7; Romans 5:1-11; John 4:5-42

Call to Worship (Psalm 95):

> *Leader:* O come, let us sing to the LORD.
>
> ***People:*** **Let us make a joyful noise to the rock of our salvation!**
>
> *Leader:* Let us come into his presence with thanksgiving;
>
> ***People:*** **Let us make a joyful noise to him with songs of praise!**
>
> *Leader:* For the LORD is a great God, and a great King above all gods.
>
> ***People:*** **In his hand are the depths of the earth; the heights of the mountains are his also.**
>
> *Leader:* O come, let us worship and bow down, let us kneel before the LORD, our Maker!
>
> ***People:*** **For he is our God, and we are the people of his pasture, and the sheep of his hand.**

Pastoral Prayer:
Living waters, flow still upon parched lands. Provide assurance to your wandering people that what lies ahead is better than the

bondage we have so recently escaped. Prophesy again telling all that we have done so that we might worship you in spirit and in truth. Nourish the land and send us to gather your harvest that all may hear your good news. Living waters, flow still among your people, gush up as a spring bearing us to eternal life. Wash us. Pour over us. Drown us in grace so we might live anew. Amen. (Scott Haldeman)

SERMON BRIEFS

LIVING IN THE IN-BETWEEN TIMES, OR TESTS AND TRUST

EXODUS 17:1-7

This text is traditionally seen as a reproach for testing God. Even the naming stories associated here refer to the Israelites' quarrelsome manner (*Meribah* meaning "quarrel" and *Massah* meaning "test"). Themes such as obedience, following God's will, and trusting in God's providence come to mind. However, the richness of the text in its fullness (chapters and chapters of wandering in the wilderness) reminds us that finding the fulfillment of God's promises is neither quick nor easy. During that journey between promise and fulfillment, understanding God's will and obeying God's guidance are challenging at best and terrifying at worst. When fear sets in, trusting God's providence is seldom first on anyone's mind. Such was the case for the Israelites during their many years of traveling from Egypt to the promised land of Canaan. They could not understand the lengthy process in which they were involved. Where was that promised land, anyway? Nor did they want to readily obey God's servant Moses when he seemed to be leading them farther and farther from any hope of survival, let alone abundance. Where was Moses leading them, and why was it taking so long? *Trust* was not the first word on anyone's lips during the many quarrels and tests that make up much of the book of Exodus.

And so, God is once again put to the test as the people question Moses' leadership, in particular the leadership that has taken them to a place with no water. In this test, Moses' leadership is confirmed when he strikes water from a rock in the presence of the elders (17:6). In this test, the Israelites' reputation as a stubborn and rebellious people is confirmed and named by Moses (17:7). But most important, in this test, God once again provides.

Even when people insist on pushing God to the very limits of patience, God responds. Even when people distrust God's leaders and refuse to obey God's guidance, God walks with us as our companion-guide. And so, through the test, the people learn trust. And among those people is a young leader, Joshua, who learns that trust along with his people—a young man who will one day become the people's leader into the promised land.

When people are living in that "in-between time," the time between promise and fulfillment, trust often wanes. When churches are experiencing growing pains, when capital campaigns are in their infancy, when parents are raising adolescents, when couples are struggling through midlife or empty nests, people are living in between promise and fulfillment. This passage can help us to remember that we are neither the first nor the last to go through such confusing times, nor are we expected to travel such roads with perfect behavior and trust. Most important, we are not traveling through the "in-between time" alone. God is with us, responding to our tests so that we might learn to trust—again and again and again. (Mary J. Scifres)

THE DIFFERENCE IT MAKES

ROMANS 5:1-11

In the first four chapters of Romans, Paul talks about justification. Beginning with chapter 5, he presents some of the results of that. There is the word *therefore*, which means that what is said depends on what was said. These verses provide a mother lode of theological ideas and concepts. Every sentence can be a sermon in itself. At the very least, there are three differences justification makes.

I. It Brings Peace (vv. 1-2)

Peace with God can happen. No longer do we need to fight against God, or run from God, or overly fear God. Instead, we can be in a loving relationship with God because of the gracious act of Christ. This peace is really a confidence in the faithfulness and goodness of God, a God who will bring us into "glory," to share with us the Kingdom.

What will be the final destiny of the true believer in Christ? Many worry about that, wondering if they are going to be accepted into God's glory. Far too often I have been asked, "Will God really give me eternal life? Can I count on it?" Paul would tell them not to be anxious about it. Be at peace with it. Through Christ, we will share "the glory of God."

II. It Brings Hope (vv. 3-5)

Paul went on to indicate that what Christ did enabled them to live with hope in the midst of life. Life was not easy. They had to endure suffering and persecution because of their faith. In that suffering, they would find the power to endure, or to resist the temptation to quit the faith. That would deepen their character, their trust in God. The result of all that? Hope, a hope that would not disappoint them. They could go on in the midst of even the difficult moments knowing that God would be with them and love them and enable them to hold on. This hope was not a whistling in the dark. It was a sure and certain hope, based on the love of God for them as shown in Christ.

To live for Christ has never been easy. In many places across our world, Christians are persecuted and sometimes martyred for their faith. As we seek to present Christ to those who do not want to hear, fight for justice that few seem to want, or minister to the needy that most avoid—how discouraging and difficult that can be. God sees, and cares, and comes to help us minister. What we do will matter—we have that hope. We must keep on following Christ. God's love will not fail us.

III. It Brings the Assurance of Love (vv. 6-11)

In some of the most amazing verses of Scripture, Paul illustrated the depth of the love of God. He said that while they were helpless, while they were sinners, Christ died for them. God did not wait for them to clean up their act before sending Christ to love them. It was as if God could not contain that great love. Instead, God let it loose in Christ. And Christ died for them in their helplessness, in their sin. As a result, they did not have to be helpless anymore. They no longer needed to live lives of sin. Christ reconciled them to God, saved their lives. What amazing love! They did not deserve it, but that did not matter. God gave it anyway.

God still gives away that amazing love. It does not matter what we have done or been, God loves us. It does not matter what we are doing with our lives now that may not be good, God still loves us. We matter to God and God will do what is needed to help us, to forgive us, to bring us into a loving relationship with God. I remember a woman who said once that she could not give her life to Christ because she was not worthy enough to do that. She had done too many wrong things with her life. This is the passage I read to her. Our worthiness is based on the grace of God that came in Christ, not on anything we have done or been. God deems us worthy to love. How can we refuse that kind of love?

What a difference the death and resurrection of Christ have made. As a result, all of us can have a confident peace with God, a sure hope in God, and everlasting love from God. (Hugh Litchfield)

THIRSTY AND HUNGRY SOULS NEED LIVING WATER AND BREAD

JOHN 4:5-42

The story of the Samaritan woman meeting Jesus is fraught with red lights flashing at every intersection. The fact that he was in Samaria lets us know he was in Gentile territory. The fact that he was speaking to a woman tells us how radically different Jesus' ministry was in comparison to that of other rabbis. No respectable rabbi would be caught, alone, talking with a woman, much less a Samaritan woman. What makes the story even more incredible is that she was a prostitute. When the disciples return and find Jesus and the woman talking, they are flabbergasted! What this story unveils is more than that Jesus was out of bounds, socially. This story conveys what happens when the parched human soul is thirsty for the Word of God, an eternal spring—the wellspring of eternal life.

I. Thirst for Acceptance (vv. 5-15)

We all have a thirst for being accepted just as we are. Jesus finds a woman of Samaria, a Gentile woman, thirsting for such acceptance. A feud between the Jews and Samaritans had been raging for hundreds of years. Accepting each other as people of the same family was unthinkable. Legend has it that the Jews and Samaritans would not get water there together but would only go at specific times of the day in order to avoid being with each other. When the woman finds Jesus sitting by the well, she is shocked that Jesus, "a Jew," would even remain there in her presence, much less ask her for a drink. Jesus demonstrates the extraordinary love of God in the midst of enormous thirst of the human soul for acceptance.

II. Thirst for Truth (vv. 16-26)

What we all need to know is that we are accepted without fear of criticism and rebuke for who we are. Because Jesus accepts the woman's presence by the very fact that he holds a conversation with her, he demonstrates how willing God is to accept people the way they are. Jesus is quite familiar with the woman's background. By Jesus' not being shocked by who she is, we see the human spirit's thirst for truth being engaged and the woman doesn't flee. Instead, she is able to have a conversation, and out of that conversation we see God reaching deep down inside of her to where she really thirsts for God's word. This is where we all thirst for God. Jesus tells her that he is the One who all humankind thirsts for. The living God, the Messiah, the Christ, is having a conversation with an "untouchable," and out of that conversation she discovers the truth about herself. But more important, she discovers the truth about God—there is nothing that can prevent God from loving and caring for people. This is a thirst we all have—the thirst for Truth.

III. Only Living Water Can Quench Our Thirst (vv. 27-42)

Water is still the most natural and most vital source for human life. Without water, the earth would dry up and die. The woman at the well went to get that kind of water. What she came back with was the water that quenches the thirst of the human soul— the good news of God in Jesus Christ.

IV. Living Bread Feeds Our Faith (vv. 27-38)

Jesus Christ is the word of God in the flesh. When we eat this bread, the bread of life, we are empowered to do the will of God. Without the Word of God to nourish our souls, we are empty. Jesus said, "My food is to do the will of [God] who sent me and to complete [God's] work." (v. 34) In Jesus Christ, God completely and fully accepts all people and saves all people. In Jesus Christ, God feeds the human soul with acceptance and quenches the thirst for life, in this world and the next world. We eat and drink at God's table and we are fed not only in this life, but we are fed for eternity. (Mike Childress)

MARCH 10, 2002

Fourth Sunday in Lent

Worship Theme: Jesus, Light of the World, makes those who have no sight to see.

Readings: 1 Samuel 16:1-13; Ephesians 5:8-14; John 9:1-41

Call to Worship (Psalm 23):

> *Leader:*   The LORD is my shepherd, I shall not want.
>
> ***People:***   **He makes me lie down in green pastures; he leads me beside still waters;**
>
> *Leader:*   He restores my soul. He leads me in right paths for his name's sake.
>
> ***People:***   **Even though I walk through the darkest valley, I fear no evil; for you are with me; your rod and your staff—they comfort me.**
>
> *Leader:*   You prepare a table before me in the presence of my enemies; you anoint my head with oil; my cup overflows.
>
> ***People:***   **Surely goodness and mercy shall follow me all the days of my life, and I shall dwell in the house of the LORD my whole life long.**

Pastoral Prayer:

Light of the World, shine bright this day; many sit in despair. Light of the World, shine bright this day; many stumble on the path. Light of the World, shine bright this day; many have lost their way. Light of the World, shine bright this day; many cannot get home. Light of the

World, shine bright this day; there are wars and rumors of wars. Light of the World, shine bright this day; there are empty stomachs while others have larders that overflow. Light of the World, shine bright this day; many have eyes that do not see while many look but do not comprehend. Light of the World, shine bright this day; lead us on to higher ground. Amen. (Scott Haldeman)

SERMON BRIEFS

AN UNUSUAL CHOICE

1 SAMUEL 16:1-13

Throughout 1 Samuel, Samuel has no more daunting task than the one found in this passage. Yet again, Samuel is commanded by God to go and anoint a king. Initially, this does not sound like such a difficult task. After all, Samuel has done it before. When Israel demanded a king, God sent Samuel to anoint the great warrior Saul as the first king of Israel. In 2 Samuel 16, however, his task is more complex. For one thing, Saul is still king. The even symbolic act of anointing another king by Samuel would seem at best a betrayal. Second, he is not exactly sure who he is looking for. Then later, when he finds David, the young boy seems an unlikely candidate. Samuel is reminded, however, that God has a much different set of criteria for those whom he calls.

By the end of chapter 15, it is clear that Saul was not working out as Israel's king. Saul had violated the Lord's commands, and though technically he was still the ruler, God had determined that he was no longer the man for the job. As chapter 16 opens, God gives directions to Samuel on finding and anointing the one whom God had chosen as the new king. No wonder Samuel was skeptical. He knew that if Saul found out, he would be killed for trying to overthrow the king. Assured of the Lord's protection and guidance, Samuel consents to travel to meet Jesse and his sons, and under the guise of offering sacrifice with the family, identify the one who is God's chosen.

Samuel takes a leap of faith. He follows God's instruction with little or no information. He merely trusts that God will let him know when it was time. Even as an incredible person of faith, it is no wonder that Samuel's humanness shines through as he meets the sons of Jesse. After all, he had anointed Saul. He remembered the characteristics of Saul that had made him such a likely candidate for king. As each son is presented to him, Samuel feels confident that he is the one. One after another, God reminds Samuel that though these men may have the outward appearance of a great king, God chooses with a different set of criteria. God chooses based on the person's heart. After meeting seven hearty sons of Jesse, Samuel is perplexed that not one of them was the chosen one. "Are these all of your sons?" Samuel asks. "There is one more son. The baby, but he is out tending the sheep."

When David arrives, he looks nothing like his brothers. He does not look like a mighty warrior—big and strong. Instead he is freckled and handsomely featured. He does not look like the kind of man whom God would choose as king, but he is. On that day, Samuel anoints David, the small, ruddy shepherd boy, as the king of the chosen people of the Lord. Surprisingly, he would be the man who would be deemed the hero of his people.

God's standards are different from humanity's standards. Humanity chooses based on what is on the outside. It is a relief to us that, unlike our society, God judges us based on the inner parts of our being, and not on our physical appearance or skill. It is liberating to know that God chooses those of us who may feel like insignificant shepherds like David. At the same time, God's standards are terrifying. God sees beyond our self-created facades. Just as God sees the inner good, God sees the inner bad. This story of God's anointing of David reminds us that we, too, are chosen people. Chosen by God for a variety of tasks. We may not exactly look the part, but God sees beyond all that is on the exterior to our soul. How gracious and humbled it feels to be chosen. (Tracey Allred)

BEFORE AND AFTER

EPHESIANS 5:8-14

I could not believe my eyes or ears. I was sitting in church one Sunday, having come back for the Christmas break at college, and there singing in the choir was Charlie. To my knowledge, Charlie hated the church. The last time I saw him, he was staggering down the sidewalk after another round with the bottle. His drinking had cost him his family, his job, and just about his life. But all that was before—before he started to attend AA and before he met Christ, my mother explained to me.

Since chapter 2:11, Paul has been reminding the Ephesians of who they were before they met Christ and who they are now after Christ. He continues that theme in this passage.

I. Children of the Light (v. 8)

Once they had been children of the dark, living only for themselves and without God. But now they had become children of the light, living in the light of God's love and grace, seeking to be and bring light, love, and life wherever they went.

A friend of mine had once been part of a bike gang called the "Dark Riders." He did drugs, and about whatever he wanted, whenever he wanted. He and his gang brought trouble wherever they went. They especially hated Christians and the church. He would ride by the church on Sunday morning and throw beer cans at people in the churchyard. But that was before he had an encounter with Christ. Afterward, he went to college to become a pastor. His first preaching engagement was at one of the churches where he had thrown beer cans. He still loved his bike, however, and joined a biking group called the "Light Riders," who went around doing good things for those in need.

II. Find What Is Pleasing to the Lord (v. 10)

Once the Ephesians lived lives only to please themselves. No pleasure or action was out of bounds. But that was before Christ. Now, they lived only to know and do that which pleased God.

This is such a simple yet profound truth. It is not trying to please God in order to gain God's favor or earn something from God; rather, it is our response to the grace and love we have already received from God. It is like a child who seeks to please a parent, not to get something from that parent or out of fear of punishment, but as a way of expressing love for all the parent has done and does. We seek now to please God out of love for God.

III. Expose and Oppose Evil (v. 11)

Once they lived in the darkness of evil, supporting and nurturing it. But now after Christ they were warriors against evil, exposing and opposing it.

My friend the biker went back to many of his old "friends" and spoke with them, shared his testimony with them. He tried to get them to see where they were heading and how they were living. He told them of a better way. Some listened. Some didn't. Some viewed being a Christian as being meek and mild all the time. But Christians are also called to be warriors in the battle against evil, which is still alive and well. Many Christians have stood against injustice, racism, the exploitation of people and the earth, exposing such evil and doing all they could to oppose it.

In our church we like to sing the great old hymn "Just As I Am." But each time we do, I remind myself and the people, "We can and do come to Christ just as we are. But don't plan to stay that way!" That's the before and there's always an after. (Bass Mitchell)

DO YOU SEE JESUS?

JOHN 9:1-41

Our lection is the story of Jesus healing the man born blind. As you reflect and study the passage, look at the people involved in the unfolding of this man's story. What is their attitude toward Jesus and this man's healing? As we examine our lives during this Lenten season, do we "see" Jesus?

I. The Disciples: The Questioners (vv. 1-7)

The disciples' question begins the story. Was the man born blind or was it his parents' sin? (v. 2). A common Jewish belief was that if one was suffering, a great sin had been committed.

Jesus tells his disciples that the blindness had nothing to do with the man's or his parents' sin. It was an opportunity for God's power to be shown. The man was healed.

We do not know how the disciples reacted to the healing, but they first raised the question we often raise about innocent people suffering. Maybe Jesus gave the answer in the healing of the man. The man born blind believed Jesus enough to go and wash. When we see or experience suffering, do we ask the questions and look to Jesus for understanding and healing? Do we give God the opportunity to show power in our lives?

II. The Neighbors: The Skeptics (vv. 8-12)

A miracle had occurred and the neighbors could not believe it. They were skeptics. How could this man born blind now see? Was it really he? Some were amazed, surprised, and/or puzzled because this just does not happen. They wanted to know what and how it happened, but the explanation was not good enough. It did not make sense to them, so they took the man to the Pharisees.

Are we like the skeptical neighbors? Do we believe that Jesus can work miracles today? Do we need an explanation for every mystery? Are we such skeptics that we do not even pray for miracles?

III. The Pharisees: Blind Believers (vv. 13-34)

The man was taken before the Pharisees. It was the Sabbath. The Pharisees had strict Sabbath laws, which Jesus broke by making clay. There was a division among the Pharisees. Some felt he could not be from God since he broke the Sabbath law. Others questioned how he could do this miracle and not be from God.

The Pharisees set about collecting facts to try to figure out how to interpret what had happened to this man. They asked the healed man, who said that Jesus was a prophet (v. 17). They asked the parents to make sure that he had been blind since birth. They questioned the healed man again; but, not liking his answers, they threw him out of the synagogue (v. 34).

The Pharisees were so blinded by their belief in the law, they could neither see nor understand the miracle. If they believed in what had happened, then the law would be wrong. They could not be wrong. How could Jesus be from God and go against their sacred law? Do we box God in, expecting God to do things only one way? What is blinding us from recognizing or doing God's work in the world? What "gods" are in the way of following God wholeheartedly?

IV. The Parents: Silent Believers (vv. 18-23)

The parents of the man born blind were questioned about his healing. They would not commit. They feared being put out of the community. How many of us are like the parents of the healed man? We know and believe, yet we are not willing to tell the good news for fear of what others may think of us or do to us. Are we "fence riders"?

V. The Man Born Blind: Seeing, Speaking, Believing

Throughout the story, the man born blind shows growing faith. Something within compelled him to go wash, and he came back seeing. When questioned by the neighbors, he had the opportunity to speak about what had happened to him. He was questioned by the Pharisees twice. Telling the story the first time, he said that Jesus was a prophet (v. 17). During the second round of questioning he returned the question, asking the Pharisees if they wanted to become Jesus' disciples. The more he spoke, the more he believed. He could not understand the Pharisees' disbelief. For his belief, the man was thrown out of the synagogue. The man is approached by Jesus, who tells him that he is God's Son and the man believes and worships him, saying, "Lord, I believe" (v. 37).

The man's life was changed physically and spiritually. He was no longer blind, but saw a new life in relationship to God through Jesus. Are we willing to tell how Jesus has changed our lives? Are we willing to risk our "status" to witness to the power of God through Jesus? How do you see Jesus? (Marcia T. Thompson)

MARCH 17, 2002

Fifth Sunday in Lent

Worship Theme: God gives life. We who believe are given, by God's pure grace, resurrection.

Readings: Ezekiel 37:1-14; Romans 8:6-11; John 11:1-45

Call to Worship (Psalm 130):

Leader:	Out of the depths I cry to you, O LORD.
People:	**Lord, hear my voice! Let your ears be attentive to my supplications!**
Leader:	If you, O LORD, should mark iniquities, Lord, who could stand?
People:	**But there is forgiveness with you, and so to you I cry.**
Leader:	I wait for the LORD, my soul waits, and in his word I hope.
People:	**For with the LORD there is steadfast love, and with him is great power to redeem.**
All:	**Let us worship God.**

Pastoral Prayer:

Breath of God, breathe in me. Breath of God, breathe in me. Breath of God, breathe in me. Call us out from the grave of self-reliance. Call us out from the grave of false security. Call us out from the grave of despair. Call us out from the grave of anxiety. Call us out from the grave of petty conflict. Call us out from the grave of unconfessed sin. Call us out from the grave of pride. Call us out from the grave of isolation. Call us out from the grave of broken promises. Call us out as you called Lazarus and make us to live again, to live as your children, assured of eternal life, enabled to give our very lives for others. In the name of the One who is the Resurrection and the Life. Amen. (Scott Haldeman)

SERMON BRIEFS

GOD CAN!

EZEKIEL 37:1-14

There is nothing as final as death in the minds of many. And some would say nothing as hopeless as seeing the skeleton of a life that once was. For many a pastor those first funerals at which he or she presides are the most frightening. Those first sermons for a deceased person are among the most difficult. One has to find words of comfort and hope. The younger the person who has passed away, the more difficult it is to share a message of God's presence in the midst of such suffering. The most frightening of all scenarios is the funeral of nonbelievers or non-actives whose families are also nonbelievers. What can a preacher possibly say to these gathered about hope and God? In the same way, the prophet is asked by God to preach to a valley full of bones. God first asks the question of faith: "Mortal, can these bones live?" The prophet replies with a classic answer, "O Lord GOD, you know." One has to love that answer, for it places the answer on God. And God further challenges the prophet in telling him to prophesy to the bones. One can imagine the enthusiasm the prophet had in preaching to a valley of bones. The message God was trying to share with the prophet was that in all things, God can! God can bring new life even to a place that appears or is dead. In the message to the house of Israel, God is sharing that even in the midst of what appears to be over, there is something good and new that can still come. To a people that had lost all hope, God speaks hope. To a people resigned to a death of sorts, including spiritual and political death, God speaks of a new life that is coming.

The coming of this new life among the dead will be God's doing. It will be God's moving among the house of Israel that will

115

bring new life to the people. It is a reminder to Israel that they have not been abandoned even though they abandoned God. The message today is for those who feel they have strayed beyond rescue or even beyond life. God can reach even those who believe themselves to be unreachable. (Eradio Valverde Jr.)

HAVE YOU GOT THE SPIRIT?

ROMANS 8:6-11

"Are you a Spirit-filled Christian?" I have heard that question a lot. Behind it is the assumption that there can be a "un-Spirit-filled Christian." I do not think Paul would agree. In these verses, he again tried to tell readers what the difference was between trusting Christ and not trusting Christ. When they trusted Christ, the Spirit came to dwell within them. That Spirit brought them life and overcame death. That Spirit gave them the hope of eternal life. That Spirit would give life to their mortal bodies. The key statement was made in v. 9: "Anyone who does not have the Spirit of Christ does not belong to him."

There are only "Spirit-filled Christians." To give ourselves to Christ is to have the Spirit come and dwell with us. Imagine Christ knocking at the door of our lives, wanting to come in. We have the freedom of choice to open the door. Then, one day we do—we trust Christ and invite him into our lives, our homes. Christ comes into the living room and sits on the sofa. But Christ wants to take a tour of the house. We don't want that—we want to keep him in the living room, but Christ is not satisfied with that. He wants to go into the dining room, the kitchen, the bedroom, and all the nooks and crannies of our houses. He keeps insisting on it, until we finally relent. The Spirit of Christ comes into our lives at conversion and dwells with us. That Spirit wants to have total control of us and keeps pressing for it. Life is a continuous process of letting the Spirit have more and more of us. We grow more like Christ—the experience of sanctification—and draw closer to him. When the Spirit dwells in us, that is what happens.

Will we let the Spirit dwell in our lives? If we have given ourselves sincerely away to Christ, we cannot help it. The Spirit is there, giving us life and hope and love. Paul said that we would still face death, our bodies would die. Sin brings that about. However, the Spirit will give us life and hope and love, and death will be defeated. What God did in Christ is more powerful than anything sin can do to us. The Spirit will give us victory.

The justification that Christ brought to us has changed our lives. This is the message of Paul in Romans. Our whole perspective of life changes. No more are we cut off from God, fearing judgment and condemnation. Now we can be at one with God, experiencing a relationship of love and grace. No longer do we live under the power and mastery of sin. Now we live under the power and mastery of God, who has died for our sin, forgiven us, and freed us from guilt. No longer do we live for the desires of the flesh, looking out for ourselves first. Now we seek the ways of the Spirit, and reach out in compassion to others. No longer do we cringe in fear in the face of death. Instead, we celebrate the victory over death that will be ours through Christ Jesus our Lord. We now have life, more abundant today and forever.

Do you have the Spirit? When we love and trust Christ, we do. (Hugh Litchfield)

SEEING AND BELIEVING

JOHN 11:1-45

This Sunday's lection is the story of the raising of Lazarus. It may seem odd for this story to be read before Easter, but with a closer look, it is perfect. In this story, God's glory is revealed yet again. Jesus is the One who gives life. It also foreshadows Jesus' death for us to see. As you study the passage, keep in mind that the word *see* is important throughout the Gospel of John and particularly in this passage.

I. Dying with Him (vv. 1-16)

The narrative begins with the explanation of Lazarus's illness and Jesus' comments to the disciples that through Lazarus, God's glory would be seen so that others may know that he is the Son of God. Jesus tells the disciples that he is going to return to Judea. The disciples were very concerned. Some of the Jews had already tried to stone him (10:31), but he had escaped harm. Why go back? Jesus explains to the disciples that Lazarus is dead and this would be an opportunity for them to believe. Thomas then makes an important and loyal statement, "Let us also go, that we may die with him" (v. 16). Do we believe enough to go and die with Jesus?

II. I Believe (vv. 17-27)

Lazarus is dead and many Jews have come to mourn his loss. Martha heard that Jesus was coming, so she went out to meet him. Martha believes that if Jesus had been there, Lazarus would not have died. Jesus tells her that he will rise again and Martha acknowledges that, because resurrection was a common belief among the Jews. Then Jesus takes things a step further. He tells her, "I am the resurrection and the life" (v. 25). Jesus brought eternal life then. He asked Martha if she believed and Martha answered that she believed that Jesus was the Messiah, the One sent by God. She knew what he said was true, although she lacked understanding. Her faith and belief were strong enough to accept the mystery. Is it easy to believe when we cannot "see"?

III. Death's Sting (vv. 28-37)

This portion of the text contains raw emotion on everyone's part. Martha tells Mary that Jesus wants to see her and Mary quickly goes to him. The mourners follow her, thinking she is going to the tomb to weep. Mary, crying, gets straight to the point with Jesus. If he only had been there her brother would not have died (v. 32). Jesus was moved and disturbed by death's power that he saw in Mary and those consoling her. It caused him to cry, too. The consolers gave a mixed review. Some of them saw Jesus crying and talked about how much he must have loved Lazarus. Others complained by saying that if he had opened the eyes of a man born blind, surely he could have kept Lazarus from dying. Are we accepting and moved by raw emotion or do we act like the consolers, trying to fix everything?

IV. Seeing Is Believing or Believing Is Seeing (vv. 38-46)

Jesus, Mary, Martha, and the consolers went to the tomb. Jesus asked for the stone to be removed. Martha questioned this and what Jesus said in reply is key to the passage: "Did I not tell you that if you believed, you would see the glory of God?" (v. 40). In this encounter we have believing as seeing. In verse 45 we get the reverse, "Many of the Jews therefore, who had come with Mary and had seen what Jesus did, believed in him." Here we have seeing as believing. For some, neither seeing nor believing works, for they are too skeptical. They are the ones who likely were complaining in v. 37 and went to the Pharisees to report on what Jesus had done (v. 46). What do we "see" and "believe" as we prepare for Easter? (Marcia Thompson)

MARCH 24, 2002

Passion/Palm Sunday

Worship Theme: Jesus, accused as false Messiah and usurping King, is faithful unto death.

Readings: Isaiah 50:4-9*a;* Philippians 2:5-11; Matthew 26:14–27:66

Call to Worship (Psalm 31):

Leader: Blessed be the LORD, for he has wondrously shown his steadfast love to me when I was beset as a city under siege.

People: **I had said in my alarm, "I am driven far from your sight." But you heard my supplications when I cried out to you for help.**

Leader: Even though my strength fails,

People: **Even in our distress,**

Leader: The Lord is my rock and my fortress.

People: **We exalt in your steadfast love.**

All: **Blessed be God forever.**

Pastoral Prayer:

O Sacred Head now wounded, have mercy on us. O Sacred Heart now wounded, grant us peace. You take away the sins of the world. You know the shock of betrayal. You know the sting of the lash. You know the marks of nails. You know the pain of being forsaken. You know the fear of death. Be with those who suffer.

Those who betray. Those who lash out and those who suffer abuse. Those who torture and those who are tortured. Those who abandon and those who are abandoned. Those who kill and those who die. Be here now. Let us tend your broken body. Let us wrap your cooling flesh. Let us apply the spices as we lay you in a borrowed grave. Let us bid you rest, good and faithful servant. Amen. (Scott Haldeman)

SERMON BRIEFS

SO WHO IS THIS SERVANT?

ISAIAH 50:4-9*a*

Even though the Old Testament reading for Palm/Passion Sunday comes from the third Servant song in Second Isaiah, it may be helpful to preach out of the context of all four (42:1-4 [5-9]; 49:1-6; 50:4-9*a*; 52:13–53:12). The first three Servant songs are commonly read on the first three days of Holy Week, followed by the fourth (and arguably most familiar) song read on Good Friday. The result of this sequential reading is a full, if not entirely clear, picture of the Servant.

Scholars continue to debate the identity of this Servant in Isaiah. Does the Servant stand for an individual, the prophet perhaps, or some representative of the people? Or is the Servant the nation of Israel as a whole, or a specially commissioned group of the faithful? Whoever this Servant is, he or she is chosen by God and commissioned to bring forth justice to the nations (42:1). The Servant will not come shouting in the streets, yet will not be silenced until his justice has been established and his teaching has been received (42:4). The Servant is called by God in the womb (49:1) and formed for the purpose of gathering God's people back to God (49:5), and to be a light to the nations (49:6). The Servant has been given God's Word of hope and restoration (50:4) and a ready ear to receive it (50:5) and to proclaim it even to those who would ridicule him for it (50:6). The Servant is firm in his trust in God (50:6). The Servant, though undesirable in appearance, will be exalted before nations (52:13-15). The Ser-

vant will be despised, know suffering and infirmity, and accept
punishment and affliction on behalf of others (53:4-5). The Servant will bear the iniquities of all and even give his life as an
offering for sin (53:10-11). It is no wonder that the church has
been eager to claim these prophetic poems celebrating God's
Servant as fulfilled in the suffering and crucifixion of Christ.

But before we preach on Isaiah's Servant songs to the church
at the beginning of Holy Week, we should consider how they
sounded to those to whom they were addressed: the Jews in exile.
According to Old Testament scholar Paul Hanson (*Isaiah 40–66.
Interpretation: A Commentary for Teaching and Preaching*
[Louisville, Ky.: John Knox Press, 1995], p. 1), Second Isaiah was
written to the Jewish community living in Babylon during the
second half of the sixth century B.C.E. These hearers lived but a
generation removed from the destruction of Judah in 586 B.C.E.,
and within sight of the eventual overthrow of Babylon by the Persians in 539 B.C.E. Israel was a captive people, bereft of promised
land and threatened with the loss of religious and cultural identity. Israel was a scattered community struggling with both physical and theological survival. How could such a people chosen by
Yahweh and once called to become a light to the nations make
sense now of its own suffering and powerlessness? How could
they live with the prospect that God's purpose for them might be
in jeopardy? Hanson argues that all of Second Isaiah is aimed at
calling Israel back to a recognition of Yahweh as the center of its
past, present, and future.

The preaching of the third Servant song from Second Isaiah
must begin here—with a proclamation of God's promised vision
of justice, namely, the reconciliation of all people and the restoration of all creation, starting with Israel. Then the church can
speak of Jesus as the personification of the Servant in Isaiah 50:4-
9a: the One given the tongue of a teacher, able to sustain the
weary with a word . . . the One who gives his back to those who
would strike him . . . the One who trusts that God will help him
even as people spit in his face.

The church would do well to claim Jesus as the Servant only
after recognizing Israel's prior claim to it. For the Servant is Isaiah's grand and startling metaphor for God's power and victory
made manifest in what seems to all the world to be weakness and

defeat. The notion that the suffering and pain, the humiliation and dislocation of the exiled Jewish community, could actually *affect* the community's ultimate restoration as well as the restoration of all things, was a word as unprecedented as it was unfathomable. And that word should strike the Christian community the same way.

On Palm Sunday, the church customarily imagines itself along "the path down from the Mount of Olives" (Luke 19:37), spreading cloaks and palm branches before Jesus, who is riding on a donkey. Congregations sing "Hosannas" in anticipation of Christ's victory on the cross, but always with a descant acknowledging the cost of such victory. On Palm Sunday, the church must manage to lament and rejoice simultaneously. It must plainly see itself as a people living in exile like the Jews, surrounded by enemies (ostensibly benign), tempted to idolatry, and constantly in danger of losing its identity as God's people. At the same time, it must also joyfully embrace the mission God has called it to, which is no less than Jesus' mission— to become a Servant to the world and, in that sacrifice, be the light to the nations God promised from the beginning.

So who is this Servant? He is the One who comes riding on a donkey toward a cross of suffering and death. He is you or I as we follow him along the way. He is the people called Israel and now called Church who are summoned by the prophet to proclaim the mystery of the world's redemption: that through suffering comes healing, through humiliation comes exaltation, through trust comes hope, and through death comes life. (Mark Price)

SELF-EMPTYING WITHOUT
SACRIFICING A SENSE OF SELF

PHILIPPIANS 2:5-11

Many of us have lived so much of our lives for others, we no longer have any idea who *we* are. Tragically, in giving, we have given up ourselves. We have lost our identity and sacrificed our sense of self. At the same time, we continue to hear the call, "Let each of you look not to your own interests, but to the interests of others" (2:4). And to make it worse, Paul enlists Christ to substantiate his appeal—"Let the same mind be in you that was in Christ Jesus" (2:5).

How, then, can we hear Paul's call, when the life of self-sacrifice turns personally destructive? When self-emptying erodes one's sense of self, how can Christ's example serve as a model for living?

In this passage, we discover significant pieces of Christ's journey that are often overlooked and may serve to strengthen a sense of self, even as we answer the call to a self-emptying life.

I. Self-knowledge and the Freedom to Give (vv. 6-7)

While Christ lives a self-emptying life, he always knows who he is. Paul asserts, "Though he was in the form of God, [he] did not regard equality with God as something to be exploited" (2:6). Christ knows he is divine, yet he does not exploit his divinity. I have often heard, "You have to know who you are before you can give yourself to someone else." Christ knows who he is. Hence, he is able to give himself to others.

Subsequently, he "emptied himself, taking the form of a slave, being born in human likeness" (2:7a). Significantly, the first two verbs are in the active voice. Christ empties and Christ takes. Christ is the agent of the action. No one *empties* or *enslaves* him. No one extracts something from him against his will. To the contrary, he empties himself, deliberately taking the form of a slave.

I confess. Slavery images make me nervous, and I tread anxiously at this point. However, one thing I find significant is the freedom that characterizes Christ's journey. Throughout the process, Christ remains in control. No one takes his identity from him. Instead, sure of who he is, he deliberately enters the world as a slave to walk side by side with all enslaved people. And even at this point, Christ maintains access to the powers he lays aside (Matt. 26:52-54). Self-emptying remains the model, yet the sense of self is never sacrificed.

II. The Rhythm of Relationships (v. 8)

Aware of who he is, Christ is in the ideal position to respond to the rhythm of relationships. In solidarity with enslaved people, he commits himself to walk with them, realizing that their journey might eventually become his own. And indeed it does. This road of relationship leads him to a hill called Calvary. Too often, we think of obedience as adherence to a set of rules not necessarily related to actual living. Here, though, Christ's obedience is connected to "being found in human form."

As a member of the human community, Christ's life is governed by the rhythm of relationships, and a life of solidarity with enslaved people demands much from him. It requires surrendering to the possibility of death. Indeed, it means dying on a cruel cross.

III. Exaltation of a Name (vv. 9-11)

Finally, in self-emptying, Christ's name is preserved. He avoids being absorbed by others and consistently maintains a sense of personal identity. He is always "Jesus," and God lifts this name above all others (2:9).

Slavery itself is not exalted. Instead, Jesus—the name of the One who joins the plight of enslaved people—is lifted up. United, but not enmeshed, Christ's identity remains clear, and God exalts his name. In response, all people are drawn to "Jesus" as Lord (2:10-11).

A self-emptying life without a sense of self destroys the wellspring from which community takes shape. Only when we know who we are can we give ourselves to others. Our Lord knows who he is, and out of this self-knowledge, he knows what he can offer others. As a result, new life is born in the barren land of enslaved living. In that place, he calls us to discover who we are, to discover our gifts and our unique talents, with the assurance that we, too, can become a source of life for others out of the wellspring of our own abundant living. (Sean A. White)

THE CRY OF GETHSEMANE

MATTHEW 26:14–27:66

I can barely pronounce the word *Gethsemane* without feeling a chill running down my spine. Immediately, the shadow of a once immense pain overflows me. It all began on a Maundy Thursday at a Baptist Church in Scarsdale, New York. The service was somber, spiritual. The last candle was flickering in the darkness, barely outlining the beautiful sanctuary and the silhouette of the soloist who was singing a spiritual, "Did You See Them Crucify My Lord?" Ever since that night, I have understood the immense pain that Jesus suffered in the garden.

The Gospel tells us very little about the deep intimate feelings of Jesus. Only a few times can he no longer contain his humanity. It is because of those weak and most tender moments that I have come to love Christ. Somehow, I then stretch out my hand to reach him. Like the beautiful ceiling fresco in the Sistine Chapel, where God stretches his hand to reach Adam, I have often wanted to do the same when I hear about Gethsemane.

This passage of Matthew has so much richness that it is impossible to touch all of its aspects in one sermon. I will limit myself to the concepts of abandonment, by his friends and his Father, and about prayers.

Christ had emptied himself of his Divinity, but his "spiritual umbilical cord" to his Father allowed him to "know" his immediate sad future. His heart was filled with the warmth of the shared supper in the Upper Room. Even though he knew too painfully well the ensuing moments, he still needed the warmth and friendship of the men he had lived with for the last three years. He chose the three closest of his flock to support and comfort him through his prayers.

But Peter, James, and John were snoring along, probably tired from the emotionally draining days. After his first long prayer, Jesus came back and awakened them. He told them that instead of sleeping they should watch and pray so that they might not enter into temptation. Couldn't Jesus understand how exhausted they were? However, Jesus probably knew that tiredness is one of the most fertile grounds for temptation to strike. Isn't it more difficult to be kind, helpful, understanding, and considerate to others when you are really tired?

That night Jesus experienced great sorrow and distress. Luke tells us that his sweat was like clots of blood that fell on the ground. One may wonder why Jesus suffered to such an extent. First, Jesus was betrayed and abandoned by his close friends. "I looked for sympathy, but there was none, for comforters, but I found none" (Ps. 69:20 NIV). He painfully remembered how David, long before him, had also walked through the Kidron Valley, going also up the Mount of Olives, barefoot and weeping. But David had friends with him, and they all went with him, barefoot and weeping in support of his humiliation. Here, Jesus, the Son of God, one of David's sons, had no such support.

Second, even God would forgo him in those most horrible moments! God with whom he was so close, whom he loved and lived with daily, since all eternity. Suddenly God would stop loving him and pour his wrath on him, for sins he had not committed. Hell need not be a burning furnace! Hell is where God is not!

That night, Jesus plumbed to the depths of the nadir. Although everyone who faces death is distressed, why did Jesus go through such an agonizing pain, a pain so great that he was with his face to the ground since he could no longer stand? It was the pain of abandonment. Although we can hardly grasp the pain Jesus must have felt, many of us have known the incredible pain of separations, be it from a parent, a sibling, a spouse, a loved one—they all contain the sting of death in them!

Jesus had known an uninterrupted fellowship and intimacy with the Father, who had been through eternity his deepest joy, even on earth. The Father had been Jesus' unending, constantly present source of support and inward strength in his short life filled with so many disappointments and controversies. A preacher once stated that "his body was being destroyed in the worst possible way, but that was a flea bite compared to what was happening to his soul." And yet, despite it all, Jesus still resorted to his buoy, the only surviving tool he mentioned during his life: prayer.

Prayer is indeed the underlying strength, the backbone of what happens in our lives, and especially in our spiritual lives. Jesus showed us that the practice of an active prayer life could have tremendous power. He showed through his actions that prayer is, above all, total attentiveness to God, with body, heart, and soul.

Jesus would simply listen to God, be in God's presence. It was a communion so deep that words had become superfluous! Love and awe were so intermingled that words could only be a bother, a handicap. True prayer is not only resting in God. Prayer becomes our daily inner Sabbath. Prayer teaches us to be in the adoring presence of the lover of our soul. Jesus had known that for all eternity, and suddenly there was nothing but a boomerang echo of his love, with nobody at the other end. The boomerang hit him at the deepest level of his soul. And yet, despite all of it, prayer gave him the strength to go through his painful ordeal. Let us not forget that, and even pray in the midst of our most agonizing pain, and even when we believe that there is a "not home" sign on the Mount of Zion.

Gethsemane was maybe a garden with many thorns, but let not the few drops of blood on your fingers prevent you from enjoying and knowing that the rose is beautiful. For God never promised you a perfect rose garden! (Christine D'haese Radano)

MARCH 29, 2002

Good Friday

Worship Theme: All those who claim to be king set themselves against the emperor.

Readings: Isaiah 52:13–53:12; Hebrews 10:16-25; John 18:1–19:42

Call to Worship (Psalm 22):

Leader: My God, my God, why have you forsaken me?

People: **O my God, I cry by day, but you do not answer; and by night, but find no rest.**

Leader: Yet you are holy, enthroned on the praises of Israel.

People: **In you our ancestors trusted; they trusted, and you delivered them.**

Leader: To you they cried, and were saved; in you they trusted, and were not put to shame.

People: **To you, O God, we cry.**

Pastoral Prayer:
You who give us the bitter cup to drink, have mercy on us. You who give power to authorities to crucify, have mercy on us. You who reign, setting yourself against all earthly empires, have mercy on us. We pray for your church and for those we have betrayed. We pray for your people who ask for you to be crucified. We pray for authorities who rule by intimidation. We pray for those who live in fear. We pray for ourselves who cannot

believe. We pray for the suffering, the abandoned, and the sick. We pray to you whom Jesus trusted unto death, and whom you have exalted. We pray in the name of the Father, the Son, and the Holy Spirit. Amen. (Scott Haldeman)

SERMON BRIEFS

THE SUFFERING SERVANT SONG

ISAIAH 52:13–53:12

This passage of Scripture is difficult for at least two reasons. First, the language of this poem is full of obscure Hebrew words with uncertain meanings; yet, even full of double entendres and rhyme to Hebrew ears, we who read this passage today get a clear message of the Servant's vicarious suffering and God's ultimate vindication of the Servant. Second, we can't be sure just who the Suffering Servant is. Over the years the Servant has been identified as a particular prophet or king. Scholars have identified the Servant as collective, the nation of Israel, or as an individual, particularly the person of Jesus. All we can say is, for Christians on Good Friday, the image of Jesus dying on the cross bears more than a striking resemblance to the sufferings of God's Servant here in Isaiah. This passage is difficult, yet powerful. This, in itself, points to the astonishing work of the Servant.

Most scholars agree that Isaiah 52 and 53 are part of what is termed Second Isaiah. It is assumed here that the corpus of Second Isaiah is chapters 40–55. Also, many scholars believe that this prophet lived during the exile in Babylon and ministered to the exiles there. The body of this text can be divided a number of ways, but I would like to suggest a particular structure. (For this structure I am indebted to Dr. James Ware, an expert in Isaiah, at the University of Evansville.)

52:13-15	The glory of the Servant described
53:1-3	The suffering of the Servant described
53:4-6	The reason for/purpose accomplished by the suffering of the Servant described

53:7-9   The suffering of the Servant described
53:10-12   The glory of the Servant described

The obvious advantage of using this structure is that it illustrates the poetic nature of the text. Another advantage is that the inner logic of the passage becomes clearer. The form is concentric, one not uncommon in rhetoric of the day. This structure may suggest that this passage was meant to be read or recited aloud. At any rate, in a concentric form the most important part is the middle. Therein is the main point of the message. Here, the middle of the passage describes the reason for and the purpose accomplished by the Servant's suffering: he suffered vicariously for "us" (Isa. 53:5).

Here is also the message of Good Friday. God's Son suffered and died for us. Synoptic Gospels put the words in the mouth of the Gentile centurion: "Truly this man was God's Son!" (Mark 15:39; Matt. 27:54); "Certainly this man was innocent" (Luke 23:47). But the Gospel of John paints the most vivid picture. Throughout the Gospel, Jesus says that his hour has not yet come. Then finally it does come . . . on the cross. In the midst of rejection, betrayal, and suffering, Jesus, in a final act of grace, "gave up his spirit" (John 19:30). By these last words of Jesus, John implies that Jesus handed over his Spirit to *those who were ready to receive.* The supreme irony is that even then, after Jesus' supreme act as the Lamb of God taking away the sins of the world, his followers still acted like sheep who went astray and who turned to their own way (Isa. 53:6). Some of Jesus' followers hid, and others simply went back home defeated. It is not until after the Resurrection in John 20:22 that the disciples actually receive the Holy Spirit from Jesus. And perhaps they do not fully receive the Spirit, even then, until Pentecost.

But suffering is *never* the end of the story. Suffering is never the final word from God for anyone. Isaiah 52:12-15 and 53:10-12 suggest that the Servant is glorified. Likewise, there is a promise that he *will* accomplish his purpose (53:11*b*). But just as the cross is not the end of the story, it is a necessary part. To behold the glory, to even catch a glimpse, we must first be made whole. This surprising, healing, and startling act of God through God's Servant changes us.

Good Friday is a time for us to reflect on the love of God, who goes to such great lengths for us. Jesus' act is free, unearned, and unmerited by us sheep. Ask: What would it take to put yourself right with God? How much would you give? Good Friday is a time to realize that God gives it all. (Kathy Armistead)

DEEP IN THE HEART OF CREATION

HEBREWS 10:16-25

I.

There is a place I love, an Episcopal retreat center in the mountains of North Carolina near Hendersonville, where early in the morning one is blessed to see the majesty and mystery of Creation—the First Act, and all the acts since.

On the lodge's front porch are rocking chairs that overlook a narrow stretch of lake, and there, most every morning, wisps of fog slide slowly across the water's veneer, caressing the lake's surface. It is the Spirit of God, of course, hovering over the face of the deep.

There is no big, banging noise to hear, only the serenity of God's presence to see, and the peacefulness of the divine Work. As the fog wafts along, one sees as if it were time itself, like an ever-flowing stream, bearing all who breathe away.

But there is something else, too. Across the lake, near the far shore, is a large white cross that is mirrored by the water. Far from appearing a mere overlay, however, the cross looks for all the world like a sword plunged deep into the lake, and deep into the heart of the Creation itself. Howsoever the Spirit is moving, it is in view of the cross. Revelation teaches us that the Lamb is slain from the foundations of the world. That there is, in the heart of the Creation itself, the cross of Jesus. And just as Bethlehem breaks history star-wise (Buechner), so Golgotha breaks history cross-ways. In the Good Friday liturgy, and in Hendersonville, you can see that.

II.

Our text from Hebrews, an alternate reading for Good Friday, offers reflection and interpretation on Jeremiah's announcement of a new covenant: in the preaching of Hebrews' author, the death of Christ has accomplished what Jeremiah proclaimed as the eternal purposes of God. The cross is perceived as deep in the heart of God's will and work, as it was anticipated by the prophet. Thus, whatever our new situation, it is based in an age-old promise. Better, our new relationship with God, coming as it does through the death of Jesus, is in fact part of the ancient intent. The death of Jesus makes good this new covenant, by which we are forgiven: freed both from the forensic requirements of the old practices, and for the enlivening obligations of living our faith.

More simply: since we are freed from sin and guilt by the perfect offering of Christ, we are able to turn our attention to the three privileges and obligations of Christian life and worship:

- We are privileged to approach God confidently, with our prayers and praises characterized by true hearts and the full assurance of our faith;
- We are further privileged, and obligated, to hold fast the confession of our faith and hope, knowing that as God is persistent and faithful, we, too, must be faithfully persistent in our testimony;
- We are obligated to help others maintain their testimony by "provoking them to good love and good deeds."

III.

One of the great affirmations of the book of Hebrews is that Jesus is both our High Priest and our sin offering. Christ opens a way into the Holy of Holies, and brings into the very presence of God the blood that atones for all sins for all time—and it is his own blood that he carries. The cross, from deep in the heart of Creation, is the avenue of the new creation, and the ensign of the new creation, besides—touching all history, and all history's children, as a reflection of God's eternal mercy and peace. (Thomas Steagald)

CAN'T WAIT FOR SUNDAY

JOHN 18:1–19:42

I. A Unique Perspective

John's perspective on the passion of Jesus is unique among the Gospels. In Matthew and Mark, Jesus suffers on the cross. In Luke, Jesus forgives from the cross. In John, Jesus reigns from the cross. Similarly, Mark describes the cross as a disaster that the Resurrection reverses. Jesus would have avoided it, praying that the Father might remove this cup from him. Even Luke, who casts the disciples in as favorable a light as possible, does not try to soften the agony of the cross very much. Jesus still prays to be delivered. In John's account, Jesus goes to the garden, not to pray, but to meet Judas. He has already asked, "What should I say—'Father, save me from this hour'? No, it is for this reason that I have come." Instead he prays, "Father, glorify your name" (12:27-28).

Throughout John's account, Jesus is positively magisterial. Knowing all, Jesus comes forward to meet the arresting party. He questions them; and when they state their purpose, he responds with a divine, "I am." They step back and fall to the ground like bowling pins. Mark only mentioned that Jesus threw himself on the ground (14:35).

Before the high priest, Jesus questions his accusers. Later, Jesus puts Pilate on trial. Pilate bounces back and forth between Jesus and the religious leaders like a ping-pong ball. In and out he goes, trying to make up his mind. Jesus tells him, "Everyone who belongs to the truth listens to my voice." John makes us feel high drama, but only Pilate's destiny is really at stake. The scene demands to know, is Pilate of the truth?

On the cross, Jesus issues orders and creates relationships. He looks after the care of his mother, entrusting her care to his beloved disciple. No cry of dereliction can be heard. The text is quite clear that the only reason he asks for a drink is to fulfill Scripture. Fulfillment is a heavy theme for John. Over and over we are told that anything bad happens in order to fulfill either Scripture or the words of Jesus, which seem to have equal weight.

John shows us a Jesus who, being lifted up, draws all people to himself. This Jesus warned that no one could take his life, instead *he* lays it down (10:17-18). The power and glory we have to wait for until Easter in the other Gospels, John gives to us on the cross. He cannot wait for Sunday.

II. Can't Wait for Sunday

John's perspective may feel foreign to us. We understand suffering, such as Mark shows us. We may approach suffering with hope of vindication, something better down the road. God will turn things around. John would have us look at our suffering and say "This was our finest hour!" (my apologies to Winston Churchill).

John would have us know that Jesus is the Son of God, and God is always in control. Jesus is, first of all, our Lord and Savior. John shows him to be confident and in control. John simply cannot wait for Sunday because the cross is Jesus' finest hour. Even in so-called defeat, he triumphs. Balancing the voices of all four Gospels, we might say that Sunday shows us the love and power of the Father, while Friday shows us the love and power of the Son.

Jesus is, second of all, an example for believers to follow. We cannot face trials with Jesus' poise, but maybe we, too, can say, "No one takes this from me, I lay it down." And maybe that will be a comfort to us. If there is a price to pay for following Jesus, we pay it willingly. Though we may seem to be on the wrong end of things at times, we, too, are triumphant. God's love and power are so strong that defeat is impossible. (David C. Mauldin)

MARCH 31, 2002

Easter Day

Worship Theme: It is the Great Sunday! The Crucified One appears, transformed, incorruptible.

Readings: Acts 10:34-43; Colossians 3:1-4; John 20:1-18

Call to Worship (Psalm 118):

> *Leader:* The stone that the builders rejected has become the chief cornerstone.
>
> *People:* **This is the LORD's doing; it is marvelous in our eyes.**
>
> *Leader:* God has raised Jesus from the grave.
>
> *People:* **Alleluia.**
>
> *Leader:* Jesus Christ is risen today.
>
> *People:* **Alleluia.**

Pastoral Prayer:

God of mysterious power, who brings forth life out of the grave, who thwarts the executioner and destroys death, show us your power today that we may live again and, renewed, may serve your world. You who raised Jesus, raise our dead. You who raised Jesus, overturn oppression. You who raised Jesus, dry our tears. You who raised Jesus, revive your church. You who raised Jesus, depose tyrants. You who raised Jesus, come again to renew your creation. (Scott Haldeman)

SERMON BRIEFS

INSIDERS AND OUTSIDERS

ACTS 10:34-43

Our text is actually a sermon. And, like all sermons, it is best understood in the larger context in which it was delivered. This message, preached by Peter, is part of the longest narrative in Acts. The story begins when Cornelius, the Gentile, Roman army officer, receives a vision from God to send for Peter. Sixty-six verses later, the drama ends with Peter's account of the events of the church at Jerusalem. Today's text is the good news of the gospel that Peter shares with Cornelius and those who are gathered with him.

This drama is a pivotal point for the entire book of Acts, and for the story of God's ongoing redemptive activity in the world. It is a drama about insiders and outsiders. It is a drama about Cornelius, an outsider whose status would be changed to that of insider, and it is about Peter, an insider who also had to change for God's purpose to be accomplished.

Peter begins his sermon with a shocking statement, "I truly understand that God shows no partiality . . . he is Lord of all." This, coming from a man who just the day before would never have thought of sharing his table, his home, or his faith with those his tradition had taught him were unclean! However, Peter was open to God. God was taking the gospel into new places, and Peter was willing to move beyond his comfort zone and go with God. The Holy Spirit worked in that meeting that day, astounding Peter and the disciples.

Who are the insiders and outsiders in our context today? For years, Christians were the insiders in North America as the Spirit moved first in New England and Virginia and then along the developing frontier. Then over time, religion became institutionalized. We wrapped our faith in the American flag and settled into our comfort zone of American cultural Christianity. But now the church is slowly dying here as people opt out of church in increasing numbers.

In the meantime, God has taken the gospel to new places. The hot spots can now be found in South America, in parts of Africa, in Korea, and even Communist China. Many of us now find ourselves on the outside, looking in.

The challenge for us today is profound. Like Peter, are we willing to have our deepest convictions challenged if needed? Are we willing to take the risk and obey when God calls, even when we do not know what that may mean? Are we willing to make the changes necessary to keep up with wherever God is currently taking the gospel?

Who are the Corneliuses in our own lives? In our church? Where might God be calling us to go if we are to keep up with the fresh wind of the Spirit? Will it be to the inner city? To our own backyards in the suburbs? Who are the "unclean" that God loves and wants to reach? There is no partiality with God. What will our faith response be? (Tracy Hartman)

BEYOND THE FRENZIED LIFE

COLOSSIANS 3:1-4

In Colossians 2, Paul refers to those who try to secure their lives in frenzied living. His description reminds me of those few days just before out-of-town company arrives to visit in our home. During those final forty-eight hours, it feels like a cyclone is roaring through our house. The washer and dryer run continuously. Dust rags fly. Showers are scrubbed. Floors are mopped, and the grass is cut. All this is done to assure that things are in order for our guests. And as far as peace goes, little is found.

Some Christians live their lives in the same manner. From Sunday school to worship to church training to Monday night Bible study to Wednesday prayer service to Thursday night visitation to the youth car wash on Saturday morning. We anxiously rush around to assure that nothing is left undone. But for what? Why the frenzied schedule? Why the chaotic lifestyle?

On the one hand, we Christians incessantly speak of the peace which passes understanding, while on the other hand, our lives look like frenzied attempts to assure that everything is in order. The specific rituals have changed since the first century, yet the purpose remains the same. We work and work, aiming to secure our position in the Kingdom. But as the apostle Paul asserts, "These [actions] have indeed an appearance of wisdom in promoting self-imposed piety, humility, and severe treatment of the body, but they are of no value in checking self-indulgence" (2:23). Instead, they promote self-indulgence while draining peace from daily living. Thankfully, this is not the way it has to be. In Christ, the frenzy calms as our identity is secured by his grace.

For two chapters, Paul contemplates the cosmic Christ and asserts his headship over all creation. He is the "image of the invisible God" (1:15), the "firstborn of all creation" (1:15), the "head of the church" (1:18), the "firstborn from the dead" (1:18), and the "head of every ruler and authority" (2:10). Indeed, he is the "all and in all" (3:11). For this reason, all who place their faith in him rest secure in his care. The frenzied life promoted by some has no place among the faithful. Persistent observance of festivals and Sabbaths, along with abstinence from handling, tasting, and touching accomplishes little more than high blood pressure and anxiety. Such things merely amount to obeying "human commands" (2:16-22).

In response, Paul asserts, "If you have been raised with Christ, seek the things that are above, where Christ is, seated at the right hand of God" (3:1). In this way, life is secured in the One who has held it together from the beginning. Instead of an identity based on arbitrary "dos" and "don'ts," identity rooted in Christ connects one to the ground of all being. Now, the apostle exhorts, "Set your minds on things that are above . . . [for] your life is hidden with Christ in God" (3:2-3). Here, one rests secure not in performance, but in promise. Here, glory awaits, for "When Christ who is your life is revealed, then you also will be revealed with him in glory" (3:4).

Secure in Christ, one abandons the frenzied quest for new life rooted in "self-indulgence" (2:23) and stands able to move beyond self-centered living. Only then may the Christian respond to the moral exhortations that follow. Fornication and greed are no longer options, for the need to dominate others vanishes when one's security rests in Christ (3:5). A life of deception no longer proves necessary, for knowledge of the Creator makes one secure just as she is (3:9-11). Our hope comes to us from the future and rests in the One who has secured the past and the present. Therefore, "Set your minds on things that are above . . . for . . . your life is hidden with Christ in God" (3:2-3), and journey beyond the frenzied life. (Sean A. White)

MARY AND HER LORD

JOHN 20:1-18

Mary Magdalene is an intriguing figure. Scripture tells us a number of things about her. She was a devout follower of Christ. A number of women followed Christ, none more closely than Mary Magdalene. She was there at the Crucifixion. She was the first to come to the tomb on resurrection Sunday. Often she is identified with the sinful woman of Luke 7:36-39. However, there is no evidence that she was that woman. What we do know is that, as soon as she met him, her life revolved around the words and ministry of Jesus.

We aren't sure of Mary's background. There are many things that we don't know about Mary. However, we do know that she loved her Lord. In fact, her love for Christ is the focus of how John begins his resurrection narration.

The Crucifixion devastated Mary. She came to the tomb early on the first day of the week filled with grief. Her love for her Lord drove her to the tomb. She needed to be there. He was the most significant part of her life. He had changed everything for her. Now she needed to be there for him, even though he was dead.

We can only imagine where her faith stood at that time. She had surely heard him speak of his resurrection. However, the disciples had also heard Jesus' words, and yet, after Peter and John saw the empty tomb, they returned to their homes. They had not fully understood what Jesus had told them.

Here we find faith and reality colliding. The reality of the Crucifixion and trust in Jesus' words concerning resurrection were at war in the minds and hearts of those who loved Jesus. All Mary knew was that her Lord was dead and placed in a tomb. Now his body was gone.

Peter and John had come and gone. Mary stayed. She had to. Her love kept her there. Little did she know that her love for Jesus would result in the strengthening of her faith. Although everything seemed lost, she would find more than she could ever imagine.

Love overcame fear as she bent over to look into the tomb. Through tear-filled eyes she saw two angels in white. They asked her why she was crying. Then Jesus stood behind her and asked her the same question, "Why are you crying?" Why, indeed! She was crying because she believed her Lord to be dead. She thought that his body had been stolen. Her love was strong; now her faith would be strengthened. Now she would understand Jesus' words. Now faith would become reality.

Jesus said to her, *"Mary."* The Lord whom she loved spoke her name. The Lord who had called her from her life of futility had now called her to a life of possibility—a life that was even stronger than death. Now all she wanted to do was hold on to him.

Jesus told her not to hold on to him. She needed to go and tell his disciples that he was alive. She did not want to let go. But she loved the Lord enough to do what he wanted.

Mary's story teaches us an important truth. Even in the darkest hour, if our love for Christ is strong and it keeps us close to him, he will come to us. He will call us by name and strengthen our faith by showing us a life full of hope and possibility. Let us love Christ even in the darkest hour. Our love will be rewarded with a strengthened faith. (Reece B. Sherman)

SPIRITUAL PREPARATION

APRIL

We enter now into the season of Easter. Easter is at the core of our faith. The day itself is charged with meaning, with hope, with excitement. Pastors can easily view Easter as an ending, the day toward which our energies flow. And yet the Scriptures call us to envision Easter as a beginning. A wise friend once made the comment, "In life, what looks like an ending is always a beginning."

Easter reminds us of that truth. Life and ministry are always filled with surprises. I shared the following meditation with a congregation recently:

God of surprises
The morning begins in grief
And ends in hope . . .
"the stone is rolled away."

God of surprises
The morning begins in darkness
And ends in the dazzling terror
Of our light . . .
"Why do you seek the living among the dead?"

God of surprises
The morning begins with burial preparations
And ends in songs of victory:
"He is not here; he is risen."

God of surprises
We had expected to honor the dead
And now we race to share the good news:
"We have seen the Lord."

In the experience of Easter
We discover the surprise to endings
That are beyond our imagining
We unexpectedly find ourselves
In the presence of the miraculous
Through faith we come to know
That all things have been made new
That Christ is risen, just as he said!

The ministry is unpredictable. As pastors we learn to analyze the past, manage the present, plan for the future. But life is full of surprises. Sometimes what looks like an ending is actually a beginning.

- Can you recall an experience in ministry that came as a surprise to you? Can you reflect on an experience that seemed like an ending, but led to a new beginning?

In Colossians 3:1-4, Paul writes:

So if you have been raised with Christ, seek the things that are above, where Christ is, seated at the right hand of God. Set your minds on things that are above, not on things that are on earth, for you have died, and your life is hidden with Christ in God. When Christ who is your life is revealed, then you also will be revealed with him in glory.

Paul calls us to seek the things that are above. But that can be difficult. Neill Hamilton writes perceptively about the pastoral ministry:

Most of us respond to a call to ministry with particular, beloved and effective clergypersons in mind. As we observe their ministry we see God challenging human life with the transforming power of the gospel. Since we long for such challenge and transformation, we suppose that people in those congregations do also . . . prospective ministers are able to sustain their dream of ministry until their first call or appointment to parish leadership after graduation and full ordination. Then the reality of the profession tumbles in on them. The reality is that the vast majority of persons in a typical congregation do not want themselves or their world to be transformed by the gospel.

It is difficult to focus on the risen life when we are burdened by the sins of the congregation and our own failures. It is difficult to seek the things that are above when we become disillusioned about life and ministry. But stay with me. I want to focus on the word *above*. There has to be an above. If there is no above, if the dead are not raised, Paul writes, "eat and drink, for tomorrow we die" (1 Cor. 15:32). It is tough to seek the things that are above, but one thing is even tougher: to make our way through life, through the work of ministry, as if there were no "above." If there is no above, then it doesn't all add up in this life. It doesn't compute. In this life there are death and disease, displacement and disappointment, downsizing and dysfunction, darkness and despair. Our feet are planted firmly in this earth, and we are stuck in, stuck to the things of the world. We live here.

But there is more to life than this life. We "seek the things that are above," the scripture says. C. S. Lewis had a marvelous comment. He said, "Aim at Heaven, and you'll get earth thrown in. Aim at earth, and you'll get neither."

Our feet are planted firmly in this earth, but we aim for heaven. We seek the things that are above. A few years ago my wife and I traveled to Ireland. The Celtic Christians of that country, in the fifth to tenth centuries, had a clear sense of the reality of "above," the "thinness" of heaven; they believed that heaven started "one foot above our heads," and so they built crosses, large stone crosses, right in the middle of the grassy fields in which they lived and farmed. The Celtic crosses were living reminders to "seek the things that are above."

When we are tempted to get bogged down in the things of this world: the dysfunction of the moment; the crisis of the day, the fad of the week, the cause of the month, the scandal of the year, there is good news for us. It is the good news of Easter. It comes to us as a gift from the God of surprises, the God who creates new beginnings out of endings, life out of death. We are invited to seek the things that are above.

- Recall your own motivations for entering pastoral ministry. Can you identify an experience that has been disillusioning for you? Can you connect with a desire to begin again, to seek the things that are above?

When we lead God's people in giving thanks for the presence of God in Holy Communion, we often begin with the words "The Lord be with you." The congregation responds, "And also with you." We continue, "Lift up your hearts." And they respond, again, "We lift them up to the Lord."

Today, seek the things that are above. Lift up your hearts! (Ken Carter)

Sources: Neill Hamilton, *Maturing in the Christian Life* (Philadelphia: Geneva Press, p. 62). C. S. Lewis, *The Joyful Christian*, p. 38. *The United Methodist Hymnal*, p. 23.

APRIL 7, 2002

Second Sunday of Easter

Worship Theme: Blessed are those who have not seen and yet believe.

Readings: Acts 2:14*a*, 22-23; 1 Peter 1:3-9; John 20:19-31

Call to Worship (Psalm 16):

Leader: The LORD is my chosen portion and my cup.

People: I bless the LORD who gives me counsel; in the night also my heart instructs me.

Leader: I keep the LORD always before me; because he is at my right hand, I shall not be moved.

People: Therefore my heart is glad, and my soul rejoices.

Leader: For you do not give me up to Sheol, or let your faithful one see the Pit.

People: You show us the path of life. In your presence we receive the fullness of joy.

Pastoral Prayer:
Ever-patient God, you raise Jesus and we hide in fear; help us to unlock the doors of the church. Ever-patient God, you send us your peace and we live in anxiety; empower us to proclaim your peace to the nations. Ever-patient God, you say to us "Fear not" and yet we tremble; assure us of your promises so that we might be a comfort to others. Ever-patient God, you understand the difficulty of belief for us who cannot see the risen Lord; quell our

doubts that we can proclaim your mercies. Ever-patient God, we await your return; come in glory—soon and very soon. Amen. (Scott Haldeman)

SERMON BRIEFS

IF WE ARE WILLING

ACTS 2:14a, 22-33

He was one of the most faithful apostles. He was also the most impulsive apostle. Peter, who had earlier denied any relationship with Jesus, is now telling Jewish believers about Jesus' resurrection and the fulfillment of God's promised outpouring of God's Spirit on all flesh. His speech is prefaced by a powerful move of God.

What a spectacle it must have been. The followers of the crucified man named Jesus appeared, to some, to be in a drunken stupor, babbling. People heard them speaking in different languages. Those who heard the commotion knew that something strange was happening. While the cacophony of sounds coming from the "apparently" inebriated and babbling people must have startled the Jews in Jerusalem for the Festival of Pentecost, the messenger must have also been a surprise. Peter was a Galilean.

Galileans were not held in high esteem by Jews from Jerusalem. Finding it difficult to pronounce certain sounds of the Hebrew and Aramaic languages, it was thought that they couldn't speak well. He spoke what some would consider biblical ebonics; a dialect considered inferior, the speech of an undesirable person. Peter and other Galileans would have been stereotyped as "natural-born rebels" who had no respect for the Jewish law. Peter was also regarded by many in a negative manner. Yet Peter was the one addressing Jews from throughout the Diaspora, in Jerusalem for the Festival of Pentecost.

Pentecost, also known as the Feast of Weeks, was an annual celebration observed seven weeks after Passover. It was a time when the Jews celebrated the completion of the grain harvest. It was during this festival when the people would offer God the "first fruits from the harvest." The festival would conclude with a meal with the poor, aliens, and Levites. Considered a time of celebration and Sabbath, Pentecost was also associated with the giving of the Law at Sinai.

Faithful, bold, and brash, Peter fulfilled a prominent role among the apostles. Before his denial of Jesus he was the lead apostle. In his memory Peter might have harbored thoughts of failing his Lord by denying Jesus, not once, but three times. He possibly remembered other instances when his humanity showed and he disappointed himself and God. But he was the one chosen to explain to the people how God was fulfilling Old Testament/Hebrew Scriptures. He became the person who explained that God's Spirit, once only bestowed upon special people, like prophets and kings, would now be poured out on all people—female and male. He would be the one to tell the crowd that Jesus was indeed the promised Christ.

It was Simon, named Peter by Jesus, who would embody the meaning of his name and become a foundation or rock of the church of Christ. This verse teaches us that just as God used Peter, with all of his human frailty, God will use us, if we are willing. (Lillian C. Smith)

DOXOLOGY AMID TRIALS

1 PETER 1:3-9

The praise of God here echoes the praise psalms of the Old Testament. Just as the OT writers praised God for God's power and strength over the Israelites' adversaries, so, too, the author of 1 Peter is writing words of encouragement to people facing trials and tribulations. Through these words of praising God, the writer is helping a scared community of faith join in a doxology of praise for the God who has spoken again through raising Jesus Christ from the dead. Because of this God, the people can have hope amid hardships, for they share in a new life in Christ.

Verse 3 speaks of a new birth. The writer here isn't talking about literally dying and being born again, but rather is trying to convey the new life and hope that are possible when one finds faith in God through Jesus Christ. This line of thinking reminds us of Jesus speaking to Nicodemus (John 3:1f). This symbolic language of a new birth quite literally makes all the difference for a believer who is facing trials, for the genuineness of a believer's faith is tested, yet he or she finds strength in the resurrection of Jesus Christ.

Verses 5-6 remind the listeners that God will keep us safe whatever persecutions come. We can be joyful, for through the trials, we are to be confident that the genuineness of our faith will be shown through this testing by fire. The imagery of gold that is tested and purified by fire reminds us that through all of our ordeals, our faith can turn out stronger and purer.

Many will ask, "Is it God who is causing the tests? Is it the devil? Are the trials just part of life?" We can probably answer yes to all three of these questions at different points in our lives; however, the focus here seems not to be on the cause of the tests, but on the results of how the tests affect one's faith. Like gold being purified, our faith is proven genuine by the results of trials. How have we responded to the hardships? What have we learned about ourselves? What have we learned about our neighbors? What have we learned about God? How is God going to work now? How are we going to mature in our faith? Has the turmoil made us rely on God more? Has our relationship with God been enriched?

God's mercy is assumed (v. 3), but our response is in question. Will we be able to praise God after the fire? We can glibly say that our faith will be found strong, no matter what the circumstance, but I would suggest that we cannot really answer this question until we have been *in* and *through* our own fire.

The promise of salvation means that God has acted in the past, in this present experience, and there is future hope, for God will act again. The fullness of God's action will not be seen until the last day. So, until the end of time, listeners are encouraged to trust in sights unseen. Keep the faith! Verse 8 talks about the indescribable and glorious joy awaiting the faithful's future in heaven. One day, the mystery of salvation will be made known to the whole of creation. Until then, though, the faithful will face trials of all sorts, and we must allow the trials to refine and purify our faith. We must love and continue to sing, "Praise God from whom all blessings flow!" (Ryan White)

PEACE FROM BEGINNING TO END

JOHN 20:19-31

The focus of this passage has often been "Doubting Thomas." Of course, he is a central figure in this narrative. He is "everyman." We cannot vilify Thomas for his desire for proof of Jesus' resurrection, because we have been there. We also want to have proof that God is alive and active in our lives. We also want to see and touch God in the midst of our circumstances.

The true focus of this text, however, is what Jesus says to his assembled and frightened disciples the first time he sees them after the resurrection. "Peace be with you!" Three times he speaks these words to the disciples, twice without Thomas and once while he is present.

From beginning to end, Jesus' life and ministry revolved around the message of peace. Even before the Messiah came, the prophet Isaiah spoke of one who would come as the "Prince of Peace" (Isa. 9:6). At his birth, the angels shouted words of praise, saying, "Glory to God in the highest, and on earth peace among those whom he favors" (Luke 2:14). Jesus told the woman who anointed his feet with her tears and the woman who was healed of her hemorrhage to "go in peace" (Luke 7:50; 8:48). As he spoke to his disciples about his imminent departure, he comforted them by saying, "Peace I leave with you" (John 14:27).

Now Jesus comes to his disciples with the words "Peace be with you." In both the Old and New Testaments *peace* means "order, harmony, and spiritual well-being." This peace was grounded in relationship with God. This is what Jesus came to give. His desire was to bring peace that could come only through relationship with God. The peace that Jesus came to give was not simply peace of mind, but peace of life.

"My peace I give you. I do not give to you as the world gives. Do not let your hearts be troubled and do not be afraid" (John 14:27*b* NIV). His peace takes away the fear that is so much a part of living. It was fear that brought the disciples together behind locked doors. And Jesus enters the room to give them the only thing that can take the fear away, "Peace be with you."

That brings us back to Thomas. Thomas was not with the disciples the first time Jesus appeared to them. Thomas needed the proof before he could enjoy the peace. He would not believe until he saw Jesus with his own eyes and touched him with his own hands. His peace was based on proof.

We so often live life with the attitude of Thomas. "God, I won't believe that you are real until you show me!" We want to see God tangibly in the circumstances of our lives. "Make this happen and we will believe." Then, like Thomas, we must hear Jesus' gentle rebuke, "Blessed are those who have not seen and yet have believed." (Reece B. Sherman)

APRIL 14, 2002

Third Sunday of Easter

Worship Theme: The Risen is present this day; we encounter Christ in the breaking of the bread.

Readings: Acts 2:14*a*, 36-41; 1 Peter 1:17-23; Luke 24:13-35

Call to Worship (Psalm 116):

Leader: I love the LORD, because he has heard my voice.

People: **God has heard our supplications.**

Leader: God inclines his ear to me.

People: **We will call on the Lord as long as we live.**

Leader: Let us worship God.

People: **Alleluia. Praise the Lord.**

Pastoral Prayer:
Blessed be God forever, who brings forth good things from the earth. And blessed be Christ, this One called Jesus, who died and was buried, who rose from the grave and visits us still around the table. We praise and bless your name for you are worthy of our praise. Open our eyes to see you in the stranger. Open our hearts to welcome the alien. Open our ears to hear the cry of the hungry. Open our hands to give to the needy. Open our minds to recognize you wherever you appear, in places unexpected, in faces unknown, that our hearts burn and we are moved to declare, "The Lord is risen indeed." Blessed be God forever. Amen. (Scott Haldeman)

SERMON BRIEFS

INVITATIONS

ACTS 2:14*a*, 36-41

The church I attended as a child ended every service with a "time of invitation." Usually, the preacher stood at the front of the church and offered words of encouragement to those who might receive Christ as their Lord and Savior. We usually sang a hymn, and during that time, anyone who wished could come forward to speak with the preacher about joining the church. As a child, my awareness of this part of the service consisted of the fact that worship was almost over, and we would be headed to lunch soon. Much later, when I was in college, I began to really understand the importance of this part of my church tradition.

In talking with a wise friend, I realized that the "time of invitation" was not simply a way of ending the service smoothly, but rather a means of providing people with time and space to respond to the call of the gospel. My friend reminded me that each time we worship, we proclaim the good news that God is always inviting us into relationship. When I began to see the gospel as invitation, I realized that God is the first and primary actor in our salvation. Then, once we are confronted with this joyous reality, the gospel demands of us some type of response.

Peter's sermon on Pentecost provides for us a model of invitation and response. As he stood to preach before the crowd gathered that day, he recounted all the wonderful acts of God in salvation history and acknowledged the new way that God was moving among them. He explained that by sending the gift of the Holy Spirit, God was assuring that all might hear and understand the story of God's relationship with the nation of Israel. The story of Jesus was central in Peter's proclamation, and the Scripture tells us that when they were confronted with their hard-heartedness toward Christ, the crowd was "cut to the heart." Their cry of penitence was "What shall we do?" It was then that Peter issued the invitation.

God's invitation to the church gathered at Pentecost, and to us today, is to respond to the gift that has been given in Christ.

Then, as now, we begin with the gracious fact that God calls us into relationship. We begin by being invited, chosen, and called by name to take our place in the kingdom of God. It is an invitation that we do not seek out for ourselves, and it is certainly not an invitation that we deserve. It is an invitation at God's initiative and by God's grace, for the most revolutionary part of Peter's sermon that day was "For the promise is for you, for your children, and for all who are far away, everyone whom the Lord our God calls to him" (v. 39).

The beginning of our life in faith is "by invitation only," but it is far from an exclusive club. This heavenly banquet is to be enjoyed by all people. As Joel had prophesied, young and old, male and female, slave and master—all are included, for human barriers no longer exist! Peter told those who thought they had been on the guest list forever, as well as those who didn't even think they were known by the host, what was required of them. In light of the invitation, he called them to response. "Repent, and be baptized . . . so that your sins may be forgiven; and you will receive the gift of the Holy Spirit" (v. 38). I'm starting to figure it out; what I thought was the end of church is only the beginning. (Wendy Joyner)

LIVING IN EXILE

1 PETER 1:17-23

Exile imagery is prominent for those of us who participate in Israel's history. Just as Israel was in exile under Babylonian rule, the writer of this text suggests that Christ's death and resurrection make it possible for others to enter into the tradition. Now, under Roman rule, the present community of faith feels abandoned and alone. How is one to live in exile?

On the basis of their salvation, the writer gives the exiles a call to action (v. 13). The imperative given in v. 17 to have "godly fear" speaks of the attitude of one's mind toward God. Obedience is a major concern in 1 Peter, for faith shows itself through obeying God. I believe that it is obedience that calls Christians to take on responsibilities. Why do we have responsibilities? Why should we care how we act? I think partly because we are obedient to the One who purposefully created us. It is out of God's purposeful creation that we are given the potential to partner with God and take on responsibilities. By obeying God we can reach our potential!

Verses 18-21 celebrate God's saving work. The writer explains God's work like ceremonial sacrifices. The price of redemption was the blood of a lamb. No doubt the tradition of sacrificing an innocent and pure lamb was the background for this line of thinking (Exod. 12:1-7; Lev. 22:19). Now Christ is the unblemished Lamb of God who has been given for our sake. Even though some may not have been part of Israel by birth, in Christ, faith has been produced and opened for Gentiles.

God continually tries to open the door for everyone to come in, and it is through Christ that this is most evident! We so often want to close the door to God for this group or that group, but we must remember that we are not the gatekeepers. Many in Jesus' time thought that they held the keys to the Kingdom, but Jesus opened the gate as he talked about Samaritans, tax collectors, and others.

Because God opens the door for all, an ethical command is given in verse 22 that is to govern all matters—*love one another from the heart*. Above all doctrine, creed, confession, or belief, love one another. Love should be as strong and as lasting as one's faith that has been tested by fire. The love that we are speaking of here is brotherly love. It is mutual and comes not from simply doing good, but from a completely transformed life.

I would bet that there are many in our churches who are constantly asking the question, "What can *I* get out of this or that?" Living in exile can be a lonely place if you think only about yourself. To live through it, you must connect yourself with others and a larger story. Love is what makes one change focus from oneself to others. The love of God permeates us and we can't help but reflect and radiate that love out of us.

Our obedience begins with God's gracious and loving self who reaches out to have a relationship with us. Obedience leads to holy living based on unselfish love. The Eternal Word persistently calls, for God has made us like imperishable seed. This means that God never gives up on us. We never turn completely rotten. Even in exile, the living Word of God is the author of new life. (Ryan White)

WHAT IF EMMAUS WERE OUR MODEL?

LUKE 24:13-35

I did not grow up in the denomination to which I now belong. The most important reason I ended up where I did is the Lord's Supper. The church where I grew up held a funeral for Jesus four times a year. Well, perhaps that is a bit harsh. We observed the Lord's Supper in a solemn and introspective manner, as good Christians should. It was our chance to reflect upon the death of our Lord and what it meant for us. There was thanksgiving, but any note of joy was absent. I was fairly stunned the first time I worshiped in the tradition that was to become my own. I found the Supper celebrated with the same focus on the Lord's death, but added was a celebration of the Resurrection. I felt something that day, something that took me two years to understand.

I. Sorrow or Joy?

What mood should dominate the Supper? Is it something to celebrate or observe? I wonder how our practice of the Lord's Supper might be different if we took the meal at Emmaus as our primary source rather than the supper in the Upper Room. Although we may not want to do that, perhaps Luke at least hoped the two might give meaning to each other. The risen Jesus walked with a pair of disciples one afternoon as they traveled to Emmaus. They did not recognize Jesus, however. Upon arriving, they persuaded him to share supper with them. He took the bread, blessed it, broke it, and gave it to them. Does that sound familiar? In that moment their eyes were opened, and they recognized him. The Lord's Supper remembers the night Jesus used a meal to explain the significance of his death. It holds his death before our mind's eye. It also recalls the afternoon the risen Jesus became known in the breaking of bread.

It takes a lot of *something* to add words to what the apostle

Paul said. When I preside at the Table, I do just that. Echoing 1 Corinthians 11:26, I proclaim to the people, "As often as you eat this bread and drink this cup, you proclaim the Lord's death *and resurrection* until he comes." I think Paul would approve. Adding "and resurrection" is probably unnecessary, but I like to be clear. We gather at the Table with joy for the same reason we call the day Jesus died *Good* Friday. The Resurrection has shown us the meaning of the cross, and we can never pretend that we do not know how the story ends—for Jesus or for us.

II. They Recognized Him

The most stunning result of Easter is that Jesus lives. This is what the Resurrection is all about. If Jesus is alive, then he can be known in the breaking of the bread. Through the Holy Spirit, he can be present with his people as they gather at his table.

Growing up I always thought the Lord's Supper was something *we* did. What made it special were our purpose and thoughts. We remembered Jesus. That is certainly true, but for me it no longer goes far enough. Today I consider the Supper a sacrament. *Sacrament* means something that God does for you, something you could not do for yourself. So what specifically does God do in the Supper? I believe the Lord Jesus communes with us in a special way. Jesus promised to be with us always, so it is not as if we are ever without his presence. Yet in the Supper, we are connected to him in a more-than-usual way. Maybe what happened at Emmaus, when they recognized him in the breaking of bread, was not a onetime event. (David C. Mauldin)

APRIL 21, 2002

Fourth Sunday of Easter

Worship Theme: Disciples of the Risen One gather, tell stories, break bread, and pray. They hold things in common and provide for those in need. Simple acts of response to so great a gift.

Readings: Acts 2:42-47; 1 Peter 2:19-25; John 10:1-10

Call to Worship (Psalm 23):

> *Leader:*   God tends to the needs of God's people.
>
> ***People:***   **God provides our daily food and drink.**
>
> *Leader:*   God leads us in paths of righteousness and renews our spirits.
>
> ***People:***   **Even in times of trouble, we have no need to fear. God is with us.**
>
> *Leader:*   Before the eyes of our foes, God celebrates us.
>
> ***People:***   **We enter God's house, praising God's name.**

Pastoral Prayer:

Good Shepherd who provides safe pasture for your own, move us to trust in your bounty so we might meet human need with generosity. You have called us into fellowship; help us to be worthy members of your body. You have poured your grace upon us; help us to open our doors and hearts to the stranger and the alien. You have spoken through the prophets; help us to hear your word anew and to speak good news among our neighbors. You spread a table before us so that we might taste your goodness; break and share us among the hungry. You were willing to suffer so that others could be free; help us to be signs of grace in a weary world. Amen. (Scott Haldeman)

SERMON BRIEFS

DAY BY DAY

ACTS 2:42-47

I believe that one of the most significant questions for us to examine is the call of the church in the world. In most public discourse, the church is at worst hypocritical and at best irrelevant. So, as the community of faith, we are forced to struggle with the identity and role of the present church.

We sometimes read these stories of the early church and wonder what went wrong. There seemed to be so much happening in their life together. God's spirit was evident in mighty ways, and the people responded in wonder and awe. We yearn for "that old-time religion" where everything was simpler and more ideal, where "all who believed were together and had all things in common" (v. 44).

As I have pondered this yearning in my own life, I have come to realize that much of what happened in the early church was not instantaneous or simple. When we read this summary statement of the church's life together, it is easy to overlook one of the most telling descriptions about how God's Spirit moved within and upon them. It is easy to overlook one of the key factors in their activities and relationship with one another. Verses 46-47 say that "*day by day,* as they spent much time together in the temple, they broke bread at home and ate their food with glad and generous hearts, praising God and having the goodwill of all the people." Day by day—how often we forget that this is part of our calling as the church, to live in relationship with God and each other day by day.

It is sometimes the "everyday" part of life in community that I overlook. I sometimes keep my eyes open for the big, transformative moment that will instantaneously change and inspire the church, only to miss the smaller, more significant miracles that

159

take place constantly. I think God was able to bless the early church through the gift of God's Spirit because they were attentive to things that happened daily. That first community spent time together taking care of the nuts-and-bolts things that would shape their lives in the image of Christ.

The earliest believers got their priorities straight about their finances and possessions. They devoted themselves to learning together. They participated in corporate worship. They prayed together, sang together, ate together and celebrated together. These earlier believers opened themselves to God's presence by being attentive to the seemingly small and sometimes mundane parts of daily life.

I think Will Campbell has captured it best in his novel *The Glad River*. It is the story of an unlikely community experienced by three soldiers during World War II. It is the story of men who shared their lives day by day.

> We had good times together. And bad. We laughed together and we cried together. We opened the club and got drunk when the season beckoned it. We sat on hot ship-decks and talked of God and quivers, and ate ripe olives at suppertime. We confessed our cares in unlikely places. We worked and piddled, sat on rushing riverbanks in the hills, and whiled away many a summer afternoon on sleeping bayous. We read books and learned to talk like each other, argued about trivial things and took hard counsel together about the things that mattered. . . . But mostly we just loved one another. (*The Glad River* [Nashville: Rutledge Hill Press], 1982, p. 309)

It is in everyday life that God chooses to bless us and to send his gifts. Perhaps our best striving is to be in community day by day—to simply love one another. (Wendy Joyner)

IS SUFFERING A PART OF FAITH?

1 PETER 2:19-25

Speaking to some who are actual slaves of Roman masters, the writer here immediately connects, calling all Christians "servants" of God. The writer seems to know the circumstances of several Christians who are slaves to harsh owners. The call is for submission—not for the sake of the authorities at hand—but for the sake of God!

What does this mean? It is a sobering thought for all of us to think that suffering is part of faith. The writer emphasizes that God is concerned about suffering unjustly (v. 19) or doing right and suffering for it (v. 20). He quickly rejects that all suffering will be validated, for he suggests that those who do wrong should expect to suffer the consequences. However, submissive suffering is grounded in the story of Jesus' passion. The writer's point is that suffering unjustly puts us in touch with God, for Christ experienced the same. Therefore, those who do suffer from injustice must look to Jesus for strength.

What are we to do, though, as Christians who are called to live as free people? It seems that people who are free would not stick around and endure any suffering. But what is freedom in Christ? We must remember Paul speaking to the church at Corinth and warning them not to use their freedoms just for freedom's sake or as a pretext for evil practices. Rather, they are to use their freedom for God and the building up of the community of faith. Freedom in Christ is only to glorify God in the face of hostility, not for the sake of "showing off" one's freedom.

Here, those who are free in Christ, but literally bound to their masters, are suffering unjustly and are encouraged to endure it for the sake of God. This doesn't seem like good advice to some of us, but the writer is very clear in saying that endurance is a virtue when suffering is undeserved like that of Jesus. We may remember Jesus' words about submitting to earthly authorities and paying taxes to Caesar.

Verse 21 calls us to follow the example of Jesus, who became a suffering servant (Isa. 53:5-12) for our sake. We are taught not to respond to insult with insult, or to threat with threat. Jesus' words are for us to love our enemy. Christ never denounced his accusers. The writer emphasizes that Christ was more than an example, for Christ took our sins away and left them on the cross. Even through hostility and slander, we must live an upright life. We are to allow God to bring cruelty to justice. Our value comes from God, not earthly powers!

Suffering is still part of our world. We may have to suffer for our faith! Those of us who call ourselves Christians should be ready to take Jesus' example seriously. Jesus always cared for the suffering. When he was the One suffering, he suffered in a way that he didn't try to hurt those who were hurting him. He responded in love. As Christians we must oppose unjust actions and words. We must support those who suffer. Just as the early Christians suffered for their beliefs, we must ask ourselves if we are subjecting the minority religious or ethnic groups to unjust persecution. Is our evangelism misguided when we persecute people of other faith traditions? Our passage tells us that we are not to handle evil with evil, but we are to submit ourselves to God. Even through suffering, the God who knows unjust suffering firsthand tells us to love. (Ryan White)

JESUS, OUR ONE AND ONLY SHEPHERD

JOHN 10:1-10

The Gospel lection connects with the other passages by the sheep-shepherd imagery. Reading this text, one might like to skip it and find another that is easier to grasp. The imagery is confusing because it is used in various ways. For example, in verse 1, there are "bandits and thieves" climbing, trying to sneak into the sheepfold. In verse 8, the thieves and bandits call at the gate for the sheep.

However, there are some powerful images that can make this text come alive. Prior to this passage is the story of the man born blind. This story ends with a statement of judgment (9:39) and leads into this passage of Jesus as the Shepherd. Jesus' coming results in judgment, but the good news is that he has come to save, not condemn. It may be helpful to look at all of chapter 10 with the overarching theme of Jesus as the Shepherd who will give his life for his sheep. The Easter message is proclaimed again. Jesus has come to save us.

I. Jesus, the Shepherd (vv. 1-6)

This portion of the text is a contrast between the thieves and bandits and the real Shepherd of the sheep. The sheep recognize the shepherd's voice. The shepherd knows each by name and leads them as they follow him. In contrast, the thieves and bandits are strangers. The sheep will not follow a stranger, but will run from the stranger because they do not know his voice.

The images of the shepherd-sheep relationship can give us assurance and comfort. Yet, we need to examine our lives because judgment and salvation are before us. Is Jesus our Shepherd? Do we listen to his voice? Do we hear our "name" and follow as Jesus leads us? Are there "bandits and thieves" that have stolen us away?

II. Jesus, the Shepherd, and the Gate (vv. 7-10)

This portion of the text points to Jesus alone as the way to eternal life. All who enter by him will find salvation, freedom, and spiritual nourishment. There are "thieves" that come, but they lead only to destruction. Jesus alone is the way. We must listen to him exclusively.

A portion of the Barmen Declaration may be helpful in the study of this passage. The Barmen Declaration (1934) was a confession of faith by the Confessing Church. It came about in Germany as Nazi ideology was corrupting Christian doctrine, claiming that the Third Reich was itself a revelation of God's will. Referring to John 14:6 and John 10:1, 9, it states:

> Jesus Christ, as he is testified to us in the Holy Scripture, is the one Word of God, whom we are to hear, whom we are to trust and obey in life and in death.
>
> We repudiate the false teaching that the church can and must recognize yet other happenings and powers, images and truths as divine revelation alongside this one Word of God, as a source of her preaching. (John Leith, ed., *Creeds of the Churches* [Louisville: John Knox Press], 1982, p. 520)

(Marcia Thompson)

APRIL 28, 2002

Fifth Sunday of Easter

Worship Theme: We are God's holy people, a royal priesthood, called to testify to the Rejected One who has now become the cornerstone of faith.

Readings: Acts 7:55-60; 1 Peter 2:2-10; John 14:1-14

Call to Worship (Psalm 31):

Leader:	In you, O LORD, we seek refuge.
People:	**Rescue us, Lord. Be a fortress to shelter us.**
Leader:	How abundant is the goodness of our God.
People:	**We bless God for God's steadfast love.**
Leader:	Let us give God our thanks and praise.
People:	**Let us worship God in the sanctuary. Alleluia.**

Pastoral Prayer:

Cornerstone of Truth, in you we see the One who sent you; be a firm foundation for your church that we may be your holy people. Cornerstone of Life, through you all things were made; reorder your creation according to your mercy that all may live in your peace. Cornerstone of Faith, your cross is a stumbling block for some, but to us who believe it is the gate through which we must pass on the way to salvation; walk with us that we might keep on keeping on. Cornerstone of Hope, even though you were rejected you now hold all things in place; share with us a sign of your promise and glory that we might endure our trials. Enfold

164

the grieving. Lift up the despairing. Bind the wounds of the broken. Fill the empty. Cornerstone of Love, be a firm foundation for your church that we may be your holy people. Amen. (Scott Haldeman)

SERMON BRIEFS

"A GOOD DEATH"

ACTS 7:55-60

There has recently been much coverage in the news media concerning end-of-life issues and the care of those facing terminal illness. I watched with interest a PBS television series entitled, "A Good Death." The host, Bill Moyers, examined many facets of end-of-life care, including palliative care, the use of both hospice and hospital settings for death and dying, as well as other concerns of seriously ill patients and their families. One of the questions that was examined throughout was "What constitutes a good death?" Answers to this question were as different as the many individuals who shared their stories, but they did seem to have one thing in common. A good death seems to be consistent with the values and priorities that a person holds in life. Perhaps the notion of a "good death" is one reason that the stories of Christian martyrs continue to speak to us.

Stephen, a man filled with the Holy Spirit and full of wisdom, sought to minister to those around him in word and deed. From the very beginning of his service in the church, he spoke the truth boldly. The synagogue leaders perceived him as a threat, and eventually, false charges were leveled against him. However, even in the midst of persecution, Stephen continued to preach the gospel. He recounted for the leaders of the synagogue the story of salvation. He showed no fear as he accused those who were hard-hearted and unwilling to receive God's grace as found in Christ. He told his story, and when the crowd was at its angriest, he glimpsed the exalted Christ enthroned as judge of the universe. Stephen was a prophet of God who spoke the truth and witnessed to the reality of God's movement in his life.

We need only read the end of the story, however, to know that prophets are not always well received. The crowd could not bear to hear the truth. They covered their ears and ran at Stephen with a shout. Laying their garments at Saul's feet, we find that they will not rest until they have silenced Stephen by stoning him to death. Yet, it is in these moments at the end of his life that we have Stephen's most eloquent witness. Stephen died a good death.

In his dying moments, we find Stephen speaking and acting in a manner that is consistent with the values and priorities he professed during his life. He places himself in Jesus' hands and asks that his spirit be received. He does not try to fight back or defend himself, but assumes a posture of trust in a secure future. He does not seek revenge upon his persecutors, but prays for their forgiveness. In comparing this passage to the passion account in the Gospel of Luke, William Willimon wrote in an article in the journal *Interpretation*, "Jesus' followers die like Jesus."

Very few of us will be called upon to die a physical death for the faith we profess to live. However, we must always be aware of the need to die a good death, no matter how the end of our lives may come. Dying a good death means showing a consistency in our beliefs and the living of our lives. It means that our priorities and our values, like those of the martyrs, are evident to all when everything else is stripped away. What kind of legacy will follow our death? It has everything to do with faithfulness in our lives. (Wendy Joyner)

A GROWING FAITH

1 PETER 2:2-10

After warning of impure food (i.e., malice, guile, envy, slander, and so forth), the writer here speaks of a growing/maturing life in faith. Basing one's initial growth on pure spiritual milk, he assures his listeners that the assured and appropriate outcome of a faithful life is salvation. The end of the growth process, or perhaps a better way of saying it is the end of a faithful life, is graced by God's salvation.

Speaking of the new life that is possible through Jesus Christ, the writer of 1 Peter tells the faithful to rid themselves of impurities and to seek a growing faith. Do you remember some of the first words of faith that you learned? Perhaps you learned "Jesus loves me, this I know." Or, "God is great, God is good, let us thank him for our food." These first words and the actions of loving Christian people may have led many of us to the start of our faith. Milk symbolizes the primary instructions needed for growth. Do we think about our primary instructions for faith? The pure starting point that the writer emphasizes is that the Lord is good.

In verses 4-10, the writer suggests that we are being built into a kind of temple. Those with faith are like living stones that God is using to build a new temple where Jesus Christ is the cornerstone. The nature of the church is a spiritual house constructed of living stones where the building takes its design from Jesus Christ.

Faith, then, is not so much a matter of believing, but a matter of obedience. We stumble when we disobey. Full of faith, we can rejoice in the unexpected and undeserved grace of God. When we don't look to Jesus as the cornerstone, we can quickly stumble and fall. Can you think of times in your life when you tried to do everything yourself? We think we can rely on our own abilities! Often, we will have to bottom out before we will ask for help.

But, notice that all of the terms here are corporate terms. To be a Christian is to live within a community of God's people. By surrounding ourselves with faithful people, we will not as easily fall into trying to do everything ourselves. This speaks to us as believers who come to God individually, but we must always remember that the Christian life must be lived out within a community.

Verse 9 continues with Old Testament imagery of a priestly people and a holy nation (Exod. 19:6). Even though most of the people in this community are Gentiles, whatever was true for the Jewish heritage is now true of them—"once not a people, now a people who have received mercy." The story is open to all. Those rejected by men are divinely chosen. These words ring out to a people who are persecuted and in exile. God is for them! The milk that we all started with is now helping us to grow into the faithful, holy nation we are called to be. (Ryan White)

SEPARATION ANXIETY

JOHN 14:1-14

Jesus is saying good-bye and giving final instructions. He speaks of betrayal and warns of Peter's denial. He has just told his friends, "Where I am going, you cannot come" (13:33). Now he speaks a word of comfort. "Do not let your hearts be troubled," he begins. "I go to prepare a place for you . . ."

Thomas responds first, asking, "How can we know the way?" Jesus answers boldly, "*I am* the way." He is also the truth and the life, and we could discuss at length the best understanding of "No one comes to the Father, except through me."

Philip responds next: "Show us the Father." Again Jesus gives a daring, yet soothing, answer, "I am in the Father and the Father is in me."

This passage offers so much material—all of it deep and resonant. The impetus behind it seems to be anxiety. The original audience for the fourth Gospel must have needed this message of comfort. Even the casual reader of John recognizes that everything Jesus says within the story line is a living word addressed to the reader. Those who first heard this Gospel read may have brought with them a variety of anxieties. Evidence throughout the Gospel and letters of John suggests they had some rough times. In the account, Jesus' friends feel anxious. Separation from Jesus is imminent. Jesus speaks, and theology comes to their rescue. Perhaps it can rescue us from the anxieties we feel about our faith from time to time. Easter is all about the presence of the risen Lord, but you may feel an absence of God in your life—at least every now and then. Might the living word speak to us?

Theology to the Rescue

As we feel anxious, the text reminds us of the close relationship between Jesus and the Father. This is the core of this passage and John's entire Gospel. Jesus says, "Believe in God, believe also in me." The place Jesus is going is the Father's house, and he goes to prepare a place for us. So close are Jesus and the Father that

Jesus himself is the way to the Father, the unique way. To know Jesus is to know the Father.

Anxiety begins to give way also as we reflect on the close relationship between Jesus and believers. This theme will continue to emerge in the Gospel as Jesus speaks of the Holy Spirit and calls his friends the branches to which he is the vine. But it starts here. Those who believe will do the works that Jesus did, even greater works (!), because of the power of God. Incredible words pour from Jesus' lips: "I will do whatever you ask in my name, so that the Father may be glorified in the Son." Having promised to come again and take his friends to God, he now promises that the power at work in him will also be at work in them.

We could summarize this passage as follows: *Do not let your hearts be troubled. God is in control, working out a plan; and you have a place in it.* The close relationship between Jesus and God means that *we* have a connection to God through Jesus. The sovereign God holds our destinies. So much in this world is beyond our control, but not God's. If Jesus is as close to God as this passage suggests, and if Jesus is as close to us as this passage suggests, then our future is secure. No room remains for anxiety, for Jesus is taking care of us. (David C. Mauldin)

SPIRITUAL PREPARATION

MAY

One of my wife's favorite pastimes, especially if we are at the beach or in the mountains, is to put together a big puzzle. At times, all of our family has gotten into the act. Some of you may share this enthusiasm. I have another friend who takes it even more seriously. He enjoys putting together the big, complex puzzles, the ones that don't even have a picture of how they will look when completed.

To put the puzzle together, you simply get started; you work on the corners, and the edges. Then you figure out the patterns, and a picture emerges. That, it seems to me, is a good way to think about ministry. As we serve among God's people, we begin to get the picture. The pieces are there, like a puzzle, but we have to put it together! And part of being a pastor of a church is saying, "I'm going to help put the pieces of this puzzle together, or, I'm going to be one of the pieces of this puzzle."

At Pentecost we are given a picture of how God's people live together. You can see that the descriptions of the early church in Acts 2:42 are essential pieces of this puzzle. They are the borders. They are how we get started in assembling a picture that makes sense.

First, the early disciples committed themselves to the teachings of the apostles.

Something remarkable had happened in the life and ministry of Jesus. And his followers were driven to talk about who he was and what he had done. They believed that Jesus of Nazareth was the Son of God, Lord, Savior, and that in his life, death, and resurrection there was the hope of salvation. The apostles, like Peter, and then Stephen, and then Paul, would summarize their beliefs, and these ended up in the New Testament. Other summaries were put together later, such as the Nicene Creed in the fourth century, and the Apostles' Creed in the sixth century. These summaries focus on who Jesus is and who we are in relation to him. They are like a ruler that keeps things straight. And without a rule, a summary, a specific body of content that has boundaries, there is no clarity of belief. Part of the strength of the early Christian movement was that they had a clear sense of who they were and what had brought them together. "This Jesus who has been crucified," the formerly timid Peter announced with boldness, "God has made him both Lord and Messiah" (Acts 2:36).

Our picture must begin with the teaching of the apostles, about who Jesus is and who we are in relation to him. Who is Jesus? The British evangelist John Stott has written that "to know Jesus is to know God; to see Jesus is to see God; to believe in Jesus is to believe in God; to receive Jesus is to receive God; to hate Jesus is to hate God; and to honor Jesus is to honor God."

They committed themselves to the teachings of the apostles. There is another way to say this: it is not enough to feel, or to do. We are also called to believe, and to teach. The image of this puzzle piece for me is a cross, but especially the arm that is extending up, toward God.

Second, the early disciples were committed to the life together.

Much of our time as pastors is given to the ministry of conflict resolution. This is the result of our human sin. God's desire is that we all be one, that we live in community. While much attention is given to the visible signs of pentecostalism in our time, I am impressed with the aftereffects of Pentecost. I want to lift up the visible fruit of Pentecost. When we know that God is One, and when we have begun to listen to each other, then we experience God's desire for us: that we live in community. The early disciples were committed to the life together. The image of this puzzle piece is again a cross, but it is the arm that is extending out, toward others.

Third, the early disciples were committed to the common meal.

In the ancient world eating together was the way barriers were broken down. Notice in the gospels how often Jesus shared meals with all kinds of people.

Will Willimon reminds us that eating together was a "mark of unity, solidarity, and deep friendship." Two things about the common meal are noteworthy: the meal was God's way of bringing people together, and it was a reminder of God's presence in our midst. They committed themselves to the common meal, to the breaking of bread. For years my wife and I have had a habit of eating breakfast together. In the evenings we are often going in different directions; we have more control over our mornings. I am quite sure that these meals are probably the glue that holds our relationship together. It was true for the first disciples of Jesus. They shared the common meal together, a blending of communion and a family night dinner. They would not have made a distinction. It was holy. And the image for this piece of the puzzle would be an altar, but there would be ordinary plates and bowls and mugs on it.

Fourth, the early disciples were committed to the prayers.

They were a community of people who prayed for each other, in temple worship and in their homes. The early Christians were committed to the prayers. It happens even now. We pray with a family, in a circle, hands joined, as someone has died, or as a youth mission team has returned safely, or as someone goes into surgery. Prayer partners stay in touch over the Internet. Men and women gather early in the morning to pray.

The early disciples changed the world because they were committed to the life of prayer. The image of a puzzle piece here would be two hands joined together, two people in prayer. The teaching of the apostles, the life together, the common meal, the prayers. When these are firmly in place, the picture begins to emerge.

But it is not finished. There are other pieces to place in there. God will frame the borders of the picture, but you and I have to complete it. How will we do that? In the season of Pentecost, we will discover our spiritual gifts as we reclaim the importance of the teaching ministry, as we experience the gift of a small Christian fellowship, as we break bread together, as we pray for one another.

The miracle of Pentecost is an emerging Christian community. This miracle can happen in any congregation, of any size. The picture of the church will not be complete without the four important pieces described in Acts 2:42: the apostles teaching, the fellowship, the breaking of bread, the prayers. One of my favorite hymns says it clearly, "I am the church. You are the church. We are the church together." (Ken Carter)

Sources: John Stott, *Basic Christianity*, p. 26. William Willimon, *Acts*, p. 41. *The United Methodist Hymnal*, p. 558.

MAY 5, 2002

Sixth Sunday of Easter

Worship Theme: Our God, Creator of all things, seen and unseen, is not far off but knows us, just as we can know the One in whom we live and move and have our being as we come together to praise our maker and serve our neighbors.

Readings: Acts 17:22-31; 1 Peter 3:13-22; John 14:15-21

Call to Worship (Psalm 66):

Leader:	Bless the Lord, O peoples, let the sound of our praise be heard,
People:	**for God has kept us among the living and has not let our feet slip.**
Leader:	Come and hear, all you who fear God, and I will tell what God has done for me.
People:	**For truly God has listened to us; God has given heed to the words of our prayers.**
All:	**Blessed be God, because of God's steadfast love for us.**

Pastoral Prayer:

   Maker of heaven and earth, who formed us from the earth and breathed into us the breath of life, we lift our voices to sing your praise. Maker of heaven and earth, who calls us to be your people, renew your covenant within us and set us upon the right path. Maker of heaven and earth, who does not disdain your creatures but visits us, loves us, knows us, be close by once more this day. Risen Christ, who pitched your tent with us, wrapping yourself in our mortal flesh, walking among us, sharing table with outcasts and doing deeds of power, we seek your face among

173

those gathered here, in breaking bread, in a stranger's smile, in a widow's tear. Risen Christ, you reside above in glory; we call upon your name for it is the foundation of our hope; return to us to judge and save. Risen Christ, you know the depth of human pain and the height of human joy; hear our cries for the hungry, the lonely, the suffering; send your comforting Spirit. Advocate, you were sent by Christ when he ascended, reside with us and grant us peace. Advocate, you enliven our hearts; assure us of God's mercy. Advocate, you transform our spirits; empower us for service and accompany us every day. Amen. (Scott Haldeman)

SERMON BRIEFS

THE GOD WHO WOULD BE FOUND

ACTS 17:22-31

At its heart, the book of Acts is a missionary story. It is a story of men and women who faithfully witness to the love and grace of God they have found in Jesus Christ. As missionaries, these early Christian witnesses were called upon to enter into the culture and lives of others. Their job was not always easy, yet it was perhaps when the human boundaries to the gospel were most visible that God's power was made most evident.

The apostle Paul was waiting in the city of Athens for Timothy and Silas to join him. As he took in his surroundings, he noticed idols everywhere. The prevalence of these idols caused him great distress, and he set out to have conversations with the devout people in the synagogue. The more he talked to the people in the synagogue, however, the more he found out about their culture. The people of Athens were enamored with new and trendy ideas or philosophies, but they had little understanding of God. The God they worshiped was unknown, even to them. They were searching, but it seemed to be a search with no hope of discovering the truth. So as Paul sought to argue the merits of the Christian faith, he shared with them the awesome mystery of the God who could indeed be found. He outlined for them one of the central mysteries of the Christian faith, the delicate balance between the transcendence of God and the imma-nence of God.

Paul began by appealing to the rational and natural side of the Athenian philosophy. He reminded them of God the Creator, whose work they could observe in the world around them. Paul preached that God is no less than the Creator of the universe. No mere vessel made by human hands can contain God, for God is vast and wonderful. God sets all boundaries of time and space, and we are utterly dependent upon this One who sustains us. God does not need humanity, Paul argued, for God gives life and breath and all things. The Athenians were right in proclaiming God as "unknown," for God transcends anything we can know or imagine.

Yet this is where the grace of the gospel is proclaimed, for Paul then shared with the Athenians that it is not God's will to remain unknown. God seeks to be close to humanity as well, thus allowing God to be found. God makes Godself immanent, close to humanity "so that they would search for God and perhaps grope for him and find him—though indeed he is not far from each one of us" (v. 27).

What a wonderful gift and a wonderful image—humanity groping for God. It is as if we are in a darkened room, with only the slight outlines of revelation to guide us, yet the revelation is there. This is Paul's faith and his invitation, to repent and to receive God's grace as found in the One who is the resurrected judge of humanity, Jesus Christ.

As we look at Paul's sermon, may we be reminded of God's thoughts toward us. In love, God is calling us into relationship before we are even aware of it. The miracle and the mystery are that God who is transcendent is also making a way to help us to find God's closeness. In our humanness, we may stumble along and grope in some really dark corners. We confess that we are unable to see the whole picture clearly. Yet, the good news is that by God's grace in Jesus Christ, we will find that God indeed is not far from us. (Wendy Joyner)

MAINTAIN YOUR FAITH

1 PETER 3:13-22

Who can harm you if you are zealous for what is right? As Paul asked, "Who can separate us from the love of God?" The writer here suggests that the victory is God's. The victory over all evil, death, and demons was made known at the Resurrection. These words of encouragement are given just in case some are starting to waver in their faith.

Have you ever wavered in your faith? This doesn't mean that you totally denounced God or turned your back on God for good. Rather, has your faith ever hit any hard times? Has your faith been shaken? This can happen throughout life. Maybe it happened when a spouse or child was killed. Maybe your job fell through. Maybe a good, faithful friend was diagnosed with cancer. Maybe you are being persecuted just because you call yourself a Christian. Whatever the case, there are times in our lives when many of us have our faith shaken and we need something to hold on to.

We are encouraged to maintain our faith. The writer gives assurance that righteous suffering concludes in divine glory. Suffering for wrongdoings is a consequence of faulty living, but like Christ, suffering for right may occur if we are following the will of God.

First Peter reminds us of the cosmic character of the passion. We are redeemed. God continually reaches down to restore the broken relationship between God and humankind. The image of water reminds us of God's saving action. The righteous Noah and his family were saved from the Flood. Now, the saving act of Christ's suffering, death, resurrection, and ascension is laid open by believers in their baptism.

Baptism reminds us that instead of someone being overtaken by water, one participates in Christ's saving us from death. We are not literally or spiritually saved through the baptism, but through baptism, Christians symbolically understand their commitment to God as a conscious expression of faith to the reality of the new life in Christ. All of us could be encouraged to "remember our baptism," for our conduct must reflect that symbol.

Doing what is right isn't always easy. Jesus was often ridiculed for his actions. But, if our focus stays on God, God's love will help us through all that life has to offer. When life seems to be at its worst, when persecution is all around, we are encouraged to maintain our faith and be ever ready to make the claim in the One who is the author and perfecter of our faith. (Ryan White)

WHERE LOVING JESUS LEADS

JOHN 14:15-21

Every act brings about a reaction. Every step leads to another step. This is true in our everyday lives, as well as our spiritual lives. What we do leads to something else. Love is no different.

Love brings about the greatest consequences of all. Love for someone leads us to go to the greatest lengths. The love between a man and a woman often leads to courtship and marriage. Many times children result from that relationship. Love for children leads to sacrifices and even loving discipline.

Loving another leads to action on an individual's part. But it also results in great blessing. Love leads to both sacrifice and gain. Love is giving and receiving.

This is what Jesus is speaking of to his disciples as they meet together in the setting described in John 14. He tells them what loving him will lead to on their part. He instructs them on what their love for him will lead them to give. He also tells them what will be given to them as a result of their love for him.

"If you love me, you will obey *what I command."* Love for Jesus will lead to obedience on their part. It will lead to keeping and guarding what Jesus taught them during his ministry with them. If they loved him, it must be more than words of assent. Their love must result in obedience. The proof of love for Jesus is found in obedience to him.

Just as devotion for Jesus leads to duty, it also leads to delight. Just as love for Jesus calls for action on our part, it also results in God acting on our behalf. Love for Jesus leads to many blessings from Jesus.

First, he promises the Holy Spirit, another Paraclete to be with us forever. Our love for Jesus means that we will not be orphaned, we will never be alone. The presence of God will be with us throughout our lives. In both struggle and celebration we will have God's Spirit beside us, helping us, leading us, comforting us.

Second, Jesus promises spiritual sight. We will see him. He will reveal himself to us. For the disciples this promise most assuredly referred to Jesus' resurrection. He would leave them but they would see him again. Yet, in the context of the text, Jesus was referring to something even beyond his appearing to them after the Resurrection. He is telling them that their spiritual eyes will be opened. They will "see" him with a new understanding. They will "see" him as they travel through life.

Third, love for Jesus results in eternal life. *Because I live, you also will live,* Jesus told them. The relationship of love will mean a relationship of life. Jesus' disciples will share in Jesus' victory over death.

Finally, love for Jesus will result in love from God and Jesus. *He who loves me will be loved by my Father, and I too will love him and show myself to him.* This does not take away from the fact that God loves the world. But the one who loves Jesus experiences a new depth of love from God and Jesus. This results in Jesus revealing himself to those whom he loves. It is love that moves God from the unknown to the known. (Reece B. Sherman)

MAY 12, 2002

Seventh Sunday of Easter

Worship Theme: The church must not stand looking up while we wait for Jesus' return; rather we must devote ourselves to prayer, to the breaking of bread, and to good works.

Readings: Acts 1:6-14; 1 Peter 4:12-14; 5:6-11; John 17:1-11

Call to Worship (Psalm 68):

> *Leader:* Let the righteous be joyful; let them exult before God!
>
> **People:** **Let God's people shout with joy!**
>
> *Leader:* Sing to God, sing praises to the Holy One!
>
> **People:** **For God is a guardian of orphans and a protector of widows.**
>
> *Leader:* God gives the desolate a home to live in and leads prisoners out to prosperity.
>
> **All:** **God gives power and strength to his people. Blessed be God forever!**

Pastoral Prayer:

Jesus Christ, Beloved Child of the Most High, you sit at the right hand of Almighty God; do not forget your church. Jesus Christ, of one being with God, sanctify us so that we might receive adoption as Children of God. Jesus Christ, Crucified and Risen One, be a balm for those who suffer. Heal the sick. Enfold the alien. Fill the hungry. Bring peace to souls and to nations in conflict. Protect all of those who are threatened—by flood or drought, by deep freeze or blazing fire, by violent rage of those far off or those close by, by the despair of poverty or the sloth of wealth. Jesus Christ, when you ascended you promised not to leave us without aid; send your Spirit now to comfort your people. Come once more, and soon, to bring justice and peace to the whole earth. Amen. (Scott Haldeman)

SERMON BRIEFS

WHAT'S NEXT?

ACTS 1:6-14

The book of Acts is the story of a beginning. It tells of the beginning of this gathering of believers we call the church. We sometimes take the beginning of the church for granted, as if those earliest followers of Christ were certain of what lay ahead. It is easy for us to forget that in those first days following Christ's resurrection, one of the most likely questions on the lips of the disciples was "What's next?"

Yet, hear the opening words of Jesus to his followers in verses 4-5 of this first chapter of Acts. "While staying with them, he ordered them not to leave Jerusalem, but to *wait* there for the promise of the Father. . . . You will be baptized with the Holy Spirit not many days from now." One of the most amazing acts of God is followed by the command to wait, and the disciples respond with a mix of curiosity and anxiety. They want to know the big picture. "Lord, is this the time when you will restore the kingdom to Israel?" However, Jesus has one final lesson for his followers. He patiently answers that the time is not theirs to know. He promises them the Spirit, commissions them as witnesses, and is lifted up into heaven before their eyes.

I can only imagine their stunned amazement as Jesus ascended to the Father. What kind of answer was that? Surely there must be some master plan, a set of instructions, or even a hint as to what the future might hold. As the disciples gazed into the heavens, they were most surely openmouthed and lead-footed. Where does one go when there is no sense of certainty in life, in vocation, in our relationship with God?

Yet, as they find themselves in a state of suspended animation, two men in white robes appear and ask them why they are just standing there, providing them with a reminder. Jesus who has been taken up to heaven will return to them. Life has not stopped. There *are* things to do—even when you don't know the details of the plan. So the disciples return to the Upper Room and constantly devote themselves to prayer.

As part of his *Interpretation* series on the book of Acts, William Willimon reminds us that "this time between ascension and Pentecost was once designated by Karl Barth as a 'significant pause' between the mighty acts of God, a pause in which the church's task is to wait and to pray, *Veni, Creator Spiritus*" (p. 20).

Reading those words reminded me of the many times we find ourselves gazing into heaven, asking "What's next?" Times when in our individual and communal lives, we find ourselves in the middle of a "significant pause," gazing into heaven and looking for guidance. Perhaps our church is at a crossroads, awaiting a major decision about our life together or the shape that our ministry will take in the future. Perhaps we are trying to discern the call of God in our lives as individuals. Maybe we are lost and afraid, knowing that more than anything we desire the presence of Jesus, and feeling frustrated that our vision is obscured by the clouds.

The gentle reprimand from the angels calls us to trust in what we do know of God and God's promises in our lives. Jesus promised us the Holy Spirit, a job for us to do, and the power with which to do it. Jesus will return to us, and in the meantime, we must wait and pray. Pray so that we might receive the gifts and guidance of God when they are sent to us in amazing and extraordinary ways. (Wendy Joyner)

HUMILITY IN SUFFERING

1 PETER 4:12-14; 5:6-11

The flow of these two sections fits together masterfully, for just when you think you are a righteous sufferer, you need to humble yourself!

Chapter 4:12-14 begins a new section of the letter. The writer is encouraging those suffering and trying to build congregational unity in the face of impending trouble. In verse 12, true suffering and true joy are said to go hand in hand. Joy with suffering? No, not because suffering is good, but because one shares in Christ's own experience. When one is ridiculed for his sake, one is blessed. Blessing doesn't come just for suffering, but because one is suffering for the right reasons.

The writer reminds us that people who are being punished or who are suffering for evil they have done must realize that there are consequences. We cannot treat their sufferings as a sign of glory. That kind of suffering is not like Christ's. People through-out the ages have tried to seek suffering in order to imitate Christ. Some have tried to make themselves martyrs for a cause, but true martyrs don't seek glory for their actions. Seeking suffer-ing is not the same. Jesus knew that suffering might occur, but suffering was not his goal. Seeking God's will and following through is not the same as seeking suffering and then saying it was God's will!

Instead, we are to seek humility amid our suffering. We are told that humility is a position before God. How can we stay humble while we suffer? The writer says that our sufferings are few and brief compared to the glory that is to come. We must keep focused on living our lives in humility, for our lives matter more than we know!

Is there any transcendent significance in our lives? Does our faith really matter? The passage answers a resounding, "Yes." God hears and knows our cares. God will come and restore us. We are all connected! Our actions have consequences—visible, invisible, and even eternal! We never know who is watching us or what effect our lives might have on others.

Jesus said that those who will lose their life for his sake will find (save) it (Luke 9:24). We must resist the devil and allow God to be in charge. Christ's victory is marked by the power of the Spirit. God supports and strengthens the faithful! Troubles will not last forever. But, in the face of persecution, we all share in Christ's suffering. Furthermore, we should be joyous, for our faith is found to be real. God will notice and is finally the victor. We must take courage. Humility comes when we can find freedom in Christ amid our suffering; for truly then, we know that we have cast ourselves in the mighty hands of God. (Ryan White)

DEFINITION OF SUCCESS

JOHN 17:1-11

This chapter of John has often been called the "high priestly prayer" of Christ. It is a multifaceted prayer. It is both petition and intercession. It is a prayer for his disciples and those who follow them. It is also a prayer of a Son to a Father. This prayer is a virtual gold mine of truths concerning prayer, relationship, and the importance of unity.

I believe that the focal point of the prayer is found in the words, *I have brought you glory on earth by completing the work you gave me to do* (v. 4 NIV). These words set the theme for the whole prayer. Jesus prays from the perspective of One who has completed the work given to him. Included in the prayer are aspects of the work he was given to accomplish.

Success is defined in many ways in today's society. Success is often associated with money, power, and position. The label of success is also given to those who accomplish certain goals, for instance, in sports or career. Usually a person is deemed a success if they have the "good things" in life: family, career, home, friends, and sufficient material possessions.

Jesus redefines success for us. To Jesus, the measure of success has to do with doing God's will. If we were to compare Jesus' life with our modern definition of success, he would fall far short. He did not have many earthly possessions. He had no place to lay his head. Many of his friends left him. And yet, Jesus is the definition of a success. He completed the work that God gave him to do. He could say that he accomplished all of the goals set for him. How many people can say that about themselves?

Jesus finished the work that God gave him to do. He did not do what others wanted him to do. As hard as they tried, he never let others take his eyes off of the work that God gave him to complete. Jesus did not do what others wanted, but what his Father wanted. We find glimpses of what that work consisted of in the words of his prayer.

First, Jesus said, *I have revealed you* (v. 6 NIV). Jesus' work included revelation. He revealed who God truly was. He took the world beyond the definition of God given to the people by the religion of his day. He presented God as one who "so loved the world." Jesus said, "If you have seen me, you have seen the Father." He revealed God's true character to humankind.

Second, Jesus said, *I gave them the words you gave me* (v. 8 NIV). The Word that was made flesh brought the words of God to us. With both authority and compassion, Jesus changed the world with his words. His words instructed, comforted, convicted, and guided. How often we think we know his words, and yet, when we read them anew, their importance and life-giving power astound us.

As he prayed, Jesus was living in the midst of his final work. Ultimately, his final work was completed on the cross when he exclaimed, "It is finished" (John 19:30).

Jesus completed the work that God gave him to do. And because he did, we enjoy a new understanding of God. We have read and meditated on his words. In completing his task, Jesus redefined success as finishing the assignment that God has given.

The question arises, what if Jesus had not completed the work that God gave him to do? What if any part of the work had been left unfinished? The significance of that question brings on new meaning when we ask, what are the consequences of tasks that we have left unfinished? (Reece B. Sherman)

MAY 19, 2002

Day of Pentecost

Worship Theme: God sends the Holy Spirit to renew the face of the whole earth.

Readings: Numbers 11:24-30; 1 Corinthians 12:3*b*-13; John 7:37-39

Call to Worship (Psalm 104):

Leader: Bless the LORD, O my soul.

People: **You set the earth on its foundations, so that it shall never be shaken.**

Leader: You make springs gush forth in the valleys; they flow between the hills, giving drink to every wild animal. By the streams the birds of the air have their habitation; they sing among the branches.

People: **O LORD, how manifold are your works! In wisdom you have made them all.**

Leader: The earth is full of your creatures. These all look to you to give them their food in due season; when you give to them, they gather it up; when you open your hand, they are filled with good things. When you hide your face, they are dismayed; when you take away their breath, they die and return to the dust.

People: **But when you send forth your spirit, they are created anew; for you renew the face of the earth.**

All: **May the glory of the LORD endure forever; let us sing praise to our God.**

Pastoral Prayer:

Spirit of the living God, renew the face of your earth. Spirit of fire, purify our hearts with your flame. Spirit of the living God, renew the face of your earth. Spirit of truth, place good news upon our tongues that we might speak a word of hope to this weary world. Spirit of the living God, renew the face of your earth. Spirit of wind, come with power to stir up our faith and move us to acts of mercy. Spirit of the living God, renew the face of your earth. Spirit of inspiration, descend upon us, anointing us to proclaim release to those in captivity. Spirit of the living God, renew the face of your earth. Amen. (Scott Haldeman)

SERMON BRIEFS

THE GIFT

NUMBERS 11:24-30

It was the forerunner of an ideal church council. After preaching to the people, Moses had a church council meeting. It was a sizable group, composed of the seventy elders of the people, all seated around the tent. One would think that a church council immediately after service is not the most ideal situation, but in this one Moses knew of the visitor on the agenda who was to come. The visitor was the Lord. The Lord spoke to Moses and delivered a gift of "the spirit that was on him (Moses)" and the spirit was distributed to the seventy elders. Upon receiving the gift, each begins to prophesy. It is apparent from the visit and the gift shared that all who had been "registered" to be in the meeting were to be about the business of God. The forty years in the wilderness were not so much a lost trek through danger and rumblings as it was to form a people of God. Each day brought newness to the understanding that God indeed was with them and guiding them. It was an arduous task for the body and also for the spirit. With each day's new understanding also came a new challenge to their faith. Those who chose to remain faithful were blessed in their belief. The biggest question for many remained, Is God truly with us? Have we been abandoned? It was only for one time, but regardless, it was a gift of speaking for God as we understand true prophecy to be. Imagine that! A church council visited by God and blessed by God with a message of what God would have happen in that setting. The same spirit that gave Moses an unshakable faithfulness had now visited the elders. That would have been enough, but the strange thing that happened was that two men not of the council are also visited and given the same gift of prophecy. The men, Eldad and Medad, did so outside the place where the other elders/officers were gathered, showing that sometimes God does work outside the box and against the norm. What church would not want to have this type of visitation even outside the church council? The reaction then might be the same today: "Moses, these men are prophesying in the camp! They're doing spiritual things normally reserved for the council outside of the council!" Moses reacts favorably, as should most pastors when they find that instead of continuing to talk about the possibility of ministry and the programs and plans, the work begins to be actually done. As many a pastor has said, oh, that all of my people were that way. (Eradio Valverde Jr.)

SETTING THE RECORD STRAIGHT ON SPIRITUAL GIFTS

1 CORINTHIANS 12:3b-13

This scripture places us at the heart of Paul's letter to the fractured, yet faithful church at Corinth. It was a church that once wore the reputation of being unruly, hard drinking, sexually promiscuous, greedy, selfish, immoral, and trendy. But now, because of the liberating power of Jesus and the movement of the Holy Spirit, it was known for its great zeal and enthusiasm for the gospel, and its unashamed passion and emotion for Jesus Christ.

Yet Corinth was a church whose zeal for the Holy Spirit had crossed the line of disobedience and dissension. Practices of the faith in several areas had become inconsistent with the intentions of God, and various religious expressions caused division among the membership. One such instance was the misunderstanding and misuse of spiritual gifts, which served as a source of chaos for many.

So, having received a letter of concern and complaint from some of the members in the Corinthian church, Paul moves to set the record straight regarding the functions of the Holy Spirit, and in particular, spiritual gifts. He does this to restore order in the church, bring clarity to its believers, and offer understanding to all.

Paul sets the record straight by stressing the following major points. First, the Holy Spirit is manifested in a variety of ways. But all these ways carry the same power, because they all come from the same source—God.

Like the church in Corinth, in many of our churches today, people have the false belief that we must have a certain gift in order to prove that we have the Holy Spirit. In particular, there are churches and believers who teach that the gift of tongues is the sole source of proving that one has the Holy Spirit, thereby devaluing the importance of the other gifts. This fallacy has caused much harm in people's lives and confusion in the church. Paul says that the gift of tongues, while a wonderful and powerful gift, is not the only spiritual gift, nor is it a prerequisite for determining whether one has the Holy Spirit. Nor is it the most powerful of the gifts. People often misinterpret that it is because it is the most visible of the gifts. But, the gift of tongues is but one of many gifts that carry the same power, and originate in the same source—God.

Second, Paul stresses that God alone is the giver of all spiritual gifts. Not only does God have variety, but God is the giver of variety, and is the same God that inspires or activates the gifts in everyone. God gives the gifts. God inspires the gifts. God activates the gifts within us to be used for God's glory. Our role is to use them obediently.

Third, Paul stresses that God has given these gifts to us for the common good. They are not given to us for a popularity contest, or so that we can strut our stuff, saying, "Hey, look what I've got, and look what you don't have!" They are given to every individual for that individual to bless, benefit, and serve the community of believers effectively and faithfully.

For we are one body, with many members. Each individual is a critical piece in a jigsaw puzzle that brings blessing and order within the community of believers. The task of the church, then, is to bring all the pieces and gifts together, operating as one. When all the members function together, understanding each other's role and purpose, then God can do, will do, and has already done marvelous things through us! (Joseph W. Daniels Jr.)

RIVERS OF LIVING WATER

JOHN 7:37-39

We find Jesus celebrating again. This time he is celebrating "on the last day of the festival, the great day" (v. 37). This Festival of Tabernacles had several aspects that made it important. First, it was also known as the Festival of Booths, where little thatch-type dwellings were built all over Jerusalem to commemorate the Exodus event. During the Exodus, the people made similar dwellings from palm branches. Each year people from all walks of life would come and build a booth in Jerusalem to live in during the festival. Their participation reminded them of the days when they were sojourners and without suitable or adequate housing.

Second, the festival was a Festival of Ingathering or simply called *The Feast*. During this time, great amounts of food were shared and everyone ate well. Also included was a ceremony where the high priest would take a container, go to the Pool of Saloam, dip out a container of water, take it to the high altar, and pour it out as an offering to God. It was during this last great act of the festival that Jesus observed this religious ceremony and cried out:

Let anyone who is thirsty come to me, and let the one who believes in me drink. As the scripture has said, "Out of the believer's heart shall flow rivers of living water."

I. The Place of Ritual in Church Life (v. 37)

Why do we leave the church on Sundays feeling no different from when we got there? Could it be that we have participated in the rituals of the church without sensing we have experienced the One who enriches worship? We must do more than just follow the worship order. Without sensing Jesus Christ's presence in worship, we perhaps can understand why our experience of church only elicits a "trickle" effect upon our lives. Jesus stood there that day and watched the people enjoying "ritual" without enjoying the One who enriches their gathering, their festivals. Maybe we also are too interested in *what* makes worship exciting rather than in *who* makes worship extraordinary. Ritual has its place in worship, but not the first place. This belongs to Christ.

II. Worship Is Not a Practice but a Way of Life (v. 38)

If all we have to live on during the week is what we experienced in the church's sanctuary, no wonder so many Christians are living unfulfilled and unfulfilling lives when they are not "in church." One of the sad realities about church life is that we put all of the eggs of faith in the basket of worship. We are fast becoming a church that entertains people instead of one that disciples people. It's time we worship God with more than our brains and eyes. It is time that we give our *hearts* to God.

III. Worship with our Whole Being (v. 39)

Jesus said, "Out of the believer's *heart* shall flow rivers of living water." The word for *heart* in Greek is *koilia,* which means "belly." In ancient thought, the intellect was thought of in terms of the heart—head knowledge. But for deeper things, things of God, the kidneys and belly were the parts of the body where deep feelings were experienced. If worship is not experienced in the deep places of our lives, then our worship has only a trickle-down effect on us. But when we give all of our being—heart, mind, and soul—to Jesus Christ, then our spirits are like a rushing river. This river flows from Christ and Christ's presence.

And this Presence is not only in our worship, this Christ is with us wherever we go and is with us always. Then our worship becomes about a way of life, and Sunday morning is all the richer for this! (Mike Childress)

MAY 26, 2002

Trinity Sunday

Worship Theme: The God who created the world is the God who saves by sending Christ and by raising Christ through the power of the Holy Spirit.

Readings: Genesis 1:1–2:4*a;* 2 Corinthians 13:11-13; Matthew 28:16-20

Call to Worship (Psalm 8):

Leader: O LORD, our Sovereign, how majestic is your name in all the earth!

People: **You have set your glory above the heavens.**

Leader: I look at your heavens, the work of your fingers, the moon and the stars that you have established, and I wonder what are human beings that you are mindful of them, mortals that you care for them?

People: **Yet you have made us a little lower than God, and crowned us with glory and honor.**

All: **O LORD, our Sovereign, how majestic is your name in all the earth!**

Pastoral Prayer:
 God who called the waters together and formed dry land to bring forth life, we praise you for all that you made and give thanks for the bounty that surrounds us. God who sustains life with your very breath and provides for us even when we turn from you, we ask this day for our daily bread and for deliverance

from evil. God who brought slaves out of the land of bondage and made them to be your people and gave to them your Law, free us now from our fetters and order our steps in the path of righteousness. God who sent to us a Savior, a babe in swaddling clothes, a teacher, a healer, a suffering servant, we worship your Christ and yet we doubt, assure us, gift us with your peace, send us your Messiah that all might be fulfilled. God who lends us your Advocate, let your Spirit rush once more through your church, transforming us for your work and empowering us for service, for praise, and for the telling of your glory to the ends of the earth. Amen. (Scott Haldeman)

SERMON BRIEFS

GOD CREATED

GENESIS 1:1–2:4a

Somewhat ironically, Genesis has become the focus of the contemporary creation/evolution debate. On the one hand, the scientific community seeks to describe the history of the natural processes that produced the world as we know it. Since the scientific method can properly deal only with measurable phenomena—and God cannot be so quantified—scientists *as scientists* cannot speak about divine purpose and authorship. *As scientists* they can neither confirm nor deny that God authored and directed the natural processes they study. On the other hand, conservative Christians attempt to employ the text of Scripture as scientific data and equate the scientists' insistence on limiting themselves to natural phenomena with the outright rejection of God. One community deals with quantity and the other with purpose. A useless argument rages between opponents speaking entirely different languages with no hope for mutual understanding.

Science can neither prove nor disprove the existence of God. Creationists cannot prove that God created the world either. Belief in a Creator God is, by definition after all, a matter of faith. Perhaps, rather than employing the doctrine of creation and the primary text upon which it is based in a childish argument, or attempting some pseudoscientific accommodation with the natural sciences, the contemporary church would benefit more from a close reexamination of the texture and nuances of the biblical doctrine. What does Genesis 1 teach the church about the God who created the world in which it lives and about how to live as God's grateful people in that world?

God created a good *world.* With roots reaching back to the idealism and Gnosticism of the first-century Hellenistic world into which it was born, Christianity has often manifested a pessimism concerning the value and worth of the real world of rocks and bodies. Doctrines of the total depravity of human beings and otherworldly pieties have taught that the physical world is, at best, illusory, if not downright evil. Such disdain for God's creation, apparent in a milder form in modern society's disconnectedness from the natural world, can hardly be more alien to Scripture's view of the created world. Genesis 1 remarks over and again that, after each phrase in the process of world creation, God paused to evaluate God's artisanship, responding each time simply and profoundly, "It is good!"

If God created a good world, how can we continue to devalue it, to abuse it, to pollute it? Some may respond that Christianity is a matter of the heart and spirit, that to worship God is to worship in spirit and in truth. True. But it is also true that God is the God of the *living,* and, at least for the span of our normal lives, we live in the world God made for us. We must be good stewards of what we have if we are to be entrusted with even greater opportunities. Any faith that is unable gratefully and responsibly to embrace the marvelous goodness of this world will be ill-prepared for the wonders of the world-to-come.

God created a world of rhythm and harmony. Were human engineers to have fashioned a world, they would likely have created climate-controlled, geometrically ordered uniformity. In a biosphere of human manufacture, temperature would likely be maintained at a constant 72° F within two or three degrees of tolerance. Moisture levels would be controlled. Periods of light and darkness would be maximized to promote the highest possible agricultural yields. Tornadoes, hurricanes, and seasons would all be eliminated. No volcanoes would erupt to destroy cities; no earthquakes would shatter foundations and topple structures.

However, no majestic mountains would be pushed up from the earth's bedrock; no children would awaken to an unexpected snow holiday; no luscious Pacific islands would arise in a miniature reprise of the original creation's separation of dry land from sea. Thank God that, judging from the world God actually created and from the account of that creation recorded in Genesis 1, God favored rhythm and harmony over stasis and monotony: darkness and light; night and day; six days of labor and a day of rest; sea and dry land; sun and moon; seasons; winds and waves.

God created a productive *world.* Contrary to the efforts of some interpreters to read Genesis 1 as an account of the *method* of God's creative activity, the text itself portrays a God who wills, who commands, and who enables, not a God who tinkers. It does not detail the physics, geology, or biology of creation. God simply says, "Let there be light," and there is! *How* light came to be from utter darkness is of no interest to Genesis. It came to be because God so willed it!

Interestingly, however, in the latter phases of creation, according to Genesis 1, the creation, itself, was privileged to participate in the further creation of the world. In two instances, God commanded and enabled segments of creation to "produce" other creatures. At God's command, the sea "brought forth" living creatures, and the earth "produced" animals. In turn, God charged the living creatures in the sea, on the land—both plants and animals—and in the air with continuing the act of creation through reproduction. In fact, God charged mankind, God's final and climactic creation, with the responsibility for participating in the creative act not only by reproducing, but also by maintaining God's creation.

Here, the biblical doctrine of creation reaches its zenith: not in the insistence that one theory describing the scientific details of the process of world-formation be accepted over another, but in God's charge to humankind, made in God's image, that we continue God's work. The meaning of the scriptural account of creation far surpasses the call for intellectual assent to the notion that the God of Israel—and not some other god, and certainly not some chance occurrence—authored the world. God made a good world; we are responsible to husband well that good world.

God built rhythm, cycles, diversity, and harmony into God's world; we are responsible for finding our place in God's rhythm, for living our lives in harmony with God's order. (Mark Biddle)

CONTACT!

2 CORINTHIANS 13:11-13

One of the common frustrations of life is needing to get in contact with someone but not being able to do so. Even with all our communication technology it's not easy to make contact sometimes. How I hate that message I so often get when using a cell phone, "The customer you have dialed does not answer or is not available at this time. Try again later." Hopefully, if you keep trying, you will make contact somehow, sometime.

Recently, an interesting and rare movie, *Contact*, was in theaters, which was based on a book by Carl Sagan, a wonderful scientist and teacher who died far too young. It's the story of Dr. Ellie Arroway, a radio astronomer who has dedicated her life to the cosmological field of SETI (Search for Extra-Terrestrial Intelligence). She uses a giant radio telescope to scan the skies for signals that might originate from intelligent beings. Raised by her father, who died when she was young, all her life Ellie feels alone and seeks to make contact. That longing lifts her eyes to the heavens. As a scientist, she does not believe in God or the supernatural. But during the course of the movie she does have a faith experience of sorts. She makes contact! A signal is heard from the distant stars, and that signal carries instructions about a machine that can be built to send someone back to the source of that message. Ellie is chosen to go. I will not spoil the ending for those of you who may want to see the movie. Ellie learns that she is not really alone, that none of us are. That knowledge changes her life, and she becomes a kind of messenger saying that contact is possible—that we are not alone.

I think every one of us is Ellie. Each of us has deep inside this longing, this need for contact, this hunger for communication, for connection with that which is beyond us. It is for me the need for contact with God. Today, Trinity Sunday, is all about that contact!

The heart of the Trinity is that God has always been seeking us, desiring a relationship with us. In other words, the Trinity helps us explain how God has sought contact with us. This in itself is an astounding claim. For as the psalmist says when he realizes how vast the universe is and how very small we are in comparison, who are we that God would take notice, would want to be close to us? Yet, God does! Imagine this: the Creator of the universe wants to contact you! Wants to talk to you! Wants to have a relationship with you!

Paul, in today's reading, tells us what God has communicated to us—grace, love, communion. In Jesus, God's grace, God's unmerited favor and acceptance come to us all. This grace comes from the love of God the Father. And best of all, the Holy Spirit, dwelling within us, gives us constant communion—contact with God. We do not have to build a machine to enable us to make this contact. God has taken the initiative. God has called! God has e-mailed us! God has come looking for us! That's what the Trinity is all about. (Bass Mitchell)

ACTIONS ARE TRUE TOOLS

MATTHEW 28:16-20

If the passion and resurrection of Jesus were to be interpreted in the form of a theater play, this scriptural passage would be the final scene of the last act! The last scene reminds me of my childhood days, watching children's programs on French television on Wednesday afternoons. The programs often included magicians. Here, Jesus does the perfect Houdini act! A few sentences and then *pfffft*—he disappears in a puff of clouds, leaving the remaining actors somewhat dumbfounded and disoriented. The script seems to have abruptly stopped! And now, what do they do? What do they say next? What do we do? What will we say next?

The script has to be written now by the disciples of Jesus. They are commanded to "make disciples." The verb μαθητεύω is in the imperative form and its root, μανθανο, means to learn with the implication of a thought accompanied by an endeavor. It denotes one who follows someone's teaching. It implies the idea of making others "active and participating learners." This is a very heavy burden. Just ask any teacher!

What is the best way to make people want to become learners, disciples? Is it through highly emotional, stadium-filled preaching? Is it by going door to door? Is it through bumper stickers? Just turn on the TV Sunday mornings to learn about the different ways of convincing people to become disciples. Is this your method of evangelization also?

People have oranized crusades and killed others, supposedly for the sake of evangelism and for the love of God. Out-of-control evangelism has resulted in people being burned at the stake or being tortured. Is evangelism not a matter of the heart, rather than a tool for oppression?

I believe in the evangelization method of Francis of Assisi: "Everywhere you go, preach the gospel. Use words if necessary." Evangelizing is not so much a matter of words, but most important, of deeds. It is not sufficient to "feel" love for God. Love is not just a feeling. Love is also a daily reality, a mathematical demonstration! Love needs not just to "be said," it also needs to "be done." On the road, the Levite spoke about his love for God, but the Good Samaritan showed it. One Easter Sunday, Pope John XXIII went to visit a prison. It was the first time in ninety years that a pope had done so. Her started his homily by saying, "Since you could not come to me, so I have come to you." That is true evangelism! Being a disciple of God is like being in court daily; you need to prove your case, your word is not sufficient.

What a heavy burden of proof on someone's shoulders! How can someone have the strength to prove this on a daily basis? Maybe Jesus knew that and maybe that is why he said, "Lo, I am with you, always." God also made that promise to Joshua: "I was with Moses, so I will be with you; I will never leave you nor forsake you" (Josh. 1:5 NIV). Before Jesus' birth, the angel said that his name would be Immanuel—God with us. Are you aware of this constant presence?

What do you do to be aware of his presence? Do you spend time with God each day? Do you, like Brother Laurence, "practice the presence of God"? Do you spend time in solitude and in silence waiting for God to speak to you? Do you give God a chance to fulfill God's promise to you, "Lo, I will be with you always?"

Jesus gave us a very difficult task. Our actions are our tools; they are our true words. His Word is his daily presence with us. (Christine D'haese Radano)

SPIRITUAL PREPARATION

JUNE

I love the summer. I hope you are enjoying these days. I understand that summer is different according to our settings and situations. Some serve in mountain communities and near lakes; the attendance swells during these months. Others serve in cities and suburbs where the folks are in and out. Some have small children, and these can be hectic days juggling parenting and pastoral roles. Some are involved on mission trips, youth retreats, and vacation Bible schools. In the summer, life goes on. In the summer, the mission of God continues.

And yet, I love the summer. I intentionally attempt to mark it off as a different time of year. I have approached the summer for the past few years with the decision to preach exclusively from the Psalms, and I have found, after a number of years, that I am working my way through some of the less familiar but nonetheless rich resources of the Psalms. The Psalms have led me to reflect with summer congregations about creation (Psalm 8), anger (Psalm 37), guilt (Psalm 51), angels (Psalm 91), depression (Psalm 120), music (Psalm 150), thanksgiving (Psalm 100), and aging (Psalm 90). I enter into these months in a more contemplative and relaxed spirit, focusing on a small number of psalms. I try to read them devotionally and then also with an eye toward the sermon. Of course, you might use this same approach in the teaching of the Psalms, and you could work with the Psalms in any season! I have discovered a number of resources that are helpful; I would mention the writings of Walter Brueggemann, Marva Dawn, and Eugene Peterson in particular. A number of the Psalms have wonderful musical implications, from praise to classical to spiritual genres of music. I find listening to the Psalms in musical forms enriches my reflection on them, and again, sometimes the music makes its way into corporate worship.

- If you were to choose ten psalms to focus on over the next three months, what would they be? Which psalm speaks most clearly to your own spirit right now?

The summer is, of course, a wonderful time to explore the wonder of God's creation. Again, the Psalms are a rich resource. In his translation of Psalm 104, Eugene Peterson renders verse 24 in this way:

> What a wildly wonderful world, GOD!
>   You made it all, with Wisdom at your side,
>   made earth overflow with your wonderful creations.
>
> (The Message)

The creation is in itself a testimony to God's glory and greatness (Psalm 8), to God's power and purpose (Genesis 1–2; Colossians 1). John Calvin, the Reformer of the church, speaks of a book of nature alongside the book of Scripture. The world, created and loved by God (John 3:16), bears witness to the God who is both the origin and the sustaining foundation of all that is, seen and unseen.

In the summer we have the opportunity to reflect on God's gift of creation. A number of our youth and children attend camps in the summer. There they encounter God in the outdoors. A number of families have a time of respite, in the mountains or along the coast or beside a lake, where the re-creating Spirit of God can bring order and rest back into their lives. This is a wonderful time of the year to read the Psalms, which remind us of God's inescapable and constant presence. God is always with us (Psalm 139).

I invite you to read these psalms in particular: 8, 19, 24, and 104. In addition, you might build into your Sabbath times during this month some exploration of God's world: a nearby lake or fishing stream; a mountain or state park; a hiking trail; a walk through a garden. Or, a visit to an art museum, or a zoo! God's creation is, to borrow an overused word, "awesome." The summer might be the time to explore it. Consider this an invitation to a contemplative practice!

- How can we move from lament (about the chaos of summer schedules) to embrace the uniqueness of this season? How can we see the emptiness of summer as a gift from God, that might nurture our awareness of the gift of creation?

Of course, we do not worship the creation (pantheism); but the One who brings creation into being; we care for the creation because of our responsibility as stewards; we take the time and find the space to contemplate God's goodness and mercy in a stream, a forest, a waterfall, an ocean wave; we listen for God's music in the stillness of creation. And we sing the words of St. Francis:

Let all things their Creator bless,
And worship him in humbleness,
O praise ye! Alleluia!
Praise, praise the Father, praise the Son,
And praise the Spirit, Three in One!
O praise ye! O praise ye!
Alleluia! Alleluia! Alleluia!

I wrote this prayer for a congregation years ago; now I offer it to you.

A Summer Prayer

O God of every time and season
we give thanks for rhythms of work and rest
for places apart that mark our years
for the eternal return of ocean waves
for the defiant posture of mountains for the hiddenness of
favorite coves
for pilgrimages made and then homecomings.

O God, for this season we are grateful for sanity regained
for blessings discovered
for those who return to us and for those who leave.

Teach us, God of wonder and creation
that your presence is woven into
the comings and goings of our lives
and having fled to our own lonely places
let us return, with Jesus,
to live and work
to heal and pray
to worship and love.
Amen.

May you know God's presence in these days of summer! (Ken Carter)

Sources: "All Creatures of Our God and King," *United Methodist Hymnal*, p. 62 (Nashville: UMPH, 1989); Ken Carter, "A Summer Prayer," *Alive Now*, July/August, 2000, p. 65.

JUNE 2, 2002

Second Sunday After Pentecost

Worship Theme: If we depend upon our own righteousness we cannot stand before God's judgment, but Christ justifies all through faith.

Readings: Genesis 6:9-22; 7:24; 8:14-19; Romans 1:16-17; 3:22*b*-28 (29-31); Matthew 7:21-29

Call to Worship (Psalm 46):

> *Leader:* God is our refuge and strength, a very present help in trouble.
>
> *People:* **Whom shall we fear? Of whom shall we be afraid?**
>
> *Leader:* There is a river whose streams make glad the city of God, the holy habitation of the Most High.
>
> *People:* **God is in the midst of the city; it shall not be moved; God will protect us when the morning dawns.**
>
> *Leader:* Come, behold the works of the LORD. God makes wars cease, breaks the bow, and shatters the spear. God burns the shields with fire and declares, "Be still, and know that I am God! I am exalted among the nations, I am exalted in the earth."
>
> *People:* **The LORD of hosts is with us; the God of Jacob is our refuge.**

Pastoral Prayer:

God, righteous judge, look not on our failures but keep your promise never again to destroy your earth. Restrain the flood-waters. Still earthquakes and volcanoes. Rescue those who suffer disaster. God, merciful Savior, look not on our failures but see in us the righteousness of Christ. Strengthen our faith. Forgive us and we will go to sin no more. God, hope of the despairing, be a firm foundation for our lives. Shelter the exposed. Humble the self-assured. Hear our cries for help. Set us to the work of your justice. Restore us to wholeness. God, maker of heaven and earth, sustain the life of this planet and all its creatures, and renew the harmony of the spheres. In the name of the One whom you raised from the dead. Amen. (Scott Haldeman)

SERMON BRIEFS

GOD IN THE REAL WORLD

GENESIS 6:9-22; 7:24; 8:14-19

In recent years, Noah, his ark, and his animals have become commercially popular. A cursory tour of the local mall will reveal numbers of Noah's ark figurines, stuffed toys, pop-up children's books, and such. The Noah's ark motif has become especially popular for decorating nurseries and preschools. A major American television network recently produced and aired a strangely modified, and presumably more entertaining, version of the Noah story. Whatever the motivation for this popularity, the commercial success of cuddly Noah toys points to a remarkably consistent human trait: our need to domesticate and tame troubling, often terrifying reality.

But the Noah story, itself, resists domestication. It is troubling. It confronts some of our most cherished security blankets. It challenges neat and long-held assumptions. It reminds us, more forcibly perhaps than any other biblical text, that the good news of salvation and the bad news of sin and judgment are inextricably intertwined. Specifically, the story of the Flood confronts us with evidence that, in the face of large-scale evil, our concepts of fairness for individuals often cannot apply. Furthermore, it reminds us that sometimes God chooses to save by painful means.

The text tells us that, because corruption and violence had reached critical proportions, God decided to wipe the slate of human history clean and start afresh with Noah and his descendants. God sent a massive flood to eradicate "all flesh." Although the Bible does not detail it, one can easily imagine the Flood engulfing children of all ages, including those too young to have been held responsible in any way for the world's decadence. The animals that drowned in the Flood were surely innocent.

Quite frankly, we must admit that this almost totalitarian aspect of God's punishment strikes us as overly harsh, indeed, as downright unfair. We might well prefer that God had employed some other, more selective techniques whereby innocent children could have been spared at least. We can always dismiss this aspect of the Noah story as evidence of ancient Israel's savagery and bloodthirstiness and argue that they simply had not yet come to a mature understanding of God's justice. But, to do so is to refuse to confront a facet of reality attested to not only in Scripture but also in our own experience.

How could God stand by and permit the Holocaust? Why does God permit the tornado to follow its path toward a crowded preschool? We comfort ourselves, correctly, with reminders that God is present in suffering and that, as Supreme Judge of all the world's rights and wrongs, God will one day set things right. But we must also accept the evidence that God has chosen not to create a cartoon world in which actions have no consequences and in which one's freedom to act has no impact on the lives of others.

Like civilization in Noah's day, Nazi Germany was corrupt and filled with violence. Like God's punitive flood, however, the Allied war effort was a blunt instrument of justice. Allied bombs killed soldiers and civilians alike—the most committed Nazi plant supervisor, and the Jewish slave-laborer, as well. The indiscriminate nature of warfare cannot be mitigated by such Orwellian doublespeak as the now-popular phrases "smart bombs" and "collateral damage." No, war is a messy means of doing justice.

Why does God choose to employ such indiscriminate means as floods and wars to guide and direct human history? Neither the

Scriptures nor experience suggests an answer to this question. Both only agree that God's intervention in human history typically has a very real-world quality. God is no cartoonist. Through their evil choices, human beings often create situations so massively evil that only drastic, if "unfair," measures can stop the spread of corruption. We may wish it were not so; no doubt the loving God wishes it were not so; but the real world is messy.

Even the good news found in the Genesis account of the Flood is stamped with a sobering imprint of the real world. Because God persists in God's good purpose for the world, and because Noah was outstandingly righteous in his generation, God chose to spare righteous Noah so that the world could be repopulated. In simplest terms, the Flood exemplifies the truth that God often saves only a remnant, that God cleanses by purging, that there is always hope, but that it often lies beyond judgment.

That version of Christianity that sees God's working in the world and in our lives in relation to stuffed animal toys and cartoons seeks to tame the Lord God, Creator and Ruler of the universe. It underestimates the horror of human evil and the seriousness of God's response. (Mark Biddle)

AMAZING GRACE!

ROMANS 1:16-17; 3:22*b*-28 (29-31)

The Romans text can be used to speak to individuals about their personal need for salvation, or it can be used to speak to the entire community about corporate sins that keep us from offering God's grace to all.

In Romans 3:21-30, Paul resumes the themes he stated in 1:16-17:

- God, who is righteous and faithful to an undeserving creation, has, in Jesus Christ, provided a way for us to become righteous and fulfill our created purpose.
- Salvation is a gift from God; it cannot be earned or deserved.
- Salvation is available to all who have faith.

However, in preaching this passage, we must not ignore what lies in between. In 1:18–3:20, Paul describes our rebellion against God and God's abandonment of us to our own devices. We have allowed someone or something, other than God, to become our Lord. All of us are worthy of God's wrath and punishment. The good news found in today's passage comes none too soon after this proclamation.

We must take care in preaching a message about personal salvation. This passage is a staple of revival preachers and of those who chide their efforts. An overemphasis on guilt and emotion may bring these negative images to mind. Conversely, Paul's complex theology tempts us to provide lengthy, intellectual interpretations. However, this approach will probably not speak to our listeners' needs. We can help listeners understand the themes of this passage by weaving them together with an authentic testimony of God's grace, or with the words of a familiar hymn.

The life of John Newton provides a good example. Newton was a naval deserter turned sea captain and slave trader in eighteenth-century England. His experiences left him a bitter man with a blasphemous reputation. After rejecting God for years, he experienced grace when he came to Christ during a violent storm at sea. God continued to be at work in Newton's life as he slowly turned from slave trader to pastor. Through his ministry, Newton influenced politicians who passed laws ending the International Slave Trade some thirty years later. His testimony shows the power of God to make us righteous and to empower us to fulfill our purpose in life.

Newton was also a gifted writer. His words have been a source of encouragement since he penned them in the early 1800s. "Amazing grace, how sweet the sound that saved a wretch like me. I once was lost, but now am found, was blind but now I see."

Pastors speaking to believers may wish to preach a more corporate message. In this case, focus may rest on corporate sins such as racism, sexism, and materialism that keep us from sharing the gospel with all people. We can remind our congregations that before God, all our artificial barriers of nationality, gender, and class are stripped away. Jesus modeled this radical message as he empowered women and the social outcasts of his day. What might it mean in the life of the church if we could confess these sins and allow God to move us beyond our comfort zones to take the message of amazing grace to those we view as "other"? (Tracy Hartman)

BY THE POWER OF THREE

MATTHEW 7:21-29

I. Three-way Justification

What did you do today? What are you doing right now? Is it important? If so, to whom is it important? It seems that prophesying, casting out demons, and doing deeds of power would be important—especially if they are being done in the Lord's name. One would think these things would be very important to God.

Christ begins this passage by dividing those who will gain entrance into heaven and those who will be turned away. Those who come to Christ having done what seems to be the Lord's work will be turned away. Those turned away offer three different justifications for why they should gain entrance into heaven: they have prophesied, they have cast out demons, and they have done deeds of power. How often are our day's tasks things that we deem important and to be the things that God would have us to do as ministers? How often do we step back and take a different view to discern whether these things are important to us or truly important to God?

II. Three-way Admonition

How shocking would it be to approach the gates of heaven and have Jesus Christ say to you, "I never knew you; go away from me; you are an evildoer"? You are a minister of the gospel of Christ, are you not? Do you not profess to live a life according to the covenants laid before not only you, but the generations who have come before you? You have dedicated your life to a commitment of serving other people in the name of Christ. How could it happen, then, that Christ, when you have used your life to serve his name, could turn you away from an eternity in heaven not only once, but three times?

There is no quicker way to completely crush a person, physically, spiritually, or eternally than to deny their acquaintance, send them away, and insult their life's work. Is there a more serious call to pay attention to the words of Christ? Is there a more serious call to live according to his example? Could anything worse ever happen to a person than what Christ foretells will happen?

So then, how is it that we keep this from happening? How do we ensure that our works are not in vain, that they truly are the works of God? How do we prevent the three-way admonition of Christ at the gates of heaven? Christ gives us a small clue—he says that one must do the will of the Father. This answer, then, begs the question, what exactly is the will of the Father?

III. Three-way Weather

In the attempt to give some clarity, Christ offers the analogy of the two houses, one built upon a foundation of rock and the other built upon sand. He again uses the numeral three in his description of the weather: *the rain fell, the floods came, and the wind blew and beat.* Perhaps the will of God is doing the kind of work that adds to the solid foundation of rock. To look at the other side of the analogy—how sad will it be to get to the point in time Christ is speaking of and be able to see the "foundation" of our lives? How much more of your foundation will be sand than rock? What are some things that you can or should be doing to make your foundation more rock than sand? (Victoria Atkinson)

JUNE 9, 2002

Third Sunday After Pentecost

Worship Theme: Risking faith, we leave the familiar and journey to the unknown, but God goes with us.

Readings: Genesis 12:1-9; Romans 4:13-25; Matthew 9:9-13, 18-26

Call to Worship (Psalm 33):

> *Leader:* Rejoice in the LORD, O you righteous.
>
> **People:** **Praise the LORD with the lyre; make melody to God with the harp.**
>
> *Leader:* Sing to him a new song and play skillfully on the strings, for the word of the LORD is upright, and all his work is done in faithfulness.
>
> **People:** **For God loves righteousness and justice; the earth is full of the steadfast love of the LORD.**
>
> **All:** **Let your steadfast love, O LORD, be upon us, even as we hope in you.**

Pastoral Prayer:

God of Mystery, you sent Abraham and Sarah far from their homes to found a new people, your people. Strengthen our belief so we can step out in faith to do your will. Tell us where we should go to heal and to serve. God of Mystery, you sent Jesus among us to show us your mercy. Assure us of your transformative presence so we might believe and be healed. Raise us from slumber to tell of your might. Let us touch you that we might be whole. God of Mystery, you will bring to fruition the New Age in your own time. Grant us peace as we wait. Grant us peace as we pray. Grant us peace as we struggle. May you come soon. Amen. (Scott Haldeman)

SERMON BRIEFS

RESPONDING IN FAITH

GENESIS 12:1-9

The Bible holds a mirror before us, so that we may see ourselves. We see in the characters on the pages of Scripture our extemes of sorrow and joy, our capacities for good and for evil, our ability to show mercy and our tendency toward spite—characteristics we all share. In a sense, the Bible invites us to consider ourselves as human beings, to ask what humanity is, and to join others in acknowledging the human condition.

One of the most striking features of the biblical book of Genesis is the relative absence of God from its pages. Apart from God's activity in creating the world and virtually destroying it just a few chapters later, God normally appears in Genesis in the lives of key human figures to make some incredible promise, as he makes to Abraham in our text, or to issue a call to some daring—and, in at least one case (the sacrifice of Isaac), troubling—act.

Never does God specify the details of the journey from the present to the realization of the promise. Never does God advise as to the wise and proper course of action for responding to the call. Never does God explain motivations, purposes, objectives, or plans of action. God rarely appears, although God is essential to the premises of the plot. The characters onstage are ever aware of God's importance, but after God abandons daily walks with humans "in the cool of the day," none have regular, intimate interaction with God. God even anesthetizes the chosen one before making a covenant with him (Genesis 15).

The text before us is a pointed demonstration of this phenomenon of God's relative absence. After appearing to Abraham to promise him land, offspring, protection, and the key role in blessing humankind, God disappears. Abraham, who remarkably responds in faith to God's call, leaves his home and family (except for his nephew Lot) in Haran, and moves south to wander among the Canaanite inhabitants who then occupied the land God had chosen to be Abraham's heritage. The contrast between God's bold promises and the realities Abraham faced could hardly have been starker.

God promised a land: Abraham found Canaan in the possession of the Canaanites. In fact, Abraham and his son Isaac after him would spend their lives as sojourners in the land God had promised. Abraham's grandson Jacob would leave the land to seek his fortune and start his family. Abraham's great-grandsons would go to Egypt, where Abraham's descendants would spend generations as slaves. Only hundreds of years later would Israel occupy as their own the land promised Abraham. God's original promise failed to mention that detail.

God promised offspring. The fact that Abraham brought his nephew Lot along with him to Canaan is a reminder of Abraham's childlessness. Perhaps Abraham thought to draft Lot into service as his heir. When Lot left Abraham to begin his own life, the role of Abraham's heir fell to a trusted servant, Eliezer. Later, Sarah would suggest the arrangement that produced Ishmael, giving Abraham a son. None of these heirs that Abraham provided for himself, however, were the heir God had intended. Very late in their lives, Isaac would be born to Abraham and Sarah—but not before Abraham's struggles to make God's promise come true had resulted in great pain and sorrow. One can easily imagine the anguish God could have spared Hagar and Ishmael had God warned Abraham against following Sarah's plan. God's original promise failed to mention the details.

Abraham wanders from place to place, perhaps to guard against staying too long in the vicinity of a given Canaanite family or clan, so as not to wear out his welcome. The account gives the impression, and one can well imagine given their status as sojourners and their ages, that Abraham and Sarah focused all their attention and strength on merely staying alive. There could be no thought of being the source of blessing for the world!

We often romanticize biblical figures. Abraham, God's friend, must have known an intimacy with God that we can never rival—

so we assume. The evidence of the account of Abraham's life paints the picture of a man who responded in faith to a magnificent call of God, but who had no more insight into the details of God's plan than we do. In fact, the entire Genesis story concentrates, not on outlining the secrets of God's plan for human history, but on the human characters and their struggle to do justice to the call of this God, who reappears every decade or so to restate or revise the old promise, or to issue some new directive.

Rather than disappointing, however, this feature of the Abraham story is perhaps the most theologically fertile and encouragingly humanistic aspect of the book. Genesis does not describe human experience as a series of divine interventions and manipulations, but as the struggle to be human, the struggle to respond to call and promise—with no map for the journey, no training wheels, no "Do Not Enter," "One Way," or "Detour" signs to mark the way. Just as we do, Abraham and the other characters in Genesis lived their lives as best they could. They didn't know what they didn't know. (Mark Biddle)

THE GOD OF THE IMPOSSIBLE

ROMANS 4:13-25

We all face impossible situations. Are you facing one right now? What in your life seems absolutely impossible? Are you having a hard time believing that God can work in your situation? Take heart; you are not alone.

In this passage, specifically in verse 17, Paul hints at three impossible situations. He also reminds us that God is able to give life to the dead and call into existence the things that do not exist.

The first and most obvious situation is Abraham's. Here is Abraham, nearly one hundred years old, when God promises him that he will become the father of many nations. God has promised to call into existence children who do not yet exist. The text tells us that despite his age, despite how impossible the situation looked, Abraham grew strong in his faith and gave glory to God, convinced that God was able to fulfill what God had promised.

The second situation that this text hints at is the resurrection of Christ. Imagine yourself as a disciple and recall the impossible nature of this time. You have just watched from afar as they crucified Jesus. You watched in horror as they nailed him to the cross, and shamefully hid your face to keep from being recognized as one of his followers. Now, you are holed up in an upper room with the others, wondering how things went so horribly wrong. Then, there is a knock at the door. Your heart is gripped with fear; it is the soldiers coming to drag you all away. But no, it is Mary, and she is talking out of her head. "He is alive," she proclaims, "the Lord is alive." It is impossible, you all say, but your feet compel you through the door as you and the others follow her back to the tomb. You dare not hope, but could it be? Has the God of the impossible given life to the dead?

And what is the third situation? Is it not our own? Verse 24 tells us that if we believe in God, who raised Jesus from the dead, it will be reckoned to us as righteousness, as well. God can give life to our deadened spirits and call into existence things in our lives that do not yet exist. What is our seemingly impossible situation? Can we, like Abraham, grow strong in our faith and give glory to God, being convinced that God can do as God promised?

A legitimate question is, How does one do this? We are tempted, as Abraham was in the birth of Ishmael, to take matters into our own hands. Instead, we must give God room and time to work. This is not a call to passivism, but rather a call to undertake useful activities within the framework of trust in God, who bases promises on love and grace. Then, we must wait and trust and see what the God of the impossible does on our behalf. (Tracy Hartman)

ONLY THE SICK SURVIVE

MATTHEW 9:9-13, 18-26

Have you ever watched the reaction on a dying person's face when the doctor walks into the hospital room? Many times, a look of hope comes across the face of the sick. The doctor is a very attractive person to those in need of medical attention. Doctors hold the secrets to wellness and the prolonging of life. Doctors would be followed to the ends of the earth, if it meant their patients could attain a higher quality of life.

In this text, Jesus is as attractive to the tax collectors and sinners as a doctor is to the dying. Jesus approaches Matthew, the tax collector, the sickest of the sick, according to the social standards of Jesus' day. All Jesus has to say is "Follow me," and without hesitation, Matthew is on his coattails.

With this introduction, Jesus' fellow dinner guests are, appropriately, sinners and tax collectors, which is a great surprise to the Pharisees. They logically assume that Jesus would be dining with the righteous and high-ranking members of society, not the lowest of the low. The Pharisees could not be more wrong. Jesus informs them that his presence on earth is for those who need him—the sick, those who need mercy. He has come for the sinners, not for the righteous.

How ironic it must have been to witness Jesus calling the Pharisees *righteous* and the tax collectors *sinners*. Surely Jesus is not using his words literally. Perhaps the way Jesus actually perceives the situation is that the tax collectors are aware of the oppression they inflict upon people; they know they are sinners. The Pharisees portray themselves to be righteous, and are not even knowing (or wanting to know) that they need Jesus. Jesus dines at the table with those who know they need him.

Likewise, as a doctor responds to the sick, Jesus responds to those who need him. Jesus fulfills a need for sinners through healing the sick. He heals the hemorrhaging woman. He brings a child back from the dead in verses 18-26. What incredible faith the hemorrhaging woman had to know that if she touched Jesus' cloak, she would be healed. Jesus' presence was seen as a threat to the synagogue and its leaders, and yet one of its leaders comes and begs for Jesus to help his dying daughter. It is not until he is at his wit's end—his daughter has died—that the leader of the synagogue realizes that Jesus is the only way to save not only his daughter, but his only quality of life, as well.

How often are we like the leader of the synagogue, handling life just fine without the help of God, until something tragic happens. Too frequently, we place too much credit in our hands and think that we don't need God or God's help and guidance. Perhaps this is why, when we do make hospital visits as ministers to family members or friends of family members who are unchurched, we so often hear pleas to God in the face of death. "I know I have not led a good life or gone to church, but if God would just get me through this one time, I promise I would be good." At this point we can be grateful for the fact, as shown in this passage, that even actions as small as grasping hold of the cloak of Christ are enough faith to save the sick and dying. (Victoria Atkinson)

JUNE 16, 2002

Fourth Sunday After Pentecost

Worship Theme: God sustains us in suffering and surprises us with unexpected gifts. Nothing is too wonderful for God to do.

Readings: Genesis 18:1-15; Romans 5:1-8; Matthew 9:35–10:8 (9-23)

Call to Worship (Psalm 116):

Leader: Gracious is the LORD, and righteous; our God is merciful.

People: **The LORD protects the simple; when I was brought low, he saved me.**

Leader: Return, O my soul, to your rest, for the LORD has dealt bountifully with you. What shall I return to the LORD for all his bounty to me?

People: **Let us lift up the cup of salvation and call on the name of the LORD.**

Leader: Let us offer to God a thanksgiving sacrifice and call on the name of the LORD. Let us make our vows to the LORD in the presence of all God's people, in the courts of the house of the LORD, in the midst of Jerusalem.

People: **Praise the LORD!**

Pastoral Prayer:
God, three in one, you visit us with good news even in the desert. Visit us this day. Reveal the mystery of your unity and

relationality. Break bread with us as we share bread with strangers. God of laughter, you embarrass us with good things. Shower us continually with your grace. God, giver of your very self, you find the lost and restore the broken. Fill us with the hope of your promise of grace. God, beloved of Jesus, you restore the suffering and break the power of death. Accompany us when we are persecuted so we endure in hope. God, maker of disciples, send us out to teach and to heal. Guide our feet to places that need good news and watch over us in unfriendly lands. We pray through Christ who sends us out and promises to return and establish justice and peace. Amen. (Scott Haldeman)

SERMON BRIEFS

A BIBLICAL COMEDY

GENESIS 18:1-15

The Bible's account of God's visit with Abraham and Sarah to announce the impending birth of Isaac is one of the most delightfully narrated vignettes in Scripture. Its theme is clear: laughter. After all, Isaac's very name means "he laughed." One might even go so far as to characterize the account as comic. Those who have made a study of comedy and laughter point out that comedy hinges on some basic incongruity. We laugh at a burly, bearded, construction worker dressed as a bride in some amateur production staged to raise funds for the local PTA because of the comical inconsistency of the sight. We laugh at Deputy Barney Fife armed with his pistol and the one bullet Sherriff Taylor allows him to carry in his shirt pocket, because of the incongruity between the lovable but incompetent Barney and our expectations of a typical law enforcement officer. We laugh at ourselves when we cannot find the eyeglasses we have perched on top of our heads.

And, if we can allow ourselves freedom from stuffy, preconceived notions that, despite the explicit evidence to the contrary, scripture is and must always be sober and somber, we can laugh along with Sarah at the events narrated in our text for the same reasons—comic incongruity. According to the text, the Lord and God, who created the entire universe, assumes human form to visit Abraham and Sarah and to seek refuge from the desert heat and refreshment before continuing the journey. In the very presence of God, neither Abraham nor Sarah recognizes the guest whom they entertain with a barbecue! Like children, Sarah and the Lord God Almighty have a "You did!"—"No, I didn't!"—"Uh-huh!" argument. But, of course, the climactic comic moment is Sarah's laughter at God's bold announcement that she, a barren nanogenarian, will give birth to a son by centenarian Abraham!

Of course, Sarah's laughter expresses her incredulity, just as Abraham's laughter had earlier. Neither Sarah nor Abraham responds at first to God's announcement with deep confidence that God is both faithful to God's promise and able to fulfill it, no matter the improbability of the means. But can any of us find fault with her reaction? The picture of a ninety-year-old first-time mother is truly ridiculously comic, isn't it?

As the story continues, Sarah's incredulous laughter becomes the laughter of rejoicing. When Isaac is, in fact, born, Sarah exclaims that now everyone—including we who read of it thousands of years later—who hears of the circumstances of Isaac's birth will laugh in astonishment. And rightly so. The fact that God is faithful and able in no way diminishes the ridiculous absurdity of the birth. To the contrary, it amplifies it! Comical words become a comic reality in the person of Isaac, "he laughed."

How do we evaluate this laughter? Is the biblical story comedy? It deals with the weighty and lofty matter of human sin and divine forgiveness, of human history and divine purpose, of human hopes and divine promises. Are these most ultimate of all questions funny?

It comes as a surprise to us, perhaps—much as Isaac's birth surprised Sarah—that the answer is a resounding yes! What can be more ridiculous than God choosing an aged, childless, Hebrew couple to be a new beginning for the human race? More incongruous than the Lord of the universe delivering an insignificant, motley group of slaves from the lordly Pharaoh of grand Egypt? Is it more incredible than God Almighty being so concerned with human beings that God becomes flesh and dwells among us? Is it more consistent with our expectations of reality than the notion that the greatest power in the universe is not political strength, or wealth, or even military might, but self-sacrificing love? More surprising than Easter Sunday morning? (Mark Biddle)

A FRIEND TO DIE FOR

ROMANS 5:1-8

The mortar fire inadvertently hit an orphanage, and a young Vietnamese girl was critically wounded. Without a blood transfusion, she would die. An American doctor and nurse tried, as best they could in limited Vietnamese, to ask if any of the other children at the orphanage would be willing to give her blood. After a moment, a small hand slowly raised, dropped back down, and hesitantly went back up again.

The doctors began the transfusion, and Heng, the young donor, began to sob. He told the doctor that he was not in pain, yet he continued to cry. With the language limitations, the Americans could not figure out what was wrong. Finally, a Vietnamese nurse arrived and spoke to the distressed child. She listened to his reply and then spoke to him in a soothing voice. Finally, a great look of relief spread over his face. The nurse explained to the Americans that the boy thought he was going to die—that he would have to give all of his blood so that the girl could live.

"But why would he be willing to do that?" the Americans asked. The nurse repeated the question to the boy, who answered simply, "She is my friend."

Today's Scripture passage tells us bluntly that it is rare for any of us to be willing to die for a righteous person or a friend. Yet, God proved God's love for us that while we were still sinners— far from a friend to God—Christ was willing to die for us.

His death gives us life in numerous ways. Through his death, Christ makes possible our justification by faith, which allows us to overcome our past and have peace with God (v. 1). As believers, we may have confidence in our hope for the future (v. 2). But even more, our position as children of God means that we can face with confidence the trials of our lives (v. 3).

Both here and in James we learn that suffering can teach us patience, and that patience or endurance produces character. As our character is strengthened, so is our hope. This hope is based in God's great love for us, which comes to us through the Holy Spirit. This love is the same love that Christ exhibited in dying for us. This is the love that transforms our past, present, and future.

Christ was willing to die for us, before we were even his friends. Now that we are his friends and more, are we willing to do the same? (Tracy Hartman)

SERVANTS AND LABORERS

MATTHEW 9:35–10:8 (9-23)

In this pericope, Matthew's emphasis on servanthood is paramount. Alongside his servant message, however, the Matthean goal of connecting Jesus to both Judaism and the Davidic line of kingship continues. This second emphasis of Matthew's Gospel may be helpful and important to note in order to alleviate confusion about the inclusion of non-Jews in Christ's kingdom (a confusion that might arise for congregations hearing 10:6). However, the first emphasis offers the primary preaching focus of this brief—that Jesus came to serve and calls Christian followers to serve in that same vein.

As Matthew concludes Jesus' Sermon on the Mount, this passage transitions into Jesus' call to the missionary work required of Jesus' followers. Even as Jesus gives authority to the disciples to heal, cleanse, and cure, Jesus does so in the context of servanthood and compassion. This missionary work is not to prove Jesus' authority so much as it is a mission to offer "compassion for them [the people], because they were harassed and helpless, like sheep without a shepherd" (9:36). In focusing this mission on the needs of Jewish sisters and brothers, Jesus is throwing quite an insult at the scribes who were present in almost every city . . . implying that they are not shepherding their flocks in the manner of

Davidic leadership. And so, the disciples are commissioned to offer that much-needed shepherding.

Likewise, American Christians today can find churches in almost any neighborhood, but good shepherding is not so common. Many congregations are without pastors, and most churches lack for leadership in one area or another. Very few churchgoers today feel overwhelmed by an overabundance of volunteers, lay ministers, or active church members. And yet, we face the very situation Jesus noticed all around him: people who feel helpless and are in need of compassion, and situations that seem hopeless in need of relief. In a time of decreasing church attendance and membership, alongside increasing violence and moral confusion, most people understand Jesus' perception of seeing a community of sheep without a shepherd. The harvest of persons in need of Christ's compassion is still very great, just as it was in Jesus' day.

Up to this point in Matthew's Gospel, Jesus had been the sole missionary in those situations of great need. Here, Jesus recognizes that God has not called him to be the lone Good Shepherd to lead and feed the lost sheep of this world. In 9:37, Jesus turns to his disciples to enlist their shepherding ministry. And soon after (10:1), he blesses them with the authority and the ability to heal and aid as Jesus had healed and aided people. And so, the first team of church servant-leaders was born.

Such shepherding could not have occurred without the blessing and guidance of Christ; and such is the case today. Compassionate and strong shepherding was desperately needed as it is needed today. Jesus could not walk and talk in a dozen villages and cities simultaneously; and such might seem to be the case today—but maybe not. For through the twelve disciples, Jesus' ministry of healing and teaching was offered throughout the Galilee. And through modern-day disciples, Jesus' ministry of healing and teaching can be offered throughout the world. Matthew's Gospel ends with the commission to take this message to the ends of the earth, and so Christians today receive not just this first commissioning of Matthew 10:7-8, but also the Great Commission of Matthew 28:16-20. (Mary J. Scifres)

JUNE 23, 2002

Fifth Sunday After Pentecost

Worship Theme: Those who proclaim the good news need not fear; though they may suffer, their reward is sure.

Readings: Genesis 21:8-21; Romans 6:1*b*-11; Matthew 10:24-39

Call to Worship (Psalm 88):

Leader: God of my salvation, when I cry out to you, incline your ear to me for my soul is full of troubles, and my life draws near to Sheol.

People: **I am like those who have no help, like those forsaken among the dead.**

Leader: I am like the slain that lie in the grave, like those whom you remember no more, for they are cut off from your hand.

People: **Every day I call on you, O LORD; I spread out my hands to you.**

Leader: Do you work wonders for the dead? Is your steadfast love declared in the grave, or your faithfulness from the Pit? Are your wonders known in the darkness, or your saving help in the land of forgetfulness?

People: **But I, O LORD, cry out to you; in the morning my prayer comes before you**.

Leader: O LORD, do not cast me off. Do not hide your face from me. My enemies surround me; my neighbors shun me. Reach out your hand to save.

Pastoral Prayer:

God who watches sparrows, keep your eye on your people that we may not perish. God who counts hairs, do not lose track of us as we sing your praise. God of the slave, the road to freedom may be filled with twists and turns; reveal the way and provide springs of water and bread for the journey. God of Isaac and Ishmael, reconcile the descendants of your chosen ones that there may be peace in our day. God of Sarah and Hagar, bring masters to repentence and servants to full stature. God of grace, dissolve our sin in your font and raise us to life everlasting. Amen. (Scott Haldeman)

SERMON BRIEFS

AN IMPROMPTU PERFORMANCE

GENESIS 21:8-21

What a soap opera! Sibling rivalry, maternal jealousy, paternal indifference, disinheritance, abandonment, the exhaustion and near death from dehydration of a banished mother and her child. Fortunately, film and television critics who object to dramatic representations of life's less nobler aspects have yet to turn their attention to censoring the Old Testament lessons read in Sunday morning worship services! It is hard to imagine a seamier story or one that subverts the believing reader's expectations to a greater degree.

Of course, the first surprising element of the story is the despicable behavior of its central figures. Any moderately sensitive reader will feel disappointment, if not revulsion, at the actions of the hero and heroine of Genesis' patriarchal narratives—Abraham and Sarah—toward Hagar and Ishmael. Hagar had not willingly become embroiled in the circumstances that nearly cost her life, after all. She was a slave. As a slave, she had not even been consulted as to whether she was in agrement with Sarah's plan to secure Abraham an heir. As the mother-to-be of Abraham's child, she surely had a valid claim to more humane treatment than Sarah meted out to her. As the mother of Abraham's firstborn, she surely deserved protection and loyalty, not rejection and banishment into the deadly desert.

Sarah, on the other hand, the maternal ancestor of all Israel, behaved in accordance only with her own selfish interests. Try as one might to justify or at least to mitigate Sarah's selfishness, her behavior remains a testament of cruelty. The moment when Sarah noticed, as though for the first time, Ishmael—some eleven years Isaac's elder—playing with her toddler as though Ishmael were the big brother—which he was—is a study in the coldness and ferocity of maternal jealousy. No slave's child was to be allowed to presume to consider himself her baby boy's big brother. She resolved immediately that both Ishmael and his mother must go to face whatever fate awaited them. Sarah's concern was only to protect Isaac's status.

Not even father Abraham is above reproach. In all his dealings with Sarah and Hagar, Abraham exhibited a striking passivity. He acquiesced to Sarah's plan to conscript Hagar as a surrogate mother; he gave Sarah carte blanche to deal with pregnant Hagar—still Sarah's slave no matter her relationship to Abraham—as she saw fit. Now, when Sarah demanded that both mother and child be banished to the desert and almost certain death, Abraham once again caved into her demands, despite his affection for Ishmael. If Sarah was harsh and cruel, Abraham was a weakling!

Clearly, one's sympathies must and do lie with Hagar, and above all, with Ishmael, the ancestor, not of Israel, but of the Arabs. Hagar's "crime" was to have been enslaved; Ishmael's was to have been born.

And yet, God intervened at the last opportunity to provide for the boy and his mother. God had not forgotten, even if Abraham and Sarah had, that Ishmael, too, was Abraham's son and, therefore, the beneficiary of God's promise to protect Abraham's offspring. God heard Ishmael's (his name means "God hears") cries and saved him.

What can possibly be the word of God in this story of cruelty, acquiescence, and abandonment? Does the Bible endorse Sarah's cruelty and Abraham's lack of backbone? What are we to learn concerning the will of God?

The best approach seems to be to take the text at face value as an honest look at those whom God called as they live out their pursuit of that calling, and at the way in which God persists in determined faithfulness to God's promise.

Obviously, the situation described here arose in the first place because Abraham and Sarah schemed, not because of God's primary plan. We will do well to acknowledge honestly this feature of the Ishmael story, and of a great number of biblical stories. Christians often conceive of God's sovereignty over the course of human affairs in absolute terms. If people were chess pieces, and God were playing alone, the game would move methodically no doubt from opening to end game in an entirely predictable way. But we are not chess pieces, and God is not the only player. We must remember that if the concept of "sin" is to have any meaning, then it must be not only a possibility but an actuality for human beings to resist, subvert, and pervert God's will.

Throughout the series of events that led up to the expulsion of Hagar and Ishmael, Abraham and Sarah acted entirely on their own initiative. Logic suggests and Scripture demonstrates that God must sometimes react to human mistakes, that God sometimes faces situations in which God's preferred plan has been rendered inoperative by human acts of rebellion or folly. God's interaction with human beings is not comparable to a master chess player's practice sessions; it is much more like the impromptu performance of a company of free-form jazz dancers.

Do our foolish or rebellious expressions of our God-given free will mean that, ultimately, God's will cannot be done? No. The amazing message of the Bible, the message of the Ishmael story, the Easter story, and virtually every story in between, is that God does not abandon God's intentions for humanity. God finds ways to bring good out of the bad situations human beings create. Sarah's word of banishment is not the final word in the Ishmael story. The final word is, in fact, "Ishmael"—God heard. God proved faithful to God's promise. In the same way, the final word in the story of Jesus is not death, but life. The final word is not sin, but forgiveness. The final word is not ours, but God's. (Mark Biddle)

CHANGING MASTERS

ROMANS 6:1*b*-11

Growing up in a Baptist church, the few few times I witnessed a baptismal service were frightening to me. It seemed as if they were trying to drown the person. I was always happy when they came up out of the water and had not died.

As I matured in the faith and had my own encounter with Christ, I began to understand that baptism was a picture of what Christ had done for us. This is what Paul was discussing in these verses. He referred to the act of baptism and connected it to the life of Christ. There was the face of *death,* that we died with Christ to that old life of sin (vv. 7-8) and are no longer under its slavery. There is *burial*, a symbol of a complete separation from the old life of sin. There is *resurrection,* a proclamation of the good news that we are living under a new master, seeking to follow the way of God (v. 4). Baptism symbolizes the truth that we came to a fork in the road and chose to take the one that led to Christ. Once we made that choice, there was no turning back. In the grace of God, we live.

There were those who were carrying that truth to the extreme. They were saying that if grace is so wonderful, let's give it a real chance to show how wonderful it is. Sin more, so grace can abound. So we do a lot of bad deeds. So what? God's grace is up to the challenge. Grace can overcome all that sin. When we are forgiven so much, people will notice how great grace is.

To that argument, Paul says simply, "By no means!" Identifying the experience of baptism with the act of justification in Christ, he said that if they had trusted Christ, they could not live that life of sin again. They were under new management; sin and death no longer had dominion over them. Instead, they had a new life that sought to live for Christ. They would seek to become what Christ desired. The big theological word for that is *sanctification.*

When I rise up to new life in Christ, will I sin again? A man had a terrible temper, but he made a commitment to Christ. A few months later, he became ready to give up on the faith. Why? His temper was still with him. He had thought that it would auto-

227

matically be taken away when he trusted Christ. He was wrong.
He should have known that he was still not perfect, that he would
have a lifetime of struggle against sin. However, there was hope
in what he said. He was upset that his bad temper had not been
overcome. He did not enjoy it. As someone has said, Christians
still sin, but they do not enjoy it as much.

When we trust Christ, we start on a new journey of our lives.
In the past, evil and sin were our traveling companions. They
ruled what we did. No more. We have changed masters. From
the moment we trust Christ, every day we seek to live life under
his leadership. (Hugh Litchfield)

CHRISTIANITY: A RELIGION OF CLIFF-HANGERS AND HORROR MOVIES

MATTHEW 10:24-39

Today's scripture makes clear for Jesus' followers that a life of
discipleship is far from easy. Post-resurrection Christians, to
whom this scripture is most clearly aimed, heard, "You will be
slandered and you might even be crucified just like me" when
they heard, "A disciple is not above the teacher. . . . If they have
called the master of the house Beelzebul, how much more will
they malign those of his household" (10:24-25). Such a harsh
warning might not be the most effective way to attract new followers, but it certainly supports followers who struggle with
fears and oppression because of their Christian faith and
actions. And almost all Christian followers know fear or timidity,
if not oppression and danger, on their faith journey.

Even American Christians, for whom the journey can be
deceptively safe, know timidity in talking about their faith lest
they be perceived as pushy; others know the fear of being
laughed at for making career or entertainment decisions based on
their Christian ethics; and increasing numbers of people feel the
awkwardness of wanting to search for God but not knowing how.
On a global basis, this scripture may seem even more relevant as
we reflect on the journey of Palestinian Christians living in
Israeli-occupied territories, Arab Christians worshiping in Mus-

lim countries, Irish Catholics seeking a voice in the Anglican world, and new Christians in emerging mission fields.

To these fears, Jesus comforts: "Do not be afraid; you are of more value than many sparrows [who are counted and known by God]" (10:31). But for most American Christians, the temptation is to claim that we are not afraid—even as we remain silent about our faith and our ethics. Lest some followers think we can be quiet about the whole Christianity thing, Jesus warns that "nothing is covered up that will not be uncovered, and nothing secret that will not become known." Any "quiet" Christian who has found herself or himself listening to the spiritual struggles of a coworker who noticed a cross necklace or lapel pin knows the truth of Jesus' words.

And so, Jesus offers instructions for our journey: "What I say to you in the dark, tell in the light; and what you hear whispered, proclaim from the housetops." These instructions were particularly challenging to the early Christian community, who knew martyrdom and exclusion on a daily basis. And yet, those days were days of rampant evangelism and church growth. The first Christians knew that they had taken on a faith that would be filled with horrors, were traveling a journey that was wrought with cliff-hangers. When one shared the gospel of Jesus Christ, one had no idea if the recipient would accept Christ, laugh aloud at the evangelist, or call the authorities. Even those who had accepted Christ were suspect, as the great Christian-killer-turned-Christian-evangelist Paul encountered when he first tried to find a place in the Jerusalem Christian community (Acts 9:26).

This pericope can be difficult to preach to a community that wants to ignore the horrible risks of living the Christian faith, or wants to pretend that God's all-loving care promises perfect endings and pat answers instead of cliff-hangers and doubts. But opening up the honest difficulties of following Christ opens up new avenues for Christian growth. Today's scripture invites such openness and growth. There is no easy way to call people to give up the desire to save their own lives and control their own destinies—such salvation and control are cornerstones of the American dream. But Christ's salvation offers the freedom to turn that control over to God since we know that even the best-laid plans cannot promise happy endings. Jesus admits that this road he lays before us is not one of peace and ease, but it is a road that will bring us growth in our love of God and neighbor, and eternal salvation in the arms of God's love and care. (Mary Scifres)

JUNE 30, 2002

Sixth Sunday After Pentecost

Worship Theme: Faith is sorely tested, the attractiveness of sin remains strong, but righteousness is now possible and God provides for those who endure.

Readings: Genesis 22:1-14; Romans 6:12-23; Matthew 10:40-42

Call to Worship (Psalm 13):

> *Leader:* How long, O LORD? Will you forget me forever? How long will you hide your face from me? How long must I bear pain in my soul, and have sorrow in my heart all day long? How long shall my enemy be exalted over me?

> *People:* **Consider and answer us, O LORD our God!**

> *Leader:* Give light to my eyes, or I will sleep the sleep of death, and my enemy will say, "I have prevailed"; my foes will rejoice because I am shaken.

> *People:* **But we trust in your steadfast love; our hearts shall rejoice in your salvation.**

> **All:** **We sing to the LORD, because God has dealt bountifully with us.**

Pastoral Prayer:

Unfathomable God, Abraham bound Isaac and raised his knife in obedience to you. Test us not in such terrifying ways. Protect children whose parents raise hands against them. Free us to do acts of mercy rather than bloody sacrifice. Provide us with grace that we can provide for others. Provide the hungry with daily bread. Provide the homeless with shelter. Provide the lonely with companions. Provide those at war with a path to reconciliation. Provide those in prison with visitors. Provide those in despair with hope. Your ways are not our ways, neither are your thoughts our thoughts. Unfathomable God, turn from your anger and show us your compassion. Amen. (Scott Haldeman)

SERMON BRIEFS

GOD PROVIDES

GENESIS 22:1-14

The narrator of the story of Isaac's sacrifice knows something Abraham and Isaac did not know; namely, that the whole affair is a test. The narrator, however, either does not know, or at least does not say, what the test question is. As a consequence, reading the story becomes a test for us, as well.

The narrator gives very few clues as to the nature of the test. We know nothing of Abraham's thinking. We are told only that God instructed Abraham to offer his only remaining son, Isaac, as a sacrifice on Mount Moriah and that Abraham arose the next morning, made preparations, and set out on the journey. What must have gone through Abraham's mind in the moments before he fell asleep that night—if he was able to sleep at all? Did he tell Sarah? Did he review the history of his relationship with the God who calls and promises, only later to ask for such a sacrifice?

God had called Abraham years before, promising him a land, a son, protection, and a key role in human history. Despite this promise, Abraham did not yet possess the land where he sojourned. He had Isaac, the promised son, to be sure. But what a maze of obstacles and dead ends Abraham had encountered before Isaac's birth. Aged, childless Abraham had brought Lot along on the journey to the promised land, hoping perhaps that his nephew could be his heir. But, Lot left soon to make his own life. So, Abraham designated a favored slave, Eliezer, as his heir, only to have God specify years later that the promise intended for Abraham to have a biological heir. Sarah's ingenious solution involving the slave Hagar produced a bona fide son and heir. But, again, years later, God informed Abraham that his cherished son, Ishmael, was not the son God had in mind. Sarah's son would be Abraham's heir. And, to make things even worse, when Isaac had indeed been born, Sarah and God conspired to force Abraham to disinherit and banish Ishmael. After all the false starts and delays and the loss of one son already, God now asked Abraham to kill the only son Abraham had left. All this time, all this pain, all these efforts to help God bring about the promise—and now, God wanted him killed!

Did Abraham's memory focus on the time, years after God had called him and before Ishmael's birth, when he had challenged God to fulfill God's promise—in effect to put up or shut up? He had begun to wonder whether there was to be any real substance to his life as God's chosen. He had doubted. But God had gone beyond making promises; God had made a covenant. Or, did Abraham's thinking dwell on the time years later when God had first declared that Ishmael was not to be the child of the promise, when God had foretold Isaac's birth? Abraham had laughed aloud at the ludicrously improbable idea that he and Sarah would have a son at their advanced ages. Abraham had laughed at God. Yet, Isaac ("he laughed") had been born as promised—and was now to be sacrificed.

What a journey of faith and doubt, of doubt and faith, Abraham had traveled. What lesson was he to have learned?

Whatever Abraham thought in the night, he arose the next morning and set out for the site intended for the sacrifice. What did he and Isaac discuss as they traveled? Did Abraham consider turning back? Did he contemplate ignoring God's directive? How could God's promise be ultimately fulfilled without Isaac? Would there be yet another miraculous birth to a woman over one hundred years old?

They reached the mountain. Isaac had no idea what was afoot. He asked his father the obvious question. Everything that they needed to make a sacrifice was on hand—except the sacrifice itself. Where is the sacrificial animal? Abraham must have winced. Where indeed. Abraham's response offers the first clue as to his thinking: "The Lord will provide."

Up the mountain they went. With remarkably restrained economy, the narrator reports the sequence of events: Abraham prepared the altar, arranged the wood, bound Isaac, laid him upon the altar, and took the knife in hand to slay his son. Just then, God spoke once more. "Stop, Abraham. I know now that you are willing to obey me even in this." Abraham's confidence that the Lord would provide proved true; instead of Isaac, Abraham offered a ram caught in a thicket. To commemorate the event, Abraham named the place "The Lord will provide."

Abraham passed the test. He had learned that no matter the delay, no matter the obstacles, no matter the improbabilities, God fulfills God's promises in God's way and on God's schedule. God provides. (Mark E. Biddle)

CHOOSING OUR PAY

ROMANS 6:12-23

The old adage says that "we get what we pay for." If we buy a cheap TV, we ought not to be surprised if it goes on the blink in a few months, or the picture is not as sharp as the one on the expensive set. If we want quality, we have to pay for it.

In a similar sense, what we get out of life depends on what we put into it. If we seek after cheap values and evil ends, we should not be surprised when life pays us back with emptiness, guilt, and meaninglessness. If we want the most out of life, we need to give ourselves to the highest and best values we can—the values seen in Christ.

This is the message Paul gives in these words of Scripture. There seem to be three movements.

I. Soldiers—Giving the Best (vv. 12-14)

Paul talked about yielding their "members" to God. This referred to a soldier's weapons, weapons offered in service. A soldier would hold nothing back in his commitment to a cause. If his life was demanded, it would be given. That was the commitment of a soldier.

Like a soldier, a disciple of Christ should yield everything to his cause. The weapons of their lives—their hands, feet, eyes, minds, hearts, lives—all needed to be committed to serving Christ. There were plenty of people who were committed to serving evil in the world. Paul stated that before Christ came to them, that was what they were doing, being instruments of wickedness. That changed. Now they were instruments of righteousness. The commitment given to evil was now transferred to Christ.

Christ held nothing back from us. We are to hold nothing back from Christ. Whatever it takes to serve, will we give it?

II. Slavery—To What or to Whom? (vv. 15-19)

What does it mean to be free? Strangely, the answer to that question is seen in the imagery that Paul used concerning slavery. Slaves were to give complete, total obedience to their master. Unfortunately, inPaul's day, many slaves did not get a chance to choose their masters. But we do! Simply put, we can choose righteousness and the way of God, or wickedness and the way of sin. Those are the choices. Whichever choices we make, the master demands our total obedience.

"I want to be free." So the cry goes out. However, the only true freedom we have is to choose to what or to whom we will be a slave. Righteousness or impurity? Good or evil? God or ourselves? All of us will serve something or someone. We are free to choose.

III. Payment (vv. 20-23)

"The wages of sin is death, but the free gift of God is eternal life in Christ Jesus our Lord" (v. 23). In other words, we get a salary for what we do with our lives. We can be a slave to things, but things will not give us love. We can serve pleasure, but its final payment is disillusionment. We can serve our work, but the work will end and we will be forgotten. We can serve ourselves, but we usually are paid back in loneliness and emptiness. Only one way will pay us what we need—that is the way of Christ. Christ brings us life, abundant and eternal. His way will bring us love, mercy, hope, peace, joy, and grace.

It is always our choice. How will we live our lives? What we get out of them in the end depends on what we put into them now. May we choose our pay wisely. (Hugh Litchfield)

WELCOMING AND BEING WELCOMED

MATTHEW 10:40-42

In this brief section of Scripture that relates to both Matthew 18:6 and 25:31-46, Jesus concludes his missionary instructions with words of comfort that "you" (the listeners) are representatives of Christ and even of God. But just as in last week's passage of Scripture, words of comfort are coupled with words of challenge to fulfill Jesus' missionary commands. And so, today's scriptures offer a message of both being *welcomed* and being *welcoming*.

There is an incredible beauty in line with Protestant theology when verse 40 is read aloud to every follower of Christ as a direct promise from Jesus: "Whoever welcomes you welcomes me, and whoever welcomes me welcomes the one who sent me." Every human being yearns to be welcomed and included, but few of us understand that yearning to come from the Christ-light living within us. Even fewer understand that God yearns to be welcomed and included. Hence, such sayings as "I stand at the door and knock" (Rev. 3:20 NIV) are sprinkled throughout Scripture to remind us of God's yearning to be in relationship with humanity.

Even more important, however, is the emphasis that we welcome God when we welcome one another, when we welcome the outsider, when we welcome the new seeker of God or the life-long Christian. Verses 41-42 move from the grammatical second person to the third person to offer that sense of instruction following the comforting second-person statements of verse 40. In the first person, we hear that we are to welcome those who prophesy in Christ's name, to welcome those who are righteous in Christ's name, and to simply offer a cup of water to the "little ones," probably meaning any and all followers of Christ, with particular emphasis on new followers. In doing so, we are fulfilling the mission work discussed throughout chapter 10, but also supporting others who are doing that same mission work for Christ.

Such welcoming sounds simple in the abstract, but is usually much more difficult when we are asked to translate our church language into the street language of our neighborhoods, or to welcome people into our churches who ask difficult questions, or to invite people into our churches who have values and lifestyles that seem to conflict with traditional church values and lifestyles. But Jesus does not demand perfection in our efforts to be welcoming; even a simple cup of cold water to a tired traveler is enough to fulfill this command, if that cup is offered with the same compassion that heralded this missionary journey back in Matthew 9:36. And so, Matthew concludes Jesus' missionary instructions with the same theme that began that journey: minister in compassion and love, and you will minister as Jesus ministered. (Mary Scifres)

SPIRITUAL PREPARATION

JULY

The New Testament teaches us that patience is a fruit of the Holy Spirit, but I confess that I am not always very patient. I sit in back of a procession of cars going down the highway; I see that one lane is closed, and the cars are backed up. I'm not always very patient. The line I have chosen in the grocery store is one where the clerk and the customer are conversing about something; they conclude their business, then the customer remembers an envelope filled with coupons.

I'm not always very patient. I'm listening to someone, and they're rambling, and in my mind I'm thinking, "*Get to the point!*" I'm not always very patient.

Patience, a fruit of the Holy Spirit, sometimes eludes me. I want it now, a minute ago, yesterday. And sometimes that spills over into my spiritual life. I wish I were farther along. I wish I had made more progress by now.

You may struggle in these same ways. You can't get a parking space; the waiter hasn't come to take your order; you may even be thinking, right now, *When is he going to get around to the point of this devotional!*

Jesus told a story about all of this. A powerless little old lady wants something.

A corrupt judge has it in his power to give her what she wants, but he really isn't inclined. "*Listen to me,*" she insists. "*Who are you?*" he replies. "*I want justice,*" she continues. "*Who is this woman?*" he asks, to no one in particular.

She doesn't give up. "*I want what is rightfully mine,*" she says. The judge knows that he is in the presence of a pest. She just doesn't get it. You can read her story in Luke 18:1-8.

Let me insert a disclaimer here. I have preached on this passage a couple of times in my ministry, although in looking back I could not quite locate the specific date. But I can tell you that this is the one sermon my children have heard very clearly, and they can almost quote the scripture. The lady asks for something, the judge says no, the lady keeps at it, the judge says no, the lady continues, the judge says no, finally the judge relents.

If you have children, you know where I'm going. Substitute child for the widow, and parent for the judge, and you've got it. Can we go to get pizza, can we go to the bookstore, to the movies, to the pool, to rent a movie, to the library?

You answer yes, when it is the appropriate answer. But sometimes the answer is "No." Or, "no, no, no, no."

But this scripture has given *power* and *hope* to my relentless children.

If it worked in the Bible, they figure, it might still be worth trying.

However, this passage is not about children who ask their parents the same question over and over. It is, Jesus tells us, in the beginning, about prayer. I like one translation of it: *pray consistently*, and *never quit*. Jesus knew, in telling this parable, that there were two enemies to the spiritual life: one is apathy, the other fatigue.

Apathy is when we don't really care; we lose interest. Many people fail in the spiritual life because they are apathetic. They just don't care. They fall away. The flame dies out. The well runs dry. The sizzle is silenced.

- Do you sense an apathy about the day-to-day ministry of which you are a part?

There is a second obstacle to the spiritual life. Fatigue. Running out of steam. Losing momentum. The battery loses power. And we can't keep going. We don't want to take another step.

These two obstacles, *apathy* and *fatigue*, prevent us from the life of prayer that Jesus wants us to have. They are obstacles to the ministry given to us by God.

What are the solutions to these obstacles?

Jesus had two guiding words. First, *pray consistently*. Consistently. Stay with it. A friend of mine would often say that about life: 90 percent of life is showing up.

In the life of prayer, be consistent. Show up before God. Make it a practice to bring your life and your losses, your problems and possibilities, your burdens and blessings before God. It is more like the mother who prays for her son every day for years, every day, than the television evangelist who has a vision of a nine-hundred-foot Jesus.

Pray consistently, Jesus says, and *never quit*. That is the second word from Jesus: *Never quit*. That's a good word for us, because sometimes we want to quit. Do you ever feel like giving up? Do you ever feel like saying, *"I quit"*?

I'll never forget one of my experiences as a youth director in an inner-city church. A dozen of us were hiking the Appalachian Trail. There were three adults. We were one day into the three-day hike when one of the counselors, mother of two of the youth, a stable person, a nurse, sat down beside the trail, buried her face in her hands, and said, *"I cannot take one more step. I cannot take one more step."*

Her tears were explosive. The other adult was the pastor. He walked over to her, sat beside her, listened, then said something to her. Then she got up, and began to walk.

- Do you ever feel like giving up? Do you ever feel like saying, *"I quit"*?

- Do you ever feel like saying, *"I cannot take one more step"*?

The great family therapist Edwin Friedman once said that one of the reasons marriages fail is that the therapist gives up. One of the reasons patients die is that the family gives up. One of the reasons teams lose is that the coach gives up.

- What are your most difficult obstacles?

In the life of prayer, Jesus says, never quit. In the parable we meet a widow who is desperate. Now, in the ancient Middle East, widows had no education, no security, no property, no status. If she had a son, a father-in-law, a father who would provide for her, she could survive. If not, Bill Hybels has noted, "she might become a beggar—the first-century equivalent of a street person or a bag lady. She would be a social outcast."

This widow is up against someone, an opponent, but she is consistent, and she doesn't quit. And the judge hears her, and out of sheer self-interest he gives her what she wants.

In the parable, it is not that the judge is like God—he is not. It is not that the older woman is like us—she is not. The point is that we should *pray consistently* and *never quit*.

Pray consistently, Jesus says. Never quit. Your prayers will make a difference.

And here's why: If a corrupt judge will finally listen to the persistent pleadings of a powerless widow, how much more will God listen to his chosen people?

God is not like the corrupt judge who has to be badgered. God is the fount of every blessing, God is the giver of every good and perfect gift. And the way we receive from God is to go to God, remembering the words of Jesus:

Pray consistently. Never quit.

One of our challenges in the ministry is to show up before God. So: *be patient*. God is working God's purpose out in you. When the obstacles of apathy and fatigue emerge in your life, recognize them for what they are. Hang in there. Never quit! (Ken Carter)

Source: Bill Hybels, *Too Busy Not to Pray*, p. 18.

JULY 7, 2002

Seventh Sunday After Pentecost

Worship Theme: God's love is steadfast and strong. God keeps the covenant, rescues us from sin despite our weakness, and asks us to bear an easy yoke, a light burden.

Readings: Genesis 24:34-38, 42-49, 58-67; Romans 7:15-25*a*; Matthew 11:16-19, 25-30

Call to Worship (Psalm 45):

> *Leader:* Your reign, O God, endures forever.
>
> **People: Your royal scepter is a scepter of equity; you love righteousness and hate wickedness.**
>
> *Leader:* God is great and showers us with love.
>
> **People: God has anointed us with the oil of gladness.**
>
> *Leader:* Our robes are fragrant with myrrh and sweet perfume.
>
> **People: We enter God's house with joy and praise God's holy name.**

Pastoral Prayer:

Lover of humanity, who makes and keeps covenant with your people, we thank you for your faithfulness. You promised land to Abraham and blessed him with wealth and posterity. Keep your promises to us—make us holy, make us your children, make us your prophets and priests in our place and time. Give us what we need each day so that we need not horde your gifts that are meant to sustain all your creatures. Forgive our shortcomings that we can start anew each day to love our neighbors. Reveal to us the structures of your justice that we might conform our world to your will. We pray for the churches that they may be places of reconciliation and healing. We pray for our political leaders that they may govern with equity and promote peace. As you have been faithful to us, help us to keep faith with you so that through us, you can feed the hungry, welcome the outsider, and comfort the grieving. Lover of humanity, who anoints us with the oil of gladness, we praise your holy name. Amen. (Scott Haldeman)

SERMON BRIEFS

A LOVE STORY

GENESIS 24:34-38, 42-49, 58-67

The Hebrew Scriptures contain many love stories. Jacob and Rachel, Samson and Delilah, Hosea and Gomer, the lovers of the Song of Songs—all these remind us of the glories (and perils) of love. The story of Isaac and Rebekah's marriage is another such story, but, like many of the others, it is more than the tale of a man and a woman. It is also the story of the love of God for the chosen people.

Unlike some other love stories, the hero plays only a small role. It seems like Isaac's lot in Scripture is to be left out of the most important moments of his life. When Abraham follows God's instructions to sacrifice his son, we never hear how Isaac felt as he trudged up the mountain beside his father. Here, when it is time for him to wed, we see he is not given a say in the matter. He does not even meet Rebekah until the matter is already arranged. This is no tale of young lovers with stars in their eyes; instead, the story focuses on the providence of God's love and on the comfort found in human love.

I. The Providence of God's Love

Our scripture is another whimsical chapter in the story of God's love for God's people. As our story begins, Abraham sends a trusted servant back to his homeland to find a wife for Isaac. Abraham's servant, who is doubtful that this journey is a good idea, prays to his master's God for a sign of the steadfast love he has heard so much about. If God truly loves Abraham, the servant prays, let the girl who is to be Isaac's wife provide a drink not only for me, but also for my camel. While it seems at first glance that this is a sensible prayer—after all, hospitality and generosity are characteristics most of us seek in a mate—the reality is a bit overwhelming. The servant had traveled with ten of Abraham's camels. Camels drink up to twenty-five gallons of water at a time. Two hundred and fifty gallons of water means a lot of trips to the well! Only a very generous and hospitable soul would agree to water a stranger's camels "until they have finished drinking."

Fortunately, God had chosen just such a woman to become Isaac's wife. When the servant approached the well, everything happened as he had prayed. His response was another prayer: "Blessed be the Lord, the God of my master Abraham, who has not forsaken his steadfast love and his faithfulness toward my master. As for me, the Lord has led me on the way to the house of my master's kin." Many years before, God made a covenant with Abraham that he would be the ancestor of a multitude of nations. Through the generosity of this girl from Nahor, the faithfulness of a servant, and several gallons of water, God proved once again steadfast love for Abraham and his descendants. Not only did God provide a mother of nations in Rebekah in order to keep the promise to Abraham, but also comfort for Isaac in a time of great sorrow.

II. The Comfort of Human Love

To understand Isaac's role in our story, we must turn back a few pages. Isaac's mother has just died. Perhaps this death turned Abraham's mind to God's promise of descendants. In any case, Abraham has determined that it is time for Isaac to marry. We do not know if Isaac agrees with, or even knows of, his father's plans. The first time he appears in our story, the marriage agreement has already been made. As Rebekah and Abraham's servant journey toward him, Isaac has made his way to the Negeb. While the

Hebrew is unclear, it suggests that Isaac was walking in the fields meditating. This *meditating* carries an understanding of lamenting, or mourning. Isaac is wandering in the fields, thinking of his mother's recent death.

When the servant and Rebekah encountered him there, Isaac brought Rebekah into his mother's tent, where "she became his wife and he loved her." And so, this chapter of the story ends, "Isaac was comforted after his mother's death." In his mother's tent, the place where Isaac first learned of love, he now learned of the comfort love can bring to a grieving heart. May we, too, find comfort in the love of those dear to us, and may we never forget to thank God, whose love provides such comfort. (Melissa Scott)

REALIZING OUR INTENTIONS

ROMANS 7:15-25*a*

I knew it was in the Bible. I heard the preacher say it many times. Jesus wanted us to love others as he had loved us. In fact, this is how people will know that we are disciples of Jesus, that we love one another (see John 13:34-35). I heard and knew all of that, but they did not know Billy. Billy was a bully who made my life miserable at school. For some reason, he had picked me out as the one to tease, harass, and harm. He was big, and he intimidated me. I would try to avoid him, but he would always find me. If someone ever asked me if I loved Billy, I would say no. I hated him.

I felt guilty about that. I knew that I should love him. That is what a follower of Jesus does. I was a follower—so the issue was settled. I was to love him. So, I determined to do just that. I would be nice to him, kind, seeking to help him anyway I could. But it did not work. Billy just laughed at me, picked on me more, kept making my life a nightmare. I knew what I needed to do—to love him—but I just couldn't.

My guess is that most of us have faced that struggle. We know what good Christians are supposed to do—we know the "Law." But, we find it so hard to keep that Law. We should not steal, but we do. We do not mean to lie, but we keep doing it. We intend to clean up our language, but those bad words keep slipping out. We don't want to—but we do.

We can identify with Paul in this passage. He was having the same inward struggle. He knew the Law, what it told him was right and wrong. He intended to do what was right, but ended up doing what was wrong. The battle inside of him to "do the right thing" was painful. He lost that battle too often. The Law looked him in the face and told him what was wrong, but the same Law did not give him the power to overcome that wrong. He felt so helpless and so ashamed of himself. He felt he was a "wretched man" and he wanted to be delivered from that slavery to sin.

This is always the dilemma of discipleship. Knowledge is good, and to discuss what is right and wrong is helpful. However, just to know that some behavior is wrong does not mean we can automatically stop it. A lot of people know the facts about the deadly dangers of smoking, but they find it too hard to break their addiction to tobacco. They want to stop, but they cannot. Good intentions, but no power to accomplish them.

What was Paul's solution? Who could deliver him? "Thanks be to God through Jesus Christ our Lord!" (v. 25). What Paul could not accomplish by his own willpower, Christ could help him accomplish. This was what it meant to be a disciple, that he did not have to follow Christ's way all by himself. Instead, the power of Christ—which comes through the Holy Spirit—would be with him. Paul alone could not do it. Paul plus Christ could.

A preacher once said that he had heard a great description of discipleship. Someone had said, "I fall down, I get up. I fall down, I get up; I fall down, I get up." That is the way it is. We try to serve Christ, and we fail and fail. We go on, then fall again. Here comes Christ—to pick us up once more. Such is the way of discipleship. It is not something we do in our own power; it is something we do with the Spirit's help.

By the way. I finally gave up and asked Christ to help me "love" Billy. I kept trying to be nice, kept taking the punishment, kept praying for help to love. Finally, Billy got tired of picking on me. He said I wasn't fun anymore, and he moved on to someone else. We did not become bosom buddies, but somehow we had a better relationship. Maybe it does work! If we depend on the power of God, we can one day realize our good intentions. (Hugh Litchfield)

STRENGTH FOR THE JOURNEY

MATTHEW 11:16-19, 25-30

This complex passage of Scripture sends most preachers running for commentaries. Douglas Hare's Matthew commentary in the Interpretation series (John Knox Press, 1993) is particularly helpful in sorting through the diverse images and wisdom sayings of this pericope. However, the preachable moment must still come from the preacher's personal insights through study and prayer. And since this passage comes immediately following the American Independence Day, the Great Invitation of vv. 28-30 seems particularly poignant. Resonating with the Statue of Liberty's words, "Give me your tired, your poor," Jesus invites God's followers to come and find strength for the journey alongside Jesus.

Every person knows that sense of exasperation Jesus expresses in vv. 16-19. John the Baptist was criticized for being too ascetic and Jesus for being too much of an aesthete! But God's wisdom is greater than all of that exasperation or conflicting criticism. And that wisdom is known clearly in knowing the Christ. "Learn from me" (v. 29) refers to the wisdom that Jesus shows as well as the wisdom that Jesus preaches, and so Christ's followers are invited to walk with Jesus on this journey, not simply listen to his preaching.

Anyone who has walked on the journey of faith knows that such a journey brings burdens and troubles. This beloved passage may seem at first to offer a promise of release from such burdens, but much like the Statue of Liberty's call to freedom, Jesus' invitation is not a promise of easy roads. Traveling the road of Christian faith, like traveling the road of political freedom, is a journey of challenge and obstacle. But these roads are also journeys of opportunity and hope. The Statue of Liberty promises a country where like-minded souls will travel the journey together. Jesus promises a journey where Christ will be our companion and our guide. God gives us rest by offering the wisdom of Christ and the companionship of Christ. Perhaps the burden is light because Jesus shares the burden with us. Perhaps the yoke is easy because Christ offers compassion and kindness to us in all of the changing circumstances of our lives. And so, the Great Invitation is great indeed, for it is an invitation to share a difficult journey with a God who loves us and walks with us each and every day. (Mary Scifres)

JULY 14, 2002

Eighth Sunday After Pentecost

Worship Theme: The Word of God is like a seed. Let us prepare the soil of our hearts and tend it carefully.

Readings: Genesis 25:19-34; Romans 8:1-11; Matthew 13:1-9, 18-23

Call to Worship (Psalm 119):

Leader: Happy are those whose way is blameless, who walk in the law of the LORD.

People: **Happy are those who keep God's decrees, who walk in the paths of righteousness.**

Leader: Your word is a lamp to my feet and a light to my path.

People: **Accept our offerings of praise, O Lord; teach us your statutes.**

Leader: With my lips I declare all the ordinances of your mouth. I delight in the way of your decrees as much as in all riches.

People: **We will delight in your statutes and we will not forget your word.**

All: **Lead us in the path of your commandments, for we delight in it.**

Pastoral Prayer:
Sower of good seed, spread a generous portion of your Word upon the fertile soil of our hearts. We will contemplate the

gospel, study the Scriptures, and meditate on your will; let no one snatch the seed away. We will let it take root and infuse our whole being; let it not wither. We will remain steadfast in spite of trouble; let it not wash away. We will commit ourselves to the life of faith; let it not be choked by worldly cares. Good Gardener, mold your clay-formed creatures more fully in your image, breathe on us your life-giving breath, sustain us with your radiance and your sweet rain. Out of us may there come an abundance of the fruits of the Spirit that we may live in right relation to our neighbors and to all the earth. Tree of Life, may we be grafted to you and be granted eternal life. Amen. (Scott Haldeman)

SERMON BRIEFS

PARTICIPATING IN GOD'S WILL THROUGH PRAYER

GENESIS 25:19-34

The story of Isaac, Rebekah, and their twin boys, Jacob and Esau, is a familiar one. When it is mentioned, images of parents playing favorites and brothers battling for blessings come quickly to mind. The beginning of the story is a much different one. It speaks of the faith of a husband and wife and of the power and perplexity of prayer. Marjorie Thompson has called prayer "a participation in willing God's will."[1] The prayers of Isaac and Rebekah illustrate this in very different ways.

I. Isaac's Prayer

Isaac and Rebekah's journey of parenthood begins with Isaac's prayer for Rebekah. She had not been able to conceive a child after their marriage. Isaac's prayer was at least partially motivated by his compassion for Rebekah. To be childless in that time was a

---

1. Marjorie Thompson, *Soul Feast* (Louisville, Ky.: Westminster/John Knox Press, 1995), p. 41.

horrible fate for a woman. Isaac must have seen her suffering and longed for its end.

Isaac's prayer also served another purpose. In praying for a child, Isaac reminded God of the promises given to his father. Abraham could not be the father of many nations unless Isaac became a father. By praying for his wife, Isaac was also "willing God's will." God had been faithful to Abraham and Sarah in granting them a child in their old age. Now God showed the same steadfast love to Isaac and Rebekah. God granted Isaac's prayer and Rebekah conceived. When we live in God's will and seek to bring it about, God is faithful to answer our prayers.

II. Rebekah's Prayer

Rebekah's prayer, which follows quickly upon her conception, is a very different prayer from that of Isaac. Rather than praying out of compassion, Rebekah prays out of despair. The children were struggling in her womb, and it seemed unbearable. Rebekah even wondered why she should continue to live if it was to be this way. Her prayer may have been out of desperation at her own pain, or perhaps it resulted from the compassion of a loving parent who would rather suffer herself than see strife and pain enter the lives of her children. Whatever her motivation, Rebekah sought out the Lord. Rather than a quiet plea or reminder of God's promise, her prayer was a demand for an answer: "If it is to be this way, why should I live?"

God's answer to Rebekah was very different, but no less certain, than the answer to Isaac. She is the first woman in the Bible to speak to God and receive a direct answer, but that answer was a bit of an enigma. Rebekah must have struggled to understand God's strange words; one brother is to be stronger than the other? My younger son will be master over the older? These words were not words of comfort; they did not serve to ease Rebekah's mind.

However, the response was one of grace and challenge. Grace meant that the weak one was to be chosen over the strong. The challenge to Rebekah was to live with the pain of children who would struggle against each other from the beginning of their lives. While we often question Rebekah's favoritism and collaboration with Jacob, perhaps that was the only course she thought she could take. God's answer to her prayer made clear God's will in the lives of her children. Rebekah's actions may have resulted from her imperfect efforts to "participate in willing God's will."

It is clear from Isaac's and Rebekah's prayers that prayer is a dangerous thing. God is faithful to answer the prayers of those who seek God's will. The responsibility we accept when we pray is to be willing to participate in bringing it about. (Melissa Scott)

THINKING AND LIVING IN FREEDOM AND LIFE

ROMANS 8:1-11

I. Freedom in Christ (vv. 1-4)

In the world, not only is humanity faced with the damaging impact and results of sin, but also the continuing stigma of "condemnation" is commonplace. Condemnation is not from God, who convicts humanity of sin. Condemnation is that continual reminder of our failure from the enemy of our soul. It is a hope-stealing satanic weapon in which a human lives in agonizing bondage to his/her past.

Paul recognizes here that those who are in Christ are not to live in the bondage of condemnation (v. 1). The believer in Christ is "freed" from the law of sin and death. Certainly, Paul was referencing the Old Testament Law's impotence to set the believer free (v. 3), but here we should look deeper to see that the application of God's Law was twisted in condemning humanity to a fate that Christ has reversed. As the power of sin and death controlled and bound the unbeliever, Jesus Christ has set him/her free with the law of the Spirit of life. Through Christ, believers do not live according to the sinful nature (since Christ has condemned sin), but believers live according to the Spirit. That is, the Spirit calls the cadence for our step and the direction for our path.

II. Setting Our Minds Properly (vv. 5-8)

If in the realm of spiritual reality, we are freed from the bondage of the control of sin and death, it remains for us to conform our thinking and viewpoint to this truth. One lives according to the sinful nature if the person has his/her mind set on the desires of that nature (v. 5). In contrast, the person who lives according to the Spirit sets his/her mind on what the Spirit desires. The question is, "What does the Spirit desire in our lives?" The mind controlled by the Spirit is life and peace while the mind after the sinful nature is death and hostility to God, refusing to submit to God, and unable to please God. Therefore, the Spirit imparts life and peace to the mind of a believer, which enables him/her to submit to God and please him. While the greatest part of this process is "God-initiated," the believer's responsibility is to "set" his/her mind on what the Spirit desires.

We "set" our minds, first in negating the wrong thoughts. We do so by taking captive thoughts that are not obedient to Christ and demolishing those that set up against the knowledge of God (2 Cor. 10:5). Second, we "set" our minds by concentrating on the proper kinds of thoughts, those that are true, noble, right, pure, lovely, excellent, and praiseworthy (Phil. 4:8). By thinking the proper thoughts and negating the wrong thoughts, we allow the Spirit to control our lives and we then "live" according to the precepts of life and peace.

III. The Results of Living in Freedom with the Proper Mind-set (vv. 9-11)

The Spirit controls believers as he lives in them (v. 9). The immediate result of the presence of the Spirit in the life of a believer is that his/her body is dead in relation to sin and the human spirit is alive because of righteousness. This dual result of the presence of the Spirit in the life of the believer, then, is death and resurrection. First, sin is put to death. Believers are made righteous in Christ in a positional sense, but, practically, sin is put to death daily by the power of the Holy Spirit. This practical expression of death to sin is the process Paul refers to as a "transformation" by renewing the mind of the believer (Rom. 12:2).

The second result of resurrection is breathing true life into the human spirit. This life is a powerful and vibrant source that flows from the power that raised Christ from the dead! That power is at work in the believer to enliven the human spirit. (Joseph Byrd)

THE SOWER, THE SEED, AND THE SOIL

MATTHEW 13:1-9, 18-23

In this passage, Matthew reports a distinct change in the approach that Jesus uses to teach people about the kingdom of God. While the author records instances of Jesus teaching through the use of analogy and other literary tools in the preceding chapters, this is the first place that Matthew records Jesus teaching in parable.

Using a framework that would have been easily understood by the people, Jesus taught about the kingdom of God. The message from this passage seems to be singular in purpose—to encourage his followers to continue in the work of spreading the message about the Kingdom even when it appears that the work is futile. Faithfully evangelize and tell others about the Kingdom even if you can't see any progress or growth.

The comparison of farming to evangelizing the world is an interesting one. Both tasks are hard, backbreaking, and sometimes thankless. To contemporary listeners the ancient practice of sowing seed without first plowing the ground is foreign. One would think that to get the best possible crop one would first select a good, aerated plot of soil and then sow the seed. Instead, the sower throws the seed with abandon, knowing that some will grow and produce a good crop. The sower threw the seed knowing that it would fall on different types of locations—rocky ground, among thorns, or good, fertile ground.

The ministry of spreading the gospel of Jesus Christ can be challenging. Many people with whom pastors interact will not accept the gift of God's grace. The process of equipping other saints for ministry, to build up the Body of Christ, can be hard. Other responsibilities compete for our attention. The administrative aspect of ministry, time-consuming as it is, has to be done.

Oh, but when a person does receive the gospel with joy and continues to believe in God's grace even in the midst of life's challenges. In my work as a campus minister, sometimes a college or university student contacts me after graduation to say that she has given her life to Jesus and all she wants to do is to live for him. Every now and then I'll receive a written note or e-mail from a student who was active in the campus ministry at Howard University. They write telling me about how they feel God moving in and directing their lives. They write about the call upon their lives. Their correspondence always surprises me because while they were in school, I really didn't see the fruit of my labor. I couldn't see how my witnessing impacted transformation in their lives. Truthfully, there were times when it seemed that they weren't even listening.

Oh, but when the seed grows. Oh, when that crop produces an abundance. What a joy! What a reason to rejoice when a seed grows into a mature plant! What a witness to God's Spirit working through the lives of God's people despite obstacles and circumstances. Humans do the planting. God provides the growth.

Jesus' message to them and to us is that of encouragement. We are to continue the work of ministry even when it appears that the reward is slow in coming. Keep on trying. Keep on sharing the good news about a good God who offers the gift of love, reconciliation, and power to everyone. Keep on planting those seeds, because, after a while, something is going to grow.

While "a first-century Galilean farmer" could have expected a normal crop return of seven and a half bushels for each bushel of seed planted, a tenfold return was considered good. The yield of a crop return of thirty-, sixty-, or even a hundredfold reflects a supernatural blessing upon the work of the farmer. God provides the increase. Get your seeds, go into the field, and start throwing. (Lillian C. Smith)

JULY 21, 2002

Ninth Sunday After Pentecost

Worship Theme: The children of God are heirs with Christ and will receive eternal life—and only God can distinguish the children of God from the children of the evil one.

Readings: Genesis 28:10-19*a;* Romans 8:12-25; Matthew 13:24-30, 36-43

Call to Worship (Psalm 139):

> *Leader:*　　O LORD, you have searched me and known me.
>
> **People:**　**You know when we sit down and when we rise up.**
>
> *Leader:*　　You discern my thoughts from far away and are acquainted with all my ways. Even before a word is on my tongue, O LORD, you know it completely. You hem me in, behind and before, and lay your hand upon me.
>
> **People:**　**Where can we go from your spirit? Or where can we flee from your presence?**
>
> *Leader:*　　If I ascend to heaven, you are there; if I make my bed in Sheol, you are there. If I take the wings of the morning and settle at the farthest limits of the sea, even there your hand shall lead me, and your right hand shall hold me fast. If I say, "Surely the darkness shall cover me, and the light around me become night," even the darkness is not dark to you; the night is as bright as the day, for darkness is as light to you.

People: **For it was you who formed me; you know all about me.**

Leader: I praise you, for I am fearfully and wonderfully made.

People: **Wonderful are your works, O God.**

Leader: Search me, O God, and know my heart; test me and know my thoughts.

People: **See if there is any wickedness in us and lead us in the way everlasting.**

Pastoral Prayer:

Tenderhearted God, we are undone by your love that catches us up and pulls us toward you. You adopt us though we have been untrue and make us heirs along with Christ of your glorious inheritance. You made us. You sustain us. You sanctify us. We try to respond. Our words fail. We find in you a perfect Father. We know you as a Mother who knows all about us and provides all that we need. Hold us close once more. Caress us. Comfort us. Take away our fears. Kiss away our tears. We are at home in you. As your children, we pray boldly. Heal our sick. Save those in trouble. Rescue the lost. Make peace. You are our all in all. Amen. (Scott Haldeman)

SERMON BRIEFS

FINDING GOD IN UNEXPECTED PLACES

GENESIS 28:10-19a

Jacob seems always to have been on his way somewhere. As a young man, that journey took him away from all that he knew, and he took the long way around to come back to the promises given to his grandfather and father by God. Along the way, he encountered God in unexpected places and in unexpected ways. Jacob's journey can help us understand our own more fully.

I. Exiled from the Familiar

As our story begins, Jacob is fleeing the only home he has ever known. He is seeking a wife from among his mother's people, but, more immediately, he is running from the anger of Esau, the brother whose birthright and blessing he had taken. Jacob is no pilgrim; he is an exile. He has little hope that his return home will be a quick one, despite his mother's promise to send for him when it was safe.

How many "Jacobs" we have in our communities today! Sometimes, our exile results from distances we have had to travel for school or work. Many of us can no longer depend on the comfort of an extended family living close by to shelter us from the worst storms of life. For many people, though, exile is a spiritual reality rather than solely a physical state. We wander through life, without a goal in mind, with no belief to sustain us, with no God to guide us. Some of us, like Jacob, have been brought up since birth to know the God of our fathers. Yet, like Jacob, we wander restlessly, until we become so weary we simply cannot go on. Our exile has brought us to a point of hopelessness; the future is too dark for us to see the path ahead.

II. Finding God in Unexpected Places

This was the case for Jacob in his exile, as well. One evening, weary from his journey, unable to see farther along the road because the sun had set, Jacob could simply travel no farther. He stopped near the city of Luz and set up camp. After making a pillow from a stone, he quickly fell asleep. As he slept, he dreamed of a ladder, or ramp, upon which the angels of God were climbing up and down. The Lord appeared beside him, identified himself as the God of Jacob's father and grandfather, and renewed the promises that had been made to Abraham. When Jacob woke from his dream, he proclaimed, "Surely the LORD is in this place—and I did not know it!" (v. 16).

"Surely the LORD is in this place!" What a strange place for God to be revealed; alongside a road, in the camp of a wanderer. Not just any wanderer, either; this was the camp of a deceitful, thieving exile. The very strangeness of this appearance is this story's greatest sign of hope for today; God does not appear only in churches and holy places. Rather, God is in exile with us, journeying with us until we come to the place and the promises God has prepared for us. The things we have done, the people we have been, have nothing to do with where and who God is. If only we could open our eyes and see our world with wonder and curiosity rather than fear and cynicism, we would know that the Lord *is* in this place, wherever we are. We, too, can find God in unexpected places.

There is a final gospel message in this story. God did not merely renew the covenant made with Abraham. He also had a promise especially for Jacob, and for us: "Know that I am with you and will keep you wherever you go, and will bring you back to this land; for I will not leave you until I have done what I have promised you" (v. 15). May we find God wherever we journey, and may we know the peace that comes through God, even in exile. (Melissa Scott)

THE LONGINGS OF THE SPIRIT

ROMANS 8:12-25

There is within us all an insatiable longing for God. For some, that longing is buried deeply in the imagined safety of the heart's interior vault, only to be brought out in times of overwhelming grief or anguish. For others, the longing expresses itself in a quiet, interior piety where the life of the Spirit is nourished in personal devotion. Still others, not content with privatized anything, load the longing for God with activist behavior; marching for justice, feeding the hungry, advocating the rights of the oppressed.

Paul knows where we live; he has our zip code. A careful reading of these verses will not allow us to consign conversation about the work of the Spirit to private speculation. Far from it. Rather here, the entire people of God is the community, the fellowship, the Body of Christ through whom and in whom the longing of the Spirit wrestles with the realities of a world still in rebellion against God.

How so? Though separated from the Christians in Rome to whom he writes, Paul insists we are a community longing to experience radical freedom. We are blessed in the United States to live in a society where freedom of expression is protected and celebrated. Political freedom, however—precious as it is—stands at a distance to the radical freedom from death and all that death represents. So radical is the freedom God gives in Christ, that Paul compares it to fear that grips every life in spiritual "bondage" (v. 15 KJV). Later in his life, Paul would write young Timothy, reminding him that "God did not give us a spirit of timidity [literally 'cowering fear'], but a spirit of power, of love and of self-discipline" (2 Tim. 1:7 NIV). Each member of the Body of Christ, the church, is spiritually a part of the entire community of believers whose longing for God finds uncommon satisfaction in the radical freedom of the Spirit.

This longing of the Spirit, nourished in soul freedom, soon meets opposition from a world longing for radical re-creation. The Spirit's freedom too soon encounters the reality of suffering (vv. 17-18). Truth to tell, none of us can navigate the waters of radical freedom and avoid the storms. Stormy weather is sure to come. For Paul, "suffering" was cosmic, spiritual, unrelenting in nature. Where we may think of suffering in terms of physical pain because of disease or spiritual anguish brought on by grief or broken relationships, suffering in the writings of the New Testament is profound suffering for the faith. Believers suffer because we live in a world at odds with God's purposes. In ignorance, the world is in opposition to the very God whose purpose is to re-create the world in the love of Christ. How ironic.

And yet, "the creature" (v. 20 KJV)—meaning all of us and all God has created—knows the futility, the struggle of life. Even so, God in love has not abandoned any of God's creation to ultimate, final alienation, fear, and death. Rather, the longing of creation for radical freedom will find its fulfillment in "the glorious liberty of the children of God" (v. 21 KJV).

This longing for radical freedom squares off in the ring of public life against creation's longing for re-creation. The environment, social justice, gender equality, violence and violent media, materialism, immorality, and racism (to name a few) are pressure points where the Spirit's longing for freedom meets the world's

longing for power. Believers who are advocates for radical freedom will suffer misunderstanding, rejection, even death.

Finally, Paul insists we live in hope, believing God alone satisfies the deepest longings within (vv. 24-25). Such hope is God's
response to the "groanings" within every life for wholeness, justice, community, and fellowship with God (v. 23). In honest
moments, all of us know what Fred Craddock has rightly called
"the groan": that insatiable, unspeakable, wordless anguish within
that longs for that which only God can supply. Here is where
hope, met personally and experienced profoundly in Christ,
allows us to live "with patience" (v. 25). We live in hope, because
such hope is the evidence of the Spirit's presence and work in our
lives and in the community of believers in which we find our
Christian identity. (Timothy L. Owings)

PLUCKING OUT WEEDS

MATTHEW 13:24-30, 36-43

The topic of who is in and who is out is an age-old one. Even
in the church, good Christians like to assign folk to the "righteous" or "unrighteous" category. Any number of items can dis-
qualify a person from God's kingdom in human eyes—skin color,
hair color, hairstyle, sexual orientation, socioeconomic class, past
history, present associations, and so forth. The list is limitless.
Sometimes church folk can be the most eager to throw someone
out of the worshiping community. But in this parable about the
weeds, otherwise known as the wheat and the tares, Jesus provides readers with an insight of God's restraint and patience
related to membership or presence in the Kingdom.

This passage and the interpretation of the parable, found in
verses 36-43, are judgment parables. As judgment parables they
provide unique insight. In verses 24-30, the kingdom of heaven is
compared to a field. The farmer has planted good seeds of grain,
but some tares, planted by an enemy, grow among the wheat.
Tares are not alien to wheat fields. They gravitate to them. Tares
are various types of weeds found in grain fields. Instead of having
the undesired weeds immediately removed from the presence of

the wheat, the farmer decides to wait until the plants are mature, fearing that premature harvesting might damage or destroy the desired plants.

It is interesting that the farmer did not enlist the help of the servants in the collection of the weeds. Even though they noticed the misfits in the fields, the farmer did not deem the servants up to the task of weeding the field. Instead, the harvesters would do the job. Could it be that humans do not have the capacity to judge other people? To be honest, every Christian resembles a tare now and then. But, to ensure that most, if not all, of the good seeds grow to maturity, the farmer allows some weeds to coexist with them. Judgment will one day come, and the weeds will be pulled from the ground and destroyed.

Only God is able to determine who is out and who is in. Judgment belongs to God alone. God is loving and patient enough to wait it out. Although tares cannot turn into wheat in the fields, within the church and in life, maybe some tare-like folk can be transformed into the likeness of Christ—inspired by interaction with some of God's wheat in the world.

The interpretation of the parable takes on a slightly different twist in verses 36-43. While the first passage encourages readers not to judge people but to continue to grow in faith in a world buffeted by evil, this passage seems to challenge believers to make sure that they remain faithful and live appropriately as people of faith. Matthew could possibly be using this parable to counter a libertine movement within the community of faith. It seems that some believers felt that they were free from restraint— moral or religious—and could act in any way.

In this passage Matthew emphasizes the reality that Jesus has the power and authority to enact judgment upon the church and the world. In the words of the spiritual, believers are told, "You better mind." It is the Son of Man who "sows the good seed." It will be the Son of Man who will send angels to pluck out the weeds, which have grown up in the midst of the Kingdom, the church. Even if children of the evil one show up and try to disguise themselves and their actions under the mask of Christianity, judgment is coming. (Lillian C. Smith)

JULY 28, 2002

Tenth Sunday After Pentecost

Worship Theme: God's reign has commenced; when we catch a glimpse of it we give up everything we have to enter into it.

Readings: Genesis 29:15-28; Romans 8:26-39; Matthew 13:31-33, 44-52

Call to Worship (Psalm 105):

Leader: O give thanks to the LORD and call on God's name.

People: **Tell of God's deeds among the peoples.**

Leader: Sing praises to God; tell of all God's wonderful works.

People: **Glory to God; we praise God's holy name.**

Leader: Let the hearts of those who seek the LORD rejoice.

People: **We lift our voices in praise to the Lord.**

Pastoral Prayer:

Wondrous Ruler, whose reign has begun yet is hidden, we seek the treasure. We catch glimpses of justice, visions of peace, and we yearn with you for their fullness. Give us another foretaste. Set the banquet before us. Bring in the hungry, the poor, and the lost. Fill us. Redeem us. Make us whole. Steadfast Lover, who has promised never to let us go, we rely on your presence in times of trouble. Heal us and all those who are sick. Comfort us and all those who suffer. Rescue us and all those who are persecuted. Let nothing separate us from you. Amen. (Scott Haldeman)

SERMON BRIEFS

WHAT GOES AROUND COMES AROUND— OR DOES IT?

GENESIS 29:15-28

Every year, I gather with a group of friends to watch the Christmas classic *It's a Wonderful Life.* Most of us greatly enjoy the movie and look forward each year to our gathering. However, one friend insists each Christmas that there is something fundamentally wrong with the film. He has no problem with the happy ending of the story, in which George, the hero, finds out how important he is to the people of his town, and Clarence, the angel, finally earns his wings. His problem is with Potter, the villain of the story. Although Potter does not succeed in his plan to ruin George, he is never arrested for, or even accused of, his evil deeds. My friend insists that this is unjust!

Next year, I will point him to today's scripture; I think this is a story he would definitely enjoy! Jacob, the ultimate trickster, finally receives a dose of his own medicine. The story begins in chapter 25 of Genesis. There, we read of Jacob's deceitfulness and greediness. Rather than offering food to a starving Esau, he sells a bowl of stew for his brother's birthright. When he finds it is time for his dying father, Isaac, to give Esau a blessing, he conspires with his mother to trick Isaac into blessing him, instead. Later, on his journey, he agrees to worship and follow God, *if* God will provide for him. Our scripture today tells of the time when Jacob, who lived by his wits, was finally outwitted.

Upon arriving at his uncle Laban's home, Jacob quickly falls in love with Laban's daughter Rachel. He agrees that he will work for his uncle for seven years in order to earn the right to marry Rachel. At the end of the seven years, a wedding does indeed take place. However, the next morning Jacob realizes that he has been given the wrong daughter in marriage. Leah, rather than Rachel, shares his tent.

There can be little question why this story was remembered through the generations by the Israelites. Stories of people "getting what is coming to them" have delighted us for years. They resonate with our sense of fairness. Many good laughs must have been shared by the Israelites as this tale was repeated around the campfire. And yet, the story has a more positive purpose than to make us feel that the trickster finally got what he deserved. It shows that human love and service can counter human deception.

Jacob was furious when he discovered the deception! He had given seven years of labor in order to be wed to the woman he loved. When he confronted Laban, Laban dismissed the deception with a weak reference to the customs of his country. "But," he said, "I will gladly give you my younger daughter in marriage as well—if you will work another seven years." Many would have been tempted to give up at this point. Working seven more years for a man who was so deceitful would be more than many could bear. However, Jacob loved Rachel. That love was strong enough to bear seven more years of work. It was even strong enough to cause some changes in Jacob's deceitful nature. He and Rachel were married the next week. Jacob could have taken his wives and belongings and fled. After all, he had a history of running from his problems. Instead, he stayed and worked the seven years he had promised.

The story of Jacob's marriage to Rachel is, of course, a story of "what goes around comes around," but it is also a tale of the powerful effect of loving and being loved. Perhaps after reading these verses, my friend will see that love does not always seek what is just; rather, it shows us that we must seek the best in ourselves and others. (Melissa Scott)

IN ALL THINGS—GOD

ROMANS 8:26-39

Paul makes no apologies for his own spiritual uncertainty. Here is a good word for preachers in this postmodern moment of history. Why? Because postmoderns glorify the uncertainty of every-thing. Truth is relative, values situational, and morality floats in the murky waters of fickle feelings. So how do we respond with hope to life that is ever-changing, always challenging, seldom pre-dictable?

For one thing, we admit up front, as Paul does (Rom. 8:26), that we are dependent on the work of the Spirit, mindful we have an incomplete grasp of complete reality. Herein is our "weak-ness"; we simply cannot fully comprehend the big picture. The good news invites us in our weakness to come clean with God, to be honest with ourselves, to confess our limitations.

How so? By first facing confessionally what we "do not know." Namely, "we do not know what we ought to pray for." Rather than collapsing under the weight of ignorance, Paul lifts up the work of the Spirit who "intercedes for us with groans that words cannot express." Here is a provocative idea for perplexing times. Where postmodernity would have us cower under the cloud of uncertainty, believers stand to their feet by faith, aware of the Spirit's work, bringing us through the noxious vapors of relativism into the freeing reality of "the mind of the Spirit."

It is here, having confessed what we "do not know" that Paul declares what is a certainty to him: "in all things God works for the good of those who love him, who have been called according to his purpose." It is in the midst of "all things" that God is always at work in the lives of those heeding that call to live for and by higher purposes.

And what are those purposes? Paul asks the question for us. "What, then, shall we say in response to this?" (v. 31 NIV). Shall we say "cynicism"? Or, "resignation"? Or, "retreat"? No. "If God is for us, who can be against us?" The good news about God is simply this: God is for us! How do we know this? Paul again anticipates our question. Verses 32-36 contain no less than five rhetorical questions, ending with Paul's quotation of Psalm 44:22, which he uses to voice the perspective of those who would col-lapse under the weight of persecution, cynicism, and despair.

"No!" cannot negate strongly enough Paul's insistence that we are not pawns on the chessboard of a failed experiment by God. Rather, "we are more than conquerors through him who loved us" (v. 37 NIV). Furthermore, we are conquerors because in "the love of God" we find our very existence, our being, our life in "Jesus Christ our Lord."

This text has many entry points for the preacher. Rather than a fatalistic "all things are good"—utter nonsense standing near the shadow of the cross—Paul calls believers to see God at work "in all things" even when all we can utter is a painful groan. The believer is not called to understand all things, but rather to live in hope through all things.

A second approach is to work from the end of the text backward. Introduce the sermon by asking, "Is there any experience in life beyond the love of God?" For some, death is such an experience. Loss numbs us and drives us to question God's love, God's care, God's purposes. At the opposite end is life. At the top of one's game, enjoying prosperity, the love of God, for some reason, is unnecessary. Where is the love of God in the present? Can we trust God in the future? These are the kinds of questions our text asks of contemporary life.

A third door into the text is the center of the text. God, who "did not spare his own Son, but gave him up for us all" (v. 32 NIV) forces us in two directions. On the one hand, we must come to the place of confessing our faith—what we "know"—in which we live believing God is at work "in all things." Our Lord's life, death, and resurrection are the foundation of such a confidence. On the other hand, we face the harsh realities of life that are often unforgiving, brutal, death-dealing. In both places, we lean our lives against God "who is for us" and in whose love we find a new and affirming way of doing life as conquerors empowered by the risen and present Christ. (Timothy L. Owings)

THE KINGDOM OF GOD

MATTHEW 13:31-33, 44-52

It should be easy to understand the Bible, or so you'd think. While there are times when the truths of biblical passages just jump out, there are other times when I have to wrestle with the text for meaning. This passage is one example of this. When I first read the passage, I remember saying to myself, "Oh, I understand," only to say a few seconds, minutes, even hours later, "What is this passage trying to communicate?"

At first glance, the parables about the mustard seed and the yeast seem to relate to the growth of the Kingdom. The Kingdom experiences a small, almost insignificant beginning, but surprisingly grows gradually into a large kingdom. The Kingdom does grow, but these parables deal with the contrast of the beginning and culmination of God's kingdom. If we take a closer look, we find even more.

These parables are similitudes. A similitude is a type of parable that uses familiar experiences to tell a story. Its familiarity to the original hearer conveyed a truth that could not be disputed. These parables reflect the use of *mashal*, a rabbinic technique of teaching in a way that would tease the mind of the hearer into deeper understanding. The hearer/listener has to wrestle with the text to comprehend the depth of its meaning.

How is it that a mustard seed, the smallest of all seeds, becomes a tree? Biologically speaking, a mustard seed should mature into a shrub, not a tree. A seed of a daisy, planted in the ground, grows into a daisy. A tulip bulb grows into a tulip, not a rosebush. But in this parable, the mustard seed becomes a tree— a tree in which the birds nest. Birds were images used to refer to Gentiles. In this parable, Jesus teaches that the kingdom of God will grow tremendously and will include, in the end, Jews and Gentiles.

A bushel of flour is a lot of flour. Anyone who has ever picked a bushel of vegetables—greens, tomatoes, and so forth—knows that a bushel of anything is a significant amount. It is heavy. Imagine working a little bit of yeast into a bushel of flour. Imagine waiting for it to grow and then being surprised at how high it rises. When the dough has risen and been baked it will feed a large crowd. In both instances, something supernatural happens. Human effort could not affect the outcome.

The kingdom of God, although it seems to have had a small beginning, will grow into something that will be hard to fathom. The kingdom of God will include and embrace numerous people, even folk deemed "undesirable" by the establishment. When the

kingdom of God has completely broken in, there will be a celebration feast for everyone who has made their home there. Do
not be fooled, although it seems that evil abounds, and that God's
kingdom is losing ground; hold on. In God's time, the end will
come. (Lillian C. Smith)

SPIRITUAL PREPARATION

❦

AUGUST

I grew up in an area that was farmland; now it is suburbia. My grandparents lived next to us, and we would often go there and play. The area surrounding their house was wooded, with lots of expanse to play in. They also had a huge attic that we would roam around and rummage through. It was delightful, and part of its attraction was that we could get lost, be by ourselves . . . or so we thought. Years later, after I had moved away, after both of my grandparents had died, I walked around their property, and into the house. No one lived there any longer. That day I made two discoveries: first, the house was much smaller than I remembered, and the attic was tiny! It was just a few easy steps from almost anywhere in the house to that attic. And second, the woods in which we played were *right next* to the house, and quite observable from a number of windows. I may have thought that I was miles away from anybody else, but in reality I was within sight of the adults in that house at all times.

Of all of the Psalms, the 139th is one of my favorites. It is one of the most personal of the Psalms. It focuses on a person and his or her relationship with God. It is the kind of conversation we rarely have with someone else, perhaps a spouse or a close friend or mentor, but when we have the conversation we never forget it. It is a psalm about the nearness of God. Augustine, one of the great saints, bishops, and teachers of the early church, said it well: *"God is nearer to us than we are to ourselves."* The 139th Psalm speaks of a God who is nearer to us than we might imagine.

I want to offer three affirmations about this *God who is nearer to us than we are to ourselves*, and within those affirmations I want to suggest three corresponding convictions about us as pastors.

The first affirmation is that God is our *Creator*. The psalmist writes:

It was you who formed my inward parts; you knit me together in my mother's womb. (Ps. 139:13)

God is our Creator; God shapes us and forms us. The psalmist continues:

My frame was not hidden from you, when I was being made in secret, intricately woven in the depths of the earth. Your eyes beheld my unformed substance. (v. 15)

This Master designer, this *God who is nearer to us than we are to ourselves*, has created each one of us, and this affirmation carries with it a belief about ourselves, expressed in the scripture as well: *I am fearfully and wonderfully made. Wonderful are your works!* (v. 14).

God is our Creator. God calls us to use our gifts, to be who we are and not someone else. The temptation is to try to emulate the legendary pastor of the congregation we are serving, or to copy the styles of those pastors who receive wide acclaim. This psalm reminds us that God *creates* us.

- Have you ever wished that you had the gifts of another pastor? Can you claim, as God's gift, some distinctive strength that is in your own life?

There is a second affirmation: God *leads* and *guides* us. The psalmist writes again:

You search me, you know me

. . . if I settle at the farthest end of the sea your right hand shall lead me

. . . you lead me in the way everlasting. (vv. 1, 9, 24)

Who are your guides in this life? The psalmist points to the One who creates us and knows us, *who is nearer to us than we are to ourselves*, as the One who also guides us. God is the One who knows the future. And God is the One who leads us into the

271

future. Even pastors who plan their futures, or attempt to, can hear this as good news!

This belief about God connects with an important need for us: to claim and use the tools that Christians have traditionally used to find the way forward: *prayer, Christian friendship and spiritual direction, the Bible*. It is unthinkable that a pastor can know God's guidance and direction apart from speaking and listening to God, sharing with and hearing from a trusted Christian friend, knowing how God has led his people in the past, by allowing Scripture to speak.

I want to touch on Christian friendship for a moment.

It is important that we allow Christian friends to be our guides, especially those persons who are farther along the path than we are, who can be our friends and mentors. Alister McGrath writes: *"There is a great* 'cloud of witnesses' who have wrestled with the issues of Christian living . . . and that we can learn from them. [As someone has put it] we are like dwarves sitting on the shoulders of giants. We see more things than them, and things that are farther away—not because we can see better than them, or because we are taller than they are, but because they raise us up, and add their stature to ours."

Christian friends—sometimes they are pastoral mentors to us—guide us; they help us to see our way forward more clearly.

- Can you recall a mentor who has been a guide to you? Can you offer a prayer of thanksgiving for that person?

There is a third affirmation: *God promises to be with us wherever we are.*

We are not alone. The psalmist asks: *Is there anyplace I can go to avoid your Spirit? f I climb to the sky, you're there! If I go underground, you're there!"* (The Message).

Two of the most remarkable days of my life are vivid reminders to me of this truth. One day was spent in the lowest city in the world, the oldest city on earth—Jericho, where Joshua fought; Jericho, where Jesus met Zacchaeus. Another day was spent sailing on Lake Titicaca, which borders Bolivia and Peru, the highest lake in the world, almost fourteen thousand feet in altitude, the bluest water I have ever seen.

In the geography of the spirit these days are symbolic of this truth that God is with us. *Because God is nearer to us than we are to ourselves!*

If I ascend to heaven, the psalmist prays to God, you are there. If I go into the depths of sheol, you are there. As pastors we can become isolated, but we are never alone. God is with us. *God is nearer to us than we are to ourselves.*

I invite you to say this affirmation:

> *God created me. I am wonderfully made.*
> *God leads and guides me. I will follow Jesus.*
> *God is with me. I am not alone.*

(Ken Carter)

Source: Alister McGrath, *Beyond The Quiet Time*, p. 9.

AUGUST 4, 2002

Eleventh Sunday After Pentecost

Worship Theme: Jesus, though in a state of grief himself, feels compassion for the crowd, heals their sick, and multiplies meager fare to satisfy their hunger.

Readings: Genesis 32:22-31; Romans 9:1-5; Matthew 14:13-21

Call to Worship (Psalm 17):

Leader: O LORD, attend to my cry; give ear to my prayer from lips free of deceit.

People: **From you let my vindication come.**

Leader: If you try my heart, if you visit me by night, if you test me, you will find no wickedness in me; my mouth does not transgress.

People: **My steps have held fast to your paths; my feet have not slipped.**

Leader: I call upon you, for you will answer me, O God; incline your ear to me, hear my words. Wondrously show your steadfast love, O savior of those who seek refuge from their adversaries at your right hand.

People: **Guard me as the apple of the eye; hide me in the shadow of your wings.**

All: **Let us worship God.**

Pastoral Prayer:

Praise Jesus. He shows compassion. While retreating from the crowds to mourn his friend John, he sees people coming to him for help and is moved to heal and teach. We lift our sick before you now. Heal them. While healing, Jesus sees the hunger of the people and is moved to feed them. From five loaves and two fishes comes enough for everyone and more besides. We tell of our hungers now. Fill our stomachs and our spirits. Be the Bread of Life for us. Take our meager resources and multiply them to feed the hungry near us and more besides. Praise Jesus. He is compassion. He laid down his very life for us to reconcile us to God and each other. We name those with whom we need to be reconciled. Break down the barriers that divide humanity. Show us how to lay down our lives. Bring peace. Praise Jesus who is our Christ, and who with God and the Spirit reigns over all with compassion and mercy. Amen. (Scott Haldeman)

SERMON BRIEFS

CHALLENGES AND BLESSINGS

GENESIS 32:22-31

This story of Jacob wrestling by the river Jabbok resonates deeply with many who hear it. It is more than the story of two "men" wrestling; it is even more than the story of the people of Israel and their tumultuous relationship with God. It is the story of each person who chooses to accept God's offer of relationship. The story tells, in a very few words, all that God does for God's people. In the struggle of life, God brings peace to those who are troubled and troubles those who have become too complacent.

All of this happens in the all-night wrestling match described in today's scripture. Jacob began this solitary, restless night full of fear. He was not sure what the next day's meeting with his brother would bring. As he wrestled with the "man" by the river, he wrestled also with his doubts and fears. Toward morning, Jacob had every reason to be content in his own power. He knew that he could continue this wrestling match for much longer.

God, however, knew that Jacob's assurance was destined to bring him trouble. "Let me go, for the day is breaking," the divine wrestler said. When Jacob would not heed the warning, God struck him on the hip trying to get away. This was not done out of anger, but out of love; God was concerned that Jacob would not survive seeing God's face (Exod. 33:20).

Often, God acts in a such a way with us. When we become too sure of ourselves, when we become content that we have a hold on God, God acts to show us our foolishness. The struggle of trying to know God is an important part of our faith. When we believe that we know God fully, God must act to show us that such knowledge is impossible. While we may not bear a physical reminder after such struggles, we will not escape untouched.

God's touch on Jacob's thigh did not end the struggle. At Jacob's insistence, God also gave Jacob a blessing. This was a special blessing, one that only God could provide—a new name. While Jacob had become confident during the struggle, the old fears were still clinging to him. He knew that this divine being with whom he wrestled could allay his fears and doubts and bring him peace. He continued in the struggle, not knowing the outcome, but knowing that the encounter itself was vital. God chose to bless his persistence in the confrontation with a new name. No longer would this one be called Jacob, the supplanter. Now, he would be Israel, which means, "the one who strives with God" or "God strives." Upon receiving this new name and blessing, Israel realized with whom he had been wrestling. "I have seen the face of God," Israel declared.

The dual meaning of Israel's name points to the nature of his, and our, relationship with God. Although God indeed strives and works for God's people, it is equally important that we are people who strive with God. God is committed to staying in the struggle. God will provide blessings and remonstrations to us as we need them. Our task is to continue the endeavor of knowing God more fully. Then, God will always work with us, as with Jacob, to comfort the afflicted and afflict the comfortable. (Melissa Scott)

WORLD IN CONFLICT

ROMANS 9:1-5

Life often moves us to extremes. The moment of great triumph too soon leads to the moment of deep depression. Mood swings are no stranger to the human species. The highs of success are often followed by the lows of failure and doubt. Having praised God for God's limitless love (Rom. 8:37-39), Paul now comes face-to-face with the reality of his own people's distance from Christ. What about the fate of people who refuse to acknowledge, much less receive, God's love in Jesus Christ? Paul, apostle to the Gentiles, is in anguish over the fate of his people, the Jews. To wrestle with this text is to plumb the depths of troubling and provocative questions.

Believers live in two worlds, two realities, two stories. More starkly defined today, the two stories in which we live collide with each other. One is the story of acquisition, the other the story of generosity; one the story of security, the other the story of sacrifice. Paul, whose personal struggle tumbles out of Romans 7:7-25, now confronts the struggle to reconcile the good news of Christ with the tradition and heritage of his own people. In midsentence, Paul blurts out, "I could wish that I myself were cursed and cut off from Christ for the sake of my brothers, those of my own race" (v. 3 NIV). We are overhearing a man freed from his past, but still haunted by the implications of the gospel for the future. "Who shall separate us from the love Christ?" (Rom. 8:35). At one level, Paul says convincingly, "Nothing!" What does the preacher do with this text?

Paul is sitting at a desk in a room in one of the port cities of western Turkey. At his feet are bags of money he has collected from the churches in Macedonia and Achaia—modern Greece—for the poor saints in Jerusalem. On the desk is the parchment on which he is writing the Letter to the Romans. By his own witness in Romans, he longs to go to Rome, but must accompany the offering for the saints in Jerusalem. He will send the letter to Rome by one of the ships at anchor; he will board another ship at anchor for Caesarea, and from there travel overland to Jerusalem. Paul is torn between Rome and Jerusalem.

Like Paul, we struggle with the demands placed on us by the two worlds in which we live—we are pulled in two directions. As believers, we are the children of God, citizens of God's kingdom. "Jesus is Lord" is far more than a casual confession; it is both the gospel reality into which we have been born again and the relationship through which we know God. On the other hand, we live as residents of planet earth, members of a common humanity in rebellion against God. We are, in Paul's words, part of a reality that is in a "bondage to decay" (Rom. 8:21), crying out for God's liberation and God's peace. Believers who take their confession "Jesus as Lord" seriously know Paul's anguish.

Second, the "truth in Christ" compels us to struggle with the present and future destiny of unbelievers. This is not the stuff of pleasant conversation or relaxed musing. Believers who live in two worlds know in the depths of their being that the future of all earthly kingdoms is precarious at best. More than any time in recent memory, the church must face the stark and bleak future of all who say a defiant "No" to God's love in Christ. Hell, so often portrayed as a place of punishment and separation, is also a present reality experienced through despair, depression, abandonment, abuse, and the deadly consequences of reckless lifestyles and self-centered choices. Paul's struggle is ours to the degree we name in love the bleak future of those who refuse God's love in Christ.

Finally, the text suggests that God is working to bring about the redemption of all creation, including those who reject the good news of Christ. Paul's litany of the Jewish people's heritage in verses 4 and 5 is a sobering reminder that God is not without a witness to God's faithfulness. As Paul reminded the Romans earlier in his letter, God's world bears witness to God's power and majesty (Rom. 1:19-20). Here—through Israel, the patriarchs, the Law, the covenants, and so forth—God continues to bear witness to God's desire that all humanity be saved. Caught up in his own rhetoric, Paul breaks into doxology: "God over all, forever praised! Amen." Even though Jews and Gentiles reject the good news in Christ, God's love is eternally faithful. (Timothy L. Owings)

IN HIS SALAD DAYS

MATTHEW 14:13-21

The end of the last century was decried as the "triumph of the therapeutic." Things haven't changed all that much in this century, either. Self-help books proliferate on bookstore shelves. We've grown complacent or apathetic in our attempts to be creative and imaginative at home by letting Martha Stewart and her clones pervade our culture through television, books, and magazines. While more and more of us believe in God, according to the latest polls, people attend mass healings in megachurches, while buying the more difficult aspects of Christ's story beneath guilt, fear, and sentimentality.

In this story, we are confronted by a mass healing, a therapeutic session rather than salvation. From a cynical viewpoint, it may very well be true that the therapeutic has triumphed over salvation. Yet, in keeping with the remainder of Matthew's Gospel, healing must take place prior to one's becoming whole.

Could similar thoughts have been on Jesus' mind while he was in the boat alone? Had he stolen himself away because of John the Baptizer's recent demise? Or was he merely getting away to a desolated place to sort things out, put his ducks in a row, and carry out a well-laid plan? Jesus was obviously a rising star; otherwise, the crowds would not have followed him as they did. Was he running away—shades of the prodigal son—only to hesitate in the moment of realization that his place was back with the crowds, no matter the cost, and to return with resolve? Like the setting sun that drops beneath the horizon only to rise more brilliantly the following morn, Jesus turned back to continue his Promethean task of embodying the good news.

Somehow, he rediscovered his resources. In contrast, the poor disciples were not nearly as resourceful as their teacher, especially since their Master is the source of all—though the twelve have yet to acknowledge and claim the fact. They doubt. They are materialists, proto-empiricists who insist on the knowledge of a person or thing before accepting its veracity. "We don't have enough ingredients to fix five thousand–plus fish sandwiches," they exclaim. "We're helpless!" Poor hungry beggars.

279

This scenario calls to mind the story of a restaurateur named Caesar. It had been a busy week at his eating establishment, and the food service truck would not arrive for another couple of days. The dining room was full of hungry patrons. The cooks were upset because they had nothing to prepare. How could they feed the clientele? Mr. Caesar entered the kitchen, toasted some bread, collected lettuce and a block of parmesan cheese, anchovies, some eggs, balsamic vinegar, olive oil, Dijon mustard, Worcestershire sauce. These he carried along with a large wooden bowl into the dining room. With a flourish that only his quick thinking and panache could pull off, he created on the spot the very salad we know today as the Caesar salad.

Everyone—from the five thousand–plus followers after Jesus to the crowd in Mr. Caesar's restaurant—was duly impressed. All ate and were satisfied. (Eric Killinger)

AUGUST 11, 2002

Twelfth Sunday After Pentecost

Worship Theme: God confounds human wisdom, using the young to lead the old, offering the grace of the covenant with Israel to Gentiles, inviting us to walk on water.

Readings: Genesis 37:1-4, 12-28; Romans 10:5-15; Matthew 14:22-33

Call to Worship (Psalm 105):

Leader: O give thanks to the LORD and call on God's name;

People: **Make known God's mighty deeds among the peoples.**

Leader: For God is mindful of his covenant forever, the covenant that he made with Abraham, his sworn promise to Isaac, which he confirmed to Jacob as a statute, to Israel as an everlasting covenant, saying, "To you I will give the land of Canaan as your portion for an inheritance."

People: **Then they were few in number, of little account, and strangers in it, wandering from nation to nation.**

Leader: But God allowed no one to oppress them; he rebuked kings on their account, saying, "Do not touch my anointed ones; do my prophets no harm."

People: **For God is faithful; God's promises are sure.**

All: **Let us worship the Holy One of Israel.**

Pastoral Prayer:

God of the Dreamer, who chooses a youth to save a family, who sets brother against brother, who bestows authority on one sold as a slave, confound us again this day. Overturn our structures of governance that exclude those who are deemed unacceptable. Open our ears to the voices of the marginalized and maligned. Shock us with your vision of power, the cross. Creator of earth and sky and sea, who calms the wind and walks on water, call us out of our lifeboats of false security again this day. Dismantle our respect for solely the rational and scientific. Open our eyes to the metaphoric and poetic. Challenge us with tests of faith. Rescue us when we succumb to doubt. Savior of all the earth, who makes a people from those who were no people, who reaches beyond the boundaries of nations to call those far off to your salvation, broaden our vision of your reign. Destroy our petty barriers to your Word. Enlarge our sense of mission. Confront us with those we have excluded from our communities. May your new age dawn. Amen. (Scott Haldeman)

SERMON BRIEFS

THE POWER OF DREAMS

GENESIS 37:1-4, 12-28

Do you remember those warm days, just before summer vacation, when the sole purpose of a classroom was to provide a place for you to daydream? I visited many places and lived many lives during those hours when my teachers were trying to instill in me the love of quadratic equations. Most of those dreams never came to be, although a few were even better in reality. All of them played an important role in the person I became.

Dreams are powerful. They take us out of our everyday lives and give us visions of a new way of being. While all of us have had dreams of some sort, there are those among us who are dreamers by nature. They take those new places they envision seriously. Faith is a matter of course for such people. To most of us, such faith is silly or scary. When confronted with such dreamers, we react in very predictable ways. The story of Joseph and his brothers exemplifies how the world often treats dreamers.

Joseph, like many seventeen-year-olds, was a dreamer. Like many dreamers, he wanted to share his dreams with the people he loved most, his family. Unfortunately, his brothers did not appreciate the dreams, which pictured Joseph in a position of power, with them kneeling before him. As is often the case, the dreams heightened the tension already present. In this case, the brothers' jealousy of their father's favorite son grew even more intense.

Soon after, Jacob sent Joseph to find his brothers, who were tending the flocks. When Joseph approached his brothers in the field, they said, "Look, here comes this dreamer! Let us kill him . . . and we shall see what will become of his dreams."

How often our society has treated dreamers this way. The most famous dreamer of our century, Martin Luther King Jr., was assassinated by those who could not imagine living in a world of equality. We are often guilty, too, of killing dreamers in more subtle ways. When we repeatedly say to a child, "Don't be ridiculous; you could never do that!" we kill the person they might have become. When we stand by quietly and watch injustices being committed around us, we are conspiring to kill the dreams of thousands who pray for a world of love and mercy.

If you remember the story, you know that Joseph's brothers did not kill him; instead, at the request of Reuben, they simply placed him in a pit in the wilderness. Many in our community would rebel at the title "dream-killer," and some would be correct in denying that name. However, each of us has been guilty of putting dreamers and dreams away where we will not be bothered by them anymore. When we quickly turn the channel at the first sight of a suffering child, we are putting them out of our minds and doing away with their dreams for shelter and a warm meal. When we ignore the cries of those who feel neglected by the church, we are putting away their dreams for "one body, united in Christ." When we do not follow a path we feel God has set before us, we are putting away our own dreams (and God's) for a better place.

While this story shows us clearly how we often respond to dreamers, it also teaches us a valuable lesson about dreams.

When Reuben returned to take Jacob from the pit, he was gone, having been sold into slavery. Not until the brothers knelt before Joseph's throne in Egypt many years later did they come to realize the truth about dreams and dreamers. They are not easily killed or put away for long. God grants dreamers the special gifts of vision and faith. If we seek to recognize these gifts rather than putting them away, then we shall truly see what will become of these dreams. (Melissa Scott)

RADICAL GOOD NEWS

ROMANS 10:5-15

Like Romans 9:1-5, this text has as its implied reader the Jews who do not believe the good news of Jesus. Read this text carefully and discover Paul moving from a reflection on the Law (vv. 5-7), to direct address—"you" (vv. 8-13)—to the more impersonal "they" (vv. 14-15). As delicately as Paul writes, trying to convince his unbelieving kinsfolk of the radical nature of simple faith in Jesus the Messiah, he cannot escape the soul anguish that gnaws within him. His is a burden that will not and cannot be lifted.

So what does he do? First, he appeals to the Law by referring to Leviticus 18:5. Rather than being simply a "head trip," the Law requires one to embrace a lifestyle governed by faith. The Greeks called Judaism a philosophy rather than a religion, because Jews lived by the words they spoke. Jews observed the Sabbath, ate kosher food, circumcised their male babies, lived together among themselves, and refused to pay homage to Caesar (a special exemption given them by Julius Caesar some forty years before the birth of our Lord). To be a Jew in the eyes of a pagan world was to embrace a Jewish lifestyle.

Second, Paul directly addresses his people by engaging in a dialogue using the diatribe form. "Do not say . . . ," "What does it say . . . ?" suggest a conversation. Here, in verses 8-13, Paul moves to the heart of the matter. The unspoken question to Jews and Greeks alike is: Who is Lord? Like Moses addressing the people as recorded in Deuteronomy 30:12-14, Paul speaks to the Jews who live so close to the Canaan of new life in Jesus Christ.

Reflecting Paul's earlier argument in Romans 3:21-23, Paul drives home his conviction that God's righteousness is at work in the human heart only by faith in Christ. To confess with one's lips "Jesus is Lord" is hard-wired to the heart's transformation by faith (Rom. 10:9-10). Everyone who trusts God by faith is God's child (v. 11 quoting Isa. 28:16). Jews and Greeks alike are saved by calling "on the name of the Lord" (v. 13, a quote of Joel 2:32).

Having cited the Law (Leviticus and Deuteronomy) and the Prophets (Isaiah and Joel), one can almost hear the change in Paul's voice as he now faces his own responsibility to his people. The apostle to the Gentiles knows in the depths of his soul that "they" have not believed because they have not heard. Why? Because they have not had anyone to tell them the good news (vv. 14-15). Catching himself in mid-sentence, he brings into his own contemporary experience and struggle the words of Isaiah 52:7, "How beautiful on the mountains are the feet of those who bring good news" (NIV). The unspoken question is: Who will do the preaching?

The preacher has several options bubbling out of this text. I mention two. The first flows from verses 5-10. Evangelism, in many quarters of mainline Protestant churches, has been the shunned stepchild of preaching. Yet every road running through postmodernity cries out for someone to speak good news. Like Paul's first-century readers, we are in daily dialogue with people who embrace multiple and less-than-satisfying lifestyles. Vainly, contemporary individuals try to "ascend to heaven" as if we can bring the divine to earth. In the affluent northern hemisphere of our globe, we have constructed economies and social structures attempting to bring humanity into the golden age fueled by information and connected by the Internet.

The good news we preach invites exhausted and frustrated men and women to heart transformation through simple faith in Jesus Christ. The law of contemporary life leaves relational and spiritual wreckage in its wake. God offers a new future and a new community in which to live. That future belongs to all who dare to say, counterculturally, "Jesus is Lord."

A second sermon opportunity appears in verses 11-15. "Everyone" may be the most misunderstood word in contemporary conversation. In these verses, Paul uses "everyone" twice, both celebrating the good news that God makes no distinction between Jew, Greek, anyone. Inclusivity, as defined by some, suggests a blurring of human differences hummed to the mantra of political correctness. The gospel's radical redefinition of inclusivity admits there are differences between "Jew" and "Greek" while championing God's gift that such differences are not barriers. The Christian gospel does not say we are all the same. To the contrary, we are male and female, Jew and Greek, rich and poor, educated and uneducated. Everyone has a place at the table. Rather than blurring our differences, the gospel celebrates them under the one lordship of Jesus Christ. (Timothy L. Owings)

FAITH IS . . . GROWING DOWN

MATTHEW 14:22-33

This is a piquant story of rootedness. Peter has "to go down" before coming up. Rise and fall. This is one of life's most prevalent themes. The thing is, however, *how* we fall. Author James Hillman reminds us that the style of coming down "remains the interesting part." How we *grow down* is the journey each of us must make to find the kingdom within.

Peter must get out of the boat. We have to get out of the house, off the couch, away from the TV, computer, and telephone to discover how gravity attracts us to put down roots.

We have to acknowledge and then confess and profess we are children of God. Peter wanted so much to become part of the brotherhood of Jesus' followers, that he requested permission to come into fellowship with the Christ by walking upon the water. Peter often was a bit hasty. You might know someone like that; someone who is eager to please, zealous to participate in whatever interests you might have, but more often than not needs to be rescued from himself or herself.

Sometimes we have trouble entering the household. We don't like the rotten branches of the family tree or the fruit they bring forth. In another Gospel story (John 21:20), Peter puts his foot in his mouth in expressing concern/angst/jealousy over the anonymous disciple's tagging along. In this instance, Jesus reprimands the rock upon whom the church would be built.

We need to find that place in life that suits our souls, whether it be in our own skins, in the wilds of Africa, on the university campus, at home, or wherever it "feels good" to live, move, and be. By the very nature, we long to be with God. Peter wanted to be with Jesus, but for some reason or other, his soul didn't feel at home on the water without his boat between it and himself. Coupled with the ferocious storm, it's little wonder Peter's psyche was tormented; thus, his "falling" was not particularly graceful—or faithful.

And here we find the good news, don't we? If we place our trust, however small, in the Lord, no matter how far we fall, our going down can be full of grace and hope. If we fall in hope, then God's love for us is made that much surer. The others immediately realize Jesus as being truly rooted in God.

Jesus' going down was not yet fully accomplished. A cross and a tomb awaited his final going down that would see his glorious rising. Likewise, Peter had yet to face the last part of growing down in his leadership of the church: his giving back to the world that which God had invested in him. And that is our lot in life: to allow our roots to be attracted by the gravity of God's heavenly kingdom; to acknowledge our place within the family of God; to live such that our souls are content in and with how we live, move, and are in the presence of God; and to reciprocate by offering our lives to the world, lives that God has invested in each of us. (Eric Killinger)

AUGUST 18, 2002

Thirteenth Sunday After Pentecost

Worship Theme: God responds to our persistence in prayer and in good works.

Readings: Genesis 45:1-15; Romans 11:1-2*a*, 29-32; Matthew 15:(10-20)21-28

Call to Worship (Psalm 133):

Leader: How very good and pleasant it is when kindred live together in unity!

People: **It is like precious oil poured upon the head, oil that runs down upon the beard.**

Leader: It is like the dew of Hermon, which falls on the mountains of Zion. For there the LORD ordained his blessing, life forevermore.

People: **We gather together to reconcile ourselves to God and one another. Let us praise the Lord!**

Pastoral Prayer:

All too-human Christ, we marvel at your choice to live among us, to share our struggles, to accept the limitations of one human life bounded by time, place, and body. You, who accepted torture and suffered execution to reconcile us to God, refused to heal the Syrophoenician woman's daughter until she boldly challenged you. We place our petitions before you with boldness this day, trusting that you will respond. Visit all the world's people with healing power. Renew the face of the whole earth with peace and justice. Let every child, woman, and man eat their fill and rest in a place they can call home this day. Bend swords into plowshares and spears into pruning hooks; let us practice war no more. Restore each one's dignity; let your very image show forth in every person's face. O Brother Christ, O Mother-God, love us with an everlasting love and bring us home. Amen. (Scott Haldeman)

SERMON BRIEFS

THE GOSPEL OF JOSEPH

GENESIS 45:1-15

Genesis 45 presents the end of a very long story. Joseph, who was sold into slavery by his brothers as a teenager, is now the chief minister of Egypt. Through a series of adventures in which Joseph repeatedly relied on God's help, he has now risen to this position of great power. When Joseph's brothers appeared before him to request food, they did not recognize him. He knew them immediately and remembered the dreams he had dreamed so long ago. Joseph could have chosen to punish his brothers for their terrible actions. Instead, he chose a different way. This is the story of great power, but it is not Joseph's power as governor that is central to the story. Instead, the power of love, of forgiveness, and of God makes this a gospel story.

I. The Power of Love

Although Joseph quickly recognized his brothers, he did not reveal himself to them. Instead, he set out schemes against them. On their first visit, he accused them of being spies and insisted that their youngest brother (the only other son of Rachel) be brought to him before he would give them food. On their second trip, he planted a silver cup in their bags and accused them of theft. However, each time his emotion overwhelmed him. On his first trip, he not only had their sacks filled with grain, he placed their money back in the sacks. On the second trip, he could no longer keep up the pretense of anger about the cup. He must know how his father and brother are; it is love for them that

289

motivates him to reveal himself. Love is more than an emotion; it is so powerful that it causes us to act in the best interest of those we love, even if they have harmed us.

II. The Power of Forgiveness

When Joseph finally revealed his identity to his brothers, they were distressed and dismayed. They must have remembered Joseph's dreams, which had angered them—dreams in which they were bowing before their brother, just as they were now. They feared retribution for their hateful actions against him so many years ago. Joseph understood that reunion with his family could only come with forgiveness. Rather than reaching out in anger, he embraced his brothers. This dreamer-turned-ruler demonstrated the fullest power of forgiveness. It is the most true demonstration of grace when we choose to forgive those who are weaker than we are. We are commanded to claim the power of forgiveness by the example of Joseph, who understood that God has given us the task of reconciliation.

III. The Power of God

Joseph's ability to forgive his brothers was a result of his understanding of the power of God. He assured his brothers that he was not angry and asked them to forgive themselves. He could do this because he saw a greater purpose in the events of his life: "God sent me before you to preserve life." Joseph knew the truth that Paul later proclaimed in his letter to the Romans: "In all things God works for the good with those who love God, who are called according to his purpose." The story of Joseph, then, is a gospel story, one in which God acts so that life, rather than death, abounds. (Melissa Scott)

NEVER GIVE UP

ROMANS 11:1-2*a*, 29-32

If Romans 9–11 forms the heart of Paul's letter, this third and last chapter of the section finds the apostle still in turmoil about the fate of his people. With sweeping finality, Paul declares, "God did not reject his people (v. 2a) . . . for God's gifts and his call are irrevocable" (v. 29a). Okay. I can accept that. But Paul does not stop—he rarely does. Rather, he goes on to say again what he has already said in Romans 3:23 ("all have sinned") by declaring God has consigned all humanity to disobedience—we are all in the same boat—for the purpose of showing mercy to all humanity—we are all equally loved.

What do we do with this text? Mind you, Paul will go to his grave longing for all Israel to be saved (Rom. 11:26). Likewise, he longs for all Gentiles to come into the experience of the grace of Christ (Rom. 10:13). Such longing for the salvation of others offers the contemporary church a challenge and a gift.

The Bible, rather than candy-coating human life, shows the human predicament without apology. The sweeping story of the Bible is of creation and the human family moving away from the God who created it in love. Eden is not a story of God rejecting humanity, but rather a story of humanity attempting to take God's place, banishing God from our present and our future. Rather than a world abandoned by God, the story of Jesus tells us God has so invested God's self in human life, God became human, born of a human mother. Like Paul, we are all descendants of people like Abraham; we all struggle with the meaning and purpose of life (Rom. 11:1). Abraham knew disappointment, ambiguity, betrayal, even death. Throughout his life, however, he did not give up on God, nor did God give up on him.

Mercy is God's gift to all who turn to God in faith. Rooted in the legal system, mercy suggests pardon, forgiveness, acquittal, redemption, a new beginning. God says we can begin again. How strange, in this moment in human history, to hear Christians joining the naysayers and brokers of gloom. For some believers, the answer is withdrawal. Put your children in private schools or, better yet, homeschool them lest their ears be filled with godless secularism. Huddle together in Christian Bible study groups, prayer meetings, weekend retreats—all designed by Christians for Christians. What discretionary time we have from the labors that pay the bills, some believe, ought to be spent in Christian fellowship, far from the maddening and death-dealing crowd.

Is that what Paul is saying here? Read the text again. The disobedience of fallen humanity, rather than being God's work, is rather God's opportunity to show lavish mercy to all who turn to God. Our job, as people who have drunk deeply of grace, is to infiltrate this culture with radical mercy, uncommon love, sacrificial involvement. Next time you read in the newspaper of an inner-city shooting, school violence, work-related crime, public mismanagement of funds, ask "Was there any Christian presence in that place?" It was Jesus who said, "You are the salt of the earth."

If God has not abandoned God's people the Jews, or the human family, why are we in the Christian community abandoning our schools, government, neighborhoods, and families to live in a world without mercy? Frank Pollard, pastor of Jackson, Mississippi's First Baptist Church, wisely put his finger on the problem when he said: "Jesus called us to be in the world and not of it. Most Christians today are of the world and not in it."

Wrestle with this text and let it wrestle with you. God's passion for creation and all humanity in creation is to demonstrate generous mercy, surprising grace, transforming love. If God has not abandoned the human family, we who say "Jesus is Lord" would be wise to get busy helping God infiltrate the world for which Christ died and rose again. (Timothy L. Owings)

UPPITY WOMEN OF FAITH, UNITE!

MATTHEW 15:(10-20) 21-28

I once bought my mother a bumper sticker, which she has tacked to the bulletin board by the phone in her kitchen. It reads, "UPPITY WOMEN OF THE WORLD, UNITE!" If bumper stickers were in existence back in Jesus' day, this Canaanite/Syrophoenician woman our Lord encountered in today's Gospel reading surely would have had one on her cart.

Even the disciples thought her bothersome. "Master, do something with her, for she is fast becoming a nuisance!" they cried. It wasn't that she was a woman. That wasn't the problem. Jesus had many female followers. From what the Gospels tell us, he encouraged women to participate in the life of the Kingdom, for he recognized their self-worth and saw that they often knew more of the mystery of God than the men did. The problem lay in the fact that this particular woman, anonymous though she must remain, was not an Israelite. She was Syrophoenician, a Canaanite—Greek, according to some. She wasn't part of the immediate program.

But, wait a minute! Jesus has been proclaimed—by his immediate followers *and* the demons he's exorcised, at any rate—to be the Son of God! The Gospel of John reminds us that Jesus was the Word of God, specifically, God in the flesh. This idea, while not a fully flowered admission in Matthew's version of the good news, is still implicit and necessary to the story. If Jesus is indeed the Christ, he and God are One. If that is so, then as Lord—and (dare we admit?) Father—Jesus is our connection to what is outside us as well as what is inside us, i.e., the kingdom of heaven.

"Master, do something about this woman. She's driving us mad with her persistent outcries!" Oh, how they begged and pleaded with him to take care of the situation. It was more than these fishermen and tax collectors' little faith and "delicate" sensibilities could handle.

I hope you can admire her persistence. She's like a woman with the twelve-year history of hemorrhaging who pushed through a crowd of well-wishers and followers to touch the hem of Jesus' robes, believing she would be healed for having done so. The Gospel of Luke recounts one of Jesus' parables, which told of a woman who kept pestering a certain judge to render a verdict on an issue of dire importance to her. She kept badgering him until he had to give in to her wishes.

This Canaanite woman (Syrophoenician in Mark) does much the same thing. She spars with Jesus until he can no longer refuse her desire that her daughter be healed of whatever demon has gripped her. This woman recognized Jesus' connectedness to the glory of our Father in heaven, and it resonated within her. With so strong a faith, it was all she could do but come to Jesus for the sake of her daughter's well-being. She understood that through Jesus her daughter could be healed and whole again.

So, uppity women, unite! Find the Christ in your life. Healing and wholeness are at hand. (Eric Killinger)

AUGUST 25, 2002

Fourteenth Sunday After Pentecost

Worship Theme: God saves and yet we participate in our salvation, as the women who draw Moses out of the water make possible the escape of Israel from slavery through the sea.

Readings: Exodus 1:8–2:10; Romans 12:1-8; Matthew 16:13-20

Call to Worship (Psalm 124):

All:	**If it had not been the LORD who was on our side . . .**
Leader:	when our enemies attacked us, they would have swallowed us up alive.
People:	**If it had not been the LORD who was on our side . . .**
Leader:	when their anger was kindled against us, the flood would have swept us away, the torrent would have gone over us, the raging waters would have drowned us.
People:	**Blessed be the LORD, who is on our side.**
Leader:	We have escaped like a bird from the snare of the fowlers; the snare is broken, and we have escaped for the LORD is on our side.
People:	**Our help is in the name of the LORD. Blessed be the LORD.**

Pastoral Prayer:

Liberator, Pharaoh, having forgotten Joseph, enslaved the Hebrews, but you heard their cry for deliverance. Deliver us from the bonds that confine us in lives of shallowness and lead us to live in abundance and with compassion. Liberator, the Egyptians benefited from the labor of slaves yet grew afraid of the strength of their captives; you hardened Pharaoh's heart and brought the nation into crisis. Deliver us from lives that depend on the exploitation of others and help us to live in harmony with the earth and in just relation to all the world's peoples. Liberator, Pharaoh ordered the death of boy-children to weaken the Hebrews; you sent your servants, Siphrah and Puah, ordinary midwives, to subvert the orders of the king. Deliver us from complicity with evil and all children from violence and help us to accomplish acts of resistance small and large that foster life. Liberator, Moses was under threat, but you preserved his life and called him out of the halls of power to be a leader of his people and to break the chains of bondage. Deliver us from forces that threaten us and lead us on a path of righteousness that we might serve you and our neighbors, bearing your good news to all. We pray in the names of God who liberates, Christ who is our Messiah, and the Spirit that goes before and behind leading us to the promised land, one God forever. Amen. (Scott Haldeman)

SERMON BRIEFS

GOD'S UNGALLANT HEROES

EXODUS 1:8–2:10

Have you ever wanted to do the right thing when the odds against you were too great? Have you ever wanted to take a stand for something you believed in strongly, but you didn't have the strength or the clout to pull it off? In our text today we meet some people I call "God's ungallant heroes." These people did what was right, but without the fierceness or drama we normally associate with heroes.

We all know and love God's gallant heroes. We think of Peter and John before the Sanhedrin, refusing to obey the council's order and saying "We cannot keep from speaking about what we have seen and heard." We think of Polycarp, one of the early Christian martyrs, who stood before the governor and refused to renounce his faith. We may think of Sir Thomas Moore, who died a traitor's death because his conscience would not let him sign the Supremacy Act, which made Henry VIII the head of the church in England. We certainly think of Martin Luther King Jr., and Rosa Parks. They took a bold public stand and suffered for doing so. All these folks, and many others, acted gallantly in the cause of right. They stood tall, spoke with conviction, and paid the price.

Not all heroes are so gallant. One that comes to mind is Oscar Schindler. His efforts to save Jews from the Holocaust were both noble and good. Outwardly, though, he made a pretext of supporting the Nazi war effort. He had to, of course. If he had taken a public stand and denounced the evils he saw, he would have simply disappeared and saved no one.

We meet more such heroes in our biblical story. First, we meet Shiphrah and Puah, the Hebrew midwives who disobeyed Pharaoh's order to kill newborn males. They did what was right. No one can deny their courage, for they put themselves in danger by their actions. When questioned, though, they offered a lame excuse, one Pharaoh may have seen through. They were in no position to stand up to Pharaoh. That would not have saved lives. So they kept a low profile, weaseled out of responsibility, and did what was right. The text explicitly states that God rewarded them.

Second, we meet Jochebed and Miriam, the mother and sister of Moses. When Jochebed could no longer hide her baby, she placed him in a specially prepared basket and floated it on the river— surely an act of desperation. When the baby was found, she became the nanny for her own son through deception. She looks far more opportunistic than gallant, but she, too, was rewarded.

These women are heroes—God's heroes. They did not make a grand scene, and they did not play from a position of strength. Nevertheless, they are worthy of our respect and emulation. They did what was right, despite everything. Contrast their actions with those of Pontius Pilate, who also wanted to avoid consequences, but who thereby failed to do right. Not everyone, after all, is a hero. Many people let circumstances become an excuse for sin. Too often we hear, "I was just following orders."

Our goal, our calling, is to gallantly stand for what is right. When possible we must unite witness and action, and few will be the times when we truly cannot. This message, therefore, is not an excuse to lie low and avoid criticism for a stand we should take. We must remember, however, that God sometimes relies on ungallant heroes. God can use *you* to do good in this world. Do not worry about making a good show, just do right. Therein lies heroism. (David C. Mauldin)

TRANSFORMED FOR OTHERS

ROMANS 12:1-8

This text, often preached as a call to individual purity, is actually a summons to the entire church to corporate transformation. The plural nouns and verbs jump out from the text: "you," "brothers," "sacrifices," "many," to name but a few. Here is a text brimming with possibilities for the preacher willing to tackle the narcissistic, self-absorbed culture in which we live.

The text has three convenient moves: *worship* (vv. 1-2), *humility* (vv. 3-5), and *gifted service* (vv. 6-8). First, the church is the living, sacrificial body of believers offering spiritual worship to God. Unlike the self-centered worship of the pagans, Christian worship is radically corporate. Paul admonishes us "to offer your bodies as living sacrifices, holy and pleasing to God." Temple Judaism and Greek-Roman paganism were no strangers to the power of sacrifice. The drill was simple: an individual offered an animal to a priest, who slaughtered it and roasted it on an altar. We know from Romans and Corinthians that one of the problems early Christians faced was the eating of sacrificial meat sold in the marketplace (Rom. 14:13-21; 1 Cor. 8:1-13).

Rabbinic Judaism, with its locus in the synagogue, countered the individualistic leanings of cultic Judaism with the communal reading of Torah, the Prophets, the hearing of a lesson or sermon, and prayers. Rather than being clergy-led, synagogue worship was lay-led and profoundly corporate.

The early church soon expressed Jesus' death on the cross in sacrificial language (Rom. 5:6-8). As a result, the church's worship moved from being focused on the offering of individual sacrifices to the offering to the risen Lord of believers as a gathered body, God's people on earth (one can hear this idea in the prayer's "Our Father" and "forgive us our trespasses as we forgive those who trespass against us"). For believers, worship is a way of being living sacrifices "transformed by the renewing of your mind." Christian worship is not a "feel good" hour from which we receive a week's worth of spiritual painkillers. Rather, worship is the sacrificial giving of ourselves, the offering to God of our lives, with the prayer that God's transforming work will confront us with the selfish, loveless existence passing for our so-called life. Christian worship is often painfully transformative, bringing our stubborn wills into conformity with God's will, yielding our narrow minds to the expansive, inclusive mind of Christ, offering our self-centered definitions of the good to the One who alone is good, even Jesus our Lord.

The text soon shifts to the results of Christian worship: humility and service. Verses 3-5 remind us that worship, rather than filling us with spiritual superiority in order to "out pious" others, actually brings us to our knees in order to receive others as Christ has received us. This, Paul says, is a "grace."

Granted, we are individuals. Paul never suggests the good news of Christ obviates or diminishes our unique personhood. To the contrary. Having offered our bodies as living sacrifices corporately, we have an individual responsibility to each other to honor, esteem, and affirm our brothers and sisters as joint inheritors, equal recipients of grace. Authentic humility flows from a life that deeply knows its gifts and its limitations. There is no place in the Christian family for either self-effacing piety or bombastic pride. Both negate the power of grace and bring reproach on both Christ and the Body of Christ, the church. Worship is both a window into the glory of God and a mirror in which we see ourselves as redeemed, saved children of God, who have in our common humanity the one denominator that binds us to each other and our risen Lord.

Worship that produces authentic humility also leads to generous service. Verses 6-8 contain Paul's laundry list of spiritual gifts as he understood them in the context of the church in Rome. Not unlike the Corinthian list of gifts (1 Cor. 12:7-11), these manifestations of the Spirit present in Rome differ in kind. Whereas the Corinthian gifts included such graces as healing, miraculous power, prophecy, discernment, and tongues, the Spirit's gifts to the Roman community seemed to be prophecy (or preaching), serving, teaching, encouraging, financial giving, leadership, and showing mercy.

Here is a good word for the contemporary church. While some would have us walk in lockstep theologically or articulate the gospel to our communities uniformly, Paul declares that the Spirit's gifts are summoned from believers in service to the world and each other. Worship, humility, and service in Christ's name mark the Christian church as belonging to Jesus Christ, her risen and present Lord. (Timothy L. Owings)

WHAT'S IN A NAME?

MATTHEW 16:13-20

I still chuckle over an editorial cartoon our newspaper carried some months ago. It was set during the presidential primaries, which coincided with the popularity of the television quiz show *Who Wants to Be a Millionaire?* The cartoon emcee asked an anonymous candidate, "Who wants to be the president?"

In our Gospel reading today, we find Jesus putting a question to his disciples. It seems appropriate, as their perception of Jesus' special kinship to God is budding. "Who do people say that the Son of Man is?" he asks them.

A number of images spring to mind. Some say Jesus is the reincarnation of John the Baptizer. With John dead, who else but Jesus could assume his mantle? Others say Jesus is Elijah, one of the great prophets whose mighty works astonished the people of his day, while some make a good argument to the effect that Jesus favors Jeremiah or one of the other prophets. Not a bad assessment, since Jesus was often unwelcome within his own community, as his prophetic predecessors had been.

"Okay. Now who do *you* say that I am? asked Jesus, putting the 64,000-denarii question to them.

Peter, who usually waded right in without first thinking to test the water, plunged in, saying, "You are the Christ, the Son of the living God!" Thinking of the quiz show *Who Wants to Be a Millionaire?* host Regis Philbin might have asked, "Final answer?"

"Congratulations!" exclaimed Jesus—for that is the ball park meaning of this beatitude—"congratulations, Peter, you figured it all out—not from any audience's help but from the revelation of my Father in heaven." What's happened? Not surprisingly, the Christ living in Peter helps him to see that Jesus is the One through whom we connect to what is outside of us, that which is beyond and seems distant to us but is in reality very much within and among us.

Now, it may be that we have been misreading ever so slightly the next bit wherein Jesus announces his plans to build the church. Peter has recognized Jesus as the Christ, the Son of the living God. He has been given a glimpse of Jesus' true nature, his *raison d'être,* by the grace and power of God the Father Almighty. In turn, Jesus identifies this disciple as Peter. Peter, of course, means "rock" in both Greek and their common tongue, Aramaic. When Jesus announces, "On this rock I will build my church," he is not referring specifically to Peter, the man; rather, Jesus is referring to the foundational acknowledgment Peter makes of Jesus as the Christ. It is Peter's *confession* of Jesus as Christ and Son of the living God on which the church is to be built.

Earlier in Matthew's Gospel, Jesus has already alluded to this very thing:

> Everyone then who hears these words of mine and acts on them will be like a wise man who built his house on rock. . . . And everyone who hears these words of mine and does not act on them will be like a foolish man who built his house on sand.

The bulwark of our faith is the confession that Jesus is the Christ. What's in a name? More than we know. (Eric Killinger)

SPIRITUAL PREPARATION

❧

SEPTEMBER

With September comes Labor Day, a day on our national calendar when we celebrate the work of men and women. Fittingly, it is a day of rest. For many, Labor Day is a holiday. Labor Day gives us the opportunity to reflect on work and rest, action and contemplation.

The Christian tradition has always valued both work and rest. The divine character of work is expressed in the saying *laborare est orare*, to work is to pray. Men and women who are created in God's image live out their vocations through daily work: this is foreseen in the ancient command: "Be fruitful and multiply, and fill the earth and subdue it; and have dominion over the fish of the sea and over the birds of the air and over every living thing that moves upon the earth" (Gen. 1:28).

The Jewish and Christian traditions have also placed a great emphasis on rest and Sabbath. In the experience of Sabbath, we are refreshed and renewed; we "catch our breath." On the Sabbath, we acknowledge that God creates and orders the world, and that life goes on even as we cease our own activities. Observance of the Sabbath is a sign of our faith and trust in God's providence. The Sabbath is also a reminder of our limitations: we cannot do it all, we are not superhuman.

- What is the relationship between work and rest in your own life? Do you value both work and rest? Do you perceive a spiritual significance in your work and in your rest?

The great theologian Karl Barth offered this commentary about work and rest:

> If man has created neither heaven nor earth nor himself; if he does not owe his existence to himself, but to the will and act of

him who bestowed it on him without his slightest cooperation; if his ability to work is not his attainment, and therefore his own property, but a free gift; if his obligation to work is not his invitation but God's commission, then he cannot and should not imagine that what is going to become of him, his future and that of his fellow man, lies in his power.

Christians, and perhaps especially pastors, have always held these two facets of life in tension. We are called to work and to rest, to labor and to contemplate. The fullness of ministry, and indeed life, is found in the wholeness of the seven days, working and resting. Pastors are sometimes tempted to neglect this pattern established by God. When we do, the result is often brokenness. All work and no rest leads to suffering within the body, mind, spirit, and community. Robert Calhoun of Yale once spoke of the "antiphony of work and worship," and indeed they constitute a natural rhythm. When out of balance, however, there are physical, economic, and spiritual consequences. The absence of work, of course, can be humiliating and dehumanizing. The absence of rest and Sabbath can also express a lack of trust and security in God's providence and can lead to physical illness and spiritual burnout.

I serve as pastor of a local church. My own experience of the past few years is that the fall is the busiest time of the year. School begins, and activity levels rise. The stewardship campaign begins. In my own tradition, The United Methodist Church, there are preparations for charge conference, which is the way we are held accountable to the denomination. The rising activity levels add to fatigue. The stewardship campaign and charge conference contribute some anxiety. The usual demands of preaching, teaching, and shepherding continue. And there is always the knowledge that just over the horizon are Advent and Christmas. For me, pastoral ministry in the fall is like running a marathon!

In such a time it is easy to lose the delicate balance between work and rest, action and contemplation. This temptation is common, for the work is always there to do. But there is a cost. If we are always working, we are not resting.

The charge to rest, to refuel, is a sermon that many of us need, whether we hear it from our spouses, our physicians, or a preacher. But there are more reasons to keep the Sabbath. Keeping the Sabbath is also an act of faith, a gesture of trust. The Sabbath is an important part of our heritage as God's people.

Walter Brueggemann has noted two critical motivations for keeping the Sabbath in an age of restlessness. We are called to rest as God rested in the act of creation (Exod. 20:11), and we are to remember, in the midst of Sabbath, "the liberation that permitted new life" (Deut. 5:15). Brueggemann observes that "the two motivations, creation in Exodus 20 and liberation in Deuteronomy 5, hold together the ordered life of God and the just intent of human life. To keep the Sabbath is to engage in an activity that holds together, sacramentally, the life of God and the life of the world in liberation."

On Labor Day, we pause to consider the meaning of work and its relationship to rest. As we begin the fall season of ministry, this relationship, this balance, is crucial.

- Take a moment to look at your fall calendar. Can you find breathing spaces, times to rest and to be re-created? Can you schedule a time, perhaps a day or two, for prayer and contemplation?

If we are rested, if we are prayerful, then our work begins to take on new meaning. We rediscover the mission to which we have been called. We are more creative. We take part in God's liberation in human lives.

Enjoy the Labor Day weekend. Reflect on your own work as a prayer to God. Seek a balance between active ministry and passive resting. Discover an ordering of a week that includes six days of work and one day of rest. (Ken Carter)

Sources: Karl Barth, *Church Dogmatics*, III, IV (Edinburgh: T & T Clark, 1975), p. 54; Walter Brueggemann, *Finally Comes The Poet* (Minneapolis: Fortress Press, 1989), p. 92.

SEPTEMBER 1, 2002

Fifteenth Sunday After Pentecost

Worship Theme: God hears our cry for deliverance and sends help, telling us the divine name so we will know who is our Savior, showering gifts upon the community, leading us in the way of the cross and bidding us follow.

Readings: Exodus 3:1-15; Romans 12:9-21; Matthew 16:21-28

Call to Worship (Psalm 105):

> *Leader:* O give thanks to the LORD, make known God's deeds of power.

> *People:* **Sing to the Lord; tell God's wonderful works.**

> *Leader:* Jacob and Rachel and Leah, and their sons and daughters, came to Egypt; Israel dwelt in the land of refuge. And the LORD made the people fruitful, made them stronger than their foes, whose hearts turned to hate the people, who dealt craftily with God's servants. The land of Egypt became a land of bondage for Israel.

> *People:* **In due time, God sent Moses, Miriam, and Aaron to rescue Israel from slavery. God brought God's people out of bondage.**

> *Leader:* Give thanks to the Lord for deeds of power.

> *People:* **Sing to the Lord; tell God's wonderful works.**

Pastoral Prayer:

Holy One of Israel, you tell your name to Moses so that he can lead your people out of Egypt. Hear the cry of your people once again. Mark us as your own. Lead us from prison to promised land. Gather all the nations at your holy mountain so we might live in peace. Crucified and Risen One, you set your face toward Jerusalem, knowing you will die there, and do not turn aside. Walk the way of sorrows with us that we might lay down our lives to receive them back from you. Rejoice at our conversion. Lament our failures and our pain. Assure us when we doubt. Rebuke us when we betray. Welcome us when we come home. Spirit of Wisdom, you fill your people with gifts for the common good. Seal us as priests. Commission us as teachers and leaders and healers. Renew us that we might persevere in your ministry, in the paths of righteousness. God, three in one, blessed are you forever. Amen. (Scott Haldeman)

SERMON BRIEFS

GOD BECOMES KNOWN

EXODUS 3:1-15

Which do you think is more important, *that* a person believes in God or *what* a person believes about God? The difference is important. How many people do you know who do not believe in God? Real atheists. I have to admit I only know about a handful. My experience seems to be consistent with various polls that suggest an overwhelming majority of Americans profess to believe in God. Now think about the people you know who believe in God. How many of them agree about what God is like?

When dealing with God, we must always leave room for different perspectives, opinions, and experiences. Nevertheless, pretty much anything that can be believed about God is believed by someone. Can everyone be right? Or are some views more right than others? The variety of views about God forces us to ask, "What can we know about God? And how can we know it?"

I. The Burning Question

Our text today is one of the great stories of the Bible, the burning bush. Moses meets God and learns God's name. The Bible does not tell us whether Moses was a religious man up to this point. His father-in-law was a priest, but nothing is mentioned about Moses himself. Whatever he was like before, Moses changed when he experienced the burning bush. Whatever he may have thought of God previously, he suddenly knew God in a direct and personal way.

How do we know about God? If we are to really know God, God is going to have to take the initiative. God communicates. God speaks and acts. In this way, God becomes known. We know almost nothing of God except what God tells us or shows us. Here Scripture is important. Moses had this incredible and wonderful encounter with God. As far as I know, no one else has encountered a burning bush that speaks with the voice of God. But through the Scriptures we share in that experience. That's what makes the Bible so powerful. It is how we share in those great moments when God becomes known. Some people say God wrote the Bible. I disagree. God did inspire the Scriptures, but God does not write books. God speaks and acts in history, in our world. The Scriptures are how we share those experiences. We know God through what God says and does. God even acts in our own lives. Given the proper perspective, and informed by the Scriptures, we can sometimes see where the hand of God has led us.

II. Toward an Answer

What can we know about God? The burning bush incident is suggestive, and what we learn there conforms to the whole witness of Scripture.

First, God sees and hears. "I have observed the misery of my people . . . I have heard their cry." This is another way of saying that God knows our circumstances. God is aware of what goes on in the world, and perhaps, God is extra attentive to those who suffer.

Second, God plans and acts. "I have come down to deliver

them," God tells Moses. God knows, and God is involved. In fact, God has a great plan for all creation that is even now still unfolding.

Third, God identifies with people. "I am the God of Abraham, the God of Isaac, and the God of Jacob." God even tells Moses, "I will be with you." God has a people. The relationship between God and God's people is called a covenant. Through baptism, you join the covenant community. In baptism God forever identifies you with Jesus Christ.

Believing God exists is important, but it is at best a first step. Knowing God is the goal. We can know God, at least well enough, because God has become known through God's own words and deeds. (David C. Mauldin)

LIVING AS A HOLY AND PLEASING SACRIFICE

ROMANS 12:9-21

In Romans 12:1, Paul urges his readers at Rome to offer their bodies as living sacrifices that are holy and pleasing to God. Such activity is the reasonable or spiritual expression of worship of God. But how does that get translated into a believer's everyday life? How does one live in such a way that he/she worships God? Romans 12:9-21 catalogs activities that guide the believer to live a worshipful life.

I. Personal Holiness (vv. 9-12)

These verses list the activities that characterize those who worship God. Paul begins with the primary issue of love, a central facet of Paul's pastoral theology. The believer must live so that his/her love is sincere, hating evil, and clinging to what is good. Finding the good in people and circumstances demands pure love that is not motivated by selfish interests. Moreover, such pure love will cause believers to be devoted to one another and honor one another. Devotion and honor are two characteristics often lost in postmodern society. Yet, the Body of Christ stands against the tide of contemporary culture and demonstrates honor toward one another.

Verse 11 exhorts that believers should not lack "zeal" and "spiritual fervor," indicating that the believer has an obligation and ability to increase and maintain a level of spiritual fervor and zeal for ministry in service to the Lord. Fatigue often comes to believers who faithfully toil and serve God, but that fatigue is not to rob believers of the excitement and energy of their faith. Verse 12 lists activities that appear to be expressions of zeal and spiritual fervor. The believer is to be joyful in hope, patient in affliction, and faithful in prayer. Zeal and fervor are then exhibited by the joy, patience, and faith of the believer.

II. Holiness in Relationships (vv. 13-21)

The personal aspects of holiness in the life of the believer are central to his/her ability to relate to others in an appropriate way. It is interesting that Paul takes greater pain and gives more time to articulate the relationships of the worshipful life of holiness. Certainly, devotion and honor with brotherly love are relational, and this is the core from which the remaining relational exhortations radiate. First, believers are to share with God's people in need, and practice hospitality. Both of these activities direct the reader to holiness of generosity toward those around him/her.

Second, Paul directs believers in the appropriate relationship with persecutors. The believer is to "bless" and not "curse." This is a reference to the teaching of Jesus (Matt. 5:44). By maintaining the posture of blessing, the believer avoids allowing bitterness to take root in his/her life. Third, Paul notes that a worshipful life that is holy and pleasing to God is one that rejoices with those who rejoice and mourns with those who mourn. Here is a description of sensitivity to the people around the believer and the believer's expressing the appropriate response.

Fourth, Paul notes that holiness is practically lived out in the lives of believers as they maintain a harmonious atmosphere in their relationships. This calls for each individual to bury pride and conceit and to develop a willingness and love for those with whom he/she would not naturally associate. The mark of the community of God is not divisions and factions, but harmony rooted in love.

Fifth, Paul takes a great deal of time to specifically deal with the believer's response when mistreated. While he has noted that the believer is to bless those who curse him/her, he articulates this even more clearly in verses 17-21. Believers are not to repay evildoers with the same kind of evil, but instead they are to try to do what is "right" in the community of believers. The goal is that the believer is to attempt to live at peace with everyone. The other reason believers are not to repay evil for evil is that avenging God's people is the business of God. The believer's response is one of care for his/her enemy. The concept here is that believers strive to overcome evil with good acts and leave vengeance to God, who will tend to such matters in the arena of judgment. This concept is as much an act of reverence toward God as it is an attitude toward one's enemy. (Joseph Byrd)

"GET THEE BEHIND ME, SATAN, AND PUSH!"

MATTHEW 16:21-28

Now that the confession has been made and the foundation poured for the church, it is time for Jesus' followers to begin coming to terms with the details of why Jesus has come here. In case we've forgotten, Jesus is who he is precisely because he was sent here to save us, to heal our fragmentary lives, and to make us whole, so we become fit for the kingdom of God. The angelic pronouncement at his conception was that he was to be named *Jesus* because his very name meant "one who saves, makes whole."

Jesus' vision for accomplishing his saving mission is met, however, by astonishment and shock. You recall perhaps the old chicken commercial in which Jim Jr., remarks he is going to "cut the fat." Someone overhears him, and word begins spreading throughout the company that people will be laid off. At the general meeting, the owner steps up to the podium and announces they will be cutting more fat—off their *chickens*—much to the relief and cheers of the workers.

A misconstruing of facts occurs in our Gospel reading. Peter doesn't perceive properly what it is that the Christ must do in order to accomplish the goal. After all, Jesus "the Savior" *is* the

Christ. We've identified him as such. He can do anything he wants. He could go out and live his days peacefully in another province. He doesn't have to die. He is the Son of the living God, by golly. And Peter, his head full of rocks, jumps in front of the Master in an attempt to restrain him.

Like a master sergeant, Jesus orders Peter to fall back in with the rest of the troops. "Get behind me, *Satan* (obstacle/stumbling block)." There is no connection here with the Prince of Darkness. I do, however, recall the story of a woman who, whenever she felt sluggish in approaching a difficult task, would say, "Get behind me, Satan, and *push!*"

It is documented that many teaching masters in oriental cultures will slap the face of a student in order for him to reach enlightenment. So it is that Jesus orders Peter back in line. It is done to encourage enlightenment and to pave the way for futher instruction. The journey on which Jesus calls us to accompany him is, after all, a lifelong learning experience. If we think along human lines by trying to save our own souls, we will lose. No kingdom of heaven. Nada. Zip. Zero. On the other hand, if we lay our egos aside, losing ourselves, in effect, for the sake of the Christ, we reap rewards beyond our wildest dreams. We become whole persons for God. (Eric Killinger)

SEPTEMBER 8, 2002

Sixteenth Sunday After Pentecost

Worship Theme: The law of God is to love, so love one another, which at times can mean confronting those who violate the covenant.

Readings: Exodus 12:1-14; Romans 13:8-14; Matthew 18:15-20

Call to Worship (Psalm 149):

Leader: Praise the LORD! Sing to the LORD a new song, praise God in the assembly of the faithful.

People: **We rejoice and praise God.**

Leader: Praise God with dancing, making melody with tambourine and lyre. For the LORD takes pleasure in God's people, adorning the humble with victory. Exult God in the sanctuary, sing for joy.

People: **We rejoice and praise God.**

Leader: Let the high praises of God be heard. For God executes vengeance on the nations and punishment on the peoples, binding their kings with fetters and their nobles with chains of iron. This is glory for all his faithful ones. Praise the LORD!

People: **We rejoice and praise God.**

Pastoral Prayer:
    God of love, who calls the church into being as a community of love, enfold us in your everlasting arms. Come among us and renew our spirits. Lift us up and hold us tight. You sent your

Spirit among God's enemies to deliver your people. Send us among the downtrodden to speak a word of hope. You gave the apostles the power to forgive sin and the duty to confront sinners. Give us a spirit of discernment to name the sins of our day and reform your church into an instrument of your love. Help us confront any who cloak their hubris in piety and any who horde the gifts you have sent to them for the benefit of all. Come among us at last to reign over the new age when all shall sit together at the welcome table and there shall be no more weeping and no more dying. In the name of One who loved perfectly. Amen. (Scott Haldeman)

SERMON BRIEFS

A DOWN 'N' DIRTY, BARE-KNUCKLES BRAWL

EXODUS 12:1-14

The teen class was having trouble with the story of the first Passover. "Wasn't God stooping to Pharaoh's level?" one boy asked. "I mean, the thing that made Pharaoh such a monster was trying to kill the Hebrew boys. Doesn't God just do the same thing?" The killing of the Egyptian firstborn disturbed some in the class. "Why couldn't God find another way to beat Pharaoh? God could have lifted him off the ground until Pharaoh gave in." This last intriguing suggestion came from a boy whose older brother had given him the idea by firsthand experience.

I cannot explain the ethical dimensions of the Passover story to the satisfaction of a half dozen teenagers, so if you were hoping for something in the way of justification for God's actions, I probably won't be much help. That's okay, though. I believe God is fully capable of justifying God's own actions. It is not as though God has to answer to us. But I believe God is loving, merciful, and compassionate. I believe even the wrath of God aims at our redemption. Because of this, I believe that in some way, someday God's justice and goodness will be clearly seen. In the meantime, though, this story can be a tough piece to fit into the puzzle of our faith.

That first boy in my class was right about one thing: God does stoop to Pharaoh's level. This story is essentially about control. God has called a people. God has crafted a nation. The story we read in Exodus describes a battle for control of that nation's destiny. In one corner stands Pharaoh, master of all Egypt. He enslaves this nation. When they continue to prosper, the gloves come off. Pharaoh orders all newborn males be killed.

God, however, stands in the other corner. God is not going to yield before Pharaoh. God fights for this nation God has made. Nine plagues come and go—nine rounds of action. Pharaoh is determined to control this people, but God says, "I will show you, Pharaoh, that I control not just this nation's destiny, but yours as well. *You* will yield to me."

If God can demonstrate control of Pharaoh's own destiny, then God will carry the day. The nation God has called will go forth at God's command to a future that God has prepared for it. So God's gloves come off, too. God gets down and dirty and fights a bare-knuckle brawl in the shadow of the great pyramids. Make no mistake. God alone is God. God alone is our Master, the Lord of our destiny, the crafter of our future.

Much is made of the connection between Passover and the Lord's Supper. After all, the supper Jesus shared with his disciples was the Passover meal, a commemoration of the brawl in the desert. Using it to explain his death, Jesus infused the meal with new meaning and significance. It speaks to us of another time when God got down and dirty, though this time the Father's only Son was the One who died. Because of the profound meaning of the cross and the Resurrection, we experience as much in the Lord's Supper as our senses can handle. We remember Jesus' death. We celebrate his resurrection and coming again. Gratitude pours from our hearts. We feel kinship with every person in the room and every Christian around the world. We experience so much meaning! At least one meaning remains exactly the same as it was for the Passover. God controls our destiny. No one else does. God alone is God. God alone is our Master, the Lord of our destiny, the crafter of our future. Amen. (David C. Mauldin)

CHRISTIAN BEHAVIOR IN THE "LAST DAYS"

ROMANS 13:8-14

This passage deals with practical aspects of the believer living by the Spirit and avoiding living by the desires of the sinful nature. The urgency of this message is demonstrated in the readers' discerning that the end times are near. This understanding and living out the exhortations reflect a spiritual maturity.

I. Understanding the Times (vv. 11-14)

The time had arrived for the believers to "wake up" because the consummation of their salvation was near. Paul is calling for believers to stir themselves from their spiritual lethargy about their lifestyle and their failure to resist the desires of the flesh. How appropriate this message is to our materialistic society today. The warning is that the night is nearly over and the day is almost here, so believers need to have a correct response and posture.

The response of believers in light of the immediacy of the end times is to put aside the deeds of darkness and put on the armor of light (v. 12). This metaphor demonstrates that certain behaviors are characteristic of the darkness. With the impending end times upon us, believers are to separate themselves from the activities that are of the worldly darkness. Moreover, believers are to prepare for spiritual warfare by putting on "armor," a clothing of oneself with the Lord Jesus Christ. Paul does not leave the deeds of darkness open for speculation or potential dilution. He lists the acts to which he refers.

Believers are to behave decently and not be involved in orgies, drunkenness, sexual immorality, debauchery, dissension, or jealousy. In other places Paul gives similar lists. Here, he is pointing out that decency moves opposite of these human activities. The list has an underlying theme of the lack of control. Orgies, drunkenness, debauchery, and sexual immorality describe a person who has lost inhibitions, allowing their carnal flesh or other substances to dictate and control their will. Dissension and jealousy seem to speak to the unbridled emotional and relational aspects of our flesh. Jealousy will cause dissension and work in opposition to the direction of the Holy Spirit in the community of faith. Believers are not to give a great deal of thought to the passions of the fallen human nature, but focus instead upon the Lord Jesus Christ whose return will signal the end times.

II. The Primary Focus for Believers for the End Times

Paul notes that believers should avoid debt, but this is hardly a lesson in budgeting or economics. The one continuing debt that believers are to maintain is that of love for one another. The commandments concerning adultery, murder, stealing, coveting, and so forth are really tributaries of the primary injunction given by Jesus Christ when he told us to love one another. Paul reminds the readers of the words of Jesus to love their neighbors as themselves. Such action does not harm one's neighbor, but truly assists him/her. Thus, when one actively loves his/her neighbor, then the whole law is fulfilled.

How empty and useless will our activities be if we fail to have love as the primary and controlling principle in our lives! Like the vices listed in verse 13 that point to people being controlled by forces beyond themselves, believers are to be controlled by love. Love is the guiding standard through the life of the believer. As the end approaches, the need for the embracing of the radical love principle of Jesus is essential. (Joseph Byrd)

IT ISN'T EASY TO GET ALONG

MATTHEW 18:15-20

It isn't easy to get along. It's especially difficult to get along in a community as small as a congregation can be. So it is not surprising that many of the materials included in the New Testament are instructions concerning how we should organize ourselves and behave within the community of faith. Most of the epistles of Paul and others in the New Testament canon are dedicated to advice on being the Body of Christ. What we often overlook, however, is that the Gospel of Matthew is written with a similar concern, a concern for how the church could more nearly embody the witness of Jesus Christ at the close of the first century.

It isn't easy to get along, even in the church. Within a few generations after Jesus' death, followers of his way recognized that, although they lived as new human beings transformed by the grace of God, they continued to struggle with the frailties and foibles of their human condition. The church, by this point in time, had a unique identity and was on its way to order and institutionalization. In this text (v. 17) we find one of two references to the *ecclesia* in Matthew's Gospel (the other reference is found in Jesus' charge to Peter in chapter 16; these are the only references to the *ecclesia* in the Gospels). Since there was, by the time of this writing, an identifiable community of believers, it is not surprising to see in Matthew's Gospel an emerging discipline for the governance of the church.

This text addresses the painful but necessary need for discipline that sometimes arises even within the church community. Jesus here realizes that, wittingly or unwittingly, we may offend a fellow member of the church. Always the Wise Psychologist as well as the Great Physician, Jesus was aware of the price to be paid for unresolved conflict in the community. The mental, physical, and emotional toll that festering hurts take upon individual lives and upon the unity of the church is great. That is why the Reformed tradition, for example, identifies church discipline along with proclamation of the Word and the sacraments as marks of the presence of the church. Therefore, although the words sound harsh, the intention of this text is to preserve the common good of the community.

What is important to note in this passage is *not* primarily the permission to practice excommunication of wayward members but the process that should be employed to try to *prevent* that extreme measure. Discipline in the church should be a community effort and should be aimed at the restoration of right relationships. Certain Christian traditions, including the Mennonite Church and the Society of Friends, practice mediation as the means to the resolution of disputes concerning ecclesiastical and secular matters. All Christians would do well to take seriously such an approach to disagreements. The ideal of church life is agreement that will result in God's confirmation and blessing of those right decisions (v. 18), God's promise to honor requests made in good faith (v. 19), and God's presence with the faithful (v. 20). These are, indeed, marks of the true church of Jesus Christ. (Beverly Zink-Sawyer)

SEPTEMBER 15, 2002

Seventeenth Sunday After Pentecost

Worship Theme: God gifts us with grace, freeing us from the law. We practice our faith in various ways and must not despise others; rather we are to forgive generously and judge not.

Readings: Exodus 14:19-31; Romans 14:1-12; Matthew 18:21-35

Call to Worship (Psalm 114):

Leader: Tremble, O earth, at the presence of the LORD, at the presence of the God of Jacob, who turns the rock into a pool of water, the flint into a spring of water.

People: Tremble, O earth, at the presence of the LORD, at the presence of the God of Jacob.

Leader: When Israel went out from Egypt, the house of Jacob from a people of strange language, Judah became God's sanctuary, Israel his dominion.

People: Tremble, O earth, at the presence of the LORD, at the presence of the God of Jacob.

Leader: The sea looked and fled; the Jordan turned back. The mountains skipped like rams, the hills like lambs. Why is it, O sea, that you flee? O Jordan, that you turn back? O mountains, that you skip like rams? O hills, like lambs?

People: Tremble, O earth, at the presence of the LORD, at the presence of the God of Jacob.

Leader: The Lord meets the people in the sanctuary; Christ comes when we gather.

People: **We enter into God's house and tremble. We worship God's holy name.**

Pastoral Prayer:
Spirit of Mercy, you wash away all we have done that offends and all we have left undone that might testify to your grace. You turn us upside down and inside out and around and around 'til we turn 'round right. Teach us your generosity that we might forgive others seventy times seven times. Teach us gratitude that we might not seek so much to be consoled as to console, not so much to be understood as to understand, not so much to speak as to listen, be comforted as to comfort. Teach us of your love so that we may love rather than judge, celebrate rather than accuse, embrace rather than exclude. Spirit of Mercy, you hover gently enough to cool our face with the breeze of your wings and you blast with strength enough to divide the sea; sweep over us now to cleanse us this day. Amen. (Scott Haldeman)

SERMON BRIEFS

NOW THAT'S RELIGION!

EXODUS 14:19-31

If uncertainty has been a big part of your life, this is a story for you. If you know frustration, confusion, even despair, this is a story for you. This story is for everyone who has ever been in an impossible situation. It challenges us to believe that God can make a way where there is no way. Some people find the miraculous aspects of the parting of the sea incredible. More people cannot really believe that God will make a way for them in this world. I am not talking about God making your plans and hopes and dreams a reality. I am talking about God working out a plan, including you in it, and making a way for you in a world fraught with uncertainty. That's what I call religion.

319

I. Ethics? History?

The author of the story about Israel crossing the Red Sea did not have a sensitive ethical orientation, by our standards. God lures Pharaoh's army into the sea in order to kill them all. You might say, "Well, at least it was an army. God fights for Israel against an aggressive army, so this is combat. Killing in combat is different from other kinds of killing." True, this is not Ananias and Sapphira. Back in verse 17, though, God tells Moses that God will harden the hearts of the Egyptians, thus drawing them into battle, in order that God might gain glory at Pharaoh's expense. The text confronts us with a picture of God with which we may not be wholly comfortable.

The author of the story also does not have a conscientious historical commitment. Some details, scholars tell us, may be exaggerated. Some 600,000 men—not including women, children, and livestock—are supposed to have made this trip, according to 12:37. The mind boggles. Not a few scholars doubt the events described ever happened at all, at least in a way we would recognize from this retelling. What events lie behind this dramatic story?

II. Religion!

We may fault the author on these counts. No doubt we would tell the story differently. Nevertheless, we have to give the author credit for one thing: this person knows what makes for good religion.

The God we meet in this story is sovereign. We may find this God complex, but here is a God not to be taken lightly. God says, "Pharaoh, quit your boasting! Moses, stop all that whining! This is my show. Here's how things are going to be." We see this in everything from the pillar of fire that separates the armies to the strong east wind that splits the sea in half. God even wins from the Egyptians a confession of faith, of sorts: "Let us flee from the Israelites, for the Lord is fighting for them against Egypt."

The God we meet in this story is not one to use power just to show off. The power serves a purpose and moves forward a plan. Here is a God deeply concerned and involved in the world. What sort of God does this kind of thing? What might it mean to you to be involved with this God?

Some people connect this story with baptism. Passing through water, being saved, emerging to a new life—these elements naturally bring baptism to mind. I would make a radical proposal: the God we meet in this story is the God we meet in the water of baptism. A sovereign God lays claim to our lives and sweeps us up into a plan that spans the ages. We emerge ready to trust God to make a way for us in this world, and not just any way, God's way. Now that's religion! (David C. Mauldin)

HANDLING OUR DISAGREEMENTS IN LOVE

ROMANS 14:1-12

This sermonic text is a postscript for Paul's letter to the church at Rome, considered by many to be the premier document of Christian theology. Having presented throughout the letter God's love for us shown through God's plan of salvation for the believer through Jesus Christ, the apostle now turns his attention to assuring that we practice this love within the fellowship of believers—particularly when potential conflicts and disagreements arise.

Often we are so focused on maintaining peace outside the body that we fail to handle the disturbances within. So often we have the mind to work for peace in the world, as we should, but sometimes we neglect the need to strengthen and develop positive relationships among believers within our own homes, churches, and communities.

As the apostle moves toward closing his profound letter, Paul wants his readers to be clear that belief in the love that Christ has for us must be practiced through the love we have for our fellow brother and sister—even when we don't always see things eye to eye. For within the Body of Christ, we don't always agree on things. We are all at the feet of Jesus, but some people are strong in the faith on certain issues, yet weak in the faith on others. There are times when a strong Christian has a view about something that's totally different from the position of a weaker believer. There are times when two believers, whether strong or weak, simply disagree.

In the text, the disagreement was over how certain special days should be observed and how the eating of certain foods should be approached. In today's world, we might find similar arguments over the proper form of worship or the proper method of baptism. A person new to the faith feels immersion is the only way, while another person, who has been in the faith longer, believes the method is less important than the actual act. Still someone else believes that children should not be baptized; while another says we must reach the "age of accountability"—whatever that age may be.

All of this spells conflict, if we are not able to approach one another and our differences in the spirit of love. Paul provides for us within the sermonic text a prescription for handling our disagreements in love.

First, he declares that we should welcome one another, even the weaker believer, for each of us is at a different level. Each of us brings a different background and history that places us at varying points along the faith journey. We need to recognize and respect this reality, and learn to support one another as we grow together in grace.

Then Paul stresses that we should be confident in our present convictions. As long as we believe passionately and sincerely that our approach to an issue is God-inspired and in line with the will of God, we need to continue in that vain. Even if our neighbor's convictions are not consistent with ours, we need to trust that God will take care of our beliefs or our neighbor's beliefs that we believe may conflict with God's will. A friend of mine used to say, "You take care of God's business; God will take care of yours."

Third, we need to break away from judging our fellow believer. We must avoid condemnation of those who disagree with our position. Disagreement should not lead to judgment. Earlier in Paul's letter, the apostle says, "Therefore, there is now no condemnation for those who are in Christ Jesus" (8:1 NIV). If Jesus doesn't condemn the believer, neither should we.

Instead, we first need to make sure that our record with God is clear. Furthermore, we need to help our brothers and sisters, and as Paul goes on to say in chapter 14, refrain from being a stumbling block to our fellow believers. For every knee shall bow to God, and every tongue confess to God. So let us take care of our own lives before God, let us encourage our neighbor to do the same, and let us handle our disagreements in love. Then we can live together in a spirit of peace and harmony. (Joseph W. Daniels Jr.)

THE ACT OF FORGIVENESS

MATTHEW 18:21-35

Occasionally, the media bring to our attention an extraordinary display of forgiveness. We have seen parents intervening in the justice system to ask the courts to spare the life of a young man who took the life of their own son. We have seen the spouse of a young teacher killed in a school shooting plead for help rather than retribution for the juvenile gunmen. We have seen former war captives and captors embrace many years after political hatreds—some long forgotten, some still fresh as open wounds—had made them enemies. Hearing of these generous acts of forgiveness, my reaction is always the same: How can they do it? How can individuals who have suffered pain and anguish and loss at the hands of another find it in their hearts to forgive the wrongdoers?

Perhaps those who have demonstrated such incredible forgiveness have learned the lesson of today's Gospel text: Jesus' lesson of heartfelt, uncalculated forgiveness. The text includes a familiar parable, one that is not at all cryptic for those who hear it. In fact, its message is extraordinarily obvious—yet extraordinarily difficult to practice. A king decides to call in the debts of his slaves. One of the slaves brought before the king owed the king an unfathomable amount of money. One talent alone represented the wages for many years of work, so the reference to "ten thousand talents" is used hyperbolically to represent a debt that could never be repaid in a lifetime, even the lifetimes of the wealthiest members of that society. The text includes no details concerning how the servant amassed such an extraordinary debt. Several scholars explain the story as based on the Gentile economic structure of contracts managed for the king by subordinate officials who served as tax collectors. Whether because of mismanagement or because of other exigencies, this servant incurred an incalculable debt.

The element of surprise occurs when the king fails to punish the servant for whatever part he had in incurring such an overwhelming debt. Both parties know that a lifetime would never be enough to repay the debt and that the sale of the servant and his family and possessions would only serve a punitive function. Rather than choosing any of the other responses to the servant's debt, the king grants an unexpected and merciful pardon when the servant throws himself on the king's mercy. But what could end there as a nice portrayal of the kingdom of heaven goes on to place a demand upon those who wish to partake of the generosity offered to children of the Kingdom. The response of the forgiven servant to his fortunate state is *not* to extend that grace to others but to deny it to one who is indebted to him. The report of the servant's behavior made its way to the king, who had the servant brought before him and, after a lecture about sharing the mercy he had been shown, condemned him to eternal torture.

The story seems outrageous until set in the context of Matthew's kingdom ethics. Matthew's primary concern is for the community of Jesus' followers, the *ecclesia.* How shall those who have been "called out" from the world live until the promised day of Jesus' coming in glory? Matthew answers that question with his unique compilation of Jesus' teachings, including his words on forgiveness that precede this parable. The introduction to the parable is Peter's question to Jesus concerning the act of forgiveness (vv. 21-22). The seventy-seven times (or seventy times seven) indicates an unfathomable offer of grace—behavior, Matthew implies, that should be characteristic of those in the community of the church. We all know what happens when forgiveness is withheld: we are eaten up by bitterness and anger, community is destroyed, and the vicious cycle of retribution continues. Someone has to stop the cycle of violence and hate. According to Jesus, "someone" is those of us who call ourselves followers of Jesus Christ, for we have been lavished with the unmerited grace of God. Our hearts have been changed within us. We can never repay or even adequately thank the Giver, but we *can* pass that grace on to others by forgiving from our hearts. (Beverly Zink-Sawyer)

SEPTEMBER 22, 2002

Eighteenth Sunday After Pentecost

Worship Theme: God is the giver of all good gifts—bread from heaven, a full day's wage to those who work only an hour, even suffering can be cause for thanks for those who know Christ.

Readings: Exodus 16:2-15; Philippians 1:21-30; Matthew 20:1-16

Call to Worship (Psalm 105):

Leader: Remember the wonderful works God has done—miracles, judgments, acts of great power.

People: We recall God's marvelous deeds.

Leader: God remembers his covenant forever, the covenant with Abraham and Sarah, the covenant with Miriam and Moses.

People: We recall God's marvelous deeds.

Leader: God brought Israel out of Egypt, brought them out with silver and gold. God spread a cloud for a covering and fire to give light by night. They asked and God supplied quails. God gave them food from heaven in abundance.

People: We recall God's marvelous deeds.

Leader: God opened the rock, and water gushed out; it flowed through the desert like a river. For God remembered the holy promise and brought the people out with joy, brought them out with singing.

People: **We recall God's marvelous deeds. Let us worship God.**

Pastoral Prayer:
Bread of Heaven, who fed our ancestors in the desert, feed us. They complained of hunger, that slavery was better than starvation. We also forget to live with an attitude of gratitude. You have blessed us richly; may we be a blessing. Bread of Heaven, who nourishes us in word and at table, feed us. Some are hungry. Fill them with good things. Some are sick. Restore them to wholeness. Some are lonely. Surround them with companionship. Some are depressed. Ignite their hope. Some are anxious. Calm their fears. Some are violent. Quell their rage. Some are rich. Upset their security. Some are alienated. Welcome them home. Bread of Heaven, who satisfies hungry hearts, feed us. Amen.

SERMON BRIEFS

THE BIRTH OF TALK RADIO— WITHOUT RADIO

EXODUS 16:2-15

Today's story from Exodus provides an exciting glimpse at the birth of talk radio. Caller One takes to the airwaves with something like this, "Yeah, hi, I'm a first-time caller. I have something to say about this Moses guy. Does he know where we're going? I'm a little tired of wandering around. Plus, I have a family. We haven't eaten anything all day, except some Moon Pies my wife brought with us from Egypt. Something has to be done." The host responds, "Thanks, caller. Listeners, I know you have heard me say this before, but it bears repeating: I know where we can find food—plenty of food. Egypt. That's all I'm going to say about that."

I. Grumbling

My reconstruction is completely accurate, except there were no radios in Bible times. If you are a stickler for history, there were no Moon Pies, either. I cannot read this story, though, without thinking of talk radio. I listen to a sports variety show; and any time a team loses, someone is going to call in and suggest the coach should be fired, if not hanged. Forget past accomplishments, championships, and reason. Frustrated fans take it out on the coach or a star player. Maybe that is human nature. Maybe it is just bad taste. Probably it is both. We see it in Exodus when the Israelites once again complain against Moses. With the Red Sea comfortably behind them, and having found water to quench their thirst, the people begin to run low on food. Hunger sets in, and the grumbling starts.

I will not judge them, because I complain when I get hungry, too. God takes their grumbling personally, however. They fault Moses and Aaron for their predicament, but God has been in charge all along. The fiery comments thrown at Moses hit God, and God takes exception. In response, however, God sends grace, not wrath. Manna from heaven will feed the people.

II. Learning to Trust

One would think the experience at the Red Sea would have taught the people to trust God more. When the bitter water was made sweet, they might have learned that God will provide. They apparently did not. Again, I do not blame them. When I was a child, my family went through some tough years. My parents got divorced; my mother got cancer; and we had no money. We got through; but because of my experience, I keep a special reserve of money in the bank in case disaster strikes. It is not a lot, but it provides a measure of comfort. Maybe that is sound financial policy. Maybe it is human nature. Either way I know I would be very uncomfortable living the way Israel had to—day-to-day. Each day enough manna falls for that day. You always have enough, but you can never store it up. If dramatic events like the Red Sea do not inspire trust, maybe the hard lessons of daily living will eventually teach them to trust God.

We may see ourselves in this story, and if we do, the question arises of how we learn to trust God. Are we weak? Will we despair and fold at the first signs of trouble? Do we have what it takes to endure and persevere? Above all, do we trust God enough to really follow the way of Jesus Christ? The way of Jesus is not easy. One can do a halfway job of it without giving up too much, in which case little trust is required. To do it right, however, requires much sacrifice and trust. I am convinced most people in church want to do it right. How, then, do we learn to trust? We learn along the way. (David C. Mauldin)

A LARGER PURPOSE

PHILIPPIANS 1:21-30

A few years ago a popular song asked, "Don't it make you sad to know that life is more than who you are?" While the writer of this song grieves the thought of his insignificance, the apostle Paul discovers hope in knowing that life is larger than himself.

Writing from prison, Paul is uncertain about his future. His destiny lies in someone else's hands. His fate rests on the whim of an unpredictable Roman government that he knows all too well. Just a few years earlier, Paul found himself scourged and thrown into prison following one of their "whims" (Acts 16:16-39). Fortunately, in response to a legal appeal, the magistrates released him the following morning. This time, however, imprisonment looks more precarious, and life itself hangs in the balance.

Like other Christians facing an uncertain future, Paul takes refuge in his faith. He reminds himself that existence is larger than physical life. He assures himself of the foundation of all existence, and finds hope in Christ. "For to me, living is Christ and dying is gain" (Phil. 1:21). In fact, Christ is the all in all, and even if he dies, Christ will sustain him. Nevertheless, such escapism fails to satisfy the apostle.

Admittedly, he desires "to depart and be with Christ," and without a doubt "that is far better" (1:23). Nevertheless, life among the faithful tips the scales and transforms his vision of the future. While he longs to go on, leaving this world behind with all of its injustices, prisons, and sufferings, Paul's existence proves larger than his own desires. He discovers that other people need him.

The sufferings persist. The shackles remain locked. But life among the faithful provides purpose. "To depart and be with Christ" may be far better, but remaining in the flesh is "more necessary" (1:24). To continue with you as you progress in the faith is more important than going to be with the Lord, Paul asserts. I will see you through to the end, but don't let me down. Live worthy of the gospel. Live in unity, walk in harmony, and strive for the faith, Paul exhorts (1:27). Then, your enemies will see their destruction, as proof of your salvation glares back at them (1:28).

The God of grace works in you as you stand firm and courageous. In fact, the very grace that works in you has enlivened *me* for years, he explains. United, Paul and the Philippians share the privilege of believing in Christ and suffering in his name (1:30).

Imprisoned for Christ, Paul's future is unclear. Life and death hang in the balance, and Paul longs to be found faithful (1:20). He longs to live boldly. At the same time, he is tempted to close shop and go on to be with the Lord. Yet, while writing to the Philippians, he senses a deeper calling. He senses that his purpose is larger than his own life.

Life is more than who he is. Unlike the popular songwriter, however, this does not make him sad. Instead, it gives Paul great hope. It points toward community, and Paul's sense of responsibility to others drives him into the future. His accountability to the Philippians provides meaning to an otherwise questionable existence.

From this point forward in his letter, Paul no longer fixates on the possibility of his own death. In living for others, he discovers hope and puts aside his own concerns about the future. Certainly, heaven will be grand, but only in its time. Until that day, and not a moment sooner, celebrating God's grace among the faithful proves eternally fruitful. (Sean A. White)

GOD'S ENDLESS GIVING

MATTHEW 20:1-16

"Life is unfair." We hear that blunt statement of reality often in our lives. We have heard it from presidents trying to explain the inequities of political life and from authors trying to help us understand why bad things happen to good people. Parents invoke the statement in attempting to explain the inscrutable complexities of life to their children, and teachers have been known to invoke it when attempting to placate unhappy students.

In this parable from Matthew's Gospel, it appears that Jesus is adding his voice to the many voices over the ages that have intoned: "Life is unfair." The parable of the laborers in the vineyard, as it is best known, is among the more familiar parables of Jesus. A landowner needed workers to pick grapes from his vineyard. Those who did such labor-intensive, seasonal work—then as now—usually were hired from pools of workers who gathered in central locations in hopes of being employed for the day. As more workers were needed, more were hired throughout the day with no specific amount of wages promised to the later workers. The unexpected twist in the story comes when all the workers are given the same wages for vastly different amounts of work. The grumbling begins, and the landowner simply responds by defending his right to be generous.

So often we, especially we who have been pastors, encounter people of faith who feel betrayed by God. They are people who have lived faithfully and worked diligently according to their understanding of God's divine laws. Then life deals them a cruel hand: the untimely death of a loved one, the loss of a job, a devastating illness, or some other tragedy. And, in their understandable anguish, they cry that life is unfair—perhaps even, God is unfair—for they have fulfilled their part of the equation while God has failed to fulfill God's. They become, they believe, the losers in a zero-sum kingdom, a kingdom based on winners and losers, a kingdom based on payment as earned. But Jesus shatters all such notions of God's kingdom in this parable. God's kingdom is not a zero-sum kingdom; it is not a world of merit. It is, instead, a world of grace and mercy where there is more than enough generosity to go around.

Life is unfair. At first glance, that seems to be the message of this parable. But the message is really the complete opposite: life—life in God's kingdom—is *more than* fair, for God's goodness to us is always far more than we can imagine or deserve. Our economic mind-set gets in the way of our understanding of this parable. We are used to systems of merit in which we tally up earnings for work done. But the kingdom of God operates not on a system of merit, but on a system of abundant grace. The opening lines of a hymn from the *Presbyterian Hymnal* capture the essence of this parable: "God whose giving knows no ending, from Your rich and endless store." Indeed, God's giving to us is endless. Now God invites us to put our calculators aside, unconcerned about how much we have earned or who is first and who is last, to receive with thanksgiving God's abundant grace and mercy. But not only that: we are also called to remember the word heard in last week's parable of the unforgiving servant, challenging us not to stop with our grateful acceptance of grace and mercy, but to extend it to others. If we are to participate fully in the Kingdom proclaimed by Jesus, we cannot help but be generous to others, as God has been generous to us. (Beverly Zink-Sawyer)

SEPTEMBER 29, 2002

Nineteenth Sunday After Pentecost

Worship Theme: Christ condescended to human form, even to death, death on a cross; happy are those who serve humbly this Lord.

Readings: Exodus 17:1-7; Philippians 2:1-13; Matthew 21:23-32

Call to Worship (Psalm 78):

> *Leader:* Give ear, O my people, to my teaching; incline your ears to the words of my mouth.
>
> ***People:*** **I will open my mouth in a parable; I will utter dark sayings from of old.**
>
> *Leader:* I will tell things that we have heard and known, that our ancestors have told us.
>
> ***People:*** **We will not hide them from our children; we will tell to the coming generation the glorious deeds of the LORD, and his might, and the wonders that he has done.**
>
> *Leader:* Tell of God's wonderful works.
>
> ***People:*** **Let us worship God.**

Pastoral Prayer:
Word of God, through whom all things were made, you renounced your glory, came down from heaven, and became a human being. Your love overwhelms us. Your example scares us. Give us this day a sign of your grace. Human One, who sojourned with us, teaching and healing, you challenged religious authori-

332

ties, overturned the order of things, valued outcasts. Your life inspires us. Your example empowers us. Let us be this day a sign of your grace. Crucified Lord, who underwent the humiliation and pain of torture and capital punishment, you descended through the depths of human anguish and visited those under the shadow of death. Your suffering eludes us. Your death overturns death's power. Exalted Savior, whom God raised to life everlasting, you ascended to God's right hand and will return again to reign with peace. Your journey is truth to us. Your triumph is ours. Come soon, we pray. Amen.

SERMON BRIEFS

JOURNEYING THROUGH THE WILDERNESS

EXODUS 17:1-7

I. From Whence Have We Come?

The story of Exodus is a story of movement, of growth and maturation. It is a story of the giving and breaking of commandments that climaxes on a mountain and culminates with a look to the promised land. Yet, before any of that, captivity must be broken and fallow deserts must be trod. The promised land is attained only through journeying the highs and lows on the mountain and in the wilderness.

The journey begins with the rule of a king, a king who did not know Joseph. A king who would continually try to beat the Israelites down, causing them to cry out to God for help. Hearing their cry, God appoints Moses to lead the Israelites out of their captivity to the promised land. On the way, the Israelites witness the ten magnificent signs that God uses to convince Pharaoh to let the Israelites go. After escaping from the pursuing Egyptians through the Red Sea, a celebration of singing and dancing commences. The songs of Moses and Miriam in chapter 15 eloquently express the gratitude of the Israelite people as they revel in their journey from bondage to freedom.

II. Where Are We Now?

But the singing and dancing stop quickly, for the Israelites now find themselves in the midst of a terrible desert where water and food are hard to find. The first three pericopes after their celebration concern the basic necessities of life. It is the last of these pericopes that will be examined.

In chapter 15, God has already turned bitter water into sweet, and provided food for the people in chapter 16, but now, in chapter 17, there is no water at all, and the Israelites are concerned that they may die of thirst. They are so thirsty that they long to go back to captivity, to go back to abuse and lack of freedom. This circumstance is so dire, the Israelites long to return to bondage. This is not a minor complaint against Moses and God.

III. Where Must We Go to Find Life?

There are three options for Moses and the Israelites. The first is to return to Egypt, to go back to their slavery. At least there they know what is going to happen each day, and apparently they have water daily. The second is to stay where they are, quarreling with Moses, and die of thirst. The third option, at least for Moses and some of the elders, is to go on ahead of the people to find water and God. God commands Moses to set out from camp, with the same rod that was used while in bondage, to a place where God will meet him and where Moses will find water so that the Israelites might live.

IV. Our Journey

By now this story should sound very familiar, for it is our story, too. We have also been a people stuck in bondage and in need of deliverance. We have seen God's wondrous signs and deeds and we have rejoiced in our freedom. And yes, we have found, and will find, ourselves in the wilderness from time to time, where there is no food, and if there is water, it's bitter.

We have the same choices today as those who came before us. We can decide that our captivity is easier, more stable and secure, and less frightening. And return to a life with fewer responsibilities, less intimacy, and more answers. Bondage is certainly easier at times—at least we know what is going to happen each day. Another choice is to sit where we are, complaining about what is now happening in our lives, longing for the good ole days, and die. Finally, we can take a risk, step out on faith, and continue the journey.

If we are to live and find the abundant life, it is this last step that we must take. The wilderness is a frightening place, but if we decide to go back to Egypt, we go back to bondage where no growth, spiritual or otherwise, takes place. Likewise, we will never reach the promised land if we stay where we are. We must continue on the journey through the wilderness toward the promised land.

But we must be careful. Before we make our decision, we must realize that the wilderness is a frightening place and going through it is brutal work. There will be times when we ask like the Israelites, "Is the Lord among us or not?" No doubt we will get the same answer. No. The Lord is not among us. For the Lord is always out in front of us, leading us in this journey, showing us where to find water that quenches our daily thirst, and meeting us so that we might find life eternal. (Scott P. Mikels)

CHRIST—A REDEMPTIVE MODEL

PHILIPPIANS 2:1-13

In the spring of 1997, my mother died after a long bout with ovarian cancer. During her illness, well-meaning friends assured us of miracles, and out of my desire to see my mother live, I believed those promises. In her quest to know God's purposes and to see God work in her life, my mother believed them, as well. Unfortunately, no miracles came, and my mother died feeling far away from God.

As I processed this experience, I could make no sense of God's absence. I could not understand why God's comforting presence seemed so far away as my mother struggled. Consequently, I wondered how long I could believe in a God who proves distant in desperate times. I wondered if my faith was a sham. I wondered if God really existed at all. I wondered if I ought to look for a different religion. Then, out of no where, I remembered the story of Jesus' own death.

I recalled how he, too, longed for God to come near. I recalled how he felt confused over God's absence. As if for the first time, I heard his cry, "My God, my God, why have you forsaken me?" (Mark 15:34). I realized that Jesus, God's Son, also looked for and did not find God. Like my mother and I, he longed to sense God's presence, and like us, he did not. In Christ, I sensed a redemptive solidarity. I found a model for living a life of faith while remaining true to existential realities. With Christ as my model, I no longer needed to look elsewhere for spiritual nourishment.

In a similar way, the apostle Paul discovers a model in Christ that redeems him during a moment of crisis. In Philippians 1, Paul acknowledges that his future is uncertain. As a prisoner, life hangs in the balance, and he struggles to come to terms with his precarious situation. In the face of possible death, he assures himself, "For to me, living is Christ and dying is gain" (1:21). Nevertheless, he confesses that he prefers death. He desires "to depart and be with Christ, for that is far better" (1:23).

Faced with hardships, imprisonment, and suffering, Paul is ready to go on. He is ready to trade the robe of flesh for the glorious robe of his resurrected Lord. At the same time, something else demands his attention. Paul does not live for himself alone, and death at this juncture seems too soon. His brothers and sisters at Philippi need him, and he needs to live for them. How, though, can he continue when life dwindles away in a Roman prison cell? How can he go on when things seem so uncertain? In Christ, Paul discovers a model of self-giving that empowers him to choose life. He then submits this model to the Philippian Christians.

After discovering great encouragement, redeeming love, and communion in the Spirit, Paul invites the Philippians to find the same. He calls them to unity of mind and love. He calls them to a life of self-giving in which the glory of the other takes precedence over the glory of self. He calls them to adopt the mind of Christ (2:2-5).

Christ, though divine, does not exploit his divinity and lord his power over others (2:6). Instead, he empties himself in the service of people. He takes sides with humanity and becomes flesh (2:7). Even when such solidarity brings him to the brink of death, he gives what this life requires.

On a cross built for the harshest of criminals, Christ takes his place. He answers the call of living for others and hangs side by side with the dregs of society (2:8). In this way, God exalts him and makes him Lord. In this way, God establishes the model of discipleship (2:9-11).

Now, Paul admonishes, "work out your own salvation with fear and trembling" (2:12). Living for oneself has its advantages, and forgetting our responsibilities to one another sounds persuasive. Nevertheless, within the human community, priorities shift. The demands of life call from another direction. Those hanging alone from the crosses of life call out to us. Will we hear their voices? Will we, like Christ, humble ourselves and walk with them along the way? With fear and trembling, let us work out our salvation. With Christ as our model, let us hear the call. (Sean A. White)

BEARING TRUE FRUIT

MATTHEW 21:23-32

This text opens with Jesus' last foray in Matthew's Gospel into the Temple, a scenario that can only lead to another confrontation with those who represent religious authority. At the opening of chapter 21, Matthew records Jesus' triumphal entry into Jerusalem and then, immediately following, his cleansing of the Temple. In between the two temple visits is the strange story of the cursing of the fig tree, pointing most likely to the fate of those so caught up in ritualistic Judaism that they have lost the ability to bear fruit (that is, to exhibit acts of true faithfulness) and are condemned to wither and die.

With that context, the conflict between Jesus and the temple leaders continues in today's text as Jesus enters the Temple for the final time before his death. In a familiar pattern of controversy-to-pronouncement, Jesus responds to a "trick" question about his authority from the "chief priests and the elders of the people" with a parable. The parable is a simple one involving two sons, both of whom are ordered to work in their father's vineyard. The first refuses to go but then changes his mind and obeys his father. The second agrees to go, but never fulfills that agreement. Even the chief priests and elders were perceptive enough to answer Jesus correctly when he asked them, "Which of the two did the will of his father?" The first son, they answered—the one who eventually changed his mind and obeyed. The kingdom of God, Jesus affirms, is made up of such individuals who truly believe and act on those beliefs, even if they are tax collectors and prostitutes and others who defy the expectations of religious insiders.

Imagine a world in which people make promises, but never fulfill them! It would be a cruel and disheartening world, indeed. Contrast that unpalatable world with the kingdom of God portrayed by Matthew. Throughout Matthew's Gospel, we see a concern for community life that reflects the Kingdom as embodied in the life, teaching, and sacrifice of Jesus Christ. The Gospel texts of the past few weeks set forth, in instruction and parable, glimpses of the content of life in God's kingdom. It is a life, according to Matthew, characterized by adherence to community discipline, the practice of unlimited forgiveness, the enjoyment of unmerited grace, and, as revealed in this text, the active expression of genuine belief.

Matthew's Jesus reminds us again and again that the kingdom of God belongs not to those who utter nice words, no matter how eloquent or righteous, but to those who demonstrate obedience to God through concern for their neighbors. To the end of his ethical teachings in the Sermon on the Mount, Jesus adds warnings about the lack of demonstrated righteousness. "Every tree that does not bear good fruit is cut down and thrown into the fire," he declared. "Thus you will know them by their fruits" (7:19-20). "Not everyone who says to me, 'Lord, Lord,' will enter the kingdom of heaven, but only the one who does the will of my Father in heaven" (7:21). Framing his Gospel with a similar call to responsibility, Matthew notes the judgment of the nations that will occur when the Son of Man comes in his glory. The unrighteous will try to defend their lack of action by saying that they never saw Jesus hungry or thirsty or in desperate need. But those who cared for "the least of these who are members of my family,"

Jesus said, were the ones who were faithful to him and will be welcomed into the kingdom prepared for them (25:34). As in Matthew's day, so in ours: there is no place in the kingdom of God for those who declare their faith with their lips, but who do not proceed to true belief that issues in action. (Beverly Zink-Sawyer)

SPIRITUAL PREPARATION

❧

OCTOBER

In my part of the country, October brings a slight chill in the air and the changing of the seasons. We have fully left summer behind, and autumn is upon us. The passage reminds me of the passage of time. The passage also points me toward the Scripture as a text that teaches me how to live in the changing of seasons, in the passage of time.

"Wisdom" writes Eugene Peterson in his introduction to the Proverbs, "is the art of living skillfully in whatever actual conditions we find ourselves" (The Message). A proverb that has spoken to me recently has a blunt directness: *"Finish your outdoor work and get your fields ready; after that, build your house"* (24:27 NIV). How can these words become wisdom for us? They speak of tending first to that which is life-sustaining. We are partners with God and with each other in the provision of our needs. The outdoor work, the planting, the readying of fields, reminds us of those matters of first priority.

- What is your outdoor work? How is God calling you to get the outdoor fields ready?

After that, the proverb has it, build the house. Some things are of secondary priority. They are wonderful, but they are not *"first things."* They can wait.

The task before us is the discernment of priorities. How does this discernment happen? As we invest time in silence, in the work of reconciliation with others and examination of self, in the study of Scripture and the practice of prayer, an appropriate order, a right sequence emerges. The Holy Spirit leads us, guides us. The gift of wisdom is offered to us.

- Do some matters before you seem to have priority over others? What is of most importance, today, in your life and ministry?

The ordering of our lives requires this gift of wisdom, to know when to act, when to wait, and how our commitments can find their proper sequence. It is not enough to do the right things. Wisdom helps us to do the right things at the right times. Not everything can be done now. Not everything should be done now. There is a time and a season for all that God calls us to be and do. The art of living skillfully is learned as we discern the ordering of these times and seasons.

We are familiar with Ecclesiastes 3:

> For everything there is a season, and a time for every matter under heaven:
> a time to be born, and a time to die;
> a time to plant, and a time to pluck up what is planted;
> a time to kill, and a time to heal;
> a time to break down, and a time to build up;
> a time to weep, and a time to laugh;
> a time to mourn, and a time to dance;
> a time to throw away stones, and a time to gather stones together;
> a time to embrace, and a time to refrain from embracing;
> a time to seek, and a time to lose;
> a time to keep, and a time to throw away;
> a time to tear, and a time to sew;
> a time to keep silence, and a time to speak;
> a time to love, and a time to hate;
> a time for war, and a time for peace. (vv. 1-8)

I have found this to be a fruitful passage in reflecting on ministry. It teaches us to be aware of the events in our own lives: there are celebrations and griefs; there are victories and defeats; there are consolations and discouragements. The passage also helps us to be sensitive to the needs of others: our pastoral ministry to others is sometimes shaped by the timing of events in their lives; our preaching takes into account the situations in which we find ourselves. The passage also serves as a corrective to the glib, positive thinking of our culture. We do not gloss over or ignore the realities of our pilgrimage through this life. Finally, this passage can be good news for us: we are invited to pray in any and all circumstances, accepting our lives as gifts from the God who enters into our time and redeems it in Jesus Christ.

- What is the time of your life, right now? Does one of the phrases from Ecclesiastes 3 describe your ministry at the moment?

If your congregation is like most, the fall can be a very busy time. One danger might be that time passes without our being aware of it. We pause for a moment, and it is Labor Day. We pause again, we are in the midst of Advent. The activities and ministries of the fall season can prohibit our attention to the inner life, to the nurturing of the heart, to the feeding of the imagination. Wisdom is a gift of God, but we must receive it. If we are preoccupied, even with many good things, we miss what the Lord wants to teach us in the events of our lives. And if the time is a blur, if all time seems the same, one day similar to the previous one and to the next, we miss the significance of what is really happening, within us and around us.

Obviously, we move through time in this way at our peril. I am reminded of the folk music classic "Cat's in the Cradle," which is set in the context of the father-son relationship. But the same could be true in areas of marriage, friendship, pastoral ministry, and relationship with God. Each day is a gift. In it God wants to teach us something, about ourselves, about those nearer to us, about life in the kingdom of God. The wise pastor listens with the heart, and sees the signs of the times. (Ken Carter)

OCTOBER 6, 2002

Twentieth Sunday After Pentecost

Worship Theme: Our righteousness is from Christ. Our bustle of works cannot earn us eternal life. Christ saves; we must simply accept the gift of grace. Then we are free to serve, even to suffer, and to obey the law in freedom, not fear.

Readings: Exodus 20:1-4, 7-9, 12-20; Philippians 3:4*b*-14; Matthew 21:33-46

Call to Worship (Psalm 19):

Leader: The heavens are telling the glory of God; and the firmament proclaims his handiwork.

People: **The law of the LORD is perfect, reviving the soul; the decrees of the LORD are sure, making wise the simple.**

Leader: The precepts of the LORD are right, rejoicing the heart; the commandment of the LORD is clear, enlightening the eyes; the fear of the LORD is pure, enduring forever; the ordinances of the LORD are true and righteous altogether.

People: **The Law of the Lord is more to be desired than gold; sweeter also than honey, and drippings of the honeycomb.**

Leader: Let the words of my mouth and the meditation of my heart be acceptable to you, O LORD, my rock and my redeemer.

People: **Let our hearts be open. Let us worship God.**

Pastoral Prayer:

Beloved of God, Rejected of Humanity, you were sent to collect the fruit of the harvest and we killed you instead, hoping to receive your inheritance through violence. We realize in horror the error of our ways. We see now you are the firstborn of God's new creation. Forgive us. Cleanse us. Create in us a clean heart that we might walk in the path of righteousness from this day forth. Forsaken One, you suffered, died, and were buried. Accompany the suffering. Assure the dying. Make whole the broken. Cornerstone of Faith, God brought you out from the grave and you ascended to glory. Raise us all on the last day when you return to renew the face of the earth. Amen. (Scott Haldeman)

SERMON BRIEFS

WHAT MORE CAN YOU SAY?

EXODUS 20:1-4, 7-9, 12-20

Is there anything left to be said about the Ten Commandments? Hundreds of books have been written about them. Yet, what can be discussed that hasn't been already? Probably not much, but we must continue to explore the fertile soil to see how God is speaking to us in the present.

1. The first commandment, "I am the Lord your God . . . you shall have no other gods before me," reminds the Israelites of what God has done and also declares what the Israelites, and we, must do. Yet, what does it mean to put God first, and who are these other gods today?

What this commandment says to this generation is that there is to be no rival for God. God must take primary importance in our lives above anything else that might attract our attention and energy. By expanding the definition of *gods,* a wide variety of "gods" begin to call out to us. For some it could be fame, fortune, or simply work. While for others it might be our view of other people or ourselves.

There is caution as well for the church, because even our communal worship of God can become a god, a rival to the true God.

2. Idols. One thing is certain, a great number of people know exactly who God is and who we are as children of God. It is this certainty that has become the idol of the modern believer. By limiting God to what we believe about God, and what we understand the Bible to teach about God, we are making God into a static being, something God definitely is not. This commandment compels us to beware of the mysterious way in which God shatters the boundaries of our understanding of, and language for, God. We must let God be God, as frightening and overwhelming as that might be.

3. This third commandment, traditionally understood to read, "You shall not take the Lord's name in vain," is incredibly valuable in present society. In a world where so much destruction and so many miracles are attributed to God, this commandment encourages us to watch what we assign to God. Likewise, we must be willing to see God in places and people where we might not normally. We must be open to the way God breaks into our everyday lives.

4. The Sabbath day is a day of remembering. Here we are reminded that we must be intentional about learning from our past mistakes and successes so that our time in the present is a holy time. Sabbath is a time of deep soul-searching and renewal. It is a time of waking up to who we are, who we are to be, and who God is. It is a day of work, a day for intense introspection and worship. It is seeing who we are and who God is and how the two fit together.

5. Honor your father and mother. Adults beware. This fifth word from God is not just about your children. Where are *your* parents? How are you treating them as you and they grow older? Have you neglected them? What are you doing to honor their lives and their years of love and dedication to you?

Likewise, children, remember that your parents have experienced some of the same things you are experiencing. There is wisdom in their years. Be willing to learn from your parents. Respect them and give them a reason to respect you as well.

6. Don't murder. For most of us, this commandment is one we are able to follow without a great deal of work. Yet, most of us have readily killed a person's spirit, their essence, their very being. Many of us can think of people who have crushed our dreams by their words. Likewise, there are people who have given us wings by challenging and encouraging us to live, and live abundantly. Will we be people who continually bring life and not death to our relationships? Will we be people who bring life to other people with whom we come into contact?

7. You shall not commit adultery. Adultery has contributed to the demise of many relationships. However, if you are married or in a committed relationship, you know that simply not committing adultery is not enough to ensure a thriving relationship. Not committing adultery is simply a boundary, but the hard work comes in what we do daily to secure a growing relationship.

8. Don't steal. Stealing is not limited to taking something from the local store. Consider these questions: How is your desire for more stuff at a lower price a means of robbing others, many of whom we never know or see? By working late, are you stealing time from your spouse or children? By degrading others, are you stealing their dignity in the eyes of others, or just losing yours? What unethical shortcuts do you take regularly to save time and money?

9. You shall not bear false witness. We have taken this to mean that we should not lie to others, but often we have not applied this commandment to ourselves. Where are those places in our lives where we are not being honest with ourselves? Where have we failed to be truthful either about our weaknesses or our strengths? Where have we shown our false self, rather than our true self? May we not deceive others or ourselves.

10. You shall not covet. When we seek something we do not have, we become dissatisfied with what we do have. What we need we have. When we start wanting something that someone else has we lose perspective on, and satisfaction with, what we do have.

May these finite insights be a platform upon which to build a more solid foundation. May these ten words continue to bring life. (Scott P. Mikels)

SERMON BRIEFS

CHRIST—NOT A PEDIGREE

PHILIPPIANS 3:4*b*-14

After finishing seminary, I worked a couple of years before deciding to return to graduate school. As I considered various institutions, I consulted with a trusted friend and former college professor. I wanted to know what kind of school would make my résumé most appealing. In response, he assured me, "When we hire a professor, we hire a person, not a pedigree." In Philippians 3, Paul's words sound similar to the comments of my college professor.

Paul places no confidence in the flesh, nor in any human accomplishment. Nevertheless, he confesses that his qualifications would place him high above the crowd. To demonstrate, he rifles off a litany of accolades:

> circumcised on the eighth day, a member of the people of Israel, of the tribe of Benjamin, a Hebrew born of Hebrews; as to the law, a Pharisee; as to zeal, a persecutor of the church; as to righteousness under the law, blameless. (3:5-6)

Without a doubt, such a résumé would place Paul on the short list of any first-century seminary hiring committee. Nevertheless, from Paul's perspective all of this is mere rubbish. It amounts to garbage!

Forget about the short list! The most important list is Christ's list, and from Christ's perspective, pedigrees amount to very little. In fact, reliance on human achievements disqualifies one from gaining Christ. Just as my college professor assured me, "We hire people, not pedigrees," so, too, Christ is in the people business. In that business, grace rules the day, while pedigrees are disposable.

Relationships built around works fall prey to manipulation, and hierarchies of affection emerge. In Christ, however, no one *wins* affection. Instead, the way of Christ is paved by faith and faith alone (3:9). By dying, and then surrendering claim to God's favor, we gain the righteousness we all desire. By faith, we trust in God's favor, and hopefully look toward the future.

Unlike the litany of Paul's accomplishments, which relies upon past realities, the way of faith is built upon a liberating grace that always looks forward. In reference to attaining "the resurrection from the dead" (3:11), Paul acknowledges that he has not obtained this goal. Instead, "I press on to make it my own" (3:12), he explains. His prized pedigree lies among the trash heap, and he forgets "what lies behind" and strains "forward to what lies ahead." He presses "toward the goal for the prize of the heavenly call of God in Christ Jesus" (3:14).

The way of Christ is a progressive experience. It orients the believer to what can be, not to what was. It is a life of hope driven by what will be, not by what is.

Relying on a list of human accomplishments lends itself to a life of anxiety. While Paul's confidence might grow as his accomplishments are announced, many of us dread that someone might ask about our qualifications. Instead of growing more assured, we worry whether our résumé will be good enough. Even if our qualifications meet the standard, the next person's may be better. The cycle is endless, and peace is hard to come by.

Following Paul's lead, we, too, can forsake our reliance on personal accomplishments, opting to have faith in God's redeeming power revealed in Christ. We, too, may trash our accolades, refusing to trust in past accomplishments. At the same time, we can say good-bye to those pieces that truly do not measure up, and we can look forward to the future. We can anticipate that day in which resurrection is reality and where competition gives way to salvation. (Sean A. White)

OWNERS OR SHARECROPPERS?

MATTHEW 21:33-46

It's October, the time of harvest. And, it's the first Sunday of October, the time when many Christians observe World Communion Sunday. Few scriptures could be more appropriate for this day than this parable of harvest. It is set in a vineyard, a common image for the kingdom of God. It concerns the state of affairs in the commonwealth of God. On this day, diverse groups within

God's family lean forward to hear a story of peculiar relevance from Jesus.

Jesus works with material that's familiar to his listeners. He uses words and images from Isaiah's "Song of the Vineyard" (Isa. 5:1-7). As in Isaiah, a landowner painstakingly establishes a vineyard. The vineyard in Isaiah yields wild grapes rather than grapes. The vineyard here produces an adequate crop, but the tenants refuse to turn over produce to the owner. Both stories present injustices that cry for remedy.

The parable's landowner affords us a glimpse of the character of God, while the tenants resemble us. God has created a wonderful world in which each of us has a place, and an opportunity for prosperity. God has attended to every detail of the creation. In this vineyard we have every reason to rejoice in the blessings that the Creator has bestowed on us and to share the riches with others and with God. No other arrangement seems fair.

Unfortunately, our story, like the story here, packs a rude surprise. We present-day tenants want to keep *all* of the produce! In fact, we, too, want to be installed as owners. We justify it in our thoughts: "We have tilled the soil, tended to the crop, kept watch over it night and day. Without us there would be no crop! Why should the owner get any of the crop, let alone the lion's share of it?"

We, like the original tenants, contemplate the distance between the owner and ourselves. We reason, "Why should we pay him? He's too far away to touch us directly. He may never come back! He has many other vineyards, and we need the produce more than he does."

The tenants in the parable are traditionally called "wicked" more for their violence than their greed. In Matthew 11:12 Jesus has already said, "From the days of John the Baptist until now the kingdom of heaven has suffered violence, and the violent take it by force." From the time of Cain and Abel we humans have shown an astonishing capacity for violence. We let no one, not even God, stand in our way.

The most amazing feature of the parable is the forbearance of the landowner. He ends up with no rent, no honor, no servants, no son, and no vineyard! This is an odd depiction of our Creator God, who has a strange vulnerability to us creatures. God comes to us in such ways that we can almost always turn God down. Frederick Buechner observes that "God puts himself at our mercy not only in the sense of the suffering that we can cause him by our blindness—and cruelty, but the suffering that we can cause him simply by suffering ourselves." When someone we love suffers, we suffer with him because the suffering and the love are one (*The Hungering Dark* [San Francisco: Harper, 1985], p. 14). Because of God's unsurpassable love for us there seem to be no limits to the self-humiliation to which the divine will descend in pursuit of us. That's love's nature.

Jesus' story says that in God's commonwealth all of us are sharecroppers, not owners. We tend the earth and its riches on the Creator's behalf. Though we have delusions of ownership, we are here only through the generosity of the Owner, who seeks tenants who will share the harvest generously.

The issue of sharing is crucial. How much of the produce are we using to build a commonwealth of justice and love, and how much are we using to feed our own worldly status? Only generous people can reflect God's image in a broken world. If we aim to be good neighbors and faithful stewards on this World Communion Sunday, we must work to put all of the crop into God's hands. The One who created it and made it grow is also the One most able to distribute the bounty for the blessing of all. (Sandy Wylie)

OCTOBER 13, 2002

Twenty-first Sunday After Pentecost

Worship Theme: God's Welcome Table awaits us—we are invited and must respond; we are welcomed and should come prepared to celebrate.

Readings: Exodus 32:1-14; Philippians 4:1-9; Matthew 22:1-14

Call to Worship (Psalm 106):

Leader: Praise the LORD! O give thanks to God whose steadfast love endures forever.

People: **Who can utter the mighty doings of the LORD, or declare all his praise?**

Leader: Happy are those who observe justice, who do righteousness at all times.

People: **Remember me, O LORD, when you show favor to your people; help me when you deliver them.**

Leader: Save me that I may see the prosperity of your chosen ones, that I may rejoice in the gladness of your nation, that I may glory in your heritage.

People: **Praise the LORD for God's steadfast love endures forever.**

Pastoral Prayer:
Steadfast Lover, you save your people but we turn away, impatient and fickle. Turn from your wrath once more and renew your covenant within us. Call us again from the idols we make and the

351

concerns that distract us from you. From our self-satisfaction, deliver us. From our self-hatred, free us. Write your law on our hearts so that we may know you more clearly, love you more dearly, follow you more nearly. Banquet Host, you set a table before us, full of your bounty, places for all. Invite us this day. We await word from your servants. We will not refuse. We search out our finery and prepare for a party. Send us to call others. To those without homes. To those without money. To those in prisons. To those in hospitals. To those who are dying. What a great day that will be. We yearn with impatience. Give us a foretaste at your table this day. And we shall be dissatisfied with anything less. We shall work tirelessly until that day comes. May it come soon, we pray. Amen. (Scott Haldeman)

SERMON BRIEFS

WHO WILL BE YOUR GOD?

EXODUS 32:1-14

I. Israel's Fall Narrative (vv. 1-6)

Moses has been gone for quite some time. The natives are getting restless. Everyone is wondering where this person is who brought them out of the land of Egypt. Without Moses they cannot proceed. So, like any faithful community, they go to the next in charge and come up with an alternate plan.

The plan is to build gods; gods who will go before them (v. 1) and gods who have brought them out of the land of Egypt (v. 4). No more of this fire and cloud stuff. In the absence of Moses (their god image presently?), they build something more tangible. The image they construct appears to be one to which they are accustomed, a calf made of gold, representing "gods."

It is difficult to tell whether these gods are to supplant Yahweh or not. In verse 4, the Israelites credit these gods with their escape from Egypt. Yet, in verse 5, Aaron speaks of a festival to the Lord. For the Israelites, and Aaron, too, there does not seem to be a problem with a multitude of deities being worshiped, despite the commandment given earlier to not have any gods before God.

II. God's Anger (vv. 7-11)

Yahweh, on the other hand, does have a problem with the perverse actions of the Israelites. The Lord accuses the Israelites of turning aside from the way that they were commanded. They have broken the first two commandments given in Exodus 20. Not only that, they have attributed to these gods the role of deliverer from Egypt. Perhaps this is why Yahweh shows no willingness to claim the Israelites as "my people."

In response to the Israelites' actions Yahweh intends to consume them, to destroy them. Yet, God leaves an opening for Moses' response in verse 11. It is in the words, "let me alone." Why would Yahweh need to say this? Does God need Moses' permission to do what God intends? It would appear that in this instance, yes, God does need Moses' permission.

III. Moses' Response (vv. 11-13)

Just as amazing as God's request for permission is Moses' unwillingness to give it. Like a good lawyer, Moses reminds God of what has already been said under oath. Moses says that these are not "my people," these are "your people." Moses goes so far as to imply that since God swore by God's own self, this covenant was binding and could not be broken.

Moses also urges God to remember the covenant that God has with Abraham, Isaac, and Israel. This "remember" is the same "remember" that is used in Exodus 2:23-24. This is the same "remember" that started this journey of deliverance. Moses is asking Yahweh to remember just as Yahweh did when Yahweh heard the Israelites cry out of their slavery.

Another argument that Moses uses is to play God against the nations watching the Israelites. What would the Egyptians say if God destroyed the people that God had just brought out of Egypt? It would not look good for God or the Israelites.

IV. God's Response (v. 14)

"And the LORD changed his mind about the disaster (RSV, repented of the evil) that he planned to bring on his people." God doesn't say this to Moses. It is simply stated in the text. God, supposedly, decides that the argument that Moses has given is a good one, and once again the Israelites become "God's people." But what of this repentance, this changing of Yahweh's mind? This is a turning, from divine justice to divine mercy. God has seen not the error of God's ways, but the essence of God's ways. God's action is compassion rather than judgment.

V. Insights

What are we to learn about the Israelites and about ourselves in this story?

First, the life of faith is very much like this episode. If you are serious about your faith in God and in your understanding of who you are and who God is, you will experience this crisis in your own journey. The question is, will you seek something less, something easier than a relationship with God, and set up for yourself a system that is concrete, a golden calf? Or will you let God be God and let the ambiguity remain, fighting off the desire for everything to make sense and be easily understood?

Second, the way to the promised land takes us through the wilderness past the mountain. The journey toward Canaan is a time of cleansing—the time when we throw off the riches accumulated in our bondage and the false gods worshiped and make our way through the desert past the mountain into the promised land.

Third, in this journey there must be a death among the people if there is to be life. Our false ideas of God must die and our false selves must die (see vv. 25-29) if we are to make it to Canaan. It is only by the destruction of our false gods and in the death of our false selves that we can continue the journey to the promised land. The wilderness is godforsaken (see Exodus 17), but the mountain is a place of god-forsaking. This is a much-needed part of the journey.

Finally, if you want to see an appropriate way to handle the difficult moments in relationships, look at Moses. In the midst of this frightening episode in which God threatens to annihilate the Israelite community, Moses has the courage to stay in the tension and confront God. This is a story of meeting the God within, of facing the moments where we would rather move to a lesser degree of intimacy, like the Israelites, because it is easier. But Moses faces God, and himself, and the relationship moves to deeper levels (see Exod. 33:12-23). (Scott P. Mikels)

"REMEMBER WHO YOU ARE AND PRESS ON"

PHILIPPIANS 4:1-9

Human relationships can be the most challenging terrain any of us traverse. As the road of life twists and turns, it is often difficult to know whether we are coming or going. As relational hills grow steeper and more treacherous, the stakes rise and the journey demands greater care and attention.

A cursory reading of Paul's letter to the Philippians reveals an intimate affection between the apostle and his fellow Christians. He begins his letter by confessing how often he thanks God for his brothers and sisters at Philippi (1:3). In the same breath, he acknowledges reciprocity, for he knows they hold him dear to their hearts (1:7). As he begins the final section, Paul addresses them as his "joy and crown" (4:1). At the same time, he verbalizes what everyone already knows—there is tension in the family.

Evidently, two women in the church have had words and conflict sharply divides them. Consequently, Paul pleads, "I urge Euodia and I urge Syntyche to be of the same mind in the Lord" (4:2). But how does Paul think this will happen? Certainly, each of us has known disrupted relationships, and we have tasted the bitterness of conflict. As a result, we know that words like, "Please make up," do little to cool the flame. What, then, does Paul imagine will help these women?

As noted, Paul shares a deep relationship with the Philippian people, and this intimacy bears deep roots. "From the first day until now," they have shared together in the gospel (1:5). In the early days, when no one lent their support, the believers at

Philippi had confidence in Paul and gave generously to him (4:15). Consequently, deep community formed among them. In calling these two women back to one another, Paul evokes the power of memory. He passionately reminds them of the past they have shared. "Help these women," he pleads, "for they have struggled beside me in the work of the gospel, together with . . . the rest of my coworkers, whose names are written in the book of life" (4:3).

In effect, Paul pleads, Look, this is who we are. This is who *you* are. Together, we have struggled as bearers of the good news. Through good times and bad we have been there for one another. Let's not give this up. Remember . . . and be reconciled. Furthermore, Paul explains, you are gentle people. Therefore, "Let your gentleness be known to everyone" (4:5).

Without a doubt, in relationships it is often difficult to remember who we are. Tempers flare. Sharp comments dart back and forth. Perspectives cloud, and the haze of conflict distorts our vision. At such times, we need someone else's perspective. We need the look of one who can see more clearly than we. We need the perspective of one not clouded by the steam rising off the road of heated conflict. In the case of Euodia and Syntyche, Paul serves this role. He mirrors back to these dear women a vision of their true identity. In spite of the conflict, they remain faithful companions in the gospel. They remain gentle people formed by the graciousness of God.

With this in mind, Paul instructs them to turn to the God of peace. With rejoicing, prayer, and thanksgiving, turn toward the Lord, and "the peace of God, which surpasses all understanding, will guard your hearts and your minds in Christ Jesus" (4:7). Stay focused, attending to those things worthy of praise (4:8). Remain steadfast, living out what you have been taught. And finally, be attentive, for "the God of peace will be with you" (4:9). Remember who you are, and press toward what you can be! (Sean A. White)

NO SHIRT, NO SHOES, NO KINGDOM

MATTHEW 22:1-14

The banquet is a favorite image for the kingdom of God in Scripture. Among the most joyous and festive feasts is a *wedding* banquet, always a celebration of profoundest meaning for us humans. The very identification of the kingdom of God with such a banquet says something important about it. The Kingdom is the location of life's greatest joy and fulfillment. In it we have fellowship with God and the saints. In it are light, perfect rest, and inexpressible happiness. It's the place for which every soul longs, even when we mortals do not know its name. Finding and knowing God is a thing of such great importance that nothing else can take its place for anyone. To miss the Kingdom is to miss everything. Therefore, entering the Kingdom is a subject to which Jesus returns again and again.

Jesus tells us amazing things about the Kingdom. First, *all* are invited. No one is excluded! Second, admission is absolutely free. Maintaining our citizenship is often costly, but it's a price we're enabled to pay and are glad to pay. Entrance, though, is ours for the asking. Third, admission is usually by way of invitation. Someone invites us—it's that simple! We may not even remember the invitation, especially if we first came into the Kingdom in the arms of our parents.

People react to the invitation in all sorts of puzzling ways. In Jesus' story the first group "will not come." The second group "makes light of it" because they're busy with worldly pursuits. Another group mistreats and even kills the messengers! The last group, a ragtag collection of the "good and bad," winds up in the banquet hall out of a variety of motives, some of which are unclear even to themselves. The hall is finally full!

It all happens by invitation. There's no royal decree, no edict from on high. God, like this king, operates only through people's free will. People are free to spurn God. We church folk who labor in some corner of the Kingdom certainly see this as our constituents and neighbors, in large numbers, pass up our best offerings in favor of pursuits that they value more. We who are in the kingdom business must always remember that we are, above all, *inviters.* Our job is to invite people—all people. It's a serious business worth our best efforts. The stakes are high, and the time is short.

Our text closes with a curious story of a man who is thrown into outer darkness simply because he isn't wearing a wedding robe! In biblical imagery, clothing sometimes signifies character or discipleship. This man may remind us that although we are invited to come to the Kingdom just as we are, there is a dress code inside the door. We cannot apply for forgiveness every morning without giving up the shortcomings for which we beg pardon.

A friend of mine attended a "blue jeans" service that started in her church. Such services are aimed at the unchurched. Worshipers dress down—way down. Food and drink are offered and are often carried into the worship space. My friend was startled to find herself beside a local rowdy who was so stirred by one of the peppy choruses that he sloshed hot coffee on her! It was not a worshipful moment *for her.* She beheld his giddy exuberance with mixed feelings. She wondered if he was simply playing a frivolous game with the grace of God. She also wondered how well equipped her church was to guide this fellow to higher levels of discipleship. John Wesley warned, "Never encourage the devil by snatching souls from him that you cannot nurture."

If there's a subject about which Matthew is deadly serious, it's God's judgment. For Matthew, Christians, as well as pagans, can find themselves in outer darkness. In fact, Jesus' words here are to *insiders.* Yes, there's a dress code in the Kingdom. We may come to the Kingdom as we are, but we who refuse to don the garments of righteousness are no better off than those who never show up. (Sandy Wylie)

OCTOBER 20, 2002

Twenty-second Sunday After Pentecost

Worship Theme: We are citizens of this world, yet we are never to confuse our patriotism with our ultimate loyalty, which is to God alone.

Readings: Exodus 33:12-23; 1 Thessalonians 1:1-10; Matthew 22:15-22

Call to Worship (Psalm 99):

> *Leader:* The LORD is king; let the peoples tremble! He sits enthroned upon the cherubim; let the earth quake!
>
> ***People:*** **The LORD is great in Zion, exalted over all the peoples**.
>
> *Leader:* Let them praise your great and awesome name.
>
> ***People:*** **Holy is the God of Israel!**
>
> *Leader:* Mighty Sovereign, lover of justice, you have established equity; you have executed justice and righteousness in Jacob.
>
> ***People:*** **Holy is the God of Israel!**

Pastoral Prayer:

Heavenly Sovereign, who is above every earthly ruler and who calls your people from every nation to proclaim your rule of justice, we render to you our thanks and praise, we pledge to you our lives, that living as citizens of history we might live also as inhabitants of an age beyond this age, an age in which all the earth lives together in peace. We give to Caesar, to our own nation, to those who govern according to the rule of law, our obedience. But to you only do we give our hearts. Ready to protest injustice, ready to struggle for the rights of the outcast, the stranger, the exploited, we stand as your prophets in our own time and place. We love you and so we feed your sheep. We shelter those without homes. We feed those who are hungry. We visit those who are shut in and those who are lonely and those in prison. We embrace those without family, those without nation, those who sojourn among us. We extend our help to those who suffer from earthquake and flood. We lift up those who live in the midst of war and those who suffer the whims of dictators. We confess the failings of our nation and pledge to work to require of our officials policies that promote justice and peace even at the expense of our own comfort. Visit us this day with your peace. May your eternal reign commence. Amen. (Scott Haldeman)

SERMON BRIEFS

BEHOLD, THE BACK OF GOD

EXODUS 33:12-23

In this pericope, two different themes are entwined tightly. The first is the continuing question of whether God will continue to be in relationship with the Israelite people. The second is a more subtle, yet intriguing, Golden Calf episode for Moses. In these verses Moses continually pushes God to define their relationship and remove any question of God's presence with him and the Israelites. In other words, he pushes God to be more tangible.

I. Moses' Questioning of God (vv. 12-16)

The Moses of these verses looks very similar to the Moses first encountered in Exodus 3–4. It is as if Moses has forgotten all that has transpired since his initial encounter with God. Moses, like the Israelites, needs God to be more well-defined, more concrete. After all that God has done with and for Moses, Moses cannot trust God to continue to lead the people and make Godself known. Granted, this is coming after the Golden Calf and God's clear distancing from the Israelites (33:1-6), but why is Moses, after his clearly deepening relationship with God (Exod. 32), questioning God's intimacy with him?

Perhaps this isn't just a need by Moses for reassurance but a strategic ploy to lump himself in with the Israelite people to ensure their part in this continuing journey. Perhaps by connecting himself so closely to the Israelites, it will ensure their abiding part in the journey and God's continuing favor upon them. If this is what is going on, Moses' brilliance and audacity can again be celebrated, because it works.

II. God's Response (vv. 17-20)

Despite the seemingly manipulative tactics by Moses to ensure the favor of God upon the Israelites, God does confirm what Moses has spoken. Yet, Moses is still not satisfied with God's response. He continues to push Yahweh for a complete revelation. It is here that Moses' concern for the Israelites is dropped and his own need for the clearest revelation of God takes precedence. Here is where Moses imitates what the Israelites have done in chapter 32. By asking God to reveal Godself, Moses is seeking the image of God, the most substantive image of God. It is as if Moses is asking God for a Golden Calf, something Moses can hold. But God will not be held (see John 20:17).

To let Moses see God in God's fullness would be a grave mistake (pun intended). To see God is to die, as is stated in verse 20. Yet, perhaps, God is saying that this death is not just physical, but spiritual as well. To see God is to be tempted to worship only what has been seen (see John 20:29). To see God would be to get stuck on the image of God rather than continuing in a dynamic relationship with God.

What God does offer, though, is even more of Godself than Moses requests. God is saying, "Moses, don't get stuck on my presence. Know who I am." It seems that God's way of seeing humanity (see 1 Sam. 16:7ff where God does not look on outward appearances, but to the heart) is the same criteria with which we are to see God.

And how will God be known? By God's character. If Moses and we are to know God, we will do so by seeing how God acts. In God's love and compassion for people God will be known. Is this not how we are known as well?

III. An Invitation to the Journey (vv. 21-23)

Finally, instead of seeing God's face, Moses merely catches a glimpse of the Almighty's backside. Yet, perhaps this is again God's way of inviting Moses to continue the journey. This glimpse is an invitation to Moses and the people of Israel to not get stuck with the image or images, but to continue pursuing God, the way they followed the cloud and fire of God's glory in Exodus 16:7, 10; 24:16-17; 34:5; and 40:34, 38. It is a bid to join God on the journey. God beckons to Moses to continue the movement toward the promised land. And the journey continues.

IV. Reflections

Interestingly enough, God's revelation comes after Moses reveals himself to God in chapter 32. Is it because Moses allows himself to be known to God that God now has the same freedom? Do we, when we truly express all of ourselves to God, even to the point of confronting God, give God the opportunity to more fully disclose Godself to us? It is this way with our relationships with other people. The more honest we are with them the more apt they will be to reveal themselves to us.

God is a God of movement and not static moments. God is continually challenging us to move in the direction of the mountain. "Don't just get stuck. Keep moving." This is a God of becoming. We have put so much emphasis on the initial encounter with Jesus that we have cut off the life of the Christian faith. It is not about that initial moment, but about the moments that occur daily. It is about inviting God to be born in you daily. It is about embracing your humanity in such a way that every moment is a new birth and a celebration of every birth. God bless your journey. (Scott P. Mikels)

IT IS GOOD TO GIVE PRAISE

1 THESSALONIANS 1:1-10

These first words of Paul's letter to the congregation at Thessalonica are tremendously important. First, these are Paul's first recorded words. This congregation, established very early in Paul's ministry (see Acts 17:1-9), remained in his heart long after he had left their community. After receiving a report from Timothy of their progress in the gospel, as well as some of their concerns (1 Thess. 3:1-10), Paul writes a letter of encouragement, dated perhaps in the late 40s, written while he was in Athens. When we read these first ten verses we are reading the thoughts of the young missionary Paul, who is writing his first words in his first letter to one of his first churches.

Second, these early words are important for us, because they establish the tone of the conversation in the letter and reveal the relationship between Paul and the congregation in Thessalonica. The opening paragraph of any document is one of the most difficult, yet most significant, portions of the entire text. The opening words set the tone for the writing, entice the listener to read, and introduce pertinent themes that will be seen later in the text. In this case, the first ten verses set the tone for the entire letter, encourage the reader to keep reading, and introduce particular themes that Paul will address throughout the epistle.

When Paul addresses the church of the Thessalonians and offers them grace and peace, he establishes the *ambience of hospitality* in this communication with young converts to the faith. Although later to become a standard greeting for much of Paul's writings, this greeting seeks to link Paul with the community, who then in turn become linked to "God the Father and the Lord Jesus Christ" (1:1). In addition, the remainder verses will use important relational phrases such as "we always thank God for all of you" (1:2 NIV). Paul reveals his deep care for the people in Thessalonica when he admits that he knows that God "has chosen you" (1:4 NIV). In addition, he reminds them of his care for them (1:5). Paul cares deeply for these people, and he is not afraid to show his feelings for them, even in the opening words of the letter. With this setting, the listener wants to hear more.

Not only do these ten verses establish an ambience of hospitality, they also are filled with *praise for the listener*. Paul's use of praise keeps the listener connected to his words and ministry. Paul praises the believers for their ability to receive the gospel of Christ (1:6), for being an example to all of the believers in Macedonia and Achaia (1:7), for the warm reception given to the missionaries (1:9), and for their deep spirituality (1:9*b*-10). Paul's words do not reveal a psychological manipulative strategy that flatters in order to receive benefits in return. Rather, these energetic words of commendation are spoken from one who has known the congregation's struggles and victories. And in this moment, Paul wants to offer his personal words of encouragement. The listener wants to hear more.

In addition, the opening words of Paul's letter are interesting to us because they function much like an overture to an opera. The goal of the overture is to introduce the various musical themes that will be heard in the remainder of the musical composition. In the same way, this beginning section, verses 1-10, *reveals themes* found in the remaining parts of Paul's letter. The themes of praise (vv. 2-4*a*), Paul's ministry (vv. 5-6*a*), persecution (vv. 6-8), Christian sanctification (v. 9), and eschatological expectation (v. 10) are introduced and the same themes will be repeated in the remainder of the letter. What does this say to you, the preacher? Do not be afraid of praise!! Something in us does not allow lavish praise. Somewhere we have been taught that praise should be used sparingly. Perhaps in the adversarial school of learning, praise is seen as too soft, too feminine. Those advocates contend that learning, if done right, should hurt and cause violence and destruction. In order to follow rigid pedagogical standards of that tradition, praise is not seen as characteristic of good teaching. Paul, obviously, does not follow that tradition.

Paul, like the best of them, could vilify others as well as the next person. Read Galatians to see Paul's other side. But, in this congregation, they do not need shaming or shouting, blaming or exhorting. They need praise and encouragement. The young believers need to be affirmed that their religious commitments have been noticed and appreciated. They need to know that they are loved by their missionary leader, Paul. Our own preaching should do no less. (Linda McKinnish Bridges)

BETWEEN A ROCK AND A HARD PLACE

MATTHEW 22:15-22

I have borrowed a well-known phrase for the title of my sermon. Senator Mark Hatfield used the phrase as the title of his 1976 book in which he discussed the struggles of Christians who are in politics. We Christians, of all people, are eternally caught "between a rock and a hard place" in such matters. That's because we have dual citizenship; we travel through this world with two passports. The tension between the earthly realm and the heavenly never goes away.

Our text is the first of four consecutive "controversy" or "confrontation" stories in Matthew, in which Jesus butts heads with religious authorities. The authorities are out to trap him. On this occasion, Jesus faces the best-laid trap of all, as the Pharisees *and* the Herodians confront him. This is an unusual mix. The Gospels mention only one other occasion (Mark 3:6) on which these two groups get together. There's little love lost between them. The Pharisees represent the religious establishment, while the Herodians represent hated Roman political domination.

In A.D. 6 Rome levied a poll tax against the Jews, a tax that sparked many clashes between Romans and Jews. The Pharisees despised the tax, while the Herodians supported it. By asking their question of Jesus, the two groups were throwing him into the classical no-win situation. By answering, Jesus would give one or the other group reason to condemn him.

The tax could be paid only in Roman coins, which contained images and inscriptions that most Jews considered blasphemous. Jesus asked for the "legal tender" with which the tax was paid. Guess who produced it? The Pharisees, who were standing in their own sacred space, took the idolatrous coin from their own pockets, thereby acknowledging their acquiescence to the emperor.

Jesus' words ring out: "Give therefore to the emperor the things that are the emperor's, and to God the things that are God's." Jesus is not dividing the world into two realms with two sovereigns. Nor is he enunciating a doctrine of separation of church and state; that issue comes out of the eighteenth-century

365

Pastoral Prayer:

God of Moses and Miriam, who led your people through the wilderness to the edge of the promised land, take us to the mountaintop that we might glimpse a land that flows with milk and honey. Give us a glimpse. Make us yearn to see the day of your coming. Miriam did not get to enter that land, but she danced for the freedom of your people. Moses did not get to enter that land, but he did many signs and wonders in your name. Martin Luther King Jr. did not enter that land, but he served you as a drum major for justice. Oscar Romero did not enter that land, but he refused to stop speaking for those who had no voice. We lift the names of these prophets before you. Fill our mouths with words of power as you spoke through them. Anoint us with a spirit of hope as you anointed them. Make us dreamers. Show us the path to the promised land. Walk with us along it. Let us be servants of your good news. To those who are poor. To those who are sick. To those who close their ears to the cries of the hungry. To those who refuse to see the suffering of their neighbors. To the church when it betrays your great commandment. To the nation when it makes war instead of justice. In the name of the One who will welcome us all when we reach your promised land, Our Messiah, Jesus Christ, who lives and reigns with you and the Spirit. Amen. (Scott Haldeman)

SERMON BRIEFS

FROM BEGINNING TO END

DEUTERONOMY 34:1-12

The story of Moses' birth and infancy is a beloved tale. It reminds us of the blessed beginning of one who would become one of God's most dedicated servants, who would lead his people out of slavery. Throughout the Hebrew Bible, we are given dozens of accounts of such glorious beginnings, but we rarely are told the end of the great prophets' stories. Moses is no exception. We are mesmerized by his wonderful beginning, but the end of Moses' story is mysterious. Yet, in the few verses in Deuteronomy

Paul's travel itinerary in Acts suggests that Paul's greatest opposition came after the Jerusalem Conference recorded in Acts 15. Could it have been that the ones who were out to ruin Paul's reputation belonged to the Jewish-Christian church in Jerusalem? If so, then the opposition is really close, and deeply complex. These are Paul's contemporaries, people who have committed themselves to the gospel just as Paul has, but with one major difference—they will consider Gentiles as Christians only if they become Jews first.

Paul does not make those claims in Asia Minor. He openly refutes the religious tradition that connects ethnic identity and the gospel. He preaches clearly that salvation comes by faith only, not by circumcision, or strict adherence to a dietary code. Paul's preaching goes against the grain of the first church. Conservative leaders of the mother church in Jerusalem have major problems with Paul's liberal interpretation. And they set out to dismantle his ministry by defaming his name.

Some believers want to connect ethnic identity with salvation, that is, to require Jewish customs as prerequisite for salvation. Other believers, within the same church, contend that racial identity is not a requirement for salvation, and that Gentiles can become Christian without having to become Jews first.

Paul is caught in the middle of the argument. His desire to take the gospel to Asia Minor, however, overrides any ethnic pride. Paul preaches the gospel without announcing anything about the results of the Jerusalem Conference. And the religious leaders in Jerusalem are angry.

In response, they cause trouble everywhere Paul goes. In this passage, Paul reminds the people in the church of the Thessalonians of his faithfulness and courage in preaching the gospel (1 Thess. 2:2); of his honesty in presentation (2:3); of his personal integrity (2:4); of his lack of impure motive (2:5-6). Rumors have been flying that Paul is in the ministry for the money, that he speaks only to please people, that he is dishonest.

In response to the accusations of the opposition, and the possible distrust of the Thessalonians, Paul defends his reputation by saying that he has come to the believers at Thessalonica like a mother nursing her children (2:7-8). This image of intimacy, of self-revelation, sets Paul apart from the hierarchy in Jerusalem.

He does not follow their lead of sharp criticism and defamation of character. Rather, he sees himself as a self-giving mother who gives of her own life sustenance freely and without remorse, who longs for intimate moments of giving and receiving, and whose intimate relationship cannot be destroyed by outside forces— even religious leaders from the church! A nursing mother image stands to revolutionize our understanding of church leadership. That image will preach! Go for it. (Linda McKinnish Bridges)

ON LOVING ONESELF

MATTHEW 22:34-46

One of the most important things about any of us is our self-concept. It has enormous bearing on all of our behavior. It affects our relationships, and our view of God. Self-concept is not a subject we learn in school. It is part of the informal education that we receive long before we ever go to school. Transactional analysis told us that there are two life positions: O.K. and NOT O.K. The majority of us start out feeling NOT O.K., and these negative feelings never go away.

Religion greatly influences people's self-image, for obvious reasons. Religion tells us who we are, and how we fit into things. Sometimes, it sends us mixed signals. In Christianity, there is a vast witness that tells us that we are NOT O.K. We are sinners. And why? Primarily because we're self-centered. We put ourselves in the place of God.

At this point, I'm puzzled. Is it true that we are spontaneously good to ourselves? *Do we love ourselves too much?* In a great many cases, I don't believe we can say yes. In fact, a mountain of evidence shows that quite often we do *not* act in our own best interests. Creatures who love themselves too much just couldn't do the things we do to ourselves!

Americans are killing themselves in record numbers—at all ages! Self-contempt is rampant. One form is through self-mutilation, which is a surprisingly common way of acting out self-hate. Another phenomenon is what one writer has called "partial suicide," whereby people systematically destroy their talents, energies, and creative qualities. Subtle forms of self-degradation, such as substance abuse and promiscuity, could also be mentioned. And what about the way many of us don't take care of our health? On and on the list goes.

It doesn't appear that we have an overabundance of self-love. In fact, it seems that low self-esteem is more common. What we need, then, is much more love in our lives and, as our text tells us, that love needs to flow in all directions—to God, and to others and to ourselves. These three are tied together: love of God, love of others, love of self.

We must draw an important distinction between being wrapped up in ourselves *and* genuinely loving ourselves. The person who is self-absorbed is vain and selfish. Genuine love of self is altogether different. It draws us out of ourselves and results in our loving God and others.

What must happen in order for us to love ourselves properly? First, we have to experience love; we have to know that we're loved. Since no one loves more than God does, we could expect to find the purest form of love in *God's love for us*. Although we may receive God's love directly from God, often it's reflected to us through others—people who care about us, affirm us, and love us unconditionally—and people whom we learn to love in return.

The Bible is a record of God's love for this world. God is the Great Lover, whose love is unconditional and unfailing. Jesus Christ is the chief expression of that love. He's a signal that God is *for* us, not against us. Jesus did not come to make us more religious, but to make us more loving. He came to draw us out of ourselves, and into a bright new future with God and our neighbors.

Yes, we're sinners. But we're also something else: we're creatures of God's own hand—objects of God's unconditional love. That love is a transforming power that draws us out of ourselves and into the world. Such love is the medicine for the healing of the nations. (Sandy Wylie)

SPIRITUAL PREPARATION

NOVEMBER

I was serving as pastor of four rural churches, a preaching circuit, and one of the churches was having its annual bazaar. My wife and I were participants in a version of *The Newlywed Game*. While the husbands were in the soundproof booths, the wives were asked this question: "What will your husband say is his favorite holiday?" We were not doing well as a team, but a light went on in my wife's mind. "Easter," she said confidently. "After all, he's a preacher—what else could he say?" We emerged from the room and took our places next to the wives. Soon the question was asked: "What is your favorite holiday?" I listened to the other responses; visions of my grandmother's turkey and dressing danced in my head. "Thanksgiving!" I answered. "Oh no!" my wife cried out, burying her head in her hands. "You're a preacher and your favorite holiday is Thanksgiving?"

As you can imagine, I have since been forced to come up with theological reasons to support my answer, which was admittedly based on less than spiritual grounds. But I've not had to search very hard. I have been drawn especially to Paul's words to the Philippians:

> I rejoice in the Lord greatly that now at last you have revived your concern for me; indeed, you were concerned for me, but had no opportunity to show it. Not that I am referring to being in need; for I have learned to be content with whatever I have. I know what it is to have little, and I know what it is to have plenty. In any and all circumstances I have learned the secret of being well-fed and of going hungry, of having plenty and of being in need. I can do all things through him who strengthens me. (4:10-13)

To embrace each day in the spirit of Thanksgiving—this is our calling. The contemplative monk Thomas Merton has been one of the great influences on my life. In speaking about a life of prayer, his words echo those of the apostle:

> In prayer we discover what we already have. You start where you are and you deepen. What you already have, and you realize that you are already there. We already have everything, but we don't know it, and we don't experience it. Everything has been given to us in Christ. All we need is to experience what we already possess.

To embrace this day in the spirit of Thanksgiving is to become more aware of what God has done for us, placed in our hands, set on the table before us. As pastors we give thanks, we learn the secret of being content, we discover that "everything has been given to us in Christ." For this reason we celebrate Thanksgiving with all God's people. And yes, we look forward with joyous anticipation to the great Feast.

- How can a spirit of Thanksgiving emerge in your own life? How would you express it, in a prayer to God? How would you respond to it, in relation to others?

November includes the celebration of Thanksgiving. For many pastors there is the additional experience during these days of the fall stewardship campaign. This can be stressful, confusing, exciting, and clarifying. The stewardship campaign is one of those few times in a pastor's life when the mission can be measured. While this should not be seen as reductionistic—ministry is more than numbers—it can also be placed, as an act of ministry, within an understanding of thanksgiving. The words of the apostle Paul and Thomas Merton can be meaningful to individuals; they can also be helpful to congregations and their leaders. If you sense that you are carrying the weight of the stewardship campaign on your shoulders, I invite you to read Philippians 4. The apostle Paul has gone ahead of us, grateful for the gifts of God's people, experiencing abundance and scarcity, trusting in the providence of God.

Providence—that is the word that undergirds a life of gratitude and thanksgiving. God provides. Some of you have ancestors who farmed; some readers may serve in agricultural communities.

Those who work the land know what it is to trust in providence, each day. One of the hymns for this season speaks of providence:

> Come, ye thankful people, come, raise the song of harvest home;
> All is safely gathered in, ere the winter storms begin.
> God our maker doth provide for our wants to be supplied;
> Come to God's own temple, come, raise the song of harvest home.
> ("Come Ye Thankful People, Come," Verse One)

The God who creates us also provides for us. The provision of our needs evokes gratitude. The harvest in this life points us to the glorious harvest in the life to come. And the knowledge that God provides in the present gives us hope for the future. In this way thanksgiving and gratitude lead to the beginnings of Advent:

> Even so, Lord, quickly come, bring thy final harvest home;
> Gather thou thy people in, free from sorrow, free from sin,
> There, forever purified, in thy presence to abide;
> Come, with all thine angels, come, raise the glorious harvest home.
> ("Come, Ye Thankful People, Come," Verse Four)

- How can you prepare, in the days of November, for the season of Advent? What are the signs of hope in your own life? In the lives of your people?

While I have hinted at this, I must conclude with a specific word about the celebration of Holy Communion (the Lord's Supper). When we proclaim the great thanksgiving, we are remembering with gratitude all that God has done for us: in creation, in covenant, in the prophets, in the person of Jesus Christ, and in the power of the Holy Spirit. We feed God's people as we offer and celebrate this meal. We understand, in moments of weakness, that we, too, are spiritually hungry. In these busy days, may you be nourished and sustained with the bread of life, Jesus Christ our Savior. Amen. (Ken Carter)

Sources: *Thomas Merton/Monk: A Monastic Tribute* (Kalamazoo: Cistercian, 1983), p. 9; *United Methodist Hymnal* (Nashville: UMPH), 1989, p. 694).

NOVEMBER 3, 2002

Twenty-fourth Sunday After Pentecost

Worship Theme: The gospel does not weigh upon us as a burdensome yoke but lightens our load so that we may serve rather than seek honor and humble ourselves to exalt the One who bestows grace.

Readings: Joshua 3:7-17; 1 Thessalonians 2:9-13; Matthew 23:1-12

Call to Worship (Psalm 107):

Leader: Let the redeemed of the LORD praise their Deliverer. God satisfies the thirsty, and the hungry are filled with good things.

People: **We cried to the LORD in our trouble, and God delivered us from our distress.**

Leader: Some sat in darkness and in gloom, prisoners in misery and in irons.

People: **We cried to the LORD in our trouble, and God delivered us from our distress.**

Leader: Some were sick, enduring affliction.

People: **We cried to the LORD in our trouble, and God delivered us from our distress.**

Leader: Let the redeemed of the LORD praise their Deliverer.

People: **Let us worship God.**

Pastoral Prayer:

God of the covenant, with your ark you divided the waters of the Jordan so your people could cross over on dry ground and enter into the land you had promised to Sarah and Abraham, to Miriam and Moses, to all your people that they might dwell in peace. We pray for peace in that land today. We pray for all your people who choose possession over peace, autonomy rather than equity, national security instead of negotiated settlements. Move again over the waters to calm the storms of violence. Open new avenues of diplomacy. Send your Spirit to renew your whole creation. Send your Spirit to us now that we might lighten the burden for the weary in our midst. Comfort those who mourn. Heal those who are sick. Bless those who are laden with self-hatred. Lift up those who feel inferior. Indict those who ridicule, neglect, or violate. Reveal the path of righteousness and order our steps in your way. Amen. (Scott Haldeman)

SERMON BRIEFS

STEPPING OUT ON FAITH

JOSHUA 3:7-17

Children fascinate me. Recently, I spent time with a ten-month-old toddler. She has developed some of her motor skills, and though standing with support is no problem, she is not so confident when it comes to letting go and standing alone. Every now and then, she will let go, and stands confidently with a slight sway, until she loses her nerve and grabs onto the nearest support. What keeps her holding on when she obviously is strong enough to stand independently? Then, I remember that for her every new experience, like standing without support, is a leap of faith. She does not have the experience to know what is going to happen when she lets go. With every new attempt, she is boldly stepping out on faith.

Stepping out alone on faith, without a guarantee of the outcome, has long been a challenge for humankind. Throughout the Scriptures, God challenges creation toward a higher level of faith.

The story of the crossing of the Jordan in Joshua 3 is no exception. The Israelites are at the end of a long journey. Their leadership has been transferred from the now deceased Moses to Joshua. They are at the threshold of conquering the land that is the fulfillment of their covenant with God. However, they must first cross the Jordan River, which is swollen out of its banks and flooding. The Lord gives the command to Joshua that a great miracle is about to take place, and that through this miracle, God will affirm Joshua's chosenness and leadership to all of Israel. Joshua is to send the priests carrying the ark of the covenant to the edge of the swelling Jordan River. As soon as they step into the water, the river will split and the Israelites can cross the river on dry land. Through this miracle, God will again demonstrate devotion to the Israelites, and the Israelites will acknowledge the special leadership of Joshua.

It is impossible to read this story without remembering Exodus 14, in which the Red Sea splits at Moses' command, allowing the Hebrews to cross, while drowning the Egyptians. Even with the similarity of the two events, there are several things that make the crossing of the Jordan starkly different. First, Joshua is not out in front commanding the river to split. Instead, God directs Joshua to give instructions to the priests, and then let them take the first step. Second, the priests had to take initiative by stepping into the river, as it still swelled. The dry land would only appear after their first step into the water. The Israelites approached the Red Sea out of desperation, as their enemy pursued them. This time, they approached the Jordan strictly on faith. They believed that God had promised Joshua a miracle. They knew that God had delivered their ancestors across the Red Sea. Yet, when it came right down to it, they had no proof of what would happen when they stepped with their most precious item into the flooding waters. Their first step, their initiative, was ultimately a leap of faith. Their feet had to touch the waters before the dry land would come. They had no proof or guarantee. They had no personal experience. They were like a child standing alone for the first time. However, they had to trust more than just themselves, they had to trust God. (Tracey Allred)

PAUL'S PERSONAL APOLOGIA: AN EXHORTING FATHER

1 THESSALONIANS 2:9-13

In the preceding section (2:1-8), Paul reveals his credentials for authentic ministry. However, his personal summary catches the ancient and modern reader by surprise. Paul describes his ministerial authority, but not in the terms of the religious bureaucracy in Jerusalem (who have been working diligently to undermine Paul's reputation with believers in Asia Minor). The terms of his defense are not couched in the cultural forms of power, where one could use images from the hierarchy of military or government. In surprising ways, Paul goes home for his metaphor of power. His defense against his opposition is first to go into the world of woman, into the feminine world of power. In first-century patriarchal society, power was made manifest in many ways, but certainly not in maternal imagery of nursing babies! Yet, it is this image of nursing and feeding babies with one's own body that becomes Paul's guiding metaphor of leadership.

In this section (2:9-13) he continues refuting the opposition, most likely identified as Jewish Christian members of the religious hierarchy in Jerusalem. Again, he chooses surprising and shocking language that does not appear to come from the traditional notion of power at all. Paul, who certainly could have borrowed images from the powerful world of military might, flourishing commerce, or governmental functions, rather fashions his style of leadership as that of a nursing mother and an exhorting father (2:11).

The role of Father in the ancient Mediterranean world was different from our modern understanding. The father had the role of religious leadership in the home. In our contemporary society, the mother holds this important position. The role of Father in ancient society was important for the religious understanding in the home. The father responded to this role of leadership in the home by exhorting, admonishing, and cheerleading the children (2:12).

Images of pastoral leadership have gone through periods of great change. For example, images such as shepherd, pastoral care giver, friend, overseer, and spiritual guide have emerged through the years. With each cultural shift of organizational strategy in the marketplace has come a new image for church leadership.

However, lodged in an ancient text written more than seventeen hundred years ago by an energetic young missionary belonging to the patriarchal culture of the Jewish and Greco-Roman world, rests an even more potent image than any of those listed above. From the world of nursery, family, mother, father, come two of the most powerful images of power. Paul makes a particular point of saying that he has come to these young believers as a mother comes to nurse her children, and as a father comes to teach his children. Straight from the world of domestication, Paul finds his images of power.

Paul resisted the conservative, narrow-minded views of the Jewish Christians in Jerusalem. He listened respectfully to the conversations at the Jerusalem Conference. He disagreed with some of the speakers and agreed with others. But, for the most part, he refused to acknowledge the control of the religious hierarchy on what he thought was his most important life work—to preach the gospel to the Gentiles.

In this same maverick style, Paul refuses to define ecclesiastical power in terms of the culture. The demands of the patriarchal structure of culture would, in time, arrange the spirit and structure of the early church (as seen in the Pastoral Epistles). But, at this moment, in the early hours of the life of the church, Paul plants his feet on the ground and refuses to borrow from the traditional places. For Paul, a good pastor is one who loves like a mother giving milk from her own breasts to her children. For Paul, a good pastor is one who loves the people like a father who spends time teaching his children, by guiding them with his teaching and constant encouragement. The early church began in the home, and the home began the early church. May we find some new models of ministry there for ourselves. (Linda McKinnish Bridges)

TRIPPING OVER TITLES

MATTHEW 23:1-12

Jack came home and announced to his wife, "Jill, let's go out and celebrate. I've been made vice president of the company!" Jill seemed unmoved, so Jack tried again: "I said I've been made vice president!"

Jill replied, "That's great, Jack. But vice presidents are a dime a dozen. Why, down at our supermarket they've got so many vice presidents that there's one in charge of prunes."

Jack wasn't about to take this, so he phoned the supermarket. "Hello, connect me to the vice president in charge of prunes." The voice at the other end replied, "Fresh prunes or processed prunes?"

This story relates to Jesus' teaching in our text. His teaching is aimed at the scribes and Pharisees. The scribes were professional clergy who were theologically educated and ordained. They were scholars and rabbis. The Pharisees were laypeople who were dedicated to keeping the Law. So this story concerns both the clergy and the laity, especially leaders. And it has this application today.

Leadership is important in every organization, including the church. Jesus faulted some religious leaders of his time, because they seemed to be focused more on their own glorification than on the glorification of God. He gave examples: they dressed ostentatiously; they grabbed the places of honor at feasts and in the synagogues; and they gloried in being saluted in the market-places, and being called "rabbi" and even "father."

This sort of thing continues today. Some clergy preach in full academic dress, sport fancy titles, drop names all over the place, and adopt pretensions.

A pastor received an honorary doctor's degree from a university. He was flattered when a few people had addressed him as "Doctor," but something happened that put it all in perspective. One day the telephone rang, and his young daughter answered. The caller asked for her father by his new title. The girl knew that her dad had been given that title, but she was confused, since the only doctors she knew were physicians. She replied, "He isn't here right now. But I think there's something you should know. He isn't the kind of doctor that will do you any good!"

Titles and social distinctions can too easily become hindrances. We sometimes too easily wind up serving them, tripping over them, and hiding behind them. Jesus tells his followers to leave them alone! In the early church, the usual salutation of Christians for each other was "brother" or "sister." This reflected the example of Jesus.

What about this title "saint"? Isn't it a pretentious title? We might be tempted to do away with it, but it's embedded in our tradition. What we need is to get a better grasp of what a saint is, in the biblical sense. We tend to see saints as people of extraordinary virtue who have little connection with other mortals. But notice how freely Paul uses that title. He writes to the saints in Rome, the saints in Corinth, the saints in Philippi, and so forth. Paul seems to be saying that *all* Christians are supposed to be saints!

But "saint" isn't a title we can claim for ourselves. It's a title that believers confer on us mainly because of our godly influence on others. Paul Tillich observed that saints are saints not because they are good, but because they are transparent for something that is larger than they are.

The standard that Jesus Christ has set for us to be saints isn't whether we are people of social importance, or title, or learning, or wealth. The standard is this: Do we conform to his spirit of service, generosity, and love? Do people see God in us?

Of all of the questions that we might ask of ourselves and others, these are the ones that ultimately matter. (Sandford Wylie)

NOVEMBER 10, 2002

Twenty-fifth Sunday After Pentecost

Worship Theme: Stay awake, be prepared, choose well how you live—for a new age is coming, the Lord returns, and we do not know the day or the hour.

Readings: Joshua 24:1-3*a*, 14-25; 1 Thessalonians 4:13-18; Matthew 25:1-13

Call to Worship (Psalm 78):

Leader:	Give ear, O my people, to my teaching; incline your ears to the words of my mouth.
People:	**Let us listen to the word of the Lord.**
Leader:	God established a decree in Jacob, and appointed a law in Israel, which he commanded our ancestors to teach to their children; that the next generation might know them, the children yet unborn, so that they should set their hope in God, and not forget the works of God, but keep his commandments.
People:	**We will tell to our children God's law that they should not lose hope.**
Leader:	For God led the Hebrews to freedom and provided them water to drink from a rock.
People:	**God is faithful to God's people; we will not lose hope.**
Leader:	With upright heart God tended God's people, and guided them with skillful hand.
People:	**God is faithful to us; let us worship God.**

Pastoral Prayer:

Hidden Savior, you live now beyond our gaze, we await your coming. Commission us to do your ministry. Empower us with your grace to save. Provide us with a foretaste of the banquet that we should not lose hope, nor fall asleep and miss your arrival. We await you. Catch us up, with all those who are being saved, those on the earth and those under the earth. Fulfill your promise to us of eternal life. As we live in expectation, visit us now with your Spirit. Restore our strength. Fill our lungs with the breath of life. Give to us the nourishment of the bread of life. Drown us in the font of your death and resurrection. Send us as salt to those who have lost the taste for life. Send us as light to those who are lost in gloom. Bring us all to the great banquet table where none shall want and all are welcomed and filled with good things. Amen. (Scott Haldeman)

SERMON BRIEFS

WHOM WILL YOU SERVE?

JOSHUA 24:1-3*a*, 14-25

Being a servant is never easy. The selfless commitment that it takes to truly serve another person, no strings attached, is extremely difficult for human beings. Perhaps this is why stories of people, such as Mother Teresa feeding starving children, and anonymous accounts of strangers running into burning homes to rescue the residents, fascinate us. There seems to be an unspoken understanding that true servanthood is almost impossible to find in our modern world. No wonder we have difficulty being in true service to God—not only understanding the ramifications of serving the Creator, but truly taking seriously the call to serve God given throughout the Scriptures.

One of the strongest calls to God's service is found in Joshua 24. As the covenant is renewed once more, this time at Shechem, Joshua, speaking on behalf of God, reminds the Israelites of their call to truly serve God. Once again, the Israelites are reminded of not only the faithfulness of God, but of their own rebellion against God. Joshua encourages the Israelites to put away the false gods of their ancestors, those who had succumbed to Canaanite worship. In a powerful appeal (v. 15), Joshua implores his Hebrew brothers and sisters to this day choose whom they will serve. No longer can the Israelites meander through their lives serving the Lord God halfheartedly, while simultaneously acknowledging other gods. Joshua says, "Today, you must choose one or the other!" Moreover, he acknowledges that he and his family have made their choice—the Lord God.

After such a passionate plea, the Israelites immediately start recanting their service of other gods. As is their habit, the Israelites get swept up in an emotional moment. Sensitive to the plea of their leader, and the reminder of their ancestors' journey, they pledge their service to the Lord. Their action reminds me of the response to an altar call at an evangelical revival. Occasionally, after a particularly powerful, emotional plea from the preacher, people make equally emotional, rash pledges of faith, without much thought of the consequences or implications. Joshua understood this part of human nature, and especially the tendency of the Israelites to sometimes shift their allegiance, as the wind blows. He would not settle for their quick choice, and goes on through verse 24 reminding them of what choosing to serve God really means. He outlines the seriousness of their choice, and the implications of their covenant. This means their love, allegiance, and total service must be to their God, and to no other. By verse 25, Joshua feels confident that the Israelites really understand, and are ready to reaffirm their covenant with God.

Joshua took seriously what it meant to serve God. Before making this covenant at Shechem, Joshua wanted the Israelites to understand the implications of their commitment to serve the one true God. It is important for us to reevaluate our commitment to serve God, as well. Like the Israelites, we too are easily distracted and give our service and attention to other things. At times, we too are easily tempted to make rash statements of faith, when our true allegiance may belong elsewhere. Joshua reminds us of our true call to service, and the importance of reevaluating our priorities and truly recommitting to the Lord God. (Tracey Allred)

CONSOLATION WITH THESE WORDS

1 THESSALONIANS 4:13-18

These words have traditionally been used to outline the final moments of Jesus' return, commonly called the Rapture. At the last day, the voice of an archangel and a trumpet will be heard, then Jesus will return, and rapture first those who have died. Then the remaining ones are to be caught in the clouds, as they meet the Lord in the air.

This section has often characterized the entire letter as primarily concerned with providing details of Jesus' return. That judgment of eschatological interpretation, unfortunately, misses the primary point. That Jesus is going to return cannot be denied; that the early church were patiently waiting cannot be denied, as well; that Paul wrote this letter to provide minute-by-minute details of a final good-bye to life, as we have known it, is to be denied.

The community's concern relates to their grief over the death of their loved ones and their confusion over the delayed parousia. These faithful Christians have been waiting for Jesus to return, as he had promised. As they wait, their relatives have begun to die. And they are confused. Jesus was supposed to return before now, they are thinking. The community of believers in Thessalonica are grieving over the death of their loved ones. They do not need a poster detailing the events of the last day on some fine graph paper. The mourners do not need a doctrine of the last days to be created by Paul. They need words of consolation for the grieving hearts.

Paul writes his words to the believers, so that they might not "grieve as others do who have no hope" (4:13). The logic is clear. Just as Jesus died and rose, so shall our loved ones, Paul says (4:14). Our loved ones will be given priority treatment, says Paul, for they will rise first (4:15). Then the beautiful, grand events will occur—archangels and trumpets. Jesus will appear. The primary phrase, although often dwarfed by the grand apocalyptic images of verse 16, is verse 17b: "And in this manner we will be *together* with the Lord at all times." The hinge word for this entire section is a small but powerful Greek preposition, which means "together" (see 4:14). This section is about being together—together with our loved ones and together with the Lord. "Therefore comfort each other with these words," Paul admonishes.

How many times have our words been inappropriate for the setting? Many times we feel the need, perhaps developed from our own insecurities, to say something profound. It seems the preacher-thing to do! So, we search for words that are not our own, borrowed from a source not our own, from someone else's experience, not our own. And the words do not match the need of the moment. We have not listened before we have spoken.

The Thessalonians were grieving. What makes Paul such an effective missionary is that he heard their grief. They did not need a lecture on the Second Coming. They did not need a play-by-play, detailed description of the end of time. They needed comfort. They needed to know that death would not separate them from their dear family members and friends. They needed to know that God was still present, even though the promise of Jesus' return had been delayed. They needed to know that death would not separate them from their loved ones or from God. They needed comfort.

The irony is clear in the history of interpretation of this passage. For those who have longed for eschatological accuracy and precision in foretelling details belonging only to heaven, those readers have demanded that Paul's letter reveal the secrets of the last days. Just as Paul's intuitive style of leadership resisted traditional forms of doctrinal orthodoxy, so do his words continue to defy structures that look for a doctrinal response to a human problem. The people are grieving, and Paul gives them comfort. The manuals will come later. First, come the words of consolation. (Linda McKinnish Bridges)

PEOPLE OF VISION

MATTHEW 25:1-13

Matthew 25 is one of the most remarkable chapters in the New Testament. It ends the last block of Jesus' teachings in Matthew.

It concerns the kingdom of God and that final fulfillment toward which the world is moving.

Jesus begins by saying, "Then the kingdom of heaven will be like this. Ten bridesmaids took their lamps and went to meet the bridegroom . . ." The parable reflects Palestinian wedding customs, and it is full of symbolism. The wedding banquet is a New Testament symbol for the kingdom of God. The bridegroom represents the Lord of the church, and the bridesmaids represent his disciples. When the five foolish maidens are locked out of the banquet hall, they represent those would-be followers of Jesus who miss out on the kingdom.

The focus of the story is on these five foolish maidens. Just how do they miss out? The answer is that they are shortsighted and unprepared. They're muddleheaded. They don't have it all together.

The Quakers use a striking word that applies to these maidens. They talk about "allthereness." In the Christian life it's important that we be truly present to what's going on—that we be "all there." The wise and foolish bridesmaids represent two types of people. One type is people who are all there. The other type is people who are not all there. Other names for these people are doers and reactors.

Reactors are people who simply don't have control of their lives. They bounce from one predicament to another—always reacting, seldom in control. The reason why they *react* rather than *do* is that they have no real vision, no plan. Since they are not on a steady course, they are easily pushed around.

Doers, on the other hand, are people of vision. They've got a plan. They get bumped around and surprised like everyone else, but they don't get knocked off course. Doers know how to lay out a plan and follow it, how to estimate and prepare.

As Christians, we're called to know where history is moving—and that means we've got to have vision. God is a God of history. God is a God of change. God always has a plan. Whether it's an individual life, a congregation, a nation, or the whole human race, God has a plan for it. Can we see where history is moving?

In the history of our nation, we see a mixture of shortsightedness and farsightedness. There were those who plundered the earth, and there were the Johnny Appleseeds. So many of the blessings that we now enjoy came about because of the philanthropic endeavors of farsighted citizens.

When we support our church and work for its betterment, we're making an investment in the future. We're being people of vision. It's good to have a strong church at our side, so that it's always there, ready to help us, our family, and our neighbors. The writer of Proverbs says, "Where there is no vision, the people perish" (29:18 KJV).

On the individual level, the questions for today are, "Are you getting ready? Can you see where history is moving for you?" People of vision know that God's time for them will finally come. Promise will give way to fulfillment. Preparation will culminate in realization.

"The bridegroom came," said Jesus, "and *those who were ready* went with him into the wedding banquet." (Sandy Wylie)

NOVEMBER 17, 2002

Twenty-sixth Sunday After Pentecost

Worship Theme: We receive grace as a gift but do not hide it away in fear. We exercise our talents to accomplish God's purposes—like Deborah, a prophet of Israel who led the people in war and ruled them in peace; and like Paul, an apostle who suffered imprisonment to spread the gospel.

Readings: Judges 4:1-7; 1 Thessalonians 5:1-11; Matthew 25:14-30

Call to Worship (Psalm 123):

> *Leader:* To you I lift up my eyes, O you who are enthroned in the heavens!
>
> *People:* **Have mercy upon us, O LORD.**
>
> *Leader:* As the eyes of servants look to the hand of their master, as the eyes of a maid to the hand of her mistress, so our eyes look to the LORD our God, so that we might receive mercy.
>
> *People:* **Have mercy upon us, O LORD.**
>
> *Leader:* Have mercy upon us, O LORD, for we have had more than enough of contempt. Our soul has had more than its fill of the scorn of those who are at ease, of the contempt of the proud.
>
> *People:* **Have mercy upon us, O LORD.**

Pastoral Prayer:
God of the Prophets, you spoke through Deborah and delivered Israel from the cruel King Jabin, raise up this day women

and men of talent and faith to lead your church. Help us to con-, front injustice and to liberate those who struggle for self-determination. Help us to recognize and call forth each other's gifts for the common good. Who can heal? Who can interpret the signs of the times? Who can discern your will? Who can preach? Who can empower? Who can speak truth? Let the fruits of your Spirit be made visible among us so that we can be about your work. There is much to be done. There is no time to be idle. Through us may peace increase. May hungers be satisfied. May anxiety cease. May war be forgotten. May discrimination end. God of the Prophets, prophesy this day. Is this the Day of the Lord? Is this the Day of Jubilee? Is this the day of when the New Jerusalem will come down from heaven? Is this the day when you will dry our tears and death shall be no more? So be it. Amen. (Scott Haldeman)

SERMON BRIEFS

UNLIKELY SAVIORS

JUDGES 4:1-7

A favorite morning activity of mine is to sit with a cup of coffee, watching a morning news program. Feature reports highlighting the extraordinary accomplishments of ordinary citizens (for example, mall Santa performs CPR on infant, elderly woman lifts vehicle off of trapped child, stranger pulls man from burning building) are my favorites. These stories are reminders that in a world that seems callous and uncaring, there are individuals willing to risk their lives to save someone else. These stories illustrate that saviors come in all shapes and sizes, and that God still intervenes, even when we least expect it.

The book of Judges captures a time in Israelite history when a savior was much needed. A generation had passed since the triumphant victory over the Canaanites and the entry into the promised land. As Moses had feared, many Israelites had forgotten the God who had given them land and victory, and now dabbled in the religion of their neighbors. Israel was on a downward spiral, because of their poor choices and weakened faith. As Moses had prophesied, God was beginning to punish the Israelites for their rebellion. It was a desperate and confusing time for Israel. They lacked direction and leadership, and they were under attack. Israel was in need of a savior.

The stories of the various judges have a common theme. First, the Israelites rebel against God by turning toward other gods, and by breaking God's commandments. Second, God calls a judge to lead the Israelites out of their desperate situation through force or wisdom. Finally, the Israelites are victorious over their enemy and return to their devotion of the one true God of Israel. These judges were, in essence, saviors sent by God. They were unlikely saviors, just as Moses had been, usually not the strongest or most courageous, and definitely not what the Israelites were expecting. Perhaps this is why they were so effective. One of the more unlikely of saviors was probably Deborah.

Little is known of Deborah's background. Even before the crisis between Jabin and the Israelites, she was a judge to whom the Israelites brought their legal concerns and arguments. There is no account in Scripture of her "call experience" with God, as there is with many of the judges. Instead, there is the simple story of rebellion by the Israelites, and action by Deborah to intervene on their behalf. Of course, she did not act alone. She summoned Barak, who reluctantly agreed to lead an army against Jabin's forces. However, the real victory occurred at the hand of another unsuspected savior, Jael, who killed the general of Jabin's army. In this story, God once again delivered God's chosen people, this time by the hands of a female arbitrator, a reluctant military leader, and a courageous wife. Israel needed a savior, and God provided three unlikely ones. As has been done many times before and since, God chose an everyday, unsuspecting trio to save God's chosen ones.

Throughout history, both individually and communally, God has offered a means of salvation. Sometimes from a flood. Sometimes through a judge. Sometimes by a shepherd turned king, and ultimately through the love and sacrifice of Jesus Christ. Just as we are still a people in need of God's saving grace, God is still a saving God. Often we find glimpses of God's grace and mercy through someone like Deborah or Barak. God's choices may seem as strange as some of the heroic feature stories that I watch on morning TV, but as God has proven again and again, it is not by our standards or choices that God chooses to save us, it is by God alone. (Tracey Allred)

WE SHALL LIVE TOGETHER THEN AND NOW

1 THESSALONIANS 5:1-11

Community life is central to Paul's understanding of church. The central theme of 1 Thessalonians is life together, both in the future realm of heaven and in the earthly realm of life in Thessalonica, Greece. Other problems, however, did emerge from the community. For example, the believers were concerned about the end of time, who would be present, and how it would happen. Paul answers their question by pointing to the basic reality of being together with loved ones and the Lord at the time of death and resurrection.

In addition, the Thessalonians are wanting to know not only how the end will occur, but also when. Paul responds to them confirming that they already know the answer, namely, that the Lord will "come like a thief in the night" (5:2) when one least expects Christ's return. Fortunate for the believers, however, is the reality that they are not walking in darkness, but in the light, and they will not be taken by surprise. In other words, the thief metaphor cannot fully be used for believers. Because of their faith, they do not have to live in fear or dread, as one fearful of the appearance of a robber. The community can live wide-awake, hopeful lives.

The ethical demands for living while one waits are important to Paul and to the community. Believers are to be alert and well-balanced (5:6), putting on "the breastplate of faith and love, and for a helmet the hope of salvation" (5:8). The ultimate understanding is that whether alive or awake, "we may live with him" (5:10).

Having that knowledge, then, what does the community do? By now Paul's response has become redundant and repetitive, but no less significant for the ancient community than for ours, as well. Again, Paul places the value of community relationship above all doctrinal information, even ethical sanctions, when he says: "Therefore encourage one another and build up each other, as indeed you are doing" (v. 11).

What is the goal of church? Most of us realize that the church is changing drastically. Church membership is in decline; denominationalism is on the wane; and yet people seem to be wanting places of sacred fellowship. As the traditional religious structures lose their centralized position in culture, we need to rethink the purpose of the faith community. What is the basic, nonnegotiable attribute of a faith community?

For Paul and this community, there is one primary responsibility of a faith community. The believers in Thessalonians are to "encourage one another and build up each other" (5:11). Perhaps church leaders need to hear this central feature of Paul's understanding of church one more time. Perhaps we need to be reminded of this constituent feature, because this is where we, as a community of faith, have most successfully missed the mark.

The newspapers are filled weekly with advertisements announcing various support groups, from Alcoholics Anonymous to those for couples with infertility concerns. People need support from other people, in order to maneuver through life's crises. This is not new. However, organized religion has been guilty of "shooting the wounded," rather than providing a hospital for healing.

As religious people, we have established high standards of acceptability and performance that we simply cannot reach. Rather than lower the standards of admission into the fellowship, we have just limited the fellowship. What if the church of the twenty-first century became the place, much like that church in Thessalonica, where believers knew clearly that their role was not to be the sole gatekeeper of respectable doctrine or ethics? Rather, the role of the believer was to focus on encouraging another in the fellowship for the purpose of building up, rather than tearing down. What a difference that would make! (Linda McKinnish Bridges)

WHO DO YOU WANT TO BE?

MATTHEW 25:14-30

J. Ellsworth Kalas in *Parables from the Backside* recounts the story of a farmer who asks, "What are you going to plant this spring, Jake? Corn?" Jake replies: "Nope, I am scared of the corn borer." Oh, says the farmer, "Will you then plant potatoes?" And Jake replies, "Nope, too much danger of potato bugs." The farmer is at a loss and says, "Well, what are you going to plant then?" Jake answers, "Nothing. I am going to play it safe."

Every time I read this parable, I wonder if Jesus had me in mind, since I am among the worst financial investors! (As a former practicing attorney and with a CPA as father, my "investor genetic makeup" is not that of a financial risk taker!) I would not even be as financially risky as the third slave, since by putting money in the ground, I feel I would take undue risks! Indeed, there could be an earthquake, mud sliding, dogs and people could find it, and so forth. But, is this a parable about risk taking, and if yes, who is the one truly taking the risks?

Is the master the one guilty of giving extravagantly? The value of the "funds to be invested" that were given to the slaves would be the equivalent of several years' worth of wages. Is the master not a fool for having entrusted such precious belongings to his servants and then disappearing from the horizon?

Some believe that the Master represents Christ, who announces to his disciples that he is going away for a while, and that during his absence, he entrusts his disciples with the valuable possession of the gospel. If this is an interpretation you trust, then, should the Master not be considered a fool for entrusting humanity with God's work? Would it not have been more "cost-efficient" for Christ to have either stayed longer on this earth, or made the parousia come a little faster?

Or, is this a parable about risk taking, but for the servants and for us?

God has entrusted us with different sets of gifts. But, when we reach out with those gifts, we risk our entitlements, and thus, our outreach will depend on our faith level. Therefore, we will respond differently. Mother Teresa stands at one end of the spectrum, giving up everything, taking every risk in the name of God for others. Should we consider that the third servant was at the other end of the spectrum, preferring to play it safe?

The Master gave the servants different "investments" to take care of. Here, we need to reflect: Do each of us receive different awards of grace, or does it mean that we have different levels of awareness of the grace bestowed upon us by God? In addition, the Master bestowed upon the first two slaves the same rewards: a congratulations for a well-done job, and also a promise that more would be given to them. Does this imply that God does not expect us to excel but only to act according to the grace given to each of us?

We can wonder why the one who was given the least was the most afraid, especially of the Master. Can we emotionally connect with the one who is overwhelmed by the wealth being given to him all at once? When we have a lot, are we not concerned about protecting what we have? Are there alarm systems in the slums or in the wealthier neighborhoods? Was the third slave intimidated by the greater gifts of the two others? Don't people sometimes refuse to do some church activities, because others seem to have done such a good job, much better than they ever could do?

Is this then a parable of "reckless protection"?

We can protect recklessly only through fear. When we worry about the loss of something, it is fear. It may be fear of losing a reputation based on false appearances, fear of life in general, and fear of God, in particular. The psalmist said that "the earth is the Lord's and everything therein." We may see God's gifts as possessions to preciously keep and protect at any and all expense. We may see life only from a "scarcity" point of view. He who fears has little, invests little, and protects a lot. And yet, they end up losing all, even God!

But is the Master in this parable God?

Indeed, God is a God of grace, and the parable has him throw the third slave into hell mercilessly. Also, our Master is not an absentee Master. God is with us always. Maybe we need to examine this parable in a more "social gospel" light! Challenging traditional interpretations is often a risky business. But, Jesus' parables were risky to start with, and often dumbfounded even his disciples. Jesus loved to "shock" his audience. In light of this, could we expect Jesus to herald the virtues of usury and the accumulation of wealth? Would the same Jesus tell you to sell everything you have and follow him, and then throw someone else in hell who does not make enough money for his master? Even if Jesus were really saying, "Blessed are the risk takers, blessed are the fearless" would he have illustrated it with such a parable?

The first two servants play the "Master's game" and surely make a side profit. We learn from William R. Herzog that retainers did the master's dirty work, and exploited their brothers for their own profit, and for the master's benefit. The elite made money, not from interests on their bank accounts, but through their exploitation of other individuals. They would make loans to the peasants for them to purchase seeds for the crop. Such interests could rise as high as 60 to 200 percent of the harvest. Peasants had to pledge their land as collateral.

The third servant may have been just the whistle-blower. He was the beneficiary of the system, but one day he just could no longer do it! Maybe we should look at the parable the way Ched Myers did: We can find Christ in the oppressed, hungry, and poor. We can meet Christ in places were most people do not go, in the "outer darkness" where the third slave is kicked. Maybe the whistle-blower is kicked out of the wealthy master's dominion, but now he is closer to Christ. Christ also was a whistle-blower, and it led him to a cross!

Who do you want to be? (Christine D'haese Radano)

NOVEMBER 24, 2002

Christ the King

Worship Theme: Jesus judges the world according to how the least of these, the hungry, the naked, the stranger, the sick, are treated. As we treat these, so we treat him.

Readings: Ezekiel 34:11-16, 20-24; Ephesians 1:15-23; Matthew 25:31-46

Call to Worship (Psalm 100):

> *Leader:*   Make a joyful noise to the LORD, all the earth.
>
> ***People:***   **Worship the LORD with gladness; come into God's presence with singing.**
>
> *Leader:*   Know that the LORD is God. It is he who made us, and we belong to him.
>
> ***People:***   **We are God's people, and the sheep of God's pasture.**
>
> *Leader:*   Enter God's gates with thanksgiving and the sanctuary with praise. Give thanks to God, bless his name.
>
> ***People:***   **For the LORD is good; his steadfast love endures forever, and his faithfulness to all generations.**

Pastoral Prayer:
In you, O Lord, we have faith. In you, rests our sure hope. You tell us what we should do and we do not believe. It seems too simple, too mundane. Feed the hungry? Give drink to the

thirsty? Welcome the stranger? Clothe the naked? Attend the sick? Visit those in prison? Is that what you want? Is that big enough for your church? We want to build buildings. We want to hold offices of prestige. We want to write position papers. We want to draw up policy. Feed the hungry? But what is so important about that? What glory does that manifest? Clothe the naked? How quaint. O Lord, forgive us. Show yourself to us. In the hungry, may we see you. In the thirsty, you. In the stranger, you. In the naked, you. In the sick, you. In the prisoner, you. Crucified One, you know us well, you have felt the depth of human pain and the shock of abandonment. Send your Spirit to turn us around, to be about your work, to meet human need that stares us in the face every day, through eyes that look alarmingly like yours. Amen. (Scott Haldeman)

SERMON BRIEFS

THE LOVING CARE OF THE SHEPHERD

EZEKIEL 34:11-16, 20-24

Who would have thought that one of the most memorable television commercials would be a simple one about how connected the world has become. In a commercial for a wireless telephone system, the star of the commercial is a shepherd. The point is that in a remote, almost inaccessible area, the world can come to him. It is a wonderful image and a wonderful sermon theme. The world can come to the Shepherd, especially the Shepherd who came to the world to save it. In biblical imagery, the shepherd was an easily recognizable figure. The good shepherd was one who could be trusted. The responsibility with which a shepherd was entrusted was understood. The shepherd who owned the sheep was the shepherd who would give his/her life for the sheep. David immortalizes the role and responsibility of a shepherd in his Twenty-third Psalm. Countless poems, hymns, songs, and other works of art reflect the image of a good shepherd. Indeed, there is a wonderful chorus in Spanish called *Las Cien Ovejas*, the hundred sheep. It is based on Jesus' story from Luke

15 of the Lost Sheep. It is sung at worship services of all types and for some is a requested funeral song. The song's main message is one of comfort, for there is no greater biblical image than the loving care of a shepherd who seeks his or her sheep. In this passage, God speaks that same word to the people of Israel. The scattered sheep will be gathered. The sheep that are in trouble will be rescued. Those who find themselves in darkness will be brought to the light. The injured will be healed. From being strangers in a strange land they will be returned home. From having come from a strange land with different food, the sheep will feast on their own food. For anyone who has spent any amount of time away from "home," the image is easy to understand. Dorothy in *The Wizard of Oz* immortalized the line that speaks the truth "There's no place like home." That simple mantra became a litany of immortal hope. Add to the splendor of a homecoming the image of God's promise of presence and protection in their midst. Yet just as promising, though, is God's call for faithfulness and justice. Those who are found to be abusive and selfish will be judged in a severe way, for to have been in a position to help and to take advantage of sister or brother goes against God. And that same prophetic voice includes the promise of the coming "David," who will rule as "prince" and "shepherd." (Eradio Valverde Jr.)

THE BEST PRAYER OF ALL

EPHESIANS 1:15-23

This passage is a prayer for the Ephesians (and us) that God might continue to bless them in every spiritual blessing. Paul is praying for nothing less than that they will grow ever closer to God, daily experiencing the depths of God's power and grace in Christ. What greater prayer could anyone pray for us than this? What greater prayer could we pray for others than this—to be ever growing closer to God?

Do you pray for your church? For other churches? For God's people all over the world? Here we find a model for such prayers. I know a church that prays every Sunday by name for another church in their community and one in another country. The ministers of those churches are mentioned by name and the laity is also included in the prayer. This act has broadened the compassion of the people of that church and made them aware of the global nature of the church.

I. Pray for Growth

Paul is also saying that being a Christian is a life of ever growing and being nurtured in the knowledge and grace of God. We are becomers, growing in our walk with God through Christ; in our understanding of what it means to be the people of God; in our power to live out the mission God has given us in Christ. Paul prays for all of this for the Ephesians, though he seems to have never met them. He had "heard of" their faith. He knows them by reputation. They are a body of believers who truly loved God and one another.

II. Pray to Grow in Love

They also love other Christians outside their own circle—"love toward all the saints." There is a tendency in the church sometimes to think that charity begins and ends at home. I see this sometimes around budget time when there is a strong feeling that we should keep our money "here at home." Our Lord is exalted—the King of all the earth—which is an important part of what *ascension* means. Our Lord loves the whole world and so should we. When any church turns in completely on itself, neglecting to give, to love beyond its own community, it begins to die. But even a church that is poor in terms of material things becomes wealthy spiritually when its heart is open to the needs of others beyond its own four walls.

III. Pray to Grow in Empowerment

Paul then talks about the power of God. This is seen clearly in the resurrection and exaltation of Christ (v. 20). Just as God raised Christ from the dead, so God raised Christ now to sit over all the earth as Lord and King, with all peoples and all spiritual forces under his feet, that is, under his command and authority. It is an echo of some of the last words of Christ in Matthew: "All power is given unto me in heaven and on earth" (28:18).

But Christ is also Head of the church, Paul reminds them. The church is his body and he serves as the Head. The head directs and controls the body. The love and power of God flow through us, so that we experience the "fullness" of Christ. The church has the awesome privilege and responsibility of being filled with Christ. This is what empowers us, what gives us our purpose, our reason for being. We do not offer doctrines or creeds to the world, but Christ. Through the church, the Body of Christ continues to live and work in the world, bringing wholeness and salvation. (Bass Mitchell)

CHRIST IN THEM ALSO

MATTHEW 25:31-46

How many more times will I need to read Jesus' parable before I stop being surprised, even dumbfounded? Will the parousia come only when Jesus' parables have been elucidated? If this is the case, it will be many more millennia before this event occurs.

Somehow this parable tends to trigger some uncomfortable feelings. We often are a mixture of sheep and goat. Many of us do not really understand what crime, hunger, thirst, nakedness, and prison are all about. For most of us, this is not part of our daily lives.

Whom do we know who is hungry and thirsty, and has no food at all? There are, of course, "those" homeless, but most of us give money to rescue organizations, and also we pay taxes, don't we? Whom do we know who is in prison? "Well, if they are there, they probably deserved it in the first place! Clothing? Oh, I always give my unused old clothes away."

But Jesus says: "Truly I say to you, to the extent that you did it to one of these brothers of mine, *even* the least *of them,* you did it to me." We often have problems seeing Jesus in others, because we are so judgmental. We refuse to even think that

Christ is with those who are downtrodden. Often, too much focus has been placed on converting or evangelizing, too much attention given to "feeding spiritually" to the detriment of human needs. We must remember, Christ is not only in your worship service on Sunday morning; Christ is also in the least of these.

But, this parable does not tell us just to be kind, give hand-me-downs, or some extra coins and toys we may not need. John Wesley in a sermon stated that "one great reason why the rich in general have so little sympathy for the poor is because they so seldom visit them. Hence it is that, according to the common observation, one part of the world does not know what the other suffers."

This parable is the "exegetical interpretation" of "Love your neighbor as yourself!" Indeed, Christ taught us to love our neighbors—not just the rich and affluent ones, but also the downtrodden and the impoverished.

Many of us tend to be goats covered with sheepskins. We do not want to be goats, but we have so much to do! We cannot *meet* people's needs, because we do not even see or hear their needs. We are too busy to see or to listen. Instead we choose to utter some prayers for "divine intervention" to replace human intervention. In some way, many of us are like Moses, saying to God: *"O my Lord, please send someone else"* (Exod. 4:13).

I once read that a visiting missionary was approached by a church member who told him that in his prayers he usually asks God, "Why don't you do something about the poverty and pain in this world?" The missionary smiled and stated that he, too, used to ask that question of God until one day he realized that God was asking him the very same question! (Christine D'haese Radano)

SPIRITUAL PREPARATION

DECEMBER

With December come Advent (the first four Sundays) and Christmas. These days have a liturgical, pastoral, and even an institutional meaning, and the fullness of these days can stretch us, even when we are at our best. The pastor is wise to enter into these days with an attention to the texts, the symbols, and even the ironies of the season.

I recall once reading the Isaiah text for the second Sunday of Advent, Isaiah 40:1-11. Of course, I was reminded of the bass solo from Handel's *Messiah,* "Comfort ye, Comfort ye, my people, says your God." I read a little farther: "The grass withers, the flower fades, but the word of our God will stand forever" (v. 8). There are times when I wonder about what actually happens in my preaching. This word reminded me of the enduring strength and power of God that undergirds my efforts, as inadequate as they are at times. The reading continued: "He will feed his flock like a shepherd." A word of comfort.

And then a transition, pointing to the awesome creativity of God, concluding with a promise: "Those who wait for the LORD shall renew their strength, they shall mount up with wings like eagles, they shall run and not be weary, they shall walk and not faint." My mind was taken back to a recent memorial service, and to the hope that these words had given to those present when spoken in the liturgy.

I continued reading into the next chapter. By now I was beyond the scope of the lectionary text, but the words were saying something to me. Then I read Isaiah 41:10:

> Do not fear, for I am with you,
> do not be afraid, for I am your God;
> I will strengthen you, I will help you . . .

405

I wrote these words in response:

In the loneliness there arises a fear,
an ache for Someone,
and out of the fear comes fatigue, and
an overwhelming sense of the Absence.

But the prophet evokes a word of hope
in this world, and for life in it.
Emmanuel stands beside us, embraces us,
the Presence meets us in our aloneness,
a Strength allows us to rise up and walk,
to run and not be weary,
even to take flight with wings,
like an eagle.

- Two primary enemies of the spiritual life are *fear* and
  fatigue. What might this statement mean to you in Advent?
  Remember the promise of the angel to Mary:

The Lord is with you. . . . Do not be afraid. (Luke 1:28, 30)

December is charged with pastoral possibility. At heart, Advent
is about waiting, preparing, making room, hearing the unusual in
the voices of the prophets. December is about stress and disappointment, loneliness and grief, but also joy and celebration,
community, and family. The preacher carries within herself this
paradox, and it is precisely at this moment, at this time of year,
that something can indeed be reborn in each of us, even religious
professionals!

In Isaiah 43:1-7, the Lord says to Israel (and to us):

Fear not, for I have redeemed you;
  I have summoned you by name;
    you are mine.
When you pass through the waters, I will be with you

As we begin a new church year, that is about the best news we
could hear. And that is the word of the Lord. It is not my word. It
is the word of the Lord.

I am with you.
At times the gospel can be summed up in a few essential words:

I am with you. These are four of the most important words we could hear, or say. That God says them to us, about us, is utterly amazing: I am with you. At Christmas we discover this truth: "They shall name him Emmanuel, which means, God with us. Which is another way of saying, "I am with you."

The words "I am with you" create relationship.
The words "I am with you" create covenant.
The words "I am with you" create communion.
This good news is for all of us—even preachers, even at Advent and Christmas!
God says, "I am with you."
Listen again to the prophet Isaiah.
Fear not, for I have redeemed you;
I have called you by name, you are mine.
When you pass through the waters, I will be with you;
and through the rivers, they shall not overwhelm you;
when you walk through fire you shall not be burned,
and the flame shall not consume you.
For I am the LORD your God, the Holy One of Israel, your Savior.
You are precious in my sight, and honored, and I love you.
Do not fear, for I am with you.

A Covenant Prayer in the Wesleyan Tradition

I give myself completely to you, God.
Assign me to my place in your creation.
Let me suffer for you. Give me the work you would have me do.
Give me many tasks, or have me step aside while you call others.
Put me forward or humble me. Give me riches or let me live in poverty.
I freely give all that I am and all that I have to you.
And now, Holy God-Father, Son and Holy Spirit,
You are mine and I am yours. So be it.
May this covenant made on earth continue for all eternity. Amen.

In Advent we are called to take the risk of birth. We can avoid such a practice by overscheduling ourselves, an easy feat this time of year. We can avoid such a practice by making our way through the season singing the familiar carols and pronouncing the knowing clichés. But we are called to take the risk of birth. That might lead us toward reconciliation with a church member with whom we are estranged (the 1 Thessalonians lection on the third Sunday of Advent is helpful here). This might lead us to listen to the prophetic critique of our own lives. This might lead us to make room in our own lives for the stranger who comes in the form of the Christ Child.

The fulfillment of the promise of Advent is the celebration of Christmas. This grounds our belief in the Incarnation, the word made flesh, full of grace and truth (John 1). We are more familiar with the Christmas stories in Matthew and Luke, which focus on Joseph and Mary, respectively; from these accounts we recall the dreams and visions, the birth of Jesus and the manger, the gifts of wise men and the praise offered by shepherds.

The story of Christ's birth is told in somewhat different fashion, however, in the Gospel of John. The central message of early Christianity, the Incarnation, was scandalous, especially to the Gnostics, who could not believe that God would take human form. This core Christian belief, that God enters into the material world of human flesh, takes on an ironic meaning at Christmas. We are often urged to avoid, protest, and rebel against the creeping materialism of the season; we are encouraged, instead, toward more "spiritual" pursuits. Such advice is ironic in light of the essential meaning of Christmas: that Jesus is the incarnation of God, the word become flesh.

What might it mean for us, during the season of Christmas, to fully embrace the Incarnation? We might begin to see our material acts of gift-giving as occasions to express human love; we might view gestures of charity as concrete demonstrations of our faith and representative ministries. We can envision our participation in the material world as a response to a God who comes to live among us, and calls us to follow Jesus.

May the peace of Christ, God with us, Emmanuel, be with you in these days! (Ken Carter)

DECEMBER 1, 2002

First Sunday of Advent

Worship Theme: The One who is coming at Christmas is not simply a human baby born two thousand years ago, but also a divine judge who will restore wholeness to the cosmos.

Readings: Isaiah 64:1-9; 1 Corinthians 1:3-9; Mark 13:24-37

Call to Worship (Psalm 80):

Leader: Give ear, O Shepherd of Israel, you who lead Joseph like a flock! You who are enthroned upon the cherubim, shine forth. Stir up your might, and come to save us!

People: **Restore us, O God; let your face shine, that we may be saved.**

Leader: O LORD God of hosts, how long will you be angry with your people's prayers? You have fed them with the bread of tears, and given them tears to drink in full measure. You make us the scorn of our neighbors; our enemies laugh among themselves.

People: **Restore us, O God of hosts; let your face shine, that we may be saved.**

Leader: You brought a vine out of Egypt; you drove out the nations and planted it. You cleared the ground for it; it took deep root and filled the land. The mountains were covered with its shade, the mighty cedars with its branches; it sent out its branches to the sea, and its shoots to the River.

Why then have you broken down its walls, so that all who pass along the way pluck its fruit?

People: **Restore us, O God of hosts; let your face shine, that we may be saved.**

Leader: Turn again, O God of hosts; look down from heaven, and see; have regard for this vine, the stock that your right hand planted. They have burned it with fire, they have cut it down; may they perish at the rebuke of your countenance. But let your hand be upon the one at your right hand, the one whom you made strong for yourself. Then we will never turn back from you; give us life, and we will call on your name.

People: **Restore us, O LORD God of hosts; let your face shine, that we may be saved.**

Pastoral Prayer:

O that you would tear open the heavens and come down, we pray, in the words of the prophet. We await you eagerly. We yearn for the culmination of your promised grace. And, as we wait, we struggle on. We proclaim and hear your Word; enliven your Word in our hearts that they might burn. We gather around your table to share bread; sanctify us in the meal, and multiply the loaf to feed a hungry world. We speak truth to power; overturn injustice. We shelter the homeless and provide clothes for the naked; help us to persevere. Enlighten us to cure the causes of poverty and not only its symptoms. Chasten us when we are self-righteous. Reveal how our comfort depends on the misery of others. Work in us so that you might find us blameless on that great day when you return. We are your elect, recipients of your grace; strengthen us as we work, and as we wait, so that we can stay awake and receive you. Amen. (Scott Haldeman)

SERMON BRIEFS

WE ARE THE BIBLE

ISAIAH 64:1-9

It is every pastor's dream to discover, to write, or to find already written, the ultimate surefire no-failure church growth manual. It would be one that would outline step by easy step the way to grow a large church. The church, at times, has indeed sought to find the ultimate marketing and publicity ploy to draw in new converts. Our bookstores' shelves are lined with the latest, and we hope, the greatest of books that offer ways to bring in new members.

Equally as important to some has been the notion of drawing in critics and enemies of the church so that they would be silent about their doubts and attacks on the church. A successful businessman and media tycoon comes to mind as someone who openly questions the need for anything religious, labeling those who follow and practice religious faith as "weaklings." Oh, we cry, to win him would be to silence him! Even better, if God would somehow make this man know that God exists, that would be enough. "Oh, if only God would come down and prove that God really exists!" How many times have we heard that or thought it ourselves?

The prophet Isaiah calls out to God with the same sort of wondering: If only you would come down in a mighty way to make yourself known! The tearing open of the heavens and God making an appearance would be fantastic some think, as does Isaiah. And make it good, Lord! Let the mountains quake and make it in a way that lets all the people throughout the world know. Yet, almost as suddenly as he wonders and asks aloud for such a sign, Isaiah sighs and says, you are the God "who works for those who wait for him. You meet those who gladly do right, those who remember you in your ways." It is here that Isaiah declares that our knowing God is in our relationship with God. God is real in our daily lives when we seek God and seek to know the way God is at work in our lives. It is in our attitude about things that can so easily be taken for granted that we declare, this is of God.

411

Isaiah, like the members of the church who watch as people fall away, knows that perhaps we have not done enough, we have continued in our sin, and through our sinfulness we are taken away. Isaiah realizes that God continues to make God's presence known through our faith and our faith in action. It is in our daily living that God's power and presence will be realized. As so many have said before, we become the sermon taken to the streets. We are the Bible and our words are the actions of a living, loving, caring God. Yet, like Isaiah, the church can declare, God is still our God and we declare that God is the "potter" and we are the "clay." All of us, "the work of your (God's) hand." The church continues to be the station where people can cry out for mercy and know that God's love is merciful, and when we are ready, God welcomes us back. (Eradio Valverde Jr.)

BRINGING ORDER TO CHAOS

1 CORINTHIANS 1:3-9

To read these words of thanksgiving to God by Paul, in a letter in which he is about to issue strong rebuke and correction, appears to be a contradiction—particularly when we consider the situation at Corinth, and a church that has abused God's love and misused God's spiritual gifts to cause division within the membership. Yet, when we pay close attention to these words of thanksgiving to God, Paul from the very beginning of this letter encourages us that even in divisive situations within the house of God or any organization, God can and God will bring order to chaos.

This is what Paul stresses as he gives thanks to God for the Corinthian church and all of its headaches, horror stories, and problems. He thanks God because he knows that within the chaos, God has already done marvelous things that can bring blessing to the multitudes. God has done the same with us. As we approach our challenges, let us give God thanks before the blessing, and let us extend encouragement to those in the struggle. In so doing, we will plant seeds of reconciliation and bring order to chaos.

In his thanksgiving, Paul does this in three primary ways. First of all, he offers hope. In his initial approach to the Corinthian church and its chaotic problems, Paul offers hope by first extending grace and peace to every reader or hearer of the letter. It is grace and peace that are sorely missing from the Corinthian fellowship. It is grace and peace that Paul, simply by his words, seeks to reestablish in the midst of the dissension and division.

God had been very gracious to the Corinthian membership. These were people who once carried a sour reputation of being unruly and highly immoral. But they were people who had experienced the liberating power of Jesus, the Christ. They needed to be reminded of this, and reminded of the peace that could pull them out from the traps of that old reputation. Every now and then, all of us need to be reminded of God's grace extended to us, so that we don't fall into old traps.

Paul offers them hope by reminding them that through grace, accompanied with the unity and love found in peace, the Corinthian church has already been enriched in every way—in all their speaking and all their knowledge. Paul reminds them that through grace they do not lack any spiritual gift. God has provided it all. Therefore, the tools for making peace and restoring order are already present within the church.

The tools for reestablishing harmony in our chaotic situations or divisive church settings is present, as well. Paul reminds us that when we remind people that God's unmerited favor is available and extended to us through Jesus Christ, good can come from bad situations, even when we don't warrant it. We need to offer hope from the start to encourage others as we seek to resolve conflicts and divisions within our churches and organizations.

Second, in Paul's thanksgiving, he reminds the church that God will keep them. When we find ourselves having to address divisiveness in the ranks, we need to encourage others and be assured ourselves that God will keep us strong to the end. For conflict resolution and reconciliation in general is not easy work. There will be times when we will feel like throwing in the towel. In Paul's situation, he had a number of divisive issues disrupting harmony in the church that were taking place at the same time. From sexual immorality to the abuse of the communion ritual,

413

and the misuse and abuse of spiritual gifts, the tension Paul was called to confront was thick. But we need to know—as the apostle stresses—that God will keep us. In God we will find strength to endure.

A colleague once told me, when I was in the midst of working to reconcile a bad situation, "You can look at this as a burden or an opportunity. If you look at it as a burden, it will be just that, a burden. But if you look at it as an opportunity, then the sky's the limit as to what God can do to fix the situation."

We need to look at our challenging situations as opportunities for God's blessing. When we know that God will keep us strong to the end, we will have strength to press on through the barriers that block us from unity and love, and bring order to chaos.

Finally, in Paul's thanksgiving, he reminds the Corinthian church (and us today) that God is faithful. For the God who has called us into fellowship with Jesus is the same God who stands ready, willing, and able to keep this fellowship sound and strong. God will do whatever is necessary to restore order out of chaos. God is faithful. The question is, will we be faithful in bringing order to the chaos? My prayer is that we will. (Joseph W. Daniels Jr.)

LIVING IN HOPE

MARK 13:24-37

In the ecumenical lectionary, this Gospel is to be read on the First Sunday of Advent, announcing one of the major themes of the season, the expectation of the coming of Christ in glory at the end of time. Mark draws on the observed natural wonders of his time to paint a scary picture of the end of the world, and the apocalyptic coming of the Son of Man. Eclipses of the sun and moon, meteors, and shooting stars provide Mark with metaphors of cataclysm that announce the appearance of the heavenly redeemer and judge. To this he adds the metaphors of the fig tree as a sign of the approaching fullness of summer, and the householder whose return the members of the house anticipate. What all this adds up to is a call to keep awake and to watch. It will depend upon the hearer's understanding of the One who is expected—the Son of Man—to determine in what way one watches and waits.

We have learned a great deal about sun, moon, and stars, since Mark painted his apocalyptic scenes, but our world is no less scary. We could come up with our own pictures of threat and disaster: we know that the ecosphere could die; we have seen cities and their populations dissolve with fervent heat. Despite the fact that we know much more about how the earth and the heavens work, we could paint far more electrifying scenarios for disaster than would have occurred to Mark: global warming, global viruses, global warfare.

What is important here, however, is not these grim projections, but the call to keep our eyes wide open and to live in *hope*. Isn't that what this is about, not living in our fears, but getting in touch with our hopes? I suppose that it is true that fear can spur us, get our attention, and wake us. But does not mere unmitigated fear finally paralyze us, make us want to run and hide or, at least, to distract ourselves? Not infrequently fear leads not to action but, over the long run, to crawling in a hole, to the sin of acedia: sloth, giving up, caving in and not caring.

Mark's little apocalypse calls us to keep awake and watch. One way to help ourselves to do that is to get in touch with our hopes. What is it, really, that we are hoping for? Some, of course, can give you quite a simple answer, and one based on a certain way of looking at Mark's apocalyptic text. "I don't really hope for much in *this* world at all. Jesus is coming soon, that is all that matters, so I'll keep my eyes on the prize." During the whole time that I was a student at Baylor University in Waco, Texas, the Davidians were encamped just outside the city, waiting for the end of the world. While I wrote term papers, fell in love, and waxed my car, they watched and waited in their uncomfortable camp. That would be one way of looking at it, and it is an apocalyptic view that takes many forms. All of them, in one way or another, tend to give up on the world of commuters and the dreams of college kids, not to mention the cultivation and care of dear mother earth.

That may be quite close to the attitude of Mark's community. They were under siege, and their future on this earth could not have looked too bright. A heightened sense of the precarious existence of human beings lies at the heart of apocalyptic writing, both in the hearts of those who produce texts like this and those who respond strongly to them.

But this text, especially if we read it on the First Sunday of Advent, need not lead us to disdain our life on earth or to watch and wait fearfully. Mark's message for us is likely: this world is passing away, we do not know what will happen tomorrow, it could all end soon. So, keep awake, keep your eyes open, and like a servant expecting the master's return, do all you can where you are for the household. That would be more like the church we love. The church knows that it is all passing away, but it lives as if every child, every sick person, every old and lonely person matters. The church watches and waits in hope, and so it is empowered to serve the One who was, and is, and is to come. So Mark could paint the most alarming picture of the end of it all, and then say that living is like seeing the signs of summer in a flowering fig tree, and like trying to be faithful in your duties day by day, not knowing when the Master will come. (Charles L. Rice)

DECEMBER 8, 2002

Second Sunday of Advent

Worship Theme: God brings comfort to God's people, sending first John the Baptizer and then One who is greater, One who brings the baptism of the Spirit.

Readings: Isaiah 40:1-11; 2 Peter 3:8-15*a;* Mark 1:1-8

Call to Worship (Psalm 85):

Leader: LORD, you were favorable to your land; you restored the fortunes of Jacob.

People: **You forgave the iniquity of your people; you pardoned all their sin.**

Leader: You withdrew all your wrath; you turned from your hot anger.

People: **Restore us again, O God of our salvation, and put away your indignation toward us.**

Leader: Show us your steadfast love, O LORD, and grant us your salvation. Let me hear what God declares, for he will speak peace to his people, to his faithful, to those who turn to him in their hearts.

People: **Show us your steadfast love, O LORD, and grant us your salvation.**

Pastoral Prayer:
   Holy Comforter, who gathered your exiled children under your wings and brought them home, shelter us this day. Speak to us

417

THE ABINGDON PREACHING ANNUAL 2002

tenderly of your promises. Speak words of assurance to those who doubt. Comfort your people. Speak words of healing to those who are ill. Comfort your people. Speak words of hope to those who despair. Comfort your people. Speak words of power to those who are abused and downtrodden. Comfort your people. Send once more prophets like John. Call us to repent. Call us to attend to the One who is coming. We ready ourselves for the new heaven and the new earth. Send the Spirit to baptize. Send the Spirit to transform. Send the Spirit to renew. Enliven your church. Humble the proud. Enfold the suffering. Feed the hungry. Comfort your people. Prepare us for the day of your coming. In the name of the One who shared our deepest suffering and who was raised to live with you where suffering is no more. Amen. (Scott Haldeman)

SERMON BRIEFS

HERE IS YOUR GOD!

ISAIAH 40:1-11

The prophets spoke words of judgment against ancient Israel, harsh, shrill, and wrath-filled words. Isaiah says this about Jerusalem and its inhabitants:

> How the faithful city has become a whore!
> She that was full of justice, righteousness lodged in her—
> but now murderers!
> Your silver has become dross, your wine is mixed with water.
> Your princes are rebels and companions of thieves. (1:21-23)

But for the prophets of ancient Israel, judgment is never the final word. Condemnation is not the goal. Destruction is not the end result. The prophets intermingled their words of judgment with words of hope, restoration, and comfort.

Chapter 40 of Isaiah marks the beginning of what scholars call Second Isaiah. Most believe that the book of Isaiah is actually a compilation of prophetic writings that come from three different time periods in the life of ancient Israel: chapters 1–39 from the preexilic period (before 587); chapters 40–55 from the exilic period (587–538); and chapters 56–66 from the postexilic period (after 538). Isaiah 40, then, marks the beginning of prophetic words addressed to the Israelites who had been captured by the Babylonians in 587 and exiled to Babylon. The Babylonian Israelites were heirs to generations of Israelites who had broken their covenant with the Lord time and time again. The Lord spoke these words to the prophets during the reign of Manasseh (687–642):

> I am bringing upon Jerusalem and Judah such evil that the ears of everyone who hears of it will tingle. I will stretch over Jerusalem. . . I will wipe Jerusalem as one wipes a dish, wiping it and turning it upside down . . . because they have done what is evil in my sight. (2 Kings 21:12-15)

The Israelites had sinned for so long and in so many ways that the words of judgment spoken by Isaiah, Jeremiah, Micah, and Habakkuk would indeed come to pass. The covenant had been broken once and for all—the Lord declared, "You are not my people and I am not your God" (Hos. 1:9). The Babylonians marched in; the presence of the Lord departed from the Temple (Ezekiel 10); the Babylonians destroyed Jerusalem and the Temple; they deported the Israelites to Babylon. The kingdom of Judah with its God enthroned in Jerusalem was no more.

But the prophetic words do not end there. In Isaiah 40, we read words of hope for the Israelite people and for Jerusalem, the city in which God's presence had dwelt among the people. "Speak tenderly to Jerusalem, and cry to her that she has served her term, that her penalty is paid" (v. 2). And Isaiah promises that God will return to the city and dwell once again among the people.

> In the wilderness prepare the way of the LORD, make straight in the desert a highway for our God . . . say to the cities of Judah, "Here is your God!" . . . He will feed his flock like a shepherd; he will gather the lambs in his arms, and carry them in his bosom, and gently lead the mother sheep. (vv. 3, 9, 11)

Imagine the impact of these words on the Israelites in exile in Babylon, wondering if they would ever see their homeland again and if God's presence was still among them. Isaiah tells the people to carve out a processional path, make the necessary preparations, because soon they will participate in the joyous return of the Lord to Jerusalem and enthronement in the Temple. They were indeed the Lord's people, and the Lord was their God.

Abraham Heschel describes Isaiah 40–55 as "prophecy tempered with human tears, mixed with a joy that heals all scars, clearing a way for understanding the future in spite of the present." The people had sinned and judgment had been carried out. There was no going back to "the way things were." But the penalty had been paid; God would begin anew with the people. Words of hope, words of comfort, words about restoration. "Lift up your voice with strength, O Jerusalem, herald of good tidings, lift it up, do not fear" (v. 9). Words of comfort to the Israelites in exile in Babylon; timeless words of hope to all generations of believers. (Nancy L. deClaissé-Walford)

IT TAKES TIME!

2 PETER 3:8-15*a*

She is alone. After sixty-one years of marriage, she is alone. After the funeral, her daughter wanted to spend the night with her, but she wanted to be alone. The pastor's parting words were, "It takes time."

They are trying again. Things got so busy. Time just flew. Then two strangers stared at each other across the breakfast table. So, they are trying to rekindle the spark in their marriage. The counselor said, "You did not get into this overnight, you won't be out of it overnight. It takes time."

Cancer was the last word she wanted to hear. They said they got it all. Today, she takes the last agonizing treatment. But what is a few minutes in light of the time it could buy her? She has decided that whether she has one day or thirty-one years, she will make the best of the time she has left. Time—our most precious possession.

Peter says the time will come (v. 10). As the first-generation Christian leaders were dying off, false teachers who scoffed at the

Second Coming were trying to elbow their way into the theology in process of the early church. Indeed, some like Mark (9:1) and Paul (1 Cor. 7:26, 29, 31) had said the time is short. False teachers scoffed at their sense of urgency. But Peter reminds them and us that God keeps his promises about Christ's return (v. 9). Sometimes, it just takes time.

Simon also reminds us that God's time is not necessarily our time. Quoting Psalm 94, he reiterates that a thousand years is like a day to God. When you think of it, it is pure arrogance on our part to think that God has to conform to our schedules and timetables. I mean, who invented time in the first place? Besides, God uses this time to allow others opportunity to repent (v. 9). We have had time to repent. Why shouldn't they? What is a few days of delay in light of eternity?

Peter also gives to us a word as to how we can prepare for the time! He describes the transition in such terms of radical transformation; surely we should take our preparation seriously. In fact, the false teachers had lost their sense of immediacy and had laxed into a libertine lifestyle, but Peter points out that we should live lives that are "holy and godly" (v. 11 NIV). We should make every effort to appear before him as "spotless, blameless and at peace" when the time comes (v. 14 NIV). We should be grateful that his delay gives us and others time to prepare (v. 15).

Then he says a most astounding thing. He states that we can actually hasten the time of Jesus' coming (v. 12). Perhaps Simon recalled our Lord's statement that the preaching of the gospel to everyone would precede his coming. If we want Christ to return soon, get out and tell the story to speed the time. As Snuffy Smith says, "Time's a wastin'." It takes time. But the time is coming. In that we find hope. We find hope in Peter's wonderful assurance that the time will come when righteousness will find a home (v. 13). Somewhere, some time, things will be right.

It is that hope that sustains the small rural church to cope with dwindling resources and changing leadership. It is that hope that sustains the inner-city church to deal with the violence that surrounds it and the members fleeing to the comfortable suburbs.

The rent is due, the washer is out, and both boys need new shoes. Her ex-husband's check is very late, again, and like last month may not come at all. She wonders how long can she keep it up. She doesn't know about tomorrow, but for one more day, this day, she has determined to live with integrity, hope, and the refusal to sink into despair. She will live one day at a time. Things will be better. The time will come. It just takes time. (Gary L. Carver)

THE WAY TO GO

MARK 1:1-8

The vigor and directness of Mark's Gospel is evident from the beginning. The Second Evangelist gets right down to it, declaring that something has happened that—worldly appearances to the contrary—has changed everything. A messenger appears, crying out in an unpromising place and pointing toward the future, "the voice of one crying in the wilderness: 'Prepare the way of the Lord, make his paths straight.' " Can that voice break through to us today? Is it a voice that we are listening for?

Far from a clearly marked *path*, the situation in this new century is more like being on a five-lane superhighway trying to read the signs in speeding unpredictable traffic. That very situation could, perhaps, make us ready to hear this voice calling out loud and clear, pointing us toward the One who speaks most clearly and calls us to take stock and walk in a new way.

The symbol of this clarity and newness is, as John the Baptist preaches, *baptism.* Jewish baptism was either for proselytes, or for ritual cleansing. John's baptism combines the motifs—initiation into a new way, and as a baptism of repentance. The voice that calls in the wilderness to prepare the way of the One who is coming is the voice that calls to baptism, to show in this dramatic action both a clean break and a new start.

Baptismal practice among the early Christians showed this dual meaning: *the old world was being left behind, something new and promising was beginning.* Paul would later develop this in terms of a dying and rising, being buried with Christ in baptism and raised with him to newness of life (Romans 6). A period of catechesis developed, a time of purging of the old ways and careful preparation for the new life in Christ; this has taken the form, in our time, of a somewhat tame Lenten observance that shows only the barest remnants of renunciation and reorientation those early Christians intended.

Fred Craddock, in one of his sermons, asks: "Have you ever heard John preach?" There are those, of course, who seem quite confident that they have heard that voice and that they know exactly what the markers of the path are. We would do well to keep in mind that neither John's message nor that of Jesus after him was unambiguous: not everyone could hear, and many who heard could not follow. Some of those who are most sure of the voice and of the way may be those who miss the way of Christ.

John the Baptist, however, points us toward the One who comes to lead us in his ways, of trust, peace, and love. That is a path we can identify, and it is the way in which Jesus himself walks and in which he leads us. It is to this life that we are called when at baptism we are "sealed by the Holy Spirit in baptism and marked as Christ's own forever." To walk in that way, in our time as in every age, is to respond to a strange voice and to walk in a new way.

It is not that John himself did not find this way ambiguous, not to mention difficult. But as Mark tells us the story right here at the start, there is One coming whom we can trust and in whose way we are called to walk. That is what baptism says: who knows where this will lead, and you can be sure that the way will not always be clear. But from this day you belong to Christ, and that is what matters. As Herbert Butterfield put it at the end of his book, *Christianity and History*, we are called to "hold to Christ and in everything else remain uncommitted." (Charles L. Rice)

DECEMBER 15, 2002

Third Sunday of Advent

Worship Theme: Rejoice and give thanks for the Light of the World is about to dawn, John tells us. The One who breaks the heavy yoke and sets us at liberty is on the way.

Readings: Isaiah 61:1-4, 8-11; 1 Thessalonians 5:16-24; John 1:6-8, 19-28

Call to Worship (Psalm 126):

> *Leader:*   When the LORD restored the fortunes of Zion, our mouths were filled with laughter, and our tongues shouted with joy.

> *People:*   **The LORD has done great things for us.**

> *Leader:*   The LORD has done great things for us, and we rejoiced. Restore our fortunes, O LORD, like the watercourses in the Negeb. May those who sow in tears reap with shouts of joy.

> *People:*   **The LORD has done great things for us.**

> *Leader:*   Those who go out weeping, bearing the seed for sowing, shall come home with shouts of joy, carrying their sheaves.

> *People:*   **The LORD has done great things for us. Let us worship God.**

Pastoral Prayer:
    Giver of all good gifts, who blesses us each day with your grace, with your Spirit, with your compassion, may your light

shine in your world this day. Bind all broken hearts. Comfort those who mourn. Turn our ashes into garlands. Change our funeral suits to festival garments. Source of Mercy, sanctify us. Keep our bodies sound. Make us blameless in your sight. Spirit of the Prophets, descend on us. Make us your instruments. To visit those who are ill. To embrace the dying. To tell of your love. To work for your justice. To set free the imprisoned. To prepare your way. To cry in the wilderness—the wilderness of despair, the wilderness of pain, the wilderness of hunger, the wilderness of rejection, the wilderness of our lives. To prepare a way for you in this wilderness. Come, we prepare for you. Come, we pray. Amen. (Scott Haldeman)

SERMON BRIEFS

GOD'S SEAL OF HOPE—THE MESSIAH

ISAIAH 61:1-4, 8-11

Reminding his readers of the origin of Harvard, writer Charles Swindoll writes that the university was founded in 1636 by John Harvard, a minister. One year later, he died and left to the university his 400 volumes and a gift of 780 pounds of sterling. His benevolence would assist in training future generations going into Christian ministry.

The original seal of the school was a shield with three open books, two facing up, the third facedown, and the Latin phrase "Veritas Christo et Ecclesia!" Translated it states, "Truth for Christ and the Church."

"The distinguished seal reminded students that truth and freedom are found only in Jesus Christ, and the display of three books represented the importance of knowledge—yet with one turned down emphasizing the limits of human reason," noted Swindoll.

He continues that, tragically, with time's passing, the once-godly philosophy of education has eroded: "Harvard's new seal carries no reference to Christ or the Church. And the book facing down has now been turned up. We can now know it all, this symbol says. There are no divine mysteries. Intellect is everything."[1]

God put his seal upon life, but unlike Harvard's seal, God's seal will never change. His seal is Jesus Christ. That seal was good yesterday, is good today, and will be good tomorrow. He is the Messiah.

I. The Seal of the Messiah—Good News

The tainting of worldwide news stems from the D-word— *depravity*. Not human failure, not human ignorance, not human foolishness but, human depravity—inbred sin, carnality. We are an ethically, morally, and spiritually bankrupt people. There is no good news to be found here. But in Jesus the offer of good news is to all people. Depravity doesn't have to reign. Sin can be broken and replaced by holiness. Good news for a lifetime.

- Peace in the chaos of living
- Forgiveness in an unforgiving world
- Hope in a fractured society
- Purity in a soiled heart
- Mercy in a merciless community

II. The Seal of the Messiah—Liberty

Jesus came to throw open the prison doors of sin and release the prisoners! The Septuagint translates this section as the opening of the eyes. Whether it is the opening of prison doors or closed eyes, liberty and freedom come now to the believer.

Someone wrote, "Great the joy when the blinding film of human tradition and religion is removed by the power of the ascended Lord through the Spirit! Great the gladness and gratitude in the possession of liberty and spiritual sight!"[2]

Those who have been the prisoners of lying, cheating, slander, immorality, disobedience, hatred, drunkenness—can be set free! The phrase "Give me liberty or give me death" takes on a whole new concept when viewed in the spiritual realm.

---

1. Charles Swindoll, *Day by Day* (Nashville: Word Publishing, 2000), p. 244.

2. W. E. Vine, *Isaiah* (Grand Rapids: Zondervan Publishing House, 1971), p. 199.

III. The Seal of the Messiah—Righteousness

Jesus came to help humankind conduct itself in a right way. Righteousness takes on God's characteristics in an ethical connotation. The rich don't oppress the poor. People see those in need and stick out a hand to help.

"The 'Holiness Code' (Lev. 17–26) shows indissoluble connection between worship and work, religious devotion and ethical practice, by combining ritual law and moral law. The injunctions within it, such as 'Thou shalt love thy neighbor as thyself: I am the Lord' (19:18), make it clear that the only holiness acceptable to God is that which involves right and just relations with all men."[3]

A righteousness lifestyle becomes the habit of the Christian. The believer wants now to follow Jesus in life, action, and faith. It is not in our own righteousness, but in his righteousness that we live, for the Messiah ushers in a righteous standard.

Is God's seal upon your life today? (Derl Keefer)

---

3. John A. Knight, *All Loves Excelling* (Kansas City: Beacon Hill Press of Kansas City, 1995), p. 40.

PAUL'S LAST-MINUTE INSTRUCTIONS

1 THESSALONIANS 5:16-24

Reading this pericope reminds me of saying good-bye to my son at the door before he leaves for school each morning. At the door, or somewhere in close proximity to the door, we go through the mother-son ritual of parting. It is a mother thing, I know that. But it has to be done. It goes something like this: "Don't forget the lunch box. Have you got all of your homework? Be sure and enjoy the day. Be safe. Have you got your gloves?" On different mornings, different adaptations of the door litany occur. When I have noticed that there was discouragement the night before or anxiety before a final examination, the words might be "hang in there until TGIF" (Thank Goodness It's Friday—where we rent a family movie and eat pizza), or "make sure you find something to smile about today."

Like the mother who wishes she had more time to have conversation with the son, she settles for these short, proverbial, morning snippets, which she hopes will be remembered sometime during the day. And as he rushes out the door and leaves her presence, she shares these loving imperatives—the kind of domestic slogans that can be imprinted in cross-stitch floss and hung on the wall in the family room.

Here at the end of Paul's letter, the situation is not that different from the mother saying good-bye to her child at the door as he leaves for school. The final words that Paul offers this beloved congregation come from his heart and his close relationship with them. The instruction has been given in the months before as he had spent time with them, worshiping and teaching in their community of faith (Acts 17). The relationship continues through the ministry of letter writing. After hearing Timothy's report, Paul writes a letter placing on paper all the words of encouragement and teaching that he has been wanting to tell them since his departure. And now, at the end of the letter, anything that has been previously omitted enters the text. Those last-minute instructions that somehow did not surface in the carefully written paragraphs of epistolary convention become piled high at the end of the letter. With love for these people Paul says to them: "Rejoice always." "Pray without ceasing." "Give thanks in all things." "Do not quench the Spirit." "Do not despise prophecy." "Test everything; hold fast to that which is beautiful." "Keep away from every kind of evil."

The pastoral (maternal) response of Paul is striking. The time is too short for long paragraphs; narrative text is too cumbersome. Short proverbial statements with aphoristic ring fit the farewell setting.

Max Ehrmann in 1927 penned the words to "Desiderata," whose form and content are similar to Paul's own words.

> Go placidly amid the noise and haste and remember what peace there may be in silence. As far as possible without surrender be on good terms with all persons. Speak your truth quietly and clearly; and listen to others, even the full and ignorant; they too have their story. . . . Be yourself. Especially, do not feign affection. . . . Take kindly the counsel of the years, gracefully surrendering the things of youth. . . . With all its sham, drudgery and broken dreams, it is still a beautiful world. Be careful. Strive to be happy.

Paul has loved this community of faith, like a mother nursing her children (2:7), as a father teaching them (2:11). When he is not with them, he feels as if he is an orphan (2:17). His words have encouraged the new converts to have hope in the coming of Christ. And perhaps most important, his words have given them comfort as they grieved the deaths of their dear loved ones. For Paul, the most important point was not the date or time of Jesus' return, not even the specific details attached to Jesus' arrival. The significance for Paul and the community of faith was that they would be with their loved ones and with Jesus at the time of Jesus' return. Relationships were the most important element of the faith.

Relationship between the dead ones, the living ones, and the One who had come once already and would come again soon would be Paul's primary word to this community. Ethical imperatives would not be dismissed as unessential, but absolutely crucial to the well-being of the community (4:1-12). Doctrinal issues were not ignored, but made subservient to the formation of the community (4:13–5:11).

Paul's benediction, offered as a conclusion to the letter, reinforces the sense of oneness within the body of believers: "May the God of peace, God's self, sanctify you completely, even the whole of you, and may your spirit and soul and body be kept without blame in the coming of our Lord Jesus" (5:23). So be it for all of us! (Linda McKinnish Bridges)

A LIVING TESTIMONY

JOHN 1:6-8, 19-28

John the Evangelist gives us a picture of John the Baptizer. In two short excerpts of this Gospel, we see that John is a messenger sent from God. This is the purpose of his place in the Gospel of John—to be a witness and forerunner of the true light sent from God, and this light will enlighten everyone, not just the religious community. John the Evangelist gives us a sneak preview of what true evangelism is: to go before the people and give a testimony to the Light. We may be surprised by what we find. Moreover, our stereotypes of evangelism can be changed as a result of finding that John the Baptizer's witness is a living testimony.

I. A Living Testimony: Setting the Record Straight
(vv. 6-8, 19)

The writer of the Gospel of John identifies the one who came to give a witness of God's light. His name is John. All we are told is that he was sent from God. His sole purpose in this Gospel is to give a testimony of what God was doing in the midst of people. The writer makes it perfectly clear that John is not the center of his message. John is a testifier, if you will, of the light that is breaking into the realm of human affairs. He is John the Baptizer and not John the Light. But when the religious leaders approach him and ask him to identify himself, perhaps they are not so sure that he isn't the light. So, they ask him, "Who are you?"

Setting the record straight is something we need to remind ourselves when giving living testimonies of the light of Jesus Christ that influences our daily living. Too often, the church and Christians may speak with an authority that belongs only to Christ. When we are confronted by those who question our motives and actions as Christians, the writer of this Gospel account reminds us that we would do well to always keep the record straight about who we are. We are *witnesses* of something and Someone who is greater than we are. The church and Christians are not the light of God in a dark world, but are those who give testimony to and are witnesses of the Light. Our language and behavior are always to be pointers to Someone who is greater than we are, thereby drawing others to Christ and not to ourselves. This was John's own understanding of setting the record straight.

II. A Living Testimony: Giving an Authentic Response
(vv. 20-23)

John, sensing the pressure of the religious community, had to respond to the question, "Who are you?" and he responded decisively: "I am not the Messiah." He didn't make any bones about it. Within the religious community, especially the church, giving an authentic response can be difficult. Weighing such issues as political correctness and social politeness can oftentimes cause us to avoid very difficult questions. Jesus didn't seem to mind difficult questions and always used an economy of words to convey what he wanted to say. Likewise, as followers of Jesus, we can find John's reply a refreshing, although risk-taking, example of what it means to give a genuine and authentic witness of our faith.

III. A Living Testimony: Demonstrating Genuine Humility (vv. 24-28)

"Who are you?" is a question we need to be asked in our own day and time. Disciples of Jesus Christ should be ready and willing to give an authentic response. We shouldn't flower it up or make excuses for ourselves. When doing the Christ's work in our respective communities, it's refreshing to know that there are those with whom our work is catching their eyes and ears. To not be effective followers of Jesus Christ is a travesty. To help bring people to their senses and address the sin that plagues all of us, with a message and work of hope, is to invite inquisitiveness on the part of the religious community. "Who are you?" "What are you doing?" or "What makes you do what you do?" are questions that require us to be honest and up-front with those who are curious, and give our answers without an "in-your-face" attitude demonstrating resentment or arrogance. And, we should be able, like John, to say who we are and, most important, *whose* we are. John's simple candor, honesty, and forthrightness in answering the Pharisee's question is a model we can all emulate. Put simply, it is a model we can emulate, genuinely and authentically. (Mike Childress)

DEECEMBER 22, 2002

Fourth Sunday of Advent

Worship Theme: Nothing is impossible for God—a virgin conceives, an old woman will have a child, and the promised descendant of David is born, One who will rule forever in a reign of peace.

Readings: 2 Samuel 7:1-11, 16; Romans 16:25-27; Luke 1:26-38

Call to Worship (Psalm 89):

Leader: I will sing of your steadfast love, O LORD, forever; with my mouth I will proclaim your faithfulness to all generations.

People: **I declare that your steadfast love is established forever; your faithfulness is as firm as the heavens.**

Leader: Let the heavens praise your wonders, O LORD, your faithfulness in the assembly of the holy ones. For who is as mighty as you, O LORD? Your faithfulness surrounds you. You rule the raging of the sea; when its waves rise, you still them.

People: **I declare that your steadfast love is established forever; your faithfulness is as firm as the heavens.**

Leader: Lord, where is your steadfast love of old, which by your faithfulness you swore to David? Remember, O Lord, how your servant is taunted; how I bear in my bosom the insults of the peoples, with which your enemies taunt, O LORD, with which they taunted the footsteps of your anointed.

People: **I declare that your steadfast love is established forever; your faithfulness is as firm as the heavens. Blessed be God forever.**

Pastoral Prayer:

God of Saul and David, who raised up kings for your people, human rulers who brought peace and war, virtue and deceit, establish your reign of peace among us. Send to us One who will show us the way of mercy and love. God of Mary and Elizabeth, who gives children to the childless, who calls women to great acts of faith, reveal to us vocations of challenge and worth that we might participate in the revelation of your mysterious will. Bless all children and those who care for them. Strengthen all families, no matter the shape, of whatever size. Empower us for service that we may shelter those who are orphaned. Welcome those who are estranged. Feed those who are hungry. Mourn with those who grieve. Console those who despair. Visit those in prison. House those without shelter. God of our ancestors, who breaks our expectations and shatters our dreams, assuage our fears and come to us to make all things new. In the name of the One you sent and who will come again, to that One and to you with the Holy Spirit, be all honor and glory, now and forever. Amen. (Scott Haldeman)

SERMON BRIEFS

TO BE GOD'S HOUSE

2 SAMUEL 7:1-11, 16

Years ago, I taught a preschool Sunday school class. Every week, the members of the class (only about three or four students) would do some type of craft, which they were encouraged to take home after Sunday school. All of them joyfully took their artwork with them each week with the exception of one child.

She always wanted to leave hers on display inside our tiny classroom. As a matter of fact, she rarely took her handiwork home, but left it taped to a wall or sitting on the table every week. Finally, I asked her why she never wanted to take her crafts home. Her response was simple. Since this is God's house, she replied, she wanted to leave her crafts for Jesus to see all week and not just on Sunday. In her preschool mind, God lived in our little white country church, and her artwork could only be enjoyed by God if she actually left it in God's house.

At the time, I laughed at the simplistic outlook of a small child of faith. In her concrete way of looking at things, she truly believed that God lived in the church in the same way that she lived in her house. Over time, when I remember this story, it reminds me of the ways that human beings often try to place humanlike conditions and characteristics on the God who created the whole universe. Though the preschooler in my class was simply drawing conclusions about God in the best way she knew how at her age, it has been my experience that adults often do the same thing. We often fail to communicate effectively with God, because we cannot move beyond the perimeters of our human experience and language. In 2 Samuel 7, a highly convicted David realizes the absurdity of his own kingly palace, when God still had no temple in which to dwell. Basking in his own riches, he desires to build a worthy place for the ark of the covenant to abide. In a somewhat confusing exchange between David, Nathan, and God, God's desire for a dwelling place is seen as quite different from David's desire to build a temple.

Though this chapter is viewed by most sources as a courtly document that was inserted later, the story of this exchange between God and David through Nathan is intriguing and revealing. It starts as King David realizes the irony in his own nice home and the lack of a dwelling place for the Lord God of Israel. At first, Nathan, the king's prophet, affirms David's desire and encourages him to carry on in building a temple. That night, however, God speaks to Nathan. First the Lord addresses the idea that David is the one who should build a temple. On the contrary, in all of David's relationship with God, God has never requested that David build a structure. Instead, God tells Nathan that God desires David (and his family) to be the house of the Lord. It is not a house made of cedar that God most desires. God wants to be "housed" in the people of David, in their lives, leadership, and legacy. David wanted to build a structure by human standards appropriate for God. God wanted to dwell in David and his people, and to be an everlasting part of this great dynasty. When it was all said and done, the reader knows that for David, it would have been easier to build a cedar structure. It was a continual struggle to house the Lord in the way that God requested, but it was an important part of the covenant.

As modern adults, we understand that God does not humanly dwell within our man-made churches. We also know that we live in a very different time from David and his dynasty. Yet, God still desires for us to be God's house. Though historically we have been reluctant, God has always sought to find new ways to dwell in us, eventually offering the most selfless attempt in Jesus Christ. We are reminded, just like David, of what God wants more than a building. God wants to be part of our lives in a significant and real way. We may not represent a dynasty of kings, but we are still God's houses. (Tracey Allred)

THE POWER OF A FINAL PRAISE

ROMANS 16:25-27

This concluding doxology, bringing to a close what many believe is the foundational writing of Christian theology, does not receive much respect in various circles of Christian thought. For on the one hand, a number of scholars state that the appearance of a doxology or a final praise is uncharacteristic of Paul's writings. Paul usually closed his writings with a benediction. While on the other hand, other scholars have struggled with the mechanics of these concluding words. Some say that the combination of phrases already used in the letter such as "will establish you" (1:11) and "my gospel" (2:16), with others reminiscent of the Pastoral Epistles, make it questionable that Paul even wrote this doxology. Still others suggest that these final reflections of this great apostle are out of place, and should appear after chapter 14, verse 23.

But in spite of the questions and concerns that arise from the theological analysis of the text, none of these comments can dampen the fire that comes from this most powerful ending to a life-transforming letter. For if we take this final praise at face value, one thing still remains clear: God is worthy to be praised! And the apostle took time before he put his pen back in the ink jar to say so.

After all that God has done to save the world from its sin, and lead us back into harmonious relationship with our Creator, Paul reminds us that we need to pause before it is all said and done to give God praise. For there is power in the praise.

There is a well-known saying that goes, "When the praises go up, the blessings come down." Well if we look at this final praise carefully, then we're left to take away from an already powerful letter great blessings to encourage us along the way.

As we look at this final praise, there is the encouragement of knowing that our God is able. The fact that God is able brings to the believer a glimmer of light in a sometimes dark world. All by itself, this fact enables us to fear no evil, even as we walk through valleys lined with death shadows.

Our God is able to see us through any danger, toil, and snare. Our God is able to heal our relationships, and fix our fractured families. Our God is able to restore peace in our communities, as well as peace throughout the world. Our God is able to bring order to our finances and healing to our tired, aching bodies. As Paul said in a moment of praise to God in his letter to the church at Ephesus, our God "is able to do immeasurably more than all we ask or imagine" (Eph. 3:20 NIV). When we realize in our hearts that God is able, we have a hope that exceeds all detrimental experiences in life. Our God is able! That's a blessing.

But then there is the assurance of knowing that our God can and will establish us and strengthen us in the good news of Jesus Christ. The "my gospel" Paul refers to is that gospel or good news of Jesus Christ that Paul in chapter 1 said he's not ashamed of. For it is the power of God for the salvation of everyone who believes.

It is personal to Paul, this gospel. Not only has he heard it with his ears, but he has seen God personally intervene in his trials to deliver him time and again. The gospel has strengthened him.

When we encounter the Lord in our hardships and sufferings, and experience God giving us the help and the strength to overcome all obstacles, barriers, and evil attempts to prevent us from being whole, then we, like Paul, will be compelled to give thanks and praise to the God who is worthy to be praised. For we've been blessed. And the redeemed of the Lord must say so.

But finally, in this final praise to a powerful letter, there is the blessing of knowing that God will travel to whatever depths God must go to save us. For as the apostle declares, God went as far as to sacrifice God's only Son for our salvation and the salvation of the world. Then God made this fact known to us, a fact that for so long was kept secret, but now is made known through the prophetic writings. And so if God went as far as giving his Son in death to save us, surely he will go to the root of our addictions, the root of our pains, the root of our past sins and shames to deliver us. In the name of Jesus, God saves. In the name of Jesus, God heals. In the name of Jesus, God reconciles. When, like Paul, we allow God to become real in our souls, we can't help but believe and obey. And then we must say, Hallelujah! Thank you, Jesus! Through our mouths, yet through our actions, it is the only response we have to offer.

It is to this God, the only wise God, that glory and honor and praise are so richly deserving. To this God we give a final praise! Amen. (Joseph W. Daniels Jr.)

BLESSED WITH THE IMPOSSIBLE

LUKE 1:26-38

As is the Evangelist's custom, Luke deliberately locates the announcement of Jesus' coming birth in a very particular time and place, the sixth month of Elizabeth's pregnancy in the Galilean town of Nazareth. The Lukan author is also careful to connect the story to what has gone before; this same messenger, Gabriel, has also brought news to Elizabeth's husband, Zechariah, of the impossible made possible, the unexpected pregnancy of his wife. Yet what is most compelling about these two announcement stories is not their connection, though Luke makes that plain, but their striking disconnection. The priest Zechariah, when he receives Gabriel's news, does not believe and is rendered unable to speak, while Mary, this teenage Galilean peasant, says "yes" to the messenger's announcement, despite her obvious fear.

In the liturgy and ritual of the church, Mary is often rendered as the gentle, meek and mild, Milquetoast handmaiden of the Lord. Yet here is a very different picture of Mary, this frightened teenager, the human vehicle who makes the incarnation of God, the Immanuel, possible. Despite her doubt and concern (v. 34), she nevertheless offers herself as a "servant of the Lord" (v. 38). Could Mary have had any idea what she was getting herself into when she said yes to the messenger of God's challenge, something the older and presumably wiser Zechariah could not do? She surely was thinking of the stares an unwed mother would receive in her village. But could she have known the difficulties of rearing a son called to a higher duty than she could ever wrap her mind around, and could she have imagined the pain at watching this son die on a cross while still a young man? She could have chosen to be bitter, not grateful, when given this message from God. This was a tremendous change in plans for her, one she would have scripted differently had she been in charge. Yet she still said, "Yes!" And it was a "yes" said despite fear and confusion, and one said in gratitude, not bitterness.

When Mary said yes to the surrender of her own plans and the acceptance of the God-given ones, she was not asked to go it alone. When God gave Mary the challenge, he gave it to her in community. Gabriel tells Mary that her relative Elizabeth has also conceived a son, though she is presumably barren (v. 36), for "nothing is impossible with God" (v. 37 NIV). Not only do these words of Gabriel reassure the frightened Mary with the story of another divine promise made and kept, they remind her that she can now turn her face toward the Judean hill country. There she will find the warm greeting of Elizabeth, another woman blessed with the impossible by God. (Laura Bugg)

DECEMBER 29, 2002

First Sunday After Christmas

Worship Theme: The mystery of God's providence is revealed in this child. The church, like the three ancient astronomers, is called to proclaim the gospel to the nations.

Readings: Isaiah 60:1-6; Ephesians 3:1-12; Matthew 2:1-12

Call to Worship (Psalm 72):

Leader: O God, judge your people with righteousness, and your poor with justice.

People: **May the mountains yield prosperity for the people, and the hills blossom in righteousness.**

Leader: May your governor defend the cause of the poor of the people, give deliverance to the needy, and crush the oppressor.

People: **May he live while the sun endures, and as long as the moon, throughout all generations.**

Leader: In the days of your servant, may righteousness flourish and peace abound.

People: **Blessed be the LORD, the God of Israel, who alone does wondrous things.**

Pastoral Prayer:
   Savior of all peoples, who took on our flesh in a stable and slept in a box made for animal feed; sages followed a star to find you,

paid you homage, and went home by another way. Be present among us. Encounter us in word, in bread, in song, in prayer. Touch us. Change us. Send us out to walk in new paths, telling your story, proclaiming good news to the nations. Light of the World, shine upon us. Shine your light of hope in the corners of gloom in our lives and throughout the streets of our cities and towns. Shine upon those who are lost to show them a new path home. Shine upon those who are ill to give them strength to decide how they shall live whole lives. Shine upon those in despair who need to make a way out of no way. Shine upon those whose homes, families, and bodies war has torn apart; reveal a path to peace. Shine upon your creation, the earth and its creatures, things seen and unseen. Burn away the mist and let us see you face-to-face so that you can wipe away our tears and make death to be no more. Light of the World, we praise your name. Amen. (Scott Haldeman)

SERMON BRIEFS

THE GLORY OF THE LORD

ISAIAH 60:1-6

Isaiah discovered in his revelation that it was God who sends his glory down to people. Without that holy glory, darkness pervades the soul. Synonyms for the word *glory* include: esteem, praise, respect, reverence, honor, dignity, worship, and eminence. All of those words are wrapped up in God, who is ready to download them on those who desire God's glory!

God's glory won't automatically splash on you; it's something that has to be desired—longed for—by us!

I. The Lord's Glory Dispels Darkness

His glory is the kind that will brighten the most densely darkened spot in the world. To change a church from a shadowy existence of gloom to a sparkling center of praise; to bring honor back to a dishonorable national existence; to shape a life ravaged by sin to a life respected by purity.

How does God dispel darkness by God's glory?

- By keeping God's promise to forgive you
- By welcoming you into the Kingdom
- By renewing mercies every day
- By exercising faith in us
- By conversing with people
- By walking with us all year
- By sharing God's eternal Word with us
- By saving us from sin

The glory of God goes from one generation to another

II. The Lord's Glory Surely Shines Inside Us

If we discover God's glory, we will discover it inside our hearts. God's glory will bring dignity—a distinctiveness or noble character—to a life that has been ravaged by sin. Though we were chained like a slave, held by sin's galling fetters in life, God came and broke those chains apart and now there is a glorious freedom from the dungeon of life. Glorious light! Holy light! Pure Sunshine! Jesus incarnated by the Holy Spirit born of a woman—flesh and divine combined—very man and very God. When invited, God comes and lives in people just like you and me! What a glorious heart we can possess! Pure heart! Righteous heart! Clean heart! Does God's glory dwell in you?

III. The Lord's Glory Radiates Outside

Because your heart throbs and swells with God, you will radiate godlike light. Christians are to become virtual lighthouses through the dark waters our spiritual vessels navigate.

Navigation on the seas has always been dangerous. Without lighthouses, shipwrecks occur frequently. Even with today's sophisticated navigational equipment, lighthouses in some areas are essential, sending forth the light to protect ships from disaster.

Writing about lighthouse keepers of past generations, Larry and Patricia Wright wrote, "Lighthouse keepers have always been a brave and dedicated crew. They have weathered the worst of storms and rescued countless seamen in distress. One regulation stipulated that a light keeper must make at least three rescue attempts. More than a job, lighthouse keeping was a way of life."[1]

More than an experience, glorifying God is a way of life for the lighthouse keeper year after year! (Derl Keefer)

---

1. Larry and Patricia Wright, *Bonfires and Beacons* (Ontario: The Boston Mills Press, 1996), p. 9.

A HOLY, CATHOLIC GOSPEL

EPHESIANS 3:1-12 (EPIPHANY)

I.

Since long before the doctrine of a "holy catholic church" was given creedal expression, the church's sacred message about Jesus has been proclaimed as having universal significance: ours is a holy, catholic gospel.

For while Jesus was born to Jewish parents, he died for the whole world. If Jesus were raised modestly in Judea as the son of a craftsman, he rose gloriously on Easter Sunday as Son of God and Lord of all the earth. Further, if at first only a few tried to understand Jesus' teaching, millions now attend to his every known word. And that original handful of disciples has been joined by multitudes seeking to follow wherever Jesus might lead.

Sunday by Sunday in all parts of the world, the "catholic" church incarnates the universal truth proclaimed on each Epiphany: that the "borders" of the original gospel drama—time, place, race—were redrawn in Christ, or obliterated altogether as the church, and the church's message of the crucified and resurrected Lord was scattered into other places and times.

Accordingly, as the story of the Magi's arrival is the narrative affirmation of the gospel's catholicity, our text announces the same universalizing message more theologically.

II.

With what could well be lyrics of ancient hymns, Paul spends the first two chapters of Ephesians singing praise to God, who has gathered up all things into the mystery of God's eternal will: all nations and races are gathered up into the sphere of God's grace. All our times and places are gathered into the realm of God's kingdom. And things, whether in heaven and earth, are gathered up into the eternal reign of God's Christ.

Now in chapter 3, Paul tells of his own commission to bring this message to those for whom it is intended: those who, in prior days, were supposed to be outside the borders of God's electing. Paul has announced that Gentiles, formerly "strangers and aliens," are now citizens with the saints, and members of the household of God.

And privileged, too! Like all other Christians, the Ephesians were blessed in Christ, and chosen in Christ, and destined in Christ even before the foundations of the world, that they might live for the praise of his glory. In sum, we who sing first sing best. But all creation will sing.

III.

That is the mystery which Paul sees clearly, knows fully. He may consider himself the least of the apostles, but if so he is the "leastest with the mostest." For this eternal mystery has not been fully known in generations past. The prophets surely glimpsed it, and proclaimed it as God's future. But the depth of the mystery—the height and width of the gospel's universality—has only been fully revealed with the preaching of the gospel and the ministrations of the church.

And we ourselves, like Paul and his Ephesian friends, have been gathered up into Christ's great commissioning: to proclaim the universality of Christ, and the glorious catholicity of the gospel. We are all of us servants of that message, according to the gift of God's grace given us by the working of God's power among us.

IV.

Cyril of Jerusalem, some three hundred years after the time of Paul, described the catholic nature of the church in this way—it sounds very much like a sermon that could be preached on Epiphany:

443

The Church, then, is called catholic because it is spread through the whole world—and because it never stops teaching in all its fullness every doctrine—and also because it brings into religious obedience every sort of person, rulers and ruled, learned and simple; and because it is a universal treatment and cure for every kind of sin whether perpetuated by soul or body. . . . (Cited in *Christian Believer: Knowing God with Heart and Mind*, p. 176)

It is a gospel surely worth singing in all the world. (Thomas Steagald)

THE USUAL SUSPECTS

MATTHEW 2:1-12

We know this story so well, we hardly know it at all. That makes it tough to preach. Where is the excitement? For a preacher who likes theology, it is an even bigger challenge. This is a warm, fuzzy story—at least until we move past verse 12. The visit of the wise men is part of Christmas. It does not have to *mean* anything. But I fear that it might. Before it was a happy theme for crèches and children's pageants, it had a purpose in Matthew's Gospel. It was supposed to *say* something important. What was it? We could conduct our investigation in a number of ways, but why don't we just round up the usual suspects for questioning?

I. The Magi

Here is a quick true/false quiz. (1) The wise men were kings. (2) There were three of them. (3) They visited the baby Jesus. (4) They met the shepherds at the manger. All four statements are potentially and probably false. The Bible does not tell us they were kings or how many there were. Jesus seems to be a bit older when they visit. He is called a child, and they find him in a house. If they met the shepherds, it was not on that silent night. Luke tells about the shepherds; Matthew, the wise men.

So who were these people? We do not know as much as we would like. Matthew calls them *magoi*, which has a range of meanings from a certain kind of Persian priest to magician to charlatan. In our story they possess secret knowledge and look to the stars to predict the future. They come from the East. Certainly they are Gentiles. In response to the star, they seek out the "one born king of the Jews." Why they would want to worship him we are not told.

II. Herod

The Herod in question is Herod the Great, who ruled Judea from 37 to 4 B.C. He was from an Idumean family that had converted to Judaism, and he built his career on total loyalty to Rome. If the Magi represent a proper response to Jesus, Herod represents the opposite. On the plus side, his inquiries with the priests and scribes become an occasion for Matthew to explain the location of Jesus' birth and link it to Old Testament prophecy. Otherwise he is despicable, trying to trick the Magi so that he can harm the child. Later he slaughters the infants of Bethlehem, à la Pharaoh. When we hear of Jesus he is "troubled."

III. God

Where is God in this story? That is always a good question to ask. Matthew makes no direct reference to God, but God is active. Whenever Scripture is fulfilled—and Matthew hits that point hard in this story—God is at work. The star also indicates God's activity. You could call this a story of God reaching out to humanity. The Magi do not have the Scriptures, but God takes the initiative and calls them. The God we find working behind these scenes is active in the world and moving with a purpose.

IV. Findings

From our inquiry, I am ready to draw a conclusion about the meaning of this story: *God has a bigger plan than we may realize.* Readers will not be surprised when they get to the end of this Gospel and find Jesus saying, "Go therefore and make disciples of all nations." They can think back to this story and see what God had in mind all along. These Magi, who seem so out of place in Jerusalem, Bethlehem, and the gospel, show up at God's invitation. Also, do not miss the irony that Herod, who had benefit of the Scriptures, missed the truth about Jesus while these stargazers and dreamers found it. Let that be a reminder to us that God works in the world in ways we do not understand or acknowledge. This story is a glimpse at the size and scope of God's objective. If our investigation is on target at all, we have to come to terms with a divine plan that includes every person, including you and me. (David C. Mauldin)

BENEDICTIONS

Advent Season

See, the former things have come to pass,
a new thing comes forth,
do you not perceive it?
Go now with new eyes,
see the signs of God,
a new day is coming.

May the comfort of God surround you,
May the presence of Christ enfold you,
May the power of the Spirit renew you,
and bring you peace.
Go forth in joy to proclaim the Lord's coming.

Have you heard the good news?
Broken hearts are bound.
Fetters are opened.
Ashes become flowers and sackcloth, glorious robes.
Go out, you are free, beloved of God.

May God sanctify you entirely,
may God keep your body and soul sound,
may God's grace make you blameless on the day when the
Lord returns.
Go now, rejoicing. Pray ceaselessly and give thanks always.

Christmas Season

Go, tell it on the mountain,
Go, tell it over the hills and everywhere,
Go, tell, that Jesus Christ is born.

May the God who visits us in flesh,
visit you and yours,
visit you in a way that makes you wonder,
visit you in a way that sustains you,
until that great day when Jesus returns.

Season After Epiphany

Grace and peace to you,
the grace and peace of God,
God's grace is not simple,
calling us to be despised by those we serve,
God's peace is not easy,
calling us to follow in the way of cross,
yet grace and peace enough to share with a weary world,
grace and peace enough to sustain you until the dawn of the
new age.

The Lord is your light and your salvation.
Whom shall you fear?
Go, be a light to all those you meet.
Go, proclaim good news to strangers.

Blessed are you.
Blessed are you when you do justice.
Blessed are you when you love kindness.
Blessed are you when you walk humbly with God.
Go now, walk in righteousness,
Walk with Christ the way of the cross,
A way of foolishness to the world,
The way of God's saving wisdom.

You are the salt of the earth,
    Go and enliven the palate of mercy.
You are the light of the world,
    Go and shine God's truth in the gloom.
Practice the fast that God desires,
    Go and break the yoke of tyranny
And you will be daughters and sons of the Most High,

Heirs of salvation.
Glory be to God.

Lenten Season

Happy are those who make confession before the Lord.
God promises us forgiveness.
Go now assured of God's grace.
Step up and out on this new day,
   look into your neighbor's eye
   and say, simply, Jesus Christ is Lord.

God loves the world.
God's Beloved, Jesus, came not to condemn but to save.
Go now in God's name.
Go now as God's eyes and ears, as God's arms and hands.
Love the world. Go, behold, go now and love the world.

Jesus bids you come and drink.
Never again will you thirst.
Slake your thirst at this well and go abroad to tell of him to others
      near and far.
Go now among your neighbors, to your friends and to your
enemies,
   and tell of the One whom we worship neither on the mountain
nor in Jerusalem,
   tell of the One who is coming, coming to renew all creation.

God does not see as we see.
God looks upon the poor and sees dignity.
God looks upon the broken and sees strength.
Go now as God sees you—as a child of the Most High.
   to proclaim that the light has come
   to tell that the darkness cannot overcome it.

Can these bones live?
You with stiff sinews, you with brittle bones, you with
shriveled heart,
   hear the word of the Lord, You shall live again!

Again, the spirit blows, quickening our breath.
  Come out of your grave and live.
  Go now, with new life, to praise God.

Love the Lord, all you saints, for God preserves the faithful.
Be strong.
Take courage.
Go with God who will preserve you until we meet again.

Were you there when they crucified my Lord?
Were you there when they crucified my Lord?
Did you tremble?
Christ has died. Christ is risen. Christ will come again.
Go now, trembling. Christ goes ahead of you.

Easter Season

Where, O Death, is thy sting?
Where, O Grave, is your victory?
God has triumphed mightily.
Go now in joy, declaring that Jesus Christ is risen.

Blessed are you who believe although you have not seen the risen
Lord
  Nor touched his hands and side.
Blessed are you, heirs of an imperishable fortune as adopted
children of your God.
Go and witness to the Risen One.

Does your heart now burn as you hear once more the story? As
we break again the bread?
The Risen One goes with you—open your hearts, open your
homes that he may be revealed.
Go now out into the world, walk the road, and beware of
strangers.

Are you afraid? Does your courage fail?
Do not fear that the tomb is empty.
The stone that the builders rejected has become the cornerstone.

The One who was crucified is alive and goes before you.
Take heart. You are a holy people. Go forth in joy.

Season After Pentecost

God watches sparrows. Surely God's eye is on you.
Christ died for you and now you live in Christ.
The Spirit descends and alights upon your head.
Go out, beloved of God, tell, heal, teach, love.
God goes with you.

Bread of Heaven, you have nourished with word and table,
Satisfied, we leave this place to feed others with bread and hope.
Sustain as we go.
Bring us back to feed once more.

May God's favor accompany you.
May Christ's love surround you.
May the Spirit's assurance keep you in joy.

Happy are those who walk in God's ways.
For God's precepts are a lamp for your feet.
Go now in God's ways.
Walk in the light and do not stumble.
Be a light to those who are lost.

Special Occasions

Transfiguration

Beloved of God, do you see the mountaintop? Can you look down, in faith, upon the promised land? Beloved of God, do you see One shining in glory? This One is Jesus our Savior. Hear the voice. This One is God's Beloved Child. Through him we are all made children of God. Go now in joy to serve.

Ash Wednesday

Who can judge?
Only Christ.
And Christ lived for you and died for you. Christ rose for you

and Christ prays for you. You are a new creation. Go out in joy—your Savior reigns.

Ascension

Jesus Christ, crucified and risen, has ascended to God.
Shall we stand looking up?

By no means—for we have the Holy Spirit to comfort and guide us, and we have a call to continue Christ's work. Go out with assurance that the Spirit is with you and look not up but around for all those who need to hear some good news this day.

Pentecost

Are you thirsty? Jesus bids you come and drink.

God knows your every need and will supply your want. God sends the Spirit to loose your tongue to speak good news. Go now to praise God and tell of the One who is risen, the One who promises grace and restores us to life.

Trinity Sunday

The grace of the Lord Jesus Christ, the love of God, and the communion of the Holy Spirit be with all of you this day and forever more.

Baptism

In the font we die Christ's death. From the font we gain Christ's life. We are dead to sin and alive to God. Go now to live, testifying to the saving love of God.

Eucharist

We break bread and meet Christ—in the eyes of a loved one, in the face of a stranger.

Christ goes with you. Christ goes before you. Christ follows you. Break bread. Go, share it with loved ones. Go, share bread with strangers. Look for Christ. Christ will appear.

Confirmation

Through the waters of baptism we pass from death to life. With an anointing of oil we feel the Spirit come upon us to renew our strength so that we might mount up with wings like eagles. You are sealed with Spirit, marked as God's own. Go out in joy.

Marriage

God's love is stronger than death, a zeal mightier than the grave. Beloved, love one another as God loves you. Go out in love, show the world whose you are. Go out with passion, share your love with neighbors and strangers. Go out in love, for you are loved with a love that is stronger than death.

(Scott Haldeman)

TEXT GUIDE[*]
THE REVISED COMMON LECTIONARY (2002—YEAR A)

Sunday	First Lesson	Second Lesson	Gospel Lesson	Psalm
1/6/02	Isa. 42:1-9	Acts 10:34-43	Matt. 3:13-17	Ps. 29
1/13/02	Isa. 49:1-7	1 Cor. 1:1-9	John 1:29-42	Ps. 40:1-11
1/20/02	Isa. 9:1-4	1 Cor. 1:10-18	Matt. 4:12-23	Ps. 27:1, 4-9
1/27/02	Mic. 6:1-8	1 Cor. 1:18-31	Matt. 5:1-12	Ps. 15
2/3/02	Isa. 58:1-9a, (9b-12)	1 Cor. 2:1-12 (13-16)	Matt. 5:13-20	Ps. 112:1-9 (10)
2/10/02	Exod. 24:12-18	2 Pet. 1:16-21	Matt. 17:1-9	Ps. 2
2/17/02	Gen. 2:15-17; 3:1-7	Rom. 5:12-19	Matt. 4:1-11	Ps. 32
2/24/02	Gen. 12:1-4a	Rom. 4:1-5, 13-17	John 3:1-17	Ps. 121
3/3/02	Exod. 17:1-7	Rom. 5:1-11	John 4:5-42	Ps. 95
3/10/02	1 Sam. 16:1-13	Eph. 5:8-14	John 9:1-41	Ps. 23
3/17/02	Ezek. 37:1-14	Rom. 8:6-11	John 11:1-45	Ps. 130
3/24/02	Isa. 50:4-9a	Phil. 2:5-11	Matt. 26:14–27:66	Ps. 31:9-16
3/29/02	Isa. 52:13–53:12	Heb. 10:16-25	John 18:1–19:42	Ps. 22
3/31/02	Acts 10:34-43	Col. 3:1-4	John 20:1-18	Ps. 118:1-2, 14-24
4/7/02	Acts 2:14a, 22-23	1 Pet. 1:3-9	John 20:19-31	Ps. 16
4/14/02	Acts 2:14a, 36-41	1 Pet. 1:17-23	Luke 24:13-35	Ps. 116:1-4, 12-19
4/21/02	Acts 2:42-47	1 Pet. 2:19-25	John 10:1-10	Ps. 23
4/28/02	Acts 7:55-60	1 Pet. 2:2-10	John 14:1-14	Ps. 31:1-5, 15-16
5/5/02	Acts 17:22-31	1 Pet. 3:13-22	John 14:15-21	Ps. 66:8-20
5/12/02	Acts 1:6-14	1 Pet. 4:12-14; 5:6-11	John 17:1-11	Ps. 68:1-10, 32-35
5/19/02	Num. 11:24-30	1 Cor. 12:3b-13	John 7:37-39	Ps. 104:24-34, 35b

[*]This guide represents one possible selection of lessons and psalms from the lectionary. For a complete listing see *The Revised Common Lectionary*.

454

Sunday	First Lesson	Second Lesson	Gospel Lesson	Psalm
5/26/02	Gen. 1:1–2:4a	2 Cor. 13:11-13	Matt. 28:16-20	Ps. 8
6/2/02	Gen. 6:9-22; 7:24; 8:14-19	Rom. 1:16-17; 3:22b-28 (29-31)	Matt. 7:21-29	Ps. 46
6/9/02	Gen. 12:1-9	Rom. 4:13-25	Matt. 9:9-13, 18-26	Ps. 33:1-12
6/16/02	Gen. 18:1-15	Rom. 5:1-8	Matt. 9:35–10:8 (9-23)	Ps. 116:1-2, 12-19
6/23/02	Gen. 21:8-21	Rom. 6:1b-11	Matt. 10:24-39	Ps. 88
6/30/02	Gen. 22:1-14	Rom. 6:12-23	Matt. 10:40-42	Ps. 13
7/7/02	Gen. 24:34-38, 42-49, 58-67	Rom. 7:15-25a	Matt. 11:16-19, 25-30	Ps. 45:10-17
7/14/02	Gen. 25:19-34	Rom. 8:1-11	Matt. 13:1-9, 18-23	Ps. 119:105-12
7/21/02	Gen. 28:10-19a	Rom. 8:12-25	Matt. 13:24-30, 36-43	Ps. 139:1-12, 23-24
7/28/02	Gen. 29:15-28	Rom. 8:26-39	Matt. 13:31-33, 44-52	Ps. 105:1-11, 45b
8/4/02	Gen. 32:22-31	Rom. 9:1-5	Matt. 14:13-21	Ps. 17:1-7, 15
8/11/02	Gen. 37:1-4, 12-28	Rom. 10:5-15	Matt. 14:22-33	Ps. 105:1-6, 6-22, 45b
8/18/02	Gen. 45:1-15	Rom. 11:1-2a, 29-32	Matt. 15:(10-20) 21-28	Ps. 133
8/25/02	Exod. 1:8–2:10	Rom. 12:1-8	Matt. 16:13-20	Ps. 124
9/1/02	Exod. 3:1-15	Rom. 12:9-21	Matt. 16:21-28	Ps. 105:1-6, 23-26, 45c
9/8/02	Exod. 12:1-14	Rom. 13:8-14	Matt. 18:15-20	Ps. 149

*This guide represents one possible selection of lessons and psalms from the lectionary. For a complete listing see *The Revised Common Lectionary*.

455

Sunday	First Lesson	Second Lesson	Gospel Lesson	Psalm
9/15/02	Exod. 14:19-31	Rom. 14:1-12	Matt. 18:21-35	Ps. 114
9/22/02	Exod. 16:2-15	Phil. 1:21-30	Matt. 20:1-16	Ps. 105:10-6, 37-45
9/29/02	Exod. 17:1-7	Phil. 2:1-13	Matt. 21:23-32	Ps. 78:1-4, 12-16
10/6/02	Exod. 20:1-4, 7-9, 12-20	Phil. 3:4b-14	Matt. 21:33-46	Ps. 19
10/13/02	Exod. 32:1-14	Phil. 4:1-9	Matt. 22:1-14	Ps. 106:1-6, 19-23
10/20/02	Exod. 33:12-23	1 Thess. 1:1-10	Matt. 22:15-22	Ps. 99
10/27/02	Deut. 34:1-12	1 Thess. 2:1-8	Matt. 22:34-46	Ps. 90:1-6, 13-17
11/3/02	Josh. 3:7-17	1 Thess. 2:9-13	Matt. 23:1-12	Ps. 107:1-7, 33-37
11/10/02	Josh. 24:1-3a, 14-25	1 Thess. 4:13-18	Matt. 25:1-13	Ps. 78:1-7
11/17/02	Judg. 4:1-7	1 Thess. 5:1-11	Matt. 25:14-30	Ps. 123
11/24/02	Ezek. 34:11-16, 20-24	Eph. 1:15-23	Matt. 25:31-46	Ps. 100
12/1/02	Isa. 64:1-9	1 Cor. 1:3-9	Mark 13:24-37	Ps. 80:1-7, 17-19
12/8/02	Isa. 40:1-11	2 Pet. 3:8-15a	Mark 1:1-8	Ps. 85:1-2, 8-13
12/15/02	Isa. 61:1-4, 8-11	1 Thess. 5:16-24	John 1:6-8, 19-28	Ps. 126
12/22/02	2 Sam. 7:1-11, 16	Rom. 16:25-27	Luke 1:26-38	Ps. 89:1-4, 19-26
12/29/02	Isa. 60:1-6	Eph. 3:1-12	Matt. 2:1-12	Ps. 72:1-7, 10-14

*This guide represents one possible selection of lessons and psalms from the lectionary. For a complete listing see *The Revised Common Lectionary*.

CONTRIBUTORS

Tracey Allred
3810 Hermitage Road, Apt. E
Richmond, Virginia 23227

Kathy Armistead
McKendree United Methodist
    Church
523 Church Street
Nashville, Tennessee 37219

Victoria Atkinson
3810 Hermitage Road, Apt. J
Richmond, Virginia 23227

Mark Biddle
Baptist Theological Seminary at
    Richmond
3400 Brook Road
Richmond, Virginia 23227

Bob Buchanan
Parkway Baptist Church
5975 State Bridge Road
Duluth, Georgia 30097

Charles Bugg
Baptist Theological Seminary at
    Richmond
3400 Brook Road
Richmond, Virginia 23227

Laura Bugg
528 Winthrop House
Harvard College
Cambridge, Massachusetts 92138

Joseph Byrd
Steward Road Church of God
1199 Stewart Road
Monroe, Michigan 48162

Kenneth Carter Jr.
Mount Tabor United Methodist
    Church
3543 Robinhood Road
Winston-Salem, North Carolina
    27106

Gary Carver
First Baptist Church of
    Chattanooga
401 Gateway Avenue
Chattanooga, Tennessee 37402-
    1504

Mike Childress
St. Andrews United Church of
    Christ
2608 Brown's Lane
Louisville, Kentucky 40220

Joseph Daniels Jr.
Emory United Methodist Church
6100 Georgia Avenue, NW
Washington, DC 20011

Nancy deClaissé-Walford
McAfee School of Theology
Mercer University
3001 Mercer University Drive
Atlanta, Georgia 30341

Christine D'haese Radano
Leigh Street Baptist Church
517 North 25th Street
Richmond, Virginia 23223

Scott Haldeman
Chicago Theological Seminary
5757 South University Avenue
Chicago, Illinois 60637

Tracy Hartman
Union Theological Seminary
3401 Brook Road
Richmond, Virginia 23227

Wendy Joyner
Fellowship Baptist Church
466A Highway 280
East Americus, Georgia 31709

Derl Keefer
Three Rivers Church of the
  Nazarene
15770 Coon Hollow Road
Three Rivers, Michigan 49093

Eric Killinger
4747 W. Waters Avenue #2703
Tampa, Florida 33614

Hugh Litchfield
North American Baptist
  Seminary
1525 South Grange Avenue
Sioux Falls, South Dakota 57105-
  1599

Linda McKinnish Bridges
Baptist Theological Seminary at
  Richmond
3400 Brook Road
Richmond, Virginia 23227

John Mathis
7 Locust Lane
Stafford, Virginia 22554

David C. Mauldin
Jackson Presbyterian Church
P.O. Box 664
Jackson, Georgia 30233

Scott Mikels
Baptist Theological Seminary at
  Richmond
3400 Brook Road
Richmond, Virginia 23227

Bass Mitchell
Route 2, Box 68
Hot Springs, Virginia 24445

Timothy Owings
First Baptist Church
P.O. Box 14489
Augusta, Georgia 30919

Mark Price
Westwood Baptist Church
8200 Old Keene Road
Springfield, Virginia 22152

Charles Rice
Drew University
The Theological School
Madison, New Jersey 07940

Mary Scifres
3810 67th Avenue Court NW
Gig Harbor, Washington 98335

Melissa Scott
2316 Mount Vernon Road SW
Roanoke, Virginia 24015-3616

Reece Sherman
Murray Hill Baptist Church
4300 Post Street
Jacksonville, Florida 32205

Lillian Smith
Director, Campus Ministry
General Board of Higher
    Education & Ministry
1001 19th Avenue, South
Nashville, Tennessee 37202-0871

Thomas Steagald
P.O. Box 427
Marshville, North Carolina 28103

Marcia Thompson
Robert's Chapel Baptist Church
P.O. Box 128
Pendleton, North Carolina 27862

Eradio Valverde
6800 Wurzbach Road
San Antonio, Texas 78240

Sean White
14206 Branched Antler Place
Midlothian, Virginia 23112

Ryan Wilson
First Baptist Church
P.O. Box 828
Columbus, Georgia 31902-0828

Sanford Wylie
New Haven United Methodist
    Church
5603 South New Haven
Tulsa, Oklahoma 74135-4100

Beverly Zink-Sawyer
Associate Professor of Preaching
    & Worship
Union Theological Seminary &
    Presbyterian School of
    Christian Education
3401 Brook Road
Richmond, Virginia 23227

INDEX

OLD TESTAMENT

NEW TESTAMENT